EVICTED

Extraordinary Praise for

EVICTED

"It doesn't happen every week (or every month, or even year), but every once in a while a book comes along that changes the national conversation. . . . *Evicted* looks to be one of those books."

—Pamela Paul, editor of the *New York Times Book Review*

"Written with the vividness of a novel, [*Evicted*] offers a dark mirror of middle-class America's obsession with real estate, laying bare the workings of the low end of the market, where evictions have become just another part of an often lucrative business model."

—Jennifer Schuessler, *New York Times*

"An essential piece of reportage about poverty and profit in urban America."

—Geoff Dyer, *The Guardian*'s Best Holiday Reads 2016

"*Evicted* is astonishing—a masterpiece of writing and research that fills a tremendous gap in our understanding of poverty. Taking us into some of America's poorest neighborhoods, Desmond illustrates how eviction leads to a cascade of events, often triggered by something as simple as a child throwing a snowball at a car, that can trap families in a cycle of poverty for years. Beautiful, harrowing, and deeply human, *Evicted* is a must-read for anyone who cares about social justice in this country. I loved it."

—Rebecca Skloot, author of *The Immortal Life of Henrietta Lacks*

"Should be required reading in an election year, or any other."

—*Entertainment Weekly*

"Powerful, monstrously effective . . . [*Evicted*] documents with impressive steadiness of purpose and command of detail the lives of impoverished renters at the bottom of Milwaukee's housing market. . . . In describing the plight of these people, Desmond reveals the confluence of seemingly unrelated forces that have conspired to create a thoroughly humiliated class of the almost or soon-to-be homeless. . . . But the power of this book abides in the indelible impression left by its stories."

—Jill Leovy, *The American Scholar*

"Gripping and important . . . Desmond, a Harvard sociologist, cites plenty of statistics, but it's his ethnographic gift that lends the work such force. He's one of a rare academic breed: a poverty expert who engages with the poor. His portraits are vivid and unsettling. . . . It's not easy to show desperate people using drugs or selling sex and still convey their courage and dignity. *Evicted* pulls it off."

—Jason DeParle, *New York Review of Books*

"Thank you, Matthew Desmond. Thank you for writing about destitution in America with astonishing specificity yet without voyeurism or judgment. Thank you for showing it is possible to compose spare, beautiful prose about a complicated policy problem. Thank you for giving flesh and life to our squabbles over inequality, so easily consigned to quintiles and zero-sum percentages. Thank you for proving that the struggle to keep a roof over one's head is a cause, not just a characteristic of poverty. . . . *Evicted* is an extraordinary feat of reporting and ethnography. Desmond has made it impossible to ever again consider poverty in America without tackling the role of housing—and without grappling with *Evicted*."

—*Washington Post*

"*Evicted* stands among the very best of the social justice books. . . . The book is meticulously reported and beautifully written, balancing statistics with family stories that draw you in and keep you there. I hope that all the people who read and loved Katherine Boo's *Behind the Beautiful Forevers: Life, Death, and Hope in a Mumbai Undercity* will give *Evicted* a chance."

—Ann Patchett, author of *Bel Canto* and *Commonwealth*

"[An] impressive work of scholarship . . . novelistically detailed . . . As Mr. Desmond points out, eviction has been neglected by urban sociologists, so his account fills a gap. His methodology is scrupulous."

—*Wall Street Journal*

"[Desmond] tells a complex, achingly powerful story. . . . There have been many well-received urban ethnographies in recent years, from Sudhir Venkatesh's *Gang Leader for a Day* to Katherine Boo's *Behind the Beautiful Forevers*. Desmond's *Evicted* surely deserves to take [its] place among these. It is an exquisitely crafted, meticulously researched exploration of life on the margins, providing a voice to people who have been shamefully ignored—or, worse, demonized—by opinion makers over the course of decades."

—*Boston Globe*

"This story is about one of the most basic human needs—a roof overhead—and yet Matthew Desmond has told it in sweeping, immersive, heartbreaking fashion. We enter the lives of both renters and landlords at shoulder height, experiencing their triumphs, struggles, cruelty, kindness, loss, and love. One hopes that *Evicted* will change public policy. It will certainly change how people respond to the world and those who inhabit it."

—Jeff Hobbs, author of *The Short and Tragic Life of Robert Peace*

"A shattering account of life on the American fringe, Matthew Desmond's *Evicted* shows the reality of a housing crisis that few among the political or media elite ever think much about, let alone address. It takes us to the center of what would be seen as an emergency of significant proportions if the poor had any legitimate political agency in American life."

—*The New Republic*

"Wrenching and revelatory . . . Other sociologists have ventured before into the realm of popular literature . . . but none in recent memory have so successfully bridged in a single work the demands of the academy (statistical studies and deep reviews of the existing literature) and the narrative necessity of showing what has brought these beautiful, flawed humans to their miseries. . . . A powerfully convincing book that examines the poor's impossible housing situation at point-blank range."

—*The Nation*

"Extraordinary . . . I can't remember when an ethnographic study so deepened my understanding of American life."

—Katha Pollitt, *The Guardian*

"This sensitive, achingly beautiful ethnography should refocus our understanding of poverty in America on the simple challenge of keeping a roof over your head."

—Robert D. Putnam, professor of public policy, Harvard University, and author of *Bowling Alone* and *Our Kids*

"Like Katherine Boo's *Behind the Beautiful Forevers,* this brilliant book is reportage with the depth and force of fiction. Its eye-opening details and data offer a new way to look at the affordable-housing crisis, the forces that perpetuate poverty, and the policies we need to fix a crazily stacked deck."

—*More* magazine

"[*Evicted*] is harrowing, heartbreaking, and heavily researched, and the plight of the characters will remain with you long after you close the book's pages. . . . Desmond's meticulousness shows how precision is not at odds with compassionate storytelling of the underprivileged. Indeed, [it] is the respect that *Evicted* shows for its characters' flaws and mistakes that makes the book impossible to forget."

—*Christian Science Monitor*

"This is an extraordinary and crucial piece of work. Read it. Please, read it."

—Adrian Nicole LeBlanc, author of *Random Family*

"A superb new book."

—Nicholas Kristof, *New York Times*

"The poverty of others brings up terrible questions of there-but-for-the-grace-of-God and what if, were your circumstances or skin color or gender different, that could be you. Your gaze pulls away. But Desmond writes so powerfully and with such persuasive math that he turns your head back and keeps it there: Yes, it could be you. But if home is so crucial a place that its loss causes this much pain, *Evicted* argues, making it possible for more of us might change everything."

—*Vice*

"*Evicted* is a rich, empathetic feat of storytelling and fieldwork."

—*Mother Jones*

"Matthew Desmond tells stories of people at their most vulnerable. The characters that populate this lyrical book, many of whom are women and children, are our true American heroes, showing great courage and mythic strength against forces that are much larger than the individual. Their stories are gripping and moving—tragic, too. It's a wonder and a shame that here, in the most prosperous country in the world, a roof over one's head can be elusive for so many."

—Jesmyn Ward, author of *Men We Reaped* and *Salvage the Bones*

"*Evicted* successfully interweaves the narratives of white characters living in a trailer park at the most southern point of Milwaukee with landlords and tenants in the sprawling black ghetto of the city's North Side. . . . Desmond's book manages to be a deeply moral work, a successful nonfiction narrative, and a sweeping academic survey—all while bringing new research to his academic field and to the public's attention."

—*Slate*

"*Evicted* is that rare work that has something genuinely new to say about poverty. Desmond makes a convincing case that policymakers and academics have overlooked the role of the private rental market, and that eviction 'is a cause, not just a condition, of poverty. . . .' Evictions have become routine. Desmond's book should begin to change that."

—*San Francisco Chronicle*

"Matthew Desmond's new book makes an undeniable case that we need to fix this all-American tragedy."

—*Huffington Post*

"[A] carefully researched, often heartbreaking book."

—*Chicago Tribune*

"*Evicted* is a striking account of a severe and rapidly developing form of economic hardship in the United States. Matthew Desmond's riveting narrative of the experiences of families in Milwaukee embroiled in the process of eviction will not only shock general readers, but it will broaden the perspective of experts on urban poverty as well. This powerful, well-written book also includes revealing portraits of profit-seeking land-lords, as well as important findings from comprehensive surveys to back up the ethnographic research. *Evicted* is that rare book that both enlightens and serves as an urgent call for action."

—William Julius Wilson, Lewis P. and Linda L. Geyser University Professor, Harvard University, and author of *When Work Disappears*

"*Evicted* should provoke extensive public policy discussions. It is a magnificent, richly textured book with a Tolstoyan approach: telling it like it is but with underlying compassion and a respect for the humanity of each character, major or minor."

—*Milwaukee Journal Sentinel*

"By immersing himself in the everyday lives of poor renters, Desmond follows in the tradition of James Agee, whose monumental 1941 book *Let Us Now Praise Famous Men* pounded the reader with clear-eyed and brutal descriptions of rural poverty in the Deep South."

—*Minneapolis Star Tribune*

"Desmond seems to be that rare person who is a dedicated and careful researcher and a phenomenal writer. The stories he tells in *Evicted* are gripping and intimate, at the same time as compelling as a novel and painstakingly illustrating how people are trapped and what the systemic implications are of that. I literally could not put it down. . . . [*Evicted*] feels like it has the potential to catalyze a movement."

—*Shelterforce*

"[A] masterful, heartbreaking book . . . The stories in *Evicted* are a haunting plea for us to do the right thing by families who ache for the simple routines that build a life—evening baths in a working tub for the kids, dinner cooked in one's own kitchen, windows and doors that keep cold and danger out, a place to call home."

—*Sojourner*

"[An] unflinching, richly detailed narrative . . . *Evicted* is an important book that provides an unvarnished account of the lives of the troubled and disorganized—some would say vulnerable—poor. It is thick with detail . . . and represents a new installment in a tradition dating back to

Jacob Riis's *How the Other Half Lives* (1890). . . . One can find passages to admire on almost every page of Desmond's book."

—*City Journal*

"An intimate and beautiful work as poignant as it is insightful . . . Often you hear that an author writes well for an academic, as if he were being graded on a curve. But Desmond is a good writer, period. His prose is vivid and energetic; his physical descriptions can be small gems."

—*Bookforum*

"A groundbreaking work . . . Desmond delivers a gripping, novelistic narrative. . . . This stunning, remarkable book—a scholar's twenty-first-century *How the Other Half Lives*—demands a wide audience."

—*Kirkus Reviews* (starred review)

"Gripping storytelling and meticulous research undergird this outstanding ethnographic study. . . . Desmond identifies affordable housing as a leading social justice issue of our time and offers concrete solutions to the crisis."

—*Publishers Weekly* (starred review)

"Highly recommended."

—*Library Journal* (starred review)

"It's hard to paint a slumlord as a sympathetic character, but Harvard professor Desmond manages to do so in this compelling look at home evictions in Milwaukee, Wisconsin, one of America's most segregated cities. . . . [Desmond] does a marvelous job telling these harrowing stories of people who find themselves in bad situations, shining a light on how eviction sets people up to fail. . . . This is essential reading."

—*Booklist* (starred review)

"*Evicted* paints a detailed and heartbreaking portrait of the country's eviction problem, and how it feeds into a cycle of poverty."

—*BuzzFeed*

"Sociology's next great hope . . . [Desmond] is positioned to intervene in the inequality debate in a big way."

—*Chronicle of Higher Education*

"The extent of Desmond's research is truly astonishing. More astonishing still is the fact that he's able to condense all of his observations and data into a single nonfiction volume that is both unsettling and nearly impossible to put down."

—*Chicago Review of Books*

"*Evicted* is more than good journalism. While Desmond's skill as a writer creates a narrative pull, his training as a sociologist forces him to ask why we haven't had more data on perhaps our most pressing domestic crisis."

—*Christian Century*

"Remarkable . . . [Desmond] has a novelist's eye for the telling detail and a keen ear for dialogue. . . . [His] book is a significant literary achievement, as well as a feat of reporting underpinned by statistical labour, with details provided in copious endnotes. It is eloquent, too, on the harm eviction does—not just to individuals but also to communities and to the quality of civic and urban life."

—*The Financial Times*

"Desmond's acute observational skills, his facility with reported dialogue and his ability to wrench chaotic stories into clear prose make *Evicted* a vivid, if sometimes grueling, read."

—*The Independent* (UK)

"A monumental and vivid study of urban poverty in America . . . *Evicted* demands attention."

—*The Sunday Times* (UK)

EVICTED

POVERTY AND PROFIT IN THE AMERICAN CITY

Matthew Desmond

B\D\W\Y
BROADWAY BOOKS
NEW YORK

FOR MICHELLE,

who's been down the line

I wish the rent
was heaven sent.

Langston Hughes,
"Little Lyric (Of Great Importance)"

CONTENTS

AUTHOR'S NOTE   xix

Prologue: Cold City   1

PART ONE

RENT

1. The Business of Owning the City   9
2. Making Rent   20
3. Hot Water   32
4. A Beautiful Collection   44
5. Thirteenth Street   53
6. Rat Hole   64
7. The Sick   80
8. Christmas in Room 400   94

PART TWO

OUT

9. Order Some Carryout   111
10. Hypes for Hire   134
11. The 'Hood Is Good   144

12. Disposable Ties   158
13. E-24   167
14. High Tolerance   177
15. A Nuisance   186
16. Ashes on Snow   197

PART THREE

AFTER

17. This Is America   207
18. Lobster on Food Stamps   215
19. Little   227
20. Nobody Wants the North Side   242
21. Bigheaded Boy   255
22. If They Give Momma the Punishment   259
23. The Serenity Club   270
24. Can't Win for Losing   282

Epilogue: Home and Hope   293

About This Project   315

ACKNOWLEDGMENTS   337
NOTES   343
INDEX   407
A READER'S GUIDE FOR *EVICTED*   419

Author's Note

This is a work of nonfiction. Most of the events described in this book took place between May 2008 and December 2009. Except where indicated in the notes, all the events that occurred within that time period were witnessed firsthand. All quotations were captured by a digital recorder or copied from official documents. The names of tenants, their children, and their relatives, as well as landlords and their workers, have been changed to protect their privacy.

Prologue

COLD CITY

Jori and his cousin were cutting up, tossing snowballs at passing cars. From Jori's street corner on Milwaukee's near South Side, cars driving on Sixth Street passed squat duplexes with porch steps ending at a sidewalk edged in dandelions. Those heading north approached the Basilica of St. Josaphat, whose crowning dome looked to Jori like a giant overturned plunger. It was January of 2008, and the city was experiencing the snowiest winter on record. Every so often, a car turned off Sixth Street to navigate Arthur Avenue, hemmed in by the snow, and that's when the boys would take aim. Jori packed a tight one and let it fly. The car jerked to a stop, and a man jumped out. The boys ran inside and locked the door to the apartment where Jori lived with his mother, Arleen, and younger brother, Jafaris. The lock was cheap, and the man broke down the door with a few hard-heeled kicks. He left before anything else happened. When the landlord found out about the door, she decided to evict Arleen and her boys. They had been there eight months.

The day Arleen and her boys had to be out was cold. But if she waited any longer, the landlord would summon the sheriff, who would arrive with a gun, a team of boot-footed movers, and a folded judge's order saying that her house was no longer hers. She would be given two options: truck or curb. "Truck" would mean that her things would be loaded into an eighteen-footer and later checked into bonded storage. She could get everything back after paying $350. Arleen didn't have $350, so she would have opted for "curb," which would mean watching the movers pile everything onto the sidewalk. Her mattresses. A floor-model television. Her copy of *Don't Be Afraid to Discipline*. Her nice glass dining table and the lace tablecloth that fit just-so. Silk plants. Bibles. The meat cuts in the freezer. The shower curtain. Jafaris's asthma machine.

Arleen took her sons—Jori was thirteen, Jafaris was five—to a homeless shelter, which everyone called the Lodge so you could tell your kids, "We're staying at the Lodge tonight," like it was a motel. The two-story stucco building could have passed for one, except for all the Salvation Army signs. Arleen stayed in the 120-bed shelter until April, when she found a house on Nineteenth and Hampton, in the predominantly black inner city, on Milwaukee's North Side, not far from her childhood home. It had thick trim around the windows and doors and was once Kendal green, but the paint had faded and chipped so much over the years that the bare wood siding was now exposed, making the house look camouflaged. At one point someone had started repainting the house plain white but had given up mid-brushstroke, leaving more than half unfinished. There was often no water in the house, and Jori had to bucket out what was in the toilet. But Arleen loved that it was spacious and set apart from other houses. "It was quiet," she remembered. "And five-twenty-five for a whole house, two bedrooms upstairs and two bedrooms downstairs. It was my favorite place."

After a few weeks, the city found Arleen's favorite place "unfit for human habitation," removed her, nailed green boards over the windows and doors, and issued a fine to her landlord. Arleen moved Jori and Jafaris into a drab apartment complex deeper in the inner city, on Atkinson Avenue, which she soon learned was a haven for drug dealers. She feared for her boys, especially Jori—slack-shouldered, with pecan-brown skin and a beautiful smile—who would talk to anyone.

Arleen endured four summer months on Atkinson before moving into a bottom duplex unit on Thirteenth Street and Keefe, a mile away. She and the boys walked their things over. Arleen held her breath and tried the lights, smiling with relief when they came on. She could live off someone else's electricity bill for a while. There was a fist-sized hole in a living-room window, the front door had to be locked with an ugly wooden plank dropped into metal brackets, and the carpet was filthy and ground in. But the kitchen was spacious and the living room well lit. Arleen stuffed a piece of clothing into the window hole and hung ivory curtains.

The rent was $550 a month, utilities not included, the going rate in 2008 for a two-bedroom unit in one of the worst neighborhoods in America's fourth-poorest city. Arleen couldn't find a cheaper place, at least not one fit for human habitation, and most landlords wouldn't rent her a smaller one on account of her boys. The rent would take 88 percent of Arleen's $628-a-month welfare check. Maybe she could make it work. Maybe they could at least stay through winter, until crocuses and tulips stabbed through the thawed ground of spring, Arleen's favorite season.

There was a knock at the door. It was the landlord, Sherrena Tarver. Sherrena, a black woman with bobbed hair and fresh nails, was loaded down with groceries. She had spent $40 of her own money and picked up the rest at a food pantry. She knew Arleen needed it.

Arleen thanked Sherrena and closed the door. Things were off to a good start.

EVEN IN THE most desolate areas of American cities, evictions used to be rare. They used to draw crowds. Eviction riots erupted during the Depression, even though the number of poor families who faced eviction each year was a fraction of what it is today. A *New York Times* account of community resistance to the eviction of three Bronx families in February 1932 observed, "Probably because of the cold, the crowd numbered only 1,000."[1] Sometimes neighbors confronted the marshals directly, sitting on the evicted family's furniture to prevent its removal or moving the family back in despite the judge's orders. The marshals themselves were ambivalent about carrying out evictions. It wasn't why they carried a badge and a gun.

These days, there are sheriff squads whose full-time job is to carry out eviction and foreclosure orders. There are moving companies specializing in evictions, their crews working all day, every weekday. There are hundreds of data-mining companies that sell landlords tenant screening reports listing past evictions and court filings.[2] These days, housing courts swell, forcing commissioners to settle cases in hallways or makeshift offices crammed with old desks and broken file cabinets—and most tenants don't even show up. Low-income families have grown used to the rumble of moving trucks, the early-morning knocks at the door, the belongings lining the curb.

Families have watched their incomes stagnate, or even fall, while their housing costs have soared. Today, the majority of poor renting families in America spend over half of their income on housing, and at least one in four dedicates over 70 percent to paying the rent and keeping the lights on.[3] Millions of Americans are evicted every year because they can't make rent. In Milwaukee, a city of fewer than 105,000 renter households, landlords evict roughly 16,000 adults and children each year. That's sixteen families evicted through the court system daily. But there are other ways, cheaper and quicker ways, for landlords to remove a family than through court order. Some landlords pay tenants a couple hundred dollars to leave by the end of the week. Some take off the front door. Nearly half of all forced moves experienced by renting families in Milwaukee are "informal evictions" that take place in the shadow of the law. If you count all forms of involuntary displacement—formal and informal evictions, landlord foreclosures, building condemnations—you discover that between 2009 and 2011 more than 1 in 8 Milwaukee renters experienced a forced move.[4]

There is nothing special about Milwaukee when it comes to eviction. The numbers are similar in Kansas City, Cleveland, Chicago, and other cities. In 2013, 1 in 8 poor renting families nationwide were unable to pay all of their rent, and a similar number thought it was likely they would be evicted soon.[5] This book is set in Milwaukee, but it tells an American story.

Evicted follows eight families—some black, some white; some with children, some without—swept up in the process of eviction. The evictions take place throughout the city, embroiling not only landlords and tenants but also kin and friends, lovers and ex-lovers, judges and lawyers, dope suppliers and church elders. Eviction's fallout is severe. Losing a home sends families to shelters, abandoned houses, and the street. It invites depression and illness, compels families to move into degrading housing in dangerous neighborhoods, uproots communities, and harms children. Eviction reveals people's vulnerability and desperation, as well as their ingenuity and guts.

Fewer and fewer families can afford a roof over their head. This is among the most urgent and pressing issues facing America today, and acknowledging the breadth and depth of the problem changes the way we look at poverty. For decades, we've focused mainly on jobs, public assistance, parenting, and mass incarceration. No one can deny the importance of these issues, but something fundamental is missing. We have failed to fully appreciate how deeply housing is implicated in the creation of poverty. Not everyone living in a distressed neighborhood is associated with gang members, parole officers, employers, social workers, or pastors. But nearly all of them have a landlord.

PART ONE

RENT

1.

THE BUSINESS OF OWNING

THE CITY

Before the city yielded to winter, as cold and gray as a mechanic's wrench, before Arleen convinced Sherrena Tarver to let her boys move into the Thirteenth Street duplex, the inner city was crackling with life. It was early September and Milwaukee was enjoying an Indian summer. Music rolled into the streets from car speakers as children played on the sidewalk or sold water bottles by the freeway entrance. Grandmothers watched from porch chairs as bare-chested black boys laughingly made their way to the basketball court.

Sherrena wound her way through the North Side, listening to R&B with her window down. Most middle-class Milwaukeeans zoomed past the inner city on the freeway. Landlords took the side streets, typically not in their Saab or Audi but in their "rent collector," some oil-leaking, rusted-out van or truck that hauled around extension cords, ladders, maybe a loaded pistol, plumbing snakes, toolboxes, a can of Mace, nail guns, and other necessities. Sherrena usually left her lipstick-red Camaro at home and visited tenants in a beige-and-brown 1993 Chevy Suburban with 22-inch rims. The Suburban belonged to

Quentin, Sherrena's husband, business partner, and property manager. He used a screwdriver to start it.

Some white Milwaukeeans still referred to the North Side as "the core," as they did in the 1960s, and if they ventured into it, they saw street after street of sagging duplexes, fading murals, twenty-four-hour day cares, and corner stores with WIC ACCEPTED HERE signs. Once America's eleventh-largest city, Milwaukee's population had fallen below 600,000, down from over 740,000 in 1960. It showed. Abandoned properties and weedy lots where houses once stood dotted the North Side. A typical residential street had a few single-family homes owned by older folks who tended gardens and hung American flags, more duplexes or four-family apartment buildings with chipping paint and bedsheet curtains rented to struggling families, and vacant plots and empty houses with boards drilled over their doors and windows.

Sherrena saw all this, but she saw something else too. Like other seasoned landlords, she knew who owned which multifamily, which church, which bar, which street; knew its different vicissitudes of life, its shades and moods; knew which blocks were hot and drug-soaked and which were stable and quiet. She knew the ghetto's value and how money could be made from a property that looked worthless to people who didn't know any better.

Petite with chestnut skin, Sherrena wore a lightweight red-and-blue jacket that matched her pants, which matched her off-kilter NBA cap. She liked to laugh, a full, open-mouthed hoot, sometimes catching your shoulder as if to keep from falling. But as she turned off North Avenue on her way to pay a visit to tenants who lived near the intersection of Eighteenth and Wright Streets, she slowed down and let out a heavy sigh. Evictions were a regular part of the business, but Lamar didn't have any legs. Sherrena was not looking forward to evicting a man without legs.

When Lamar first fell behind, Sherrena didn't reach automatically for the eviction notice or shrug it off with a bromide about business being business. She hemmed and hawed. "I'm gonna have a hard time doing this," she told Quentin when she could no longer ignore it. "You know that, don't you?" Sherrena frowned.

Quentin stayed quiet and let his wife say it.

"It's only fair," Sherrena offered after a few silent moments of deliberation. "I feel bad for the kids. Lamar's got them little boys in there. . . . And I love Lamar. But love don't pay the bills."

Sherrena had a lot of bills: mortgage payments, water charges, maintenance expenses, property taxes. Sometimes a major expense would come out of nowhere—a broken furnace, an unexpected bill from the city—and leave her close to broke until the first of the month.

"We don't have the time to wait," Quentin said. "While we waiting on his payment, the taxes are going up. The mortgage payment is going up."

There was no hedging in this business. When a tenant didn't pay $500, her landlord lost $500. When that happened, landlords with mortgages dug into their savings or their income to make sure the bank didn't hand them a foreclosure notice. There were no euphemisms either: no "downsizing," no "quarterly losses." Landlords took the gains and losses directly; they saw the deprivation and waste up close. Old-timers liked recalling their first big loss, their initial breaking-in: the time a tenant tore down her own ceiling, took pictures, and convinced the court commissioner it was the landlord's fault; the time an evicted couple stuffed socks down the sinks and turned the water on full-blast before moving out. Rookie landlords hardened or quit.

Sherrena nodded reassuringly and said, almost to herself, "I guess I got to stop feeling sorry for these people because nobody is feeling sorry for me. Last time I checked, the mortgage company still wanted their money."

SHERRENA AND QUENTIN had met years ago, on Fond Du Lac Avenue. Quentin pulled up beside Sherrena at a red light. She had a gorgeous smile and her car stereo was turned up. He asked her to pull over. Sherrena remembered Quentin being in a Daytona, but he insisted it was the Regal. "I ain't trying to pull nobody over in *the Daytona*," he'd say, feigning offense. Quentin was well manicured, built but not muscular, with curly hair and lots of jewelry—a thick chain, a thicker bracelet, rings. Sherrena thought he looked like a dope dealer but gave him her real number anyway. Quentin called Sherrena for three months before she agreed to let him take her out for ice cream. It took him another six years to marry her.

When Quentin pulled Sherrena over, she was a fourth-grade teacher. She talked like a teacher, calling strangers "honey" and offering motherly advice or chiding. "You know I'm fixing to fuss at you," she would say. If she sensed your attention starting to drift, she would touch your elbow or thigh to pull you back in.

Four years after meeting Quentin, Sherrena was happy with their relationship but bored at work. After eight years in the classroom, she quit and opened a day care. But "they shut it down on a tiny technicality," she remembered. So she went back to teaching. After her son from an earlier relationship started acting out, she began homeschooling him and tried her hand at real estate. When people asked, "Why real estate?" Sherrena would reply with some talk about "long-term residuals" or "property being the best investment out there." But there was more to it. Sherrena shared something with other landlords: an unbending confidence that she could make it on her own without a school or a company to fall back on, without a contract or a pension or a union. She had an understanding with the universe that she could strike out into nothing and through her own gumption and intelligence come back with a good living.

Sherrena had bought a home in 1999, when prices were low. Riding the housing boom a few years later, she refinanced and pulled out $21,000 in equity. Six months later, she refinanced again, this time pulling $12,000. She used the cash to buy her first rental property: a two-unit duplex in the inner city, where housing was cheapest. Rental profits, refinancing, and private real-estate investors offering high-interest loans helped her buy more.

She learned that the rental population comprised some upper- and middle-class households who rent out of preference or circumstance, some young and transient people, and most of the city's poor, who were excluded both from homeownership and public housing.[1] Landlords operated in different neighborhoods, typically clustering their properties in a concentrated area. In the segregated city, this meant that landlords focused on housing certain kinds of people: white ones or black ones, poor families or college students.[2] Sherrena decided to specialize in renting to the black poor.

Four years later, she owned thirty-six units, all in the inner city, and took to carrying a pair of cell phones with backup batteries, reading *Forbes*, renting office space, and accepting appointments from nine a.m. to nine p.m. Quentin quit his job and started working as Sherrena's property manager and buying buildings of his own. Sherrena started a credit-repair business and an investment business. She purchased two fifteen-passenger vans and started Prisoner Connections LLC, which for $25 to $50 a seat transported girlfriends and mothers and children to visit their incarcerated loved ones upstate. Sherrena had found her calling: inner-city entrepreneur.

SHERRENA PARKED IN front of Lamar's place and reached for a pair of eviction notices. The property sat just off Wright Street, with empty lots and a couple of street memorials for murder victims: teddy bears, Black & Mild cigars, and scribbled notes lashed to tree trunks. It was a four-family property consisting of two detached two-story buildings, one directly behind the other. The houses were longer than they were wide, with rough-wood balconies painted blue-gray like the trim and vinyl siding that was the brownish-white of leftover milk in a cereal bowl. The house facing the street had two doors, for the upper and lower units, and a pair of wooden steps leading to each, one old with peeling paint, the other new and unvarnished.

Lamar lived in the lower unit of the back house, which abutted the alley. When Sherrena pulled up, he was outside, being pushed in a wheelchair by Patrice, whose name was on the other eviction notice. He had snapped on his plastic prosthetic legs. An older black man, Lamar was wiry and youthful from the waist up, with skin the color of wet sand. He had a shaved head and a thin mustache, flecked with gray. He wore a yellow sports jersey with his keys around his neck.

"Oh, I got two at the same time," Sherrena tried to say lightly. She handed Lamar and Patrice their eviction notices.

"You almost been late," Patrice said. She wore a headwrap, pajama pants, and a white tank top that showed off her tattoo on her right arm: a cross and a ribbon with the names of her three children. At twenty-four, Patrice was half Lamar's age, but her eyes looked older. She and her children lived in the upper unit of the front house. Her mother, Doreen Hinkston, and her three younger siblings lived below her, in the bottom-floor unit. Patrice creased her eviction notice and jammed it into a pocket.

"I'm fixin' to go to practice," Lamar said from his seat.

"What practice?" Sherrena asked.

"My kids' football practice." He looked at the paper in his hand. "You know, we fixin' to do the basement. I'm already started."

"He didn't tell me about that," Sherrena replied, "he" being Quentin. Sometimes tenants worked off the rent by doing odd jobs for landlords, like cleaning out basements. "You better call *me*. Don't forget who the boss is," Sherrena joked. Lamar smiled back at her.

As Patrice began pushing Lamar down the street, Sherrena went over a checklist in her head. There were so many things to deal with— repairs, collections, moves, advertisements, inspectors, social workers, cops. The swirl of work, a million little things regularly interrupted by some big thing, had been encroaching on her Sunday soul food dinners with her mom. Just a month earlier, someone had been shot in one of her properties. A tenant's new boyfriend had taken three pumps to the chest, and blood had run down him like a full-on faucet. After police officers had asked their questions and balled up the yellow tape,

Sherrena and Quentin were stuck with the cleanup. Quentin set on it with a couple guys, rubber gloves, and a Shop-Vac. "Here you come with a boyfriend that I don't know anything about?" Sherrena asked the tenant. Quentin dealt with messes; Sherrena dealt with people. That was the arrangement.

Then, a few days after the shooting, another tenant phoned Sherrena to say that her house was being shut down. Sherrena didn't believe it until she pulled up and spotted white men in hard hats screwing green boards over her windows. The tenants had been caught stealing electricity, so the We Energies men had disconnected service at the pole and placed a call to the Department of Neighborhood Services (DNS). The tenants had to be out that day.[3]

In Milwaukee and across the nation, most renters were responsible for keeping the lights and heat on, but that had become increasingly difficult to do. Since 2000, the cost of fuels and utilities had risen by more than 50 percent, thanks to increasing global demand and the expiration of price caps. In a typical year, almost 1 in 5 poor renting families nationwide missed payments and received a disconnection notice from their utility company.[4] Families who couldn't both make rent and keep current with the utility company sometimes paid a cousin or neighbor to reroute the meter. As much as $6 billion worth of power was pirated across America every year. Only cars and credit cards got stolen more.[5] Stealing gas was much more difficult and rare. It was also unnecessary in the wintertime, when the city put a moratorium on disconnections. On that April day when the moratorium lifted, gas operators returned to poor neighborhoods with their stacks of disconnection notices and toolboxes. We Energies disconnected roughly 50,000 households each year for nonpayment. Many tenants who in the winter stayed current on their rent at the expense of their heating bill tried in the summer to climb back in the black with the utility company by shorting their landlord. Come the following winter, they had to be connected to benefit from the moratorium on disconnection. So every year in Milwaukee evictions spiked in the summer and early fall and dipped again in November, when the moratorium began.[6]

Sherrena watched the DNS hard hats march around her property. There were few things that frustrated landlords more than clipboard-in-hand building inspectors. When they were not shutting down a property, they were scrutinizing apartments for code violations. Upon request, DNS would send a building inspector to any property. The service was designed to protect the city's most vulnerable renters from negligent landlords, but to Sherrena and other property owners, tenants called for small, cosmetic things—and often because they were trying to stop an eviction or retaliate against landlords. Sherrena thought about the money she had just lost: a few thousand dollars for electrical work and unpaid rent. She remembered taking a chance on this family, feeling sorry for the mother who had told Sherrena she was trying to leave her abusive boyfriend. Sherrena had decided to rent to her and her children even though the woman had been evicted three times in the past two years. "There's me having a heart again," she thought.

SHERRENA DROVE OFF Wright Street and headed north. Since she was in this part of town, she decided to make one more stop: her duplex on Thirteenth and Keefe. Sherrena had let a new tenant move in the previous month with a partial rent and security deposit payment.

The tenant was sitting on her stoop in a long-sleeved flannel shirt, hushing a colicky baby and talking with her mother, who was leaning against a car. Seeing Sherrena, the young woman wasted no time. "My son is sick because my house is cold," she said. Her voice was tired. "The window have a hole in it, and I've been waiting patiently. I mean, I'm ready to move."

Sherrena tilted her head, confused. The window had a hole, not a crater, and it was warm enough outside that children were still swimming in Lake Michigan. How could the house be cold?

"I done called the city," the mother added, peeling herself off the car. She was slender and tall, her hair frizzed by the late-summer humidity.

Sherrena took a breath. There were worse houses on the block, but Sherrena knew her place on Thirteenth Street wasn't up to code. She would say almost no house in the city was, a commentary on the mismatch between Milwaukee's worn-out housing stock and its exacting building code. Thanks to the tenant's mother, an inspector would arrive in a few days. He would jiggle the stair banister, photograph the hole in the window, shimmy the unhinged front door. Every code violation would cost Sherrena money.

"That wasn't right for you to do that," Sherrena said, "because I was working with her."

"Then fix the window," the mother replied.

"We will! But if she don't call us to let us know—"

"She don't have no phone, that's why I called!" the mother interrupted.

As the conversation grew louder, a crowd gathered. "Who's she?" a young boy asked. "Landlord," came a reply.

"I didn't know you were going to call the building inspector, Momma," the tenant said, nervously.

"It's too late now. The damage is done," Sherrena said. She shook her head and, hands on her hips, looked at the young woman with the baby. "It's always the ones that I try to help that I have the problems out of. And I'm not saying that you a problem, but it's just that, somebody else is involved, and you the one living here. So it puts you in a spot."

"Well, let me ask you something." The tenant's mother stepped closer and the crowd with her. "If this was your daughter and these were your grandkids, what would you do?"

Sherrena didn't step back. She looked up at the mother, noticing her gold front tooth, and answered, "I would have definitely made a connection with the landlord and not called the city."

Sherrena pushed past the crowd and stepped briskly to her car. When she got home, she opened the door and yelled, "Quentin, we done walked straight into some bullshit!"

Sherrena sat down in her paper-cluttered home office. The office was one of five bedrooms in Sherrena and Quentin's home, which sat in a quiet middle-class black neighborhood off Capitol Drive. The house had a finished basement with an inset Jacuzzi tub. Sherrena and Quentin had furnished it with beige leather furniture, large brass and crystal light fixtures, and gold-colored curtains. The kitchen was spacious and unused, since they ate out most days. Typically the only things in the refrigerator were restaurant doggie bags.

"Huh?" Quentin called back, coming down the stairs.

"The girl downstairs at Thirteenth Street? Her momma done called the building inspector. . . . Her mother was outside talking *shit*!"

Quentin listened to the story and said, "Put her out."

Sherrena thought about it for a moment, then agreed. She reached in a drawer and began filling out a five-day eviction notice. The law forbade landlords from retaliating against tenants who contacted DNS. But landlords could at any time evict tenants for being behind on rent or for other violations.

By the time Quentin and Sherrena pulled the Suburban onto Thirteenth Street, night had fallen. The apartment door was open. Sherrena walked right through it without knocking and handed the young tenant an eviction notice, saying, "Here. I hope you get some assistance."

A man followed Sherrena out the door and stood on the unlit porch. "Excuse me," he called out as Sherrena met Quentin in the street. "You're *evicting* her?"

"She told me she wanted to move, so that let me know she wasn't going to pay anything else," Sherrena answered.

"She told you she wanted the windows fixed."

Quentin interjected, looking at Sherrena, "He ain't got nothin' to do with it."

"I got *everything* to do with it, blood. This my stepdaughter here!"

"You don't even stay here though, man!" Quentin yelled back.

"Ain't nobody want to live like that. . . . Fuck you mean, I don't have nothing to do with it?"

Quentin opened the Suburban's door and pulled out his security belt, equipped with handcuffs, a small baton, and a canister of Mace the size of a small fire extinguisher. Quentin had been here before. There was the tenant who told him he was going to take his security deposit out of Quentin's pocket. There was the one who said he was going to shoot him in the face.

The tenant's mother joined the stepfather on the dark porch. "Are you evicting her?" she asked.

"She didn't pay her rent," Sherrena said. "Do *y'all* have her rent to pay?"

"I don't give a shit, man," the stepfather was saying almost to himself. What he didn't give a shit about wasn't the eviction but whatever was going to transpire there, at that very moment, on that dark street.

"I don't either!" Quentin shot back.

"I'll whip that motherfuckin' ass, nigga. . . . Don't say I ain't got nothin' to do with it."

"*You don't!*" Sherrena yelled as Quentin tugged her back to the Suburban. "You don't!"

Days after the tenant left, Sherrena took a call from a caseworker at Wraparound, a local social services agency. The caseworker had a client who needed a place to live with her two boys. Wraparound would pay her security deposit and first month's rent, which sounded good to Sherrena. The new tenant's name was Arleen Belle.

2.

MAKING RENT

Sometime after Sherrena paid him a visit with her eviction notice, Lamar was back in his apartment on Eighteenth and Wright, playing spades with his two sons and their friends. As always, they sat around a small kitchen table, slapping the playing cards hard on the wood or sending them spinning with a calm flick of the wrist. The neighborhood boys knew they could show up at Lamar's place day or night for a bite to eat, a drag off a blunt if they were lucky, and a romping game of spades.

"You ain't got no more spades, Negro?"

"Look, we gonna set they ass."

Lamar was partnered with Buck. At eighteen, Buck was the oldest of the crew and went by Big Bro. They sat across from each other, playing Luke, Lamar's sixteen-year-old son, and DeMarcus, one of Luke's closest friends. Eddy, Lamar's younger son at fifteen, worked the stereo while four other neighborhood boys stood around, waiting their turn at spades. Lamar sat in his wheelchair. His prosthetic legs, each one foot to top-shin, stood beside his bed, casting a humanlike shadow on the rough wood floor.

"Police crazy," Buck offered, inspecting his hand. He was finishing high school and working part-time in its cafeteria, where he had to wear a hairnet to cover his thick cornrows. Buck slept at his parents' house but lived at Lamar's. If someone asked him why, he would study his size twelve boots and just say, "'Cause." The boys usually walked to the store or football practice together, strutting nine- or ten-deep down Wright Street. Being stopped by the Milwaukee PD had become routine. This was why, when someone made a run to the weed spot, he usually went alone. "Next time, I'm a be like, 'What you stoppin' me for?'" Buck went on. "'Cause you have a right to ask 'em. . . . They gotta see, smell, hear, or something."

"They ain't gotta see *nothing*," Lamar replied.

"Yes they do, Pops! They teachin' me this at *schooool*."

"They teaching you wrong, then."

DeMarcus laughed and put a cigarette lighter to a blunt he had just licked shut. He drew in and passed it. The game got under way—quick at first, then slower as players' hands thinned. "When the police come up," Buck persisted, "even if they pull you over, you ain't even gotta let your window down. You just gotta roll it down a little bit."

"It ain't that sweet." Lamar grinned.

"Na, Pops!"

"Don't be trying to *change* things, man," cut in DeMarcus, who had just been arrested—because of his "slick mouth," according to Lamar. "A hard head makes a soft ass."

The laughter lifted higher when Lamar added, "Can't call me collect." He took a drag off the blunt. "Baby boy," his voice was tender, "I'm fifty-one. If it's happened, I been through it."

"The police ain't protecting us," Buck said.

"I feel you on that. But all polices are not the same. . . . If I was in the neighborhood, and it was rough, I'd want the police to clean that shit up too." Lamar tossed out the king of diamonds and looked left to DeMarcus. "Go 'head, son. Get it outcha hand." The ace had already been played, and he figured DeMarcus had the queen. DeMarcus looked back at Lamar, poker-faced through thick glasses.

"Pops, your *neighborhood* protect you. . . . If somebody comes through shooting, everybody on the block, everybody who got, haulin' off shootin'."

"Man, I'm a Vietnam veteran. I know I can shoot."

Lamar had joined the navy in '74, after seeing a commercial. He was seventeen. The navy was a blur of boring oceans, exotic locations, shore-leave parties, pills, and blown checks. Lamar couldn't see why all the floppy-haired college students down in Madison had gone crazy over Vietnam, getting their noggins thumped by police batons and blowing up a university building. Lamar was having a blast. He was dishonorably discharged in 1977.

"But a bullet ain't got no *eyes*," Lamar continued. "Man, look here, we went to court with DeMarcus." The game stopped while Lamar told the story. Before DeMarcus's case was called, Lamar said, they had watched a teenager sentenced to fourteen years for accompanying his older brother when he beat a crackhead to death. "He's in the courtroom bawlin' his eyes out."

"They on some bull 'cause he a little black boy," Buck said.

"Well, then that should make you think, being black."

As Buck laughed, DeMarcus slapped his card down: the eight of spades. "Ah! That's what my *momma* taught me," he yelled. Next to all other suits, the spade was the most powerful. DeMarcus slid the book to his pile.

"Damn," Lamar said. Then he looked back at Buck. "It ain't worth it, doing stupid stuff. . . . Prison ain't no joke. You gotta fight every day in prison, *for your life*."

"I know. But when I get mad, to the extent that I wanna do something, ain't nothing stoppin' me."

"You better grow up, kid." As Buck took a long hit off the blunt, Lamar added, "And you need to slow down, *smokerrr*." He drew the last word out, using a high-pitched, tinny voice.

Buck laughed so hard he lost his hit, but the point got through. "I'm straight," he demurred the next time the blunt was offered.

When his sons were at school, Lamar listened to oldies while he cleaned and drank instant coffee with sugar. He pushed forward in his wheelchair, set the brake, and swept the dirt into a long-handled dustpan. Instead of stacking the boys into a single bedroom, Lamar had given Luke one bedroom and Eddy the other, their twin beds resting on metal frames. Lamar's bed sat in the corner of the living room. On the other side was a moss-green couch, team photographs from past football seasons, white silk flowers, and a small fish tank with guppies. The apartment was spare and tidy, full of light. Its pantry bordered on obsessive-compulsive. The Spam was stacked neatly in its place; the cereal boxes lined up at attention; the cans of soup and beans organized by kind and all forward-facing. Lamar had repurposed a Clos du Bois wine rack to hold a small stereo, dishes, and the Folgers can where he kept his tobacco and Midnight Special rolling papers.

The place had come a long way. When Lamar first came to look at the apartment, it was a mess, with maggots sprouting from unwashed dishes in the kitchen. But Lamar needed a home—he and his sons had been sharing a room in the basement of his mother's house; she gave all of them a nine p.m. curfew—and saw the place had promise. Sherrena had waived Lamar's security deposit. She thought he would be approved for Supplemental Security Income (SSI), a monthly stipend for low-income people who are either elderly or have mental or physical disabilities. But that hadn't worked out yet.

After school let out for the day, the boys would start showing up at Lamar's—sometimes with and sometimes without Luke and Eddy. Most evenings, by nightfall, everyone would have chipped in for a blunt or two and the cards would come out. Lamar's approach with his sons, and the boys he treated like sons, was open and avuncular. "You can't hide nothing from God," he told them, "so don't hide it from your daddy. Do what you do at home. . . . I'd rather for you to do it at home around me than out there on them street corners." As

Lamar smoked and laughed with the boys, he handed down advice about work, sex, drugs, cops, life. When the boys complained about girls, Lamar would try to even the scales. "You been talking about girls, but it's the men, though, that be messin' up on them." Lamar reviewed the boys' report cards and nagged them about finishing their homework. "They think I'm partying with them. I'm watching them." Lamar could watch them because he was not always away, pulling a long shift. Plenty of people on his block worked; the boys hardly saw those people except when they dashed to their cars, uniforms pressed.

LAMAR HAD WORKED several jobs after leaving the navy. He worked as a janitor at multiple places. He drove a forklift and poured chemicals for Athea Laboratories. After he lost his legs, he applied for SSI but was twice denied because, Lamar recalled being told, he could still work in his condition. Lamar wouldn't argue with that, but good jobs were scarce.

Milwaukee used to be flush with good jobs. But throughout the second half of the twentieth century, bosses in search of cheap labor moved plants overseas or to Sunbelt communities, where unions were weaker or didn't exist. Between 1979 and 1983, Milwaukee's manufacturing sector lost more jobs than during the Great Depression—about 56,000 of them. The city where virtually everyone had a job in the postwar years saw its unemployment rate climb into the double digits. Those who found new work in the emerging service sector took a pay cut. As one historian observed, "Machinists in the old Allis-Chalmers plant earned at least $11.60 an hour; clerks in the shopping center that replaced much of that plant in 1987 earned $5.23."[1]

These economic transformations—which were happening in cities across America—devastated Milwaukee's black workers, half of whom held manufacturing jobs. When plants closed, they tended to close in the inner city, where black Milwaukeeans lived. The black poverty rate rose to 28 percent in 1980. By 1990, it had climbed to 42 percent. There used to be an American Motors plant on Richards and Capitol, on the city's predominantly black North Side. It has been replaced by a Walmart. Today in Milwaukee, former leather tanneries line the banks of the Menominee River Valley like mausoleums of the city's golden industrial age; the Schlitz and Pabst breweries have been shuttered; and one in two working-age African American men doesn't have a job.[2]

In the 1980s, Milwaukee was the epicenter of deindustrialization. In the 1990s, it would become "the epicenter of the antiwelfare crusade." As President Clinton was fine-tuning his plan to "end welfare as we know it," a conservative reformer by the name of Jason Turner was transforming Milwaukee into a policy experiment that captivated lawmakers around the country. Turner's plan was dubbed Wisconsin Works (or W-2), and "works" was right: If you wanted a welfare check, you would have to work, either in the private sector or in a community job created by the state. To push things along, child-care and health-care subsidies would be expanded. W-2 meant that people were paid only for the hours they logged on a job, even if that job was to sort little toys into different colors and have the supervisor reshuffle them so they could be sorted again the next day. It meant that noncompliers could have their food stamps slashed. It meant that 22,000 Milwaukee families would be cut from the welfare rolls. Five months after Milwaukee established the first real work program in the history of welfare, Clinton signed welfare reform into federal law.[3]

When W-2 fully replaced Aid to Families with Dependent Children in 1997, it provided two types of monthly stipends: $673 for beneficiaries who worked and $628 for those who didn't or couldn't, usually because of a disability. Because Lamar didn't work, he received the lesser amount, known as W-2 T. After paying $550 in rent, Lamar had $78 for the rest of the month. That amounted to $2.19 a day.

When Lamar's welfare benefits started, right after he moved into Sherrena's apartment, he had mistakenly received two checks. In its *Rights and Responsibilities* guide, the Wisconsin Department of Children and Families informed clients who have been overpaid:

"You may have to repay benefits you receive by mistake regardless of whether it is your fault or the agency's fault."[4] Tell that to a single father trying to raise two teenage boys on a welfare check. Lamar cashed both checks and bought Luke and Eddy shoes, clothes, and school supplies, along with curtains and furniture for their new apartment. "Of course I spent it. Got my name on it," he had said when a caseworker contacted him after discovering the error. The caseworker deducted the overpayment from Lamar's next check, causing him to fall a month behind on rent.

Lamar thought the basement job he had done for Sherrena and Quentin was worth $250. The basement was covered with mildewed clothes, trash, and dog shit, reminding him of a recurring dream he had where he would crawl into a strange, shadowed basement to buy dope. He refused to ask any of the boys for help, thinking the work beneath them. He cleaned the basement alone, working until his stubs grew too sore. It took him a week. Sherrena credited him $50 for it. He still owed her $260.

It would have been impossible to get caught up in time by making extra payments. What Lamar had after the rent was paid went to household necessities (soap, toilet paper) and the phone bill. So Lamar sold $150 of food stamps for $75 cash, the going rate in Milwaukee. The refrigerator and pantry would be empty by the end of the month, but Luke and Eddy could ask their grandma for a plate. The other boys already knew to leave Lamar's food alone.

It still wasn't enough. If Lamar wanted to keep his home, he needed another hustle. He spotted one when Patrice moved out. Patrice didn't put up much of a fight after Sherrena delivered her eviction notice. She had moved upstairs from the lower unit, a two-bedroom, where she and her three small children had been living with her mother, Doreen, and Patrice's younger siblings. When Patrice was served the pink papers, she and her children simply moved back downstairs.

When Lamar found out, he figured Sherrena would need to repaint the unit. He asked her to let him do it. Sherrena agreed, saying she would have Quentin drop off the supplies. "Tell him to bring extra, baby. I'm putting together a crew."

Buck and DeMarcus showed up, along with Luke, Eddy, and a half dozen other neighborhood boys who had come to see Lamar's home as their own. They spread out in the spacious two-bedroom apartment, dipped roller and brush into a five-gallon bucket, and started slathering the walls. They worked earnestly and with a quiet seriousness. After a while, some tossed their hoodies and shirts on the floor, painting bare-chested.[5]

Lamar paused to take in the scene. Just the previous winter, he had climbed into an abandoned house, high on crack. When the high wore off, he found he couldn't climb out; his feet had frozen. Lamar kept partying after returning home from the navy. In the mid-1980s, crack hit the streets of Milwaukee, and Lamar started smoking it. He got hooked. His coworkers at Athea knew it because he wouldn't have cigarette money a couple days after payday. Lamar remembered losing his job and apartment. After that, he took Luke and Eddy to shelters and abandoned houses, tearing up the carpet so they could have a blanket at night. Luke and Eddy's mother was around back then, but her addiction eventually consumed her, and she gave up her boys. Lamar ate snow during the days he was trapped in the abandoned house. His feet swelled purple and black with frostbite until they looked like rotten fruit. He was delirious when, on the eighth day, he jumped out of an upper-floor window. He would say God threw him out. When he woke up in the hospital, his legs were gone. Except for two brief relapses, he had not smoked crack since.

"I'm blessed," Lamar said, looking at Luke and Eddy. The white paint misting from the rollers freckled their black skin. "My boys okay."

THE FOLLOWING MONTH, Sherrena was driving through heavy rain. Traffic sounded like a thousand mop buckets being tossed out the back door. She was headed to a meeting of the Milwaukee Real Estate

Investors Networking Group (RING), at the Best Western Hotel by the airport, on the far South Side of the city. Fifty people showed up, including investors, mold assessors, lawyers, and other players in real estate, but the majority of the people in the room were landlords. Men, mostly—young men in ties, many the sons of landlords but taking notes anyway; foot-tapping middle-aged men in leather jackets and boots; older men in caps and flannel shirts with knuckles like tree knots.[6] Sherrena stood out as a woman, and especially as a black woman. Besides her friend Lora, who had moved from Jamaica thirty years ago, Sherrena was the only black person in the room. Almost everyone else was white, with names like Eric, Mark, or Kathy.

A couple of generations ago, a gathering like this would have been virtually unheard-of. Many landlords were part-timers: machinists or preachers or police officers who came to own property almost by accident (through inheritance, say) and saw real estate as a side gig.[7] But the last forty years had witnessed the professionalization of property management. Since 1970, the number of people primarily employed as property managers had more than quadrupled.[8] As more landlords began buying more property and thinking of themselves primarily as landlords (instead of people who happened to own the unit downstairs), professional associations proliferated, and with them support services, accreditations, training materials, and financial instruments. According to the Library of Congress, only three books offering apartment-management advice were published between 1951 and 1975. Between 1976 and 2014, the number rose to 215.[9] Even if most landlords in a given city did not consider themselves "professionals," housing had become a business.

The evening's speaker was Ken Shields, from the Self Storage Brokers of America. After selling his insurance company, Shields had begun looking for a way to get into real estate. He started out with rooming houses, which meant he started out renting mainly to poor single men. "Very nice cash flow. But I no longer have them." The room chuckled. "I made some good money, and I mean, I love to get money, but I'm still just as happy not running around and dealing with some of these dregs of society who live in rooming houses."[10] Sherrena, who owned a couple of rooming houses, laughed along with the room. Then Shields found self-storage. "It's got the residual incomes of an apartment building, but," he lowered his voice, squinted, "you don't have *the people*. You just got their stuff! . . . This is the sweetest spot in the whole American economy. A receptacle for an enormous cascade of money."

The landlords loved Ken Shields, even if he did live in Illinois. When he finished his speech, the room broke into applause. The RING president, a mustached man with a full pouch for a stomach, stood up clapping. When there wasn't a speaker, he often organized round robins. One such evening, a woman from Lead and Asbestos Information Center, Inc., had started off by announcing, "There is money to be made on lead," to a room of landlords who more often lost money trying to abate it. One landlord asked whether he would have to report the presence of asbestos to the city or the tenants if he tested for it. "No, you don't," the woman had said.

The conversation moved on and someone else had asked about garnishing wages. A lawyer informed the room that a landlord was allowed to garnish a tenant's bank account and up to 20 percent of his or her income, but the last $1,000 was exempt. And welfare recipients were off-limits.

"How about intercepting their tax refund?" Sherrena had asked.

The lawyer looked a bit stunned. "Noooo, only the government can do that."

Sherrena already knew that. She had looked into it before. Her question wasn't a question; it was a message to Eric, Mark, Kathy, and everyone else in the room that she would do almost anything to get the rent. Many white landlords knew money could be made in the inner city, where property was cheap, but the thought of collecting payments on the North Side, let alone passing out eviction notices, made them nervous. Sherrena wanted them to know that she could help. For the right price, she would manage their property or consult with them about where to buy in the ghetto; she would be their broker to black Milwaukee. After that meeting, white landlords had surrounded Sherrena, who had worn a denim jacket with MILLION DOLLAR BABY $ bedazzled in rhinestones on the back. She poked fun as she collected business cards: "Don't be afraid of the North Side!"

As people started to leave, Sherrena and Lora found a quiet spot in the hallway. "I got drama," Sherrena began. "Drama for your *momma*! Me and Lamar Richards are going at it again—the man with no legs. He shorted me on my rent this month."

"How much?" Lora's voice, with soft traces of the island accent, belonged to a librarian. She was older than Sherrena and that night was elegantly dressed in dark slacks, gold earrings, and a layered red blouse. She folded her fur-lined coat on her lap.

"Thirty dollars." Sherrena shrugged. "But that's not it. It's the principle. . . . He already owes me two sixty for that bad job for the painting."

When Lamar and the boys had finished painting, he called Sherrena, and she came over. She noticed that the boys had not filled in the holes; had dripped white paint on the brown trim; had ignored the pantry. Lamar said Quentin had not dropped off hole-filler or brown paint. "You're supposed to go and ask for it, then," Sherrena snapped back. She refused to credit Lamar a cent toward his debt.

"And then," Sherrena continued, "he did his bathroom floor over without my knowledge and deducted thirty dollars out of the rent." When painting, Lamar had found a box of tile in Patrice's old place and had used it to retile his bathroom floor, securing each piece with leftover paint. "I told him, 'Do not—do not *ever* deduct any more rent from me ever again!' Plus, how can you deduct when you *owe* me?"

Lora recrossed her legs. "He's a player, that's all he is. Time for him to go. . . . They just try to take, take, take, take, take."

"The thing is"—Sherrena circled back to Lamar's painting job—"I would have *never* paid anybody two sixty to do that."

"I can get painting done in five rooms, thirty bucks a room, a hundred and fifty dollars."

"No, no, no. Our people do it for twenty dollars a room, twenty-five at the most."

"Exactly."

"As far as I'm concerned, he still owes the two sixty. Excuse me, now it's two ninety."

The old friends laughed. It was just what Sherrena needed.

3.

HOT WATER

Lenny Lawson stepped out of his trailer park office to burn a Pall Mall. Smoke drifted up past his mustache and light-blue eyes and disappeared above a baseball cap. He looked out over the rows of mobile homes bunched together on a skinny strip of asphalt. Almost all the trailers were lined up in the same direction and set a couple steps apart. The airport was close, and even longtime residents looked up when planes came in low, exposing their underbellies and rattling the windows. Lenny had spent his entire life in this place, all forty-three years of it, and for the past dozen years he had worked as its manager.

Lenny knew the druggies lived mostly on the north side of the trailer park, and the people working double shifts at restaurants or nursing homes lived mostly on the south side. The metal scrappers and can collectors lived near the entrance, and the people with the best jobs—sandblasters, mechanics—congregated on the park's snobby side, behind the office, in mobile homes with freshly swept porches and flowerpots. Those on SSI were sprinkled throughout, as were the older folks who "went to bed with the chickens and woke up with the chickens," as some park residents liked to say. Lenny tried to house the sex offenders near the druggies, but it didn't always work out. He had had to place one near the double shifters. Thankfully, the man never left his trailer or even opened the blinds. Someone delivered food and other necessities to him every week.

College Mobile Home Park sat on the far South Side of the city, on Sixth Street, off College Avenue.[1] It was bordered on one side by overgrown trees, shrubs, and sandpits and, on the other, by a large truck distribution center. It was a fifteen-minute walk to the nearest gas station or fast-food restaurant. There were other trailer parks nearby, surrounded by streets with modest tawny brick homes and sharply pitched roofs. This was the part of Milwaukee where poor white folks lived.

The Menominee River Valley cuts through the middle of the city and functions like its Mason-Dixon Line, dividing the predominantly black North Side from the predominantly white South Side. Milwaukeeans used to joke that the Sixteenth Street Viaduct, which stretches over the valley, was the longest bridge in the world because it connected Africa to Poland. The biggest effort to change that came in 1967, when two hundred demonstrators, almost all of them black, gathered at the north end of the viaduct and began walking to Poland to protest housing discrimination. As the marchers approached the south side of the bridge, they heard the crowd before they saw it. Chants of "Kill! Kill!" and "We want slaves!" rose up above the rock-and-roll music blasted from loudspeakers. Then the crowd appeared, a deep swell of white faces, upwards of 13,000 by some counts. Onlookers hurled bottles, rocks, piss, and spit down on the marchers. The black demonstrators marched; the white mob pulsed and seethed—and then something released, some invisible barrier fell, and the white onlookers lurched forward, crashing down on the marchers. That's when the police fired the tear gas.

The marchers returned the next night, and the night after that. They walked the Sixteenth Street Viaduct for two hundred consecutive nights. The city, then the nation, then the world took notice.

Little changed. A 1967 *New York Times* editorial declared Milwaukee "America's most segregated city." A supermajority in both houses had helped President Johnson pass the Civil Rights Act of 1964 and the Voting Rights Act of 1965, but legislators backed by real estate lobbies refused to get behind his open housing law, which would have criminalized housing discrimination. It took Martin Luther King Jr. being murdered on a Memphis balcony, and the riots that ensued, for Congress to include a real open housing measure later that year in the 1968 Civil Rights Act, commonly called the Fair Housing Act.[2]

The white, working-class South Side had, since the 1930s, made room for a small number of Hispanic families, whose men had been recruited to work in the tanneries. In the 1970s, the Hispanic population began to grow. Instead of putting up another fight, whites began moving out, pushing farther south and west. Poland became Mexico, a small enclave on the near South Side of the city. The North Side remained black. The East and West Sides of the city, as well as the far South, where Lenny's trailer park sat, belonged to the whites. Open housing law or not, Milwaukee would remain one of the most racially divided cities in the nation.[3]

Lenny stamped out his cigarette and ducked back into the office, which was situated in the middle of the trailer park, near its only entrance and exit. It was a cramped and windowless space, paper-cluttered and lit by a naked bulb screwed into the ceiling. The old fax machine, calculator, and computer were covered with grease smudges. In the summer, a wet spot grew on the thin maroon carpet under the leaky air-conditioning unit. In the winter, a space heater buzzed softly on a plastic bucket. Over the years, Lenny had added some flourishes: stag antlers, a Pabst Blue Ribbon plaque, a poster of a flushed pheasant.

"Hey," Lenny greeted Susie as he took a seat behind his desk.

Susie Dunn was on her feet, as usual, sorting mail into the mailboxes that made up one side of the office. She was not placing letters in their boxes as much as punching them in there, fast and hard. It was her way. When Susie smoked, she sucked the cigarette down, keeping her hand close to her mouth. She couldn't talk without also sweeping or scrubbing or rearranging patio furniture. It was as if she'd fall over, like a toy top, if she stopped spinning. Susie's husband liked to call her the Queen of the Trailer Park. Other people settled for Office Susie, so as not to confuse her with Heroin Susie.

"Here's your unemployment check," Susie said to a letter. "Now, why don't you pay some rent? . . . If she don't pay her rent, she ain't gonna be living here much longer. She can move back to the South Side or live in the ghetto."

The office door opened and in walked Mrs. Mytes, barefoot. At seventy-one, she was a taut and un-frail woman with a shock of cotton-white hair, a face crisscrossed with wrinkles, and no teeth.

"Hey, granny," Lenny said with a smile. He, like everyone else in the park, thought Mrs. Mytes was crazy.

"Guess what I did today? I threw a bill in the garbage can!" Mrs. Mytes looked at him sidelong with her bunched-up face. She had almost yelled the words.

"Hmm. Is that right?" Lenny answered, looking at her.

"I'm no dummy!"

"Hmm, well, I've got some bills for you. You can pay mine."

"Ha!" Mrs. Mytes said, walking out to start her day pushing a grocery cart and collecting cans. Mrs. Mytes paid the bills with her SSI check. She cashed in the cans to give her mentally challenged adult daughter snack money or, after a nice haul, a trip to Chuck E. Cheese's.

Lenny grinned and went back to his paperwork until the door swung open again. People who got half an ear everywhere else got a full one from Lenny. It was up to him to keep track of rents and maintenance requests, to screen tenants and deliver eviction notices. But it was also up to him to listen to the trailer park, to know it—know who was current and who was behind, who was pregnant, who was mixing their methadone with Xanax, whose boyfriend had just been released. "Sometimes I'm a shrink," he liked to say. "Sometimes I'm the village asshole."

THE OWNER OF the trailer park was named Tobin Charney. He lived seventy miles away, in Skokie, Illinois, but visited the trailer park every day except Sunday. He paid Office Susie $5 an hour and reduced her rent to $440. Tobin waived Lenny's rent and paid him a salary of $36,000 a year, in cash. Tobin had a reputation for being flexible and understanding. But no one thought him a pushover. A hard man with squinting eyes and an unsmiling face, he had a gruff, hurried way about him. He was seventy-one, the same age as Mrs. Mytes, and worked out regularly, keeping a gym bag in the trunk of his Cadillac. He was not chummy with his tenants or amused by them; he did not pause to ruffle their children's hair. He did not pretend he was anything he was not. His father had been a landlord and at one point owned almost 600 units. All Tobin desired was one address and 131 trailers.

But in the final week of May 2008, he found himself on the verge of losing them. All five members of Milwaukee's Licenses Committee had refused to renew Tobin's license to operate the trailer park. Alderman Terry Witkowski, a longtime South Sider with a pinkish face and silver hair, was leading the charge. Witkowski pointed to the 70 code violations that Neighborhood Services had documented in the past two years. He brought up the 260 police calls made from the trailer park in the previous year alone. He said the park was a haven for drugs, prostitution, and violence. He observed that an unconnected plumbing system had recently caused raw sewage to bubble up and spread under ten mobile homes. The Licenses Committee now considered the trailer park "an environmental biohazard."

On June 10, the city council, called the "Common Council" in Milwaukee, would vote. If the Licenses Committee's decision stood, Tobin would be out of a job and his tenants would be out of a home.

That's when the newspeople showed up with gelled hair and shoulder-mounted cameras that looked like weapons. They interviewed residents, including some outspoken critics of Tobin.

"The media paints us as ignorant half-breeds," Mary was saying to Tina outside her trailer.

"They said this was the 'shame of the South Side,'" Tina replied.

Both women had been in the park for years, and both had strong, windblown faces. "My son hasn't slept because of this," Mary went on. "Neither have I or my husband. . . . You know, I work two jobs. I work hard. I mean, I can't afford to go anywhere else."

Mrs. Mytes walked up and put her face right up next to Tina's. Tina took a step back. "That son of a bitch!" Mrs. Mytes began. "I'm gonna call the alderman, and I'm gonna give him a piece of my mind! That son—"

"See, but that won't help," Tina cut in.

"I'm gonna go, and I'm gonna give that alderman a piece of my mind," Mrs. Mytes replied. "That little son of a bitch!"

Tina and Mary shook their heads as Mrs. Mytes stomped off. Then Mary turned serious. "And to be told to move to the North Side is not funny," she said. "It's not funny." She shook a little and broke eye contact to keep from crying.

That was the heart of it, what trailer park residents feared the most. When Mary and Tina and Mrs. Mytes and the whole trailer park talked about having to leave, what they were talking about was the possibility of having to move into the black ghetto. Office Susie was one of several residents who had previously lived on the North Side, where her adult son had had a gun stuck in his face. "The alderman said this is a ghetto slum," she vented. "I'll show you a ghetto!" The situation twisted Susie's stomach so much that her son hid her pain pills, fearing she'd swallow a handful.

The trailer park had ten days before the final vote. So tenants hosted a barbecue for the media, began calling local representatives, and started to recite what they would say to the Common Council. Rufus the junk collector, with his trim red beard and distant blue eyes, wrote up his comments and practiced. "And then I'll say, 'Who has been behind on their rent, five hundred dollars?' And the hands will go up. And I could keep going: 'Seven hundred? A thousand?' And all the hands would go up." Rufus planned to end his speech by saying, "This is no slumlord. This is not a bad man."

If his speech didn't work and the trailer park was closed, Rufus was planning to put a reciprocating saw to the trailers and sell the aluminum.

TOBIN WORKED WITH his tenants. He let them pay here and there. When tenants lost their jobs, he let some of them work off the rent. He would sometimes tell Lenny, "They may be slow paying, but they're good people." He lent a woman money to attend her mother's funeral. When the police picked up the drunks responsible for cutting grass and collecting litter in the trailer park, Tobin bailed them out of jail.

Tobin's negotiations with tenants were rarely committed to writing, and sometimes tenants remembered things differently from the way Tobin did. A tenant would say she owed $150 and Tobin would say it was $250 or $600. Tobin once forgot that a tenant paid a year's worth of rent in advance after winning a workers' compensation claim. Trailer park residents had a word for this: being "Tobined." Most chalked this up to old age or forgetfulness, though Tobin was only forgetful in one direction.

It took a certain skill to make a living off the city's poorest trailer park, a certain kind of initiative. Tobin's strategy was simple. He would walk right up to a drug addict or a metal scrapper or a disabled grandmother and say, "I want my money." He would pound on the door until a tenant answered. It was almost impossible to hide the fact that you were home. It was hard to hide much of anything. Office Susie knew when your check arrived; she put it in your mailbox. And Lenny could plainly see if you had enough money to buy cigarettes or beer or a new bike for your kid but not enough to pay the rent. When a tenant opened the door, Tobin would thrust out his hand and say, "You got something for me?" Sometimes he knocked for several minutes. Sometimes he walked around the trailer, slapping the aluminum siding. Sometimes he asked Lenny or another tenant to rap on the back door while he assailed the front. He called tenants at work, even talking to their supervisors. When caseworkers or ministers would call and say "Please" or "Wait just a minute," Tobin would reply, "Pay me the rent."

Tobin was not going to forgive and forget losing hundreds or thousands of dollars or settle for half of what he was owed or price a trailer below market value. When tenants fell behind, he had three options. He could let it slide and watch his income fall, he could begin eviction proceedings, or he could start a conversation.

Option one was a non-option. Tobin was a landlord to make a living, and if he was too lenient he could lose his business. But Tobin also did not evict most tenants who owed him. Pushing tenants out and pulling new ones in cost money too. In an average month, forty of Tobin's tenants were behind—nearly one-third of the trailer park. The average tenant owed $340.[4] But Tobin only evicted a handful of tenants each month. A landlord could be too soft or too hard; the money was in the middle, with the third route, and his tenants were grateful for it, though often not at first.

Jerry Warren wasn't. Jerry used to ride with the Outlaws, a biker gang, and was covered in tattoos, several of which he had acquired in prison. Eviction notice in hand, Tobin had whapped the side of Jerry's trailer, an aqua-blue 700-footer Jerry had painted himself. Jerry balled up the notice and threw it in Tobin's face, yelling, "Tobin, I don't give a shit about this fucking eviction! And Lenny, I don't care how old you are. I'll still take to whooping your ass something good!" Lenny and Jerry exchanged words, but Tobin was unfazed. He had begun a conversation, and a few days later, after he had cooled off, Jerry would pick it up.[5] He offered to clean up the trailer park and attend to some maintenance concerns if Tobin canceled the eviction. Tobin accepted the offer.

He took a different tack with Larraine Jenkins. A month before the Licenses Committee had rejected Tobin's renewal application, he had given her a ride to eviction court in the Cadillac. Larraine received SSI for learning impairments attributed to a childhood fall out of an attic window. Her monthly check was $714. Her monthly rent was $550, utilities not included. Larraine had been late with the rent several times before Tobin finally took her to court. "It's just hard to give up that rent," Larraine admitted. "You've got to wonder if the street people don't have the right idea. Just live on the street. Don't have to pay rent to nobody." She sat in the passenger's seat, while another tenant named Pam Reinke, a pregnant woman with straight-cut bangs and freckles, sat in the back. In court, Tobin offered them both stipulation agreements, a civil court's version of a plea bargain. If they stuck to a tight payment schedule, Tobin would dismiss the eviction. If they deviated, Tobin could obtain a judgment of eviction and activate the sheriff's eviction squad (with something called a "writ of restitution") without having to take Larraine or Pam to court again.

Throughout his fight with Witkowski, Tobin had worried that tenants would hold their money until the fate of the trailer park was settled. But most tenants went right on paying. Larraine wasn't one of them. Already behind, she had withheld June's rent because she didn't know if the park would be shut down. If she had to move anyway, she figured, she might as well pocket the $550. Larraine was pushing her luck. Besides owing back rent, she had been one of the critics who had appeared on the nightly news, where she admitted to seeing prostitutes and drug dealers in the park. (Phyllis Gladstone, the most vocal supporter of Witkowski, had put Larraine up to it.)[6] When Tobin found out about everything, he recalled that Larraine hadn't fulfilled her stipulation agreement. That meant he could ask the sheriff's eviction squad to remove her. So he did.

Soon, a letter from the Milwaukee Sheriff's Office arrived in Larraine's mailbox. Printed on a bright-yellow sheet of paper was the following message:

CURRENT OCCUPANT

You are hereby notified that the Milwaukee County Sheriff's Office has a court order (Writ of Restitution/ Assistance) requiring your immediate removal from the premises. <u>Failure to vacate immediately will be cause for the Sheriff to remove your belongings from the premises.</u>

If an eviction is necessary, risk of damages or loss of property shall be borne by you, the defendant, after delivery by the Sheriff to the place of safekeeping. Movers will not take food left in your refrigerator or freezer. <u>REMOVE FOOD ITEMS.</u>

The words had terrified Larraine. It showed. Her emotions projected onto her face like a movie screen. When she was happy, she beamed, flashing a gap-toothed smile; and when she was depressed, her whole face drooped as if being pulled down by a hundred tiny lead sinkers. At fifty-four, Larraine lived alone in a clean, white trailer, though she prayed to one day be reunited with her two adult daughters and her grandson, who, along with God, occupied the center of her universe. She was tub-bellied, with a broad face and freckled white skin. Years ago, she had been gorgeous and liked to dress in a way that made boys lean out of their car windows. Larraine still cared about her appearance and would leave her eyeglasses at home because she thought they made her look "like a dead fish." When she wanted to look nice, she put on jewelry she had acquired as a young woman, using safety pins to expand the necklace chains so they fit.

Smelling of sweat and vinegar, her brown hair in disarray, Larraine stepped into the office, wringing the yellow paper like a dishrag. After a brisk exchange, Tobin led Larraine outside and called after Susie.

"Susie? Susie!" Tobin yelled.

"What, Tobin?"

"Take her to the bank, will ya? She's gonna get some money for the rent."

"Come on," Susie said, stepping briskly to her car.

When Susie returned with Larraine, Tobin was in the office, shuffling through papers. "How much?" he asked Susie.

"I have four hundred," Larraine answered.

"I'm not calling off the eviction," Tobin said, still looking at Susie. Larraine owed another $150 for that month.

Larraine just stood there.

Tobin turned to Larraine. "When can you get me the other one fifty?"

"Tonight, okay—"

Tobin cut her off: "Okay. You give it to Susie or Lenny."

Larraine didn't have it. She had used $150 of her rent money to pay a defaulted utility bill with the hope of having her gas turned back on. She wanted to take a hot shower, scrub away the smell. She wanted to feel clean, maybe even something closer to pretty, like she used to feel when she danced on tables for men, back when her daughters were babies. She wanted the water to soothe the pain of her fibromyalgia, which she likened to "a million knives" going up her back. She had prescriptions for Lyrica and Celebrex but didn't always have enough for the copay. Hot water would help. But $150 wasn't enough. We Energies accepted her money but didn't turn on her gas. Larraine felt stupid for paying.

Susie made out a receipt on a piece of scrap paper and stapled it to Larraine's eviction notice. "You should go ask your sister for the rest," she suggested, picking up the fax machine's phone and dialing a number she knew by heart. "Yes. Hello? I need to stop an eviction at College Mobile Home Park," Susie said to the Sheriff's Office. "For Larraine Jenkins in W46. She took care of her rent." Office Susie had canceled the sheriff deputies, but Tobin could reactivate them if Larraine didn't come up with the rest of what she owed.

Larraine sulked back to her trailer. It was so hot inside that she thought lukewarm water might run in the shower. She didn't turn on the fan; fans made her dizzy. She didn't open a window. She just sat on the couch. She called a few local agencies. After several unsuccessful tries, she said blankly to the floor, "I can't think of anything else." Larraine lay down on the couch, tried to ignore the heat, and slept.

4.

A BEAUTIFUL COLLECTION

The day the Common Council was to decide the fate of the trailer park, Tobin Charney, dressed in a polo shirt, tan slacks, and brown loafers, sat in the middle of a front-row bench next to his wife and lawyer. Large pink marble columns stretched up toward a beamed ceiling with an intricate maroon-and-yellow pattern. A large oak desk rested in the front of the room, facing fifteen smaller oak desks assigned to each alderperson and spaced several feet apart. The night before, the lawyer had submitted an addendum to the council. It came in too late for most alders to read, so the lawyer stood and cleared his throat. The addendum, he informed the room, included ten steps Tobin would take in the immediate and near future. He would enroll in a daylong landlord training class offered by the city, hire a twenty-four-hour security service and an independent management company, evict nuisance tenants, and address the property-code violations. He would not retaliate against tenants who spoke out against him. And he would sell the trailer park within a year.

"The people in this park are vulnerable: elderly, disabled, children," the lawyer concluded, noting that Tobin had "worked diligently" with Alderman Witkowski to "draw up the terms of the agreement."

The Common Council was not happy with this midnight deal, and they argued with one another as sunlight beamed through the chamber's stained-glass windows. One alderman called it a "gentleman's agreement." Another asked if all citizens, when called to account, could simply produce a ten-point plan. Finally, Alderman Witkowski rose to speak.

"Mr. Charney has allowed a good mobile home park to move to something like this," he began. "I have four mobile home parks in my district, and this is the only one with these types of problems." He looked over his glasses at the lawyer. "They aren't *all* elderly, disabled, and children, sir. But"—he turned back to his colleagues—"there are people with limited means and limited abilities. They would be forced to move out." Witkowski was no friend of Tobin's, but he was satisfied with the terms of the addendum.

The debate rose up again, energetic and sharp. Tobin remained seated in the back, holding his wife's hand and looking annoyed.

The president called for a vote.

After the hearing, Tobin drove to the trailer park. He did not call everyone together to announce the resolution. He did not slide into a chair in the office and let out a sigh. He began evictions. The council had agreed to let Tobin keep his license only if he took drastic steps to improve the park, including forcing the troublemakers out.

When city or state officials pressured landlords—by ordering them to hire an outside security firm or by having a building inspector scrutinize their property—landlords often passed the pressure on to their tenants.[1] There was also the matter of reestablishing control. The most effective way to assert, or reassert, ownership of land was to force people from it.[2]

"Where did my twenty-eight-day notices go?" Lenny asked. He was in the office searching through piles of papers. With a twenty-eight-day "no cause" termination notice, landlords did not need to provide a reason for the eviction. It was an ideal way to remove nuisance tenants who were current on their rent. Turning to Tobin, he said, "You got a lot of twenty-eight-day notices to fill out."

"They owe me back rent," Tobin replied. "Give them a five-day."

"They," in this case, meant Pam and her family. After driving Pam to eviction court, Tobin had asked her to talk to the newspeople. She was thirty years old and seven months pregnant, with a midwestern twang and a face cut from a high school yearbook photo. She made for a sympathetic case. But now Tobin was cleaning house.

Tobin looked up. "Lenny, I hope the money isn't coming in slow because of this," he said.

"It's not, surprisingly," Lenny replied. "I just filled out my spreadsheets, and we're looking good."

Office Susie added, "I had a beautiful collection."

Pam tried changing Tobin's mind by signing over the $1,200 check she had just received as part of Obama's economic stimulus act. She thought it would be enough, mainly because she thought she owed $1,800. But Tobin said she owed something more like $3,000, and Office Susie told him Pam smoked crack. Tobin accepted Pam's stimulus check but moved forward with the eviction anyway. Pam's family had lived in the trailer park for two years.

Pam and her boyfriend, Ned Kroll, ended up in one of Tobin's trailers because he gave it to them. Pam and Ned had been considering moving to Milwaukee from Green Bay to be closer to Pam's ailing father when they spotted an ad Tobin had taken out in the local paper. They drove down to have a look.

When Pam and Ned arrived at College Mobile Home Park, Tobin and Lenny offered them the "Handyman Special," a free mobile home. Under this arrangement, tenants owned the trailers, and Tobin owned the ground underneath them. He charged the owners "lot rent," which was equivalent to what his renters paid. But unlike the renters, families who owned their trailers were responsible for upkeep. In theory, a family could at any time move their trailer elsewhere. But the owners knew that in practice this was impossible. Towing expenses exceed $1,500 and setting up the trailer somewhere else could cost double that. When owners were evicted and inevitably left their trailer behind, Tobin would reclaim it as "abandoned property" and give it to someone else.

At the time that Pam was facing eviction, all but twenty trailers in the park were owner-occupied. The only benefit to owning your trailer was psychological. "I moved here so I can own a home, even if it's on wheels," one of Pam's neighbors liked to say.[3]

Tobin's mobile-home giveaways sped things up—he could fill recently vacated trailers, sometimes even junk trailers, in weeks if not days—but hard-up families found the trailer park on their own too.

In Milwaukee and cities across the country, as affordable rental stock has been allowed to deteriorate and eventually disappear, low-income families have rushed to occupy cheap units. Nationwide, vacancy rates for low-cost units have fallen to single digits.[4] Lenny's office phone rang daily with people inquiring about availability. The phone rang before the newspeople came, and it rang after they left. The month the story aired, the trailer park had zero vacancies. "The park is filled up," Lenny said with a chuckle. "And we still got people calling." The rent rolls that Lenny kept for Tobin showed that in an average month only five trailers sat vacant, which would put Tobin's vacancy rate below 4 percent.[5] The high demand for the cheapest housing told landlords that for every family in a unit there were scores behind them ready to take their place. In such an environment, the incentive to lower the rent, forgive a late payment, or spruce up your property was extremely low.

"FIGURES," NED HAD mumbled past a dangling cigarette when he found out Pam was pregnant with another daughter. He had made a son once, when he was sixteen, with a Mexican girl he'd met at a ZZ Top concert. But the girl's family blotted him out, and Ned hardly thought about that boy anymore unless "La Grange" came on the radio. "After that, maybe I got punished," he once mused. "No more boys." The new one would make five daughters if you counted Pam's two black girls, which Ned sometimes did.

Pam and Ned had met in Green Bay, after Pam's father asked Ned to tune up his Harley. Ned was ten years older than Pam, with grease under his fingernails, brown stubble, and long hair, balding in the front. He was the kind of man who took satisfaction in leaving the bathroom door open and scratching himself in public.

Pam already had two daughters: Bliss, born when Pam was twenty-three, and Sandra two years after that. Their father, a black man, was a drug dealer whom Pam had met when she was nineteen. Pam later learned that she was one of several girlfriends.

"Tell about the time that Dad hit you with a bottle and blood was coming out of your head," Sandra once asked her mother as they drove to a food pantry. She was six when she said this.

Pam forced a sad smile. "You weren't old enough to remember that."

"Yes, I was," replied Sandra. Sandra was the one who would squash a cockroach with a loose shoe while the other girls shuddered and clung to one another. She and Bliss were the only black children in the trailer park. Once, one of their neighbors hung a Nazi flag in his front window. Lenny didn't permit that, but he was okay with the Confederate flag as long as it was displayed underneath Old Glory.

"No, you were just a baby. Now, Bliss, she was. She got so used to it. She always saw blood just pour out of me."

Pam found a way to leave him. She began working as a certified nursing assistant, emptying bedpans, mopping up puke, and rotating the invalids to prevent bedsores. She learned how to cook pots of spaghetti and macaroni salad. Her mother had died in a car accident when Pam was in high school and had never got around to teaching her. Her father hadn't either; he spent a lot of time in prison on drug and drunk-driving charges. Pam's brother was doing better too. He was taking methadone and said he didn't miss heroin.

It was a time of promise and rebirth, a time of putting one foot steadily in front of the other. Then the ground shifted beneath. One day Pam answered the phone. A voice was saying that her brother was dead. Pam asked how. The voice said overdose. He was twenty-nine. Pam screamed into the phone. Then she hung up and dialed another number to ask for something to keep her from drowning.

The words to describe the drug—"crack," "rock"—gave off the impression that it was a gnarled, craggy thing. But when you held it in your hand, it could be smooth and elegant. It could look like a piece of Chiclets gum, the kind that slides into a child's cupped hand out of the quarter-turn machine. All those years with the drug dealer, Pam had stayed away from it. She saw how it turned people, saw what they would do for it. But she also saw the way it helped people forget. "There was not a day that went by that I wasn't fucked up on something," Pam remembered. "And sometimes I'd be like, 'Wow. I haven't even cried for him yet.' But I didn't. Before I would, I'd go and get high."

That's when she met Ned.

That first year, crack was the force that held them together. They lived for it and by it, raising the girls along the way. Soon they began selling it. A year after meeting, they were caught and convicted. Ned, who had a previous drug charge, did prison time. It was Pam's first felony. She was sentenced to four years' probation and made to sit for ten months in a jail cell, where, finally, she cried.

When Pam got out, she tried to stay sober. She moved in with the straightest friend she knew in Green Bay, but while Pam was in jail, the friend had developed a habit. "Everybody, everybody I know in fucking Green Bay is fucking on dope," Pam vented. She asked her father to wire her $500 so she could move and, to her surprise, he did. But Green Bay was a small town, and Pam soon crossed paths with one of her former dealers. "He got me hooked right back on."

Pam and Ned reconnected after he was released, and Pam soon discovered she was pregnant. Ned demanded a paternity test, which confirmed the baby was his. They settled on a name: Kristen. Soon, Ned's daughter from another woman came to live with them. Laura had a small nose and freckles, and was one year older than Bliss. A few months after Laura moved in, Ned left her, Pam, and the other girls with a woman they had just met in the drug scene. Pam and the girls spent the night at the woman's house, then the next night, and the night after that. Pam eventually walked Laura to her mother's house and knocked on the door. She remembered standing at the door and telling Laura's mother: "I'm about to have this baby. I'm homeless right now. Your old man left me. I have no money, no food, no nothing for your kid. I'm scared. . . . Can you please take your daughter?"[6]

Laura's mother stayed on the phone, gave them a bag of canned food, and shut the door. Pam and the girls stayed at the woman's house. Ned came back a month later.

WHEN TOBIN TOLD Pam and Ned he was keeping their rebate check and still evicting them, he brought along a security detail. But nobody caused a scene, even though Tobin only gave them twenty-four hours to leave before he called the sheriff. Ned might have raised hell if he didn't have an outstanding warrant for his arrest, stemming from another drug charge. Pam and Ned blamed each other for the eviction.

"You cracked it up," Ned snapped at Pam.

"*You* cracked it up," Pam shot back. "Talking about me. I handed you all the money. . . . You got us evicted."

"Move, bitch."

"It's *you*, Ned."

"You can move."

"I can't. It's you." Pam stopped. "I don't know. Is it really me? Is it me who has the problem? I don't know. Maybe it is. Am I the one that fucked up?"

They sold their only possessions worth anything—the television and the computer, Pam's Christmas gift. They would need the extra cash. Each month Pam worked thirty hours a week for her welfare check of $673 and received $390 in food stamps. On a good day Ned brought in $50 cash for customizing and repairing motorcycles. Pam's money was Pam's money and Ned's was Ned's. They kept separate bank accounts and split the bills down the middle.

After jail, Pam had had a difficult time finding work with her recent drug conviction. She finally was hired by Quad Graphics, a commercial printing plant. Quad had a reputation for hiring people with records and without high school diplomas, provided they were willing to work the third shift. Pam was. She ran the warm, humming machines from seven p.m. to seven a.m.

Quad Graphics was in Sussex, a forty-minute drive from the trailer park. Pam relished the commute. It was her time, time away from Ned and the kids.

Then her car gave out at the worst time—winter—when money was tightest. Ned had been working with a construction crew, which all but shut down in the colder months. They didn't have enough money to repair the car, and Pam lost her job. That's when they fell behind with Tobin. Emergency Assistance got them through one month. A couple months later, in February, Pam gave Tobin $1,000 that she received from her tax refund. But they were still in the red. Pam could have given Tobin more, but she wanted to get back to Quad, which meant she needed a car. She bought one for $400, but a week later Ned heard a clicking sound and told Pam to offload it before the engine threw a rod.

And a lot of money went to dope. There were mornings when Pam would come home from working the third shift to find Ned at Heroin Susie's or wide-awake in the living room, on the tail end of an all-night bender, with women passed out on the couch. There were evenings when Pam got so high she couldn't walk.

The computer and television sold, the rest of their things shoved into garbage bags, Pam walked across the row and asked Scott if she and her family could stay with him until they got back on their feet. Or at least until the baby came. Scott was a heroin user approaching forty. He lived with Teddy, an older man he had met when both were staying at the Lodge. Pam trusted them around the girls, even if Scott

did pass out in front of them once. Scott and Teddy said yes and didn't
even ask for money.

Tobin huffed when Office Susie told him that Pam and Ned were
staying with Scott and Teddy. He had agreed to rent Scott and Teddy's
trailer to Scott and Teddy, nobody else. Tobin gave Scott and Teddy
an eviction notice, tacking on Pam and Ned's rental debt to Scott and
Teddy's bill. Eviction could be contagious that way.

5.

THIRTEENTH STREET

Arleen didn't mind Thirteenth Street. There was a bodega owned by Arabs on one end of her block and a bar for old men on the other. She could walk Jafaris to school. Arleen could have done without the hypes—crack addicts—who'd recently moved into the abandoned house next door, but a few more houses down a girl was learning to play the violin.

Her new apartment was coming along too. There was a time when the house was a stately thing. Built in Greek Revival style, it was two stories of sandstone block with twin columns supporting an awning over the front door. A pair of picture-frame windows, adorned with peaked pediments, faced the street, as did a larger second-story window whose pane opened on hinges. But over the years the house had deteriorated. One column base was settling, causing the overhead awning to slope sideways. The columns, porch, and window pediments had been painted ash-gray, and an imposing iron-barred outer door had been installed. Arleen didn't like walking up the front steps, with their flaking paint and mismatched stair rails on either side, so she always used the side entrance.

Arleen had thrown herself into making the apartment a home. The previous tenants had left behind a large armoire, a bedroom dresser, a bed, and a refrigerator. There was even more in the basement: dishes, clothes, an upholstered chair. Arleen put it all to use, rearranging the furniture and stacking the dishes next to her nice porcelain plates, the ones she had been given years ago by a domestic-violence shelter. She claimed the front bedroom and gave the boys the one in the back, placing their twin mattresses on the ground and organizing clothes in dresser drawers. She unpacked a stereo and listened to old-school hip-hop tracks on burned CDs, her favorite being 2Pac's "Keep Ya Head Up." In the kitchen, she hung a humble drawing of black farm-ers hoeing a row. Over the bathroom door, she affixed a sign that she had found at a drugstore: TODAY WORRIED YOU YESTERDAY AND ALL IS WELL.

In the basement Arleen had also come across rollers, brushes, and a five-gallon bucket of white paint. She lugged everything upstairs, tied a wrap around her head, and gave the walls a fresh coat. She went ahead and painted the stairwell leading to the upstairs unit too. The job complete, she lit a stick of incense to mask the paint smell and looked around. She felt pleased with herself, content.

The days passed, and Arleen and her boys settled into their new home. After school, Jori sometimes challenged other neighborhood boys to a game of cans, Jafaris looking on. Using a basketball, Jori and his competitor tried to hit soda cans flattened on the sidewalk, earn-ing more points for farther shots. He was a lanky boy, whose arms and fingers seemed to be growing faster than the rest of him, a condition he tried to conceal under oversized sweatshirts and coats. He wore his hair natural and had a relaxed, agreeable way about him. But Jori was fiercely loyal to his momma. If Arleen needed to smile, Jori would steal for her. If she was disrespected, he would fight for her. Some kids born into poverty set their sights on doing whatever it takes to get out. Jori wasn't going anywhere, sensing he was put on this Earth to look after Arleen and Jafaris. He was, all fourteen years of him, the man of the house.

Jafaris was a big kid, the biggest in his kindergarten class. While Jori was all knees and elbows, Jafaris had a round chest and defined shoulders, with high cheekbones and cornrows that always needed redoing. When Jafaris grew bored, he would scavenge the basement or back alley for anything he could find—mop handles, rusted tools, dog leashes, pieces of plywood—and pretend they were tanks and helicopters locked in battle. After dinner, Arleen would watch reruns with the volume turned low, or read through Jafaris's Individualized Education Program (IEP) evaluations, or flip through her prayer book. Some nights, she climbed the stairs and opened the upper unit's unlocked door to give herself a little privacy. Arleen liked that the upstairs unit was vacant. She preferred things quiet.

One day, a friend gave Arleen a cat: a half-black, half-white thing. After Sherrena said they could keep it, Jori named him Little and began feeding him table scraps. Jori laughed when Little would spring at a loose shoelace or gulp down a ramen noodle. Jafaris would pick him up and press his nose against his ear. Both boys especially loved it when Little caught a mouse. He would drag the thing to the middle of the room and smack it around. The mouse would take different routes, trying to figure out what Little wanted. *Bat! Bat!* The mouse would tumble and roll with every swat. At some point, the pathetic creature would burrow under Little's arm, hiding. Little would let the mouse rest and warm itself. Then he might reach down and grab the creature with his mouth and throw it into the air and, enjoying the effect, do it again and again. Eventually the mouse would just lie there motionless, and Little would look at it with cool disgust, wondering why the creature didn't get back up.

JORI OPENED THE door and called out, "He havin' an asthma attack." Jori had walked Jafaris home from school. Arleen stayed on the love seat waiting to see how bad it was. When it was a small attack, Jafaris's mouth opened and closed like a caught fish. When it was a medium attack, he made an *O* with his mouth. When it was bad, his lips curled back, and he breathed through his nubby teeth.

Jafaris walked through the door making the *O* face. He shrugged off his backpack and leaned on the love seat like an old man after climbing a flight of stairs.

"Jafaris, go get me my bag," Arleen said.

The boy nodded and went to the bedroom. When he came back, Arleen pulled out the albuterol and shook it. Jafaris put his mouth to the inhaler and breathed in. But their timing was off. "Blow it out! Don't be playing with me," Arleen snapped.

Jafaris missed the next try too, but the third filled his lungs. He held his breath, puffing out his cheeks the way children do before jumping into a pool. His mother counted: "One . . . two . . . three . . ." At ten, Jafaris exhaled, took a breath in, and smiled. Arleen smiled back.

She gave Jafaris albuterol every morning and every evening. Before bed, he got prednisone, a steroid, through a PARI Proneb Ultra nebulizer with plastic tubing and an airplane-cabin mask. Arleen called it "the breathing machine." Jafaris's asthma had been improving. Arleen remembered when she used to rush Jafaris to the hospital every week.

Jafaris's father had given him his name, and lately Arleen had been worried he might have given him other things too. His father had "learning disabilities and anger issues," and Jafaris was beginning to exhibit similar characteristics at school. He excelled at reading but struggled with other subjects, and he pushed his classmates around. He had been evaluated but didn't qualify for additional help. Some teachers had suggested medications, which made Arleen bristle: "I don't like medicine. I'm totally against Ritalin. I think he needs more one-on-one attention. . . . I don't want to medicate him until he's seen a counselor and done gone through that."

Arleen had met Jafaris's father at the movie theater at the Mayfair Mall, when she was working the concession stand. "It just kind of happened," Arleen recalled. "We weren't in no real relationship." They tried for one, but Arleen discovered he could be a violent man. He went to prison soon after she left him. He gave Jafaris little else beyond life.

It had been the same way with Arleen's father. He had left after impregnating her mother, who was only sixteen when she had Arleen. Arleen's grandmother served food in the cafeteria at Columbia St. Mary's Hospital, but her mother rarely worked outside the home. She received assistance and later married a man who held down a job. That man became a minister, which was the reason Arleen tried never to set foot in a church.

When Arleen moved out at seventeen, she threw away the hand-me-down clothes her mother had made her wear to school. *"Dingdong,"* her classmates would taunt when she walked past in recycled bell-bottoms. Arleen put rubber bands on the bottom of her jeans, but that only made the kids laugh harder. When she dropped out before finishing high school, her mother said nothing. "She didn't care."

Arleen moved in with a family that paid her to babysit their children. During that time, she met the man who would become the father of her eldest child, Gerald, whom she took to calling Ger-Ger. After Arleen discovered she was pregnant with Ger-Ger, her man got entangled with the law. "I didn't know nothing about having a boyfriend in and out of jail all the time. So when I met somebody else," during one of the times Ger-Ger's father was locked up, "I just left him alone."

That someone else was Larry. He was a lean man with calm eyes and a wide brow. Larry had taught himself how to be a mechanic and earned money fixing cars in a back alley. On paydays, he would take Arleen out for Chinese food, her favorite. She would read the long menu but order the same thing every time: sesame chicken. They were poor and in love, and soon Arleen was pregnant with another son. They named him after Larry but called him Boosie. Larry and Arleen had three more children after that, a daughter and two more sons, letting Arleen's mother name their youngest. "Jori." They liked it.

"Will you marry me?" Larry asked one day.

Arleen laughed. She thought he was joking and said no. "He wasn't talking about no big marriage, wasn't even talking about at the courthouse," Arleen remembered. But he was not joking. When she realized this, Arleen dropped her smile and said she would have to think about it. What gave her pause was not Larry but his mother and sister. "They always thought they knew more . . . I was never good enough in they eyes."

After that, Larry started running around. It crushed Arleen, but when he came back, she always held the door open. Until one day he didn't come back. They had been together for seven years. This time, the other woman was someone Arleen considered a friend.

That happened years ago. Sometimes, Larry parked outside of where Arleen was staying. She'd climb in his van, and they'd drive around and talk, mostly about Jori. From time to time, Larry took Jori to church or let him spend the night or swelled his lip for getting in trouble at school. When Jori spotted Larry driving by in the neighborhood, he'd holler, "There go my daddy!" and run after him.

When Larry walked out on her and the kids, Arleen was working at the Mainstay Suites, by the airport. In despair, she quit and began relying on welfare. Sometime later she found work cleaning the Third Street Pier restaurant, but then her mother died suddenly. The grief overwhelmed her, and she left that job too. She later regretted going back on welfare, but it was a dark time.

When she moved onto Thirteenth Street, Arleen was receiving W-2 T, owing mainly to her chronic depression. She received the same stipend in 2008 that she would have when welfare was reformed over a decade earlier: $20.65 a day, $7,536 a year. Since 1997, welfare stipends in Milwaukee and almost everywhere else have not budged, even as housing costs have soared. For years, politicians have known that families could not survive on welfare alone.[1] This was the case before rent and utility costs climbed throughout the 2000s, and it was even more true afterward.

Arleen had given up hoping for housing assistance long ago. If she had a housing voucher or a key to a public housing unit, she would spend only 30 percent of her income on rent. It would mean the difference between stable poverty and grinding poverty, the difference between planting roots in a community and being batted from one place to another. It would mean she could give most of her check to her children instead of her landlord.

Years ago, when she was nineteen, Arleen rented a subsidized apartment for $137 a month. She had just had Ger-Ger and was grateful to be out of her mother's house. She could make her own decisions. So when a friend asked Arleen to give up her place and move in with her, Arleen decided to say yes. She walked away from a subsidized apartment and into the private rental market, where she would stay for the next twenty years. "I thought it was okay to move somewhere else," she remembered. "And I regret it, right now to this day. Young!" She shook her head at her nineteen-year-old self. "If I would've been in my right mind, I could have *still* been there."

One day on a whim, Arleen stopped by the Housing Authority and asked about the List. A woman behind the glass told her, "The List is frozen." On it were over 3,500 families who had applied for rent assistance four years earlier. Arleen nodded and left with hands in her pockets.[2] It could have been worse. In larger cities like Washington, DC, the wait for public housing was counted in decades. In those cities, a mother of a young child who put her name on the List might be a grandmother by the time her application was reviewed.[3]

Most poor people in America were like Arleen: they did not live in public housing or apartments subsidized by vouchers. Three in four families who qualified for assistance received nothing.[4]

If Arleen wanted public housing, she would have to save a month's worth of income to repay the Housing Authority for leaving her subsidized apartment without giving notice; then wait two to three years until the List unfroze; then wait another two to five years until her application made it to the top of the pile; then pray to Jesus that the person with the stale coffee and heavy stamp reviewing her file would somehow overlook the eviction record she'd collected while trying to make ends meet in the private housing market on a welfare check.

THE UPSTAIRS UNIT on Thirteenth Street didn't sit vacant for long. Sherrena moved a young woman into the apartment soon after the paint had dried on Arleen's walls. Trisha was her name.

Arleen and Trisha began talking and sharing meals. Arleen could be quiet and cautious around new people, guarded, but Trisha was an open book. She told Arleen that this was her first real home in eight years. Her last real home belonged to her sister, who had asked her to leave after Trisha told her what their father had done to her. Trisha then started sleeping in shelters and abandoned houses, but mostly she went home with men. At sixteen, she learned to use her skinny frame, her flush of wavy black hair, her copper skin, a mix of black, Mexican, and white blood. The year before, when she was twenty-three, Trisha had had a baby but signed him over to her sister because she was using. Crack, mostly. After the baby came, Trisha found Repairers of the Breach, a local homeless outreach that helped her get on SSI.

Trisha was illiterate and fragile. Jori once reduced her to tears by asking, "You special or something?" But she was also laid-back and sweet. Most of all, she was there. When Arleen and Trisha wanted a smoke to stave off boredom or, at the end of the month, hunger, Trisha used spare change to buy loose cigarettes at the corner store or fished stubs from standing ashtrays outside of fast-food joints. When Arleen needed to run an errand, Trisha would watch the boys, and Jori, who saw Trisha as an equal or a lesser, but certainly not as an adult, would tell her to watch her mouth around Jafaris. "I was born to be cussing," Trisha would reply.

One day, Arleen and Trisha watched a U-Haul truck pull up. Three women and a man walked up to the apartment and gave Arleen's door a knock. Sensing who they were, Arleen cracked the door and wedged her leg and foot behind it, in case they tried to push through.

A young woman introduced herself as the previous tenant and said she had come to collect her things. The armoire, dresser, and refrigerator all belonged to her.

Arleen told the young woman that Sherrena had thrown everything out. The woman looked doubtful, but Trisha backed her up. The previous tenant and her people left before discovering the lie. Once they were gone, Arleen and Trisha nodded at each other.[5]

After that, Trisha took to telling people that the women were old friends, that they had met outside a corner store years ago, when Trisha was just a girl and Arleen had told her, "You a pretty female." There was more to the story—about Arleen meeting Trisha's mother in prison, about Trisha waking up in the hospital and Arleen being there—but it was all in Trisha's head. It was hard to know if she believed it or not.

Trisha came to Sherrena through Belinda Hall, who was the best thing to happen to Sherrena in a long time. A black woman, not yet thirty, with a round face and glasses, Belinda ran her own business, working as a representative payee responsible for handling the finances of SSI beneficiaries found incapable of managing on their own. Sherrena liked finding tenants through social service agencies, which often vouched for tenants and put up some cash. But Belinda was a special catch. "I've been helping this girl as much as possible because I want her to *fill up* my properties," Sherrena reflected. "The rent comes directly from her every month. So that's a damn good situation to be in." Sherrena told Belinda that she would empty out all of her units if she wanted them for her clients. "I'm serious. Because I know I would get my money." Trisha was the fourth tenant Belinda had given Sherrena since the two women had met three months earlier.

Those poor and disabled enough to receive SSI but not clean enough to be welcomed into public housing made up Belinda's client base.[6] Belinda estimated that rent payments took between 60 and 70 percent of her typical client's monthly income. Many clients had little left over after Belinda paid for rent, utilities, and food.[7] Because stable and affordable housing was a major problem for Belinda's clients, she cultivated friendships with landlords, whom she could then call upon in an emergency. Belinda once phoned Sherrena around five a.m. because the heat in one of her client's buildings had gone out and she needed to relocate her that day. The faster Belinda could address clients' housing problems, the more clients she could take on—and the more money she could make. Belinda charged each client $37 a month for her services. When she met Sherrena, Belinda had 230 clients.

What Belinda could offer Sherrena and other landlords was steady, reliable rental income, and what Belinda got in return was a growing customer base, which meant more money in her pocket.

"PRESS 1 TO leave a voice message." Sherrena pressed 1. "Arleen, this is Sherrena calling. I'm calling to find out if you had your rent. Remember we agreed that you were going to pay a little bit over to get caught up with the three twenty you owed for—" Sherrena stopped herself from finishing the sentence with "your sister's funeral costs." She went on: "Um, I will be expecting the six hundred and fifty. Go 'head and give me a call."

Arleen didn't regret what she had done. Usually when there was a funeral, she couldn't even afford to buy Jafaris new shoes and would just scrub his best ones. She had missed funerals in the past because Jori and Jafaris didn't have anything to wear. But this was her sister—not in the biological sense but in the spiritual sense. They were close. She had long been a sickly girl, overweight and diabetic; her heart quit after she'd been hospitalized for pneumonia and a series of other health complications.

Arleen didn't have the money, but neither did anyone else. She would have been ashamed of herself if she hadn't pitched in. She gave half of her check to Sherrena and the other half to New Pitts Mortuary.

Sherrena felt bad when she heard about Arleen's sister. She made her new tenant a deal. Arleen could stay if she paid $650 for three months to recover the lost rent. Even if Arleen signed over her entire welfare check each month, she would still be short. But Sherrena was betting that Arleen could put in a few calls to family members or non-profit agencies. Arleen took the deal because she had no other option.

Sherrena and Quentin were in the Suburban when Arleen called around the beginning of the next month. Sherrena hung up and looked at Quentin. "Arleen said her check didn't come."

This was a half-truth. Arleen had received a check, but not for $628. She had missed an appointment with her welfare caseworker, completely forgetting about it. A reminder notice was mailed to Atkinson, or was it Nineteenth Street? When Arleen didn't show, the caseworker "sanctioned" Arleen by decreasing her benefit.[8] Arleen could have given Sherrena her reduced check, but she thought it was better to be behind and have a few hundred dollars in her pocket than be behind and completely broke.

Quentin kept his eyes on the road. "Story of they life," he said.

6.

RAT HOLE

Three generations of Hinkstons lived in the brownish-white house on Eighteenth and Wright, the one in front of Lamar's. Doreen was the mother hen. Broad-shouldered and broad-bellied, she was a moonfaced woman with glasses and dark-brown freckles flecking her lighter cheeks. For as long as she could remember, she had been overweight and tended to move slowly through her days. Doreen had four children—Patrice, Natasha, C.J., and Ruby, ages twenty-four, nineteen, fourteen, and thirteen—and three grandchildren from Patrice: ten-year-old Mikey and his two younger sisters: Jada, four; and Kayla Mae, two. There was also a dog, Coco, a football-sized ankle-biter loyal only to Natasha.

After Patrice received Sherrena's eviction papers and moved herself and her children from their upper unit to the downstairs apartment where Doreen lived with Natasha, C.J., and Ruby, all eight Hinkstons (and Coco) found themselves living together in a small, cramped space. Patrice, Natasha, and C.J. responded by spending as much time as they could out of the house, walking the block in good weather or passing evenings in the back apartment, playing spades with Lamar. But at night, everyone packed in. Patrice claimed the smaller of the two bedrooms. If she was going to pay half the rent, she argued, then she should get one bedroom to herself, even if it didn't have a door. In the other bedroom, Doreen and Natasha shared the bed while Ruby curled up in a chair at night. Mikey bedded down with C.J. on a sheetless single mattress in the living room, next to the glass table and head-high piles of clean and dirty clothes that didn't fit in the bedrooms. Patrice's daughters slept in the dining room on a single mattress, its corners split open, exposing innards of springs and etiolated foam.

No one slept well. Natasha had a habit of kicking Doreen in her sleep, and Doreen had a habit of rolling over on Natasha or stealing Natasha's pillow and hitting her with it when she tried to tug it back. The older children often missed the early-morning school bus. The little ones fell asleep at random times throughout the day. Doreen would come out of the kitchen to find their tiny heads resting on the table or some piece of clothing on the floor.

The worst night's sleep always came on the eve of your birthday. If you fell asleep that night, you could be sure that Patrice would sneak into your room and smear mayonnaise or ketchup on your face. For the past six years, the Hinkstons hadn't been able to celebrate Christmas—they didn't have the money. But on your birthday, you woke up smiling with goo on your face and a cake on the table. The Hinkstons loved pranking one another. Once Natasha put pepper in Patrice's underwear. Patrice retaliated by sneaking Ruby out of the house on a day Natasha was put in charge of watching her younger sister. When Natasha noticed Ruby was gone, she spent the next several hours patrolling the neighborhood, frantically searching.

The Hinkstons' rear door was off its hinges. The walls were pockmarked with large holes. There was one bathroom. Its ceiling sagged from an upstairs leak, and a thin blackish film coated its floor. The kitchen windows were cracked. A few dining-room windows had disheveled miniblinds, broken and strung out in all directions. Patrice hung heavy blankets over the windows facing the street, darkening the house. A small television sat on a plywood dresser in the living room, next to a lamp with no shade.

After Patrice had moved downstairs, Sherrena discovered that she had been pirating electricity. The meter-repair bill would cost $200, and Sherrena refused to pay it while Patrice was living with Doreen. "I ain't incurring shit," she said. "They black asses are gonna incur everything, or they gonna be cold this winter." It took the Hinkstons a couple months to save $200; during that time the back of the house, including the kitchen, was without power. Everything in the refrigerator spoiled. The family ate dinners out of cans: ravioli, SpaghettiOs.

The Hinkstons treated the refrigerator, sour-smelling and sitting tomblike in the kitchen, like they treated the entire apartment: as something to endure, to outlast. It was how they saw the mattresses and small love seat too, each deep-burrowed with so many roaches they planned to leave them all behind when they moved out. The roaches were there when the Hinkstons moved in: crawling the sinks, the toilet, the walls, filling kitchen drawers. "They were rushers," Sherrena said about Doreen's family. "They moved in on top of roaches."

BEFORE THE HINKSTONS had moved into Sherrena's apartment off Wright Street, they'd lived for seven years in a five-bedroom house on Thirty-Second Street. It wasn't perfect, but it was spacious and the landlord was decent. They pooled their money to make rent: $800 a month. Patrice was serving up lunch at a fast-food joint, and after dropping out, Natasha had started working too. Doreen hadn't completed high school either, though she had learned to type seventy-two words a minute at Job Corps years back. Patrice almost finished high school, making it to the eleventh grade even after having Mikey at fourteen, but in the end she started working full-time to help the family stay afloat. At sixteen, Natasha began logging twelve-hour shifts at Quad Graphics for $9.50 an hour, sometimes falling asleep on the printing machines. They didn't ask her age, and she didn't offer it.

Doreen's monthly income was $1,124: $437 from a state-funded child support supplement and $687 from SSI, which she received for an old leg injury. In eighth grade, she had broken her hip on Easter Sunday—her new wedge high heels did her in—and the fracture had never quite healed. Maybe it would have if her father had rushed her to the hospital instead of keeping her home for several days. The old man hated doctors. When his knees began going out, he just sawed off a kitchen table leg and used it for a cane.

On Thirty-Second Street, the Hinkstons became a neighborhood feature. The children ran in and out of neighbors' homes, and from her front steps Doreen got to know the other families on her block. She would rock and laugh with the grandmothers and yell at the neighborhood boys when they terrorized stray cats. When summer arrived, the children would buy bottle rockets from a neighbor and shoot them off in the street. Every so often, Doreen would host a party and invite everyone.

Then one August day in 2005, Doreen turned on the television and saw New Orleans underwater. A muddy expanse filled the city, and black bodies bobbed past folks on rooftops. She immediately called her best friend, Fanny, asking her to come over. Doreen and Fanny were shocked by what they saw on the news. "This is a total disgrace," Doreen remembered thinking. After a few restless nights, Doreen felt called to do something more for the flood victims than fret and pray. She left Patrice in charge and boarded a southbound bus with Fanny. She was forty-one. Patrice was twenty.

It wasn't like her to do something like this. She was a soft-humming stoop-sitter. "I don't go no further than my front porch," Doreen said. But there were moments along the way when she struck out against life's current, like the January night in 1998 when she hurriedly packed up and moved the family to Illinois without telling anyone. She needed to get away from C.J. and Ruby's father, who would go on to serve a long sentence upstate.

After two days on the bus, Doreen and Fanny found themselves in Lafayette, Louisiana. They joined dozens of other volunteers, passing out blankets and serving food.

The trip caused the Hinkstons to fall a month behind in rent. But they had been long-term tenants and their landlord was loyal. "He wasn't sweating me," Doreen recalled. The landlord told her to pay him back when she could. Doreen gave him extra when she had it, $100 here and there. She worked to clear her debt, but then something would happen and she'd come up short. Months passed; then years.

One early spring night in 2008 two neighborhood boys on Thirty-Second Street shot at each other. Bullets zipped through the Hinkstons' front door, shattering its window. Natasha, who was seventeen at the time, was sweeping up the glass when the police arrived. They asked to take a look inside. To hear the Hinkstons tell it, the officers ransacked their house, looking for guns or drugs. (Patrice speculated that a neighbor associated with one of the shooters had pinned the crime on the three young men who were staying with the Hinkstons at the time: Patrice's and Natasha's boyfriends as well as a cousin.) All the police found was a mess: dishes piled high in the sink, overflowing trash cans, flies. The Hinkstons were not the tidiest family, and to make matters worse, they had thrown a party the night before. There were less superficial problems too, like the plywood board the landlord had haphazardly nailed over a sagging bathroom ceiling. Perhaps because of the mess, or because Patrice began snapping at the officers around two a.m., or because they believed the Hinkstons had played a role in the shooting—whatever the case, the police called Child Protective Services, who called the Department of Neighborhood Services (DNS), who dispatched a building inspector, who issued orders to the landlord, who filled out a five-day eviction notice, citing unpaid rent. Doreen had only managed to get halfway caught up when the shooting happened. There had never been a need to rush.

After the court commissioner stamped their eviction judgment, the Hinkstons needed to find another place quickly. They searched on their own—but without a car or the Internet their reach was limited. They sought help from social workers, and one put them in touch with Sherrena. She showed them the apartment off Wright Street, and they hated it. "I wouldn't advertise it to a blind person," Patrice said. But anyplace, the family figured, was better than the street or a shelter; so they took it. Sherrena handed Doreen the keys on the spot, along with a rent receipt dashed off on a scrap of paper. Doreen tucked the scrap with PAID $1,100, RENT + SECURITY DEPOSIT into her Bible.

POOR FAMILIES WERE often compelled to accept substandard housing in the harried aftermath of eviction. Milwaukee renters whose previous move was involuntary were almost 25 percent more likely to experience long-term housing problems than other low-income renters.[1] Doreen said she took Sherrena's apartment because her family was desperate. "But we not gonna be here long." Eviction had a way of causing not one move but two: a forced move into degrading and sometimes dangerous housing and an intentional move out of it.[2] But the second move could be a while coming.

The Hinkstons began looking for new housing soon after moving into Sherrena's place, calling the numbers on rent signs and leafing through apartment listings in the *RedBook*, a free glossy found at most inner-city corner stores. But their previous move had left them exhausted, and Doreen's fresh eviction record wasn't helping matters. Patrice soon moved into the second-floor unit upstairs, and everyone breathed easier for a time. Fall arrived, and the Hinkstons settled into the neighborhood but always considered their stay temporary, even as the months rolled by, one after the other. It wasn't like on Thirty-Second, where Doreen had made it a point to get to know her neighbors and watch over the neighborhood boys. At the time of Patrice's eviction, six months after the family had relocated to Eighteenth and Wright, the only neighbor Doreen knew by name was Lamar—and his name was all she really knew about him. "I don't even go to anybody's houses, like I used to," Doreen said about her new neighborhood. "I used to get up and go to visitors. Now I just . . . stand around." When winter set in, weeks would pass without Doreen so much as stepping outside.

"The public peace—the sidewalk and street peace—of cities is not kept primarily by the police, necessary as police are. It is kept primarily by an intricate, almost unconscious, network of voluntary controls and standards among the people themselves, and enforced by the people themselves." So wrote Jane Jacobs in *The Death and Life of Great American Cities*. Jacobs believed that a prerequisite for this type of healthy and engaged community was the presence of people who simply were present, who looked after the neighborhood. She has been proved right: disadvantaged neighborhoods with higher levels of "collective efficacy"—the stuff of loosely linked neighbors who trust one another and share expectations about how to make their community better—have lower crime rates.[3]

A single eviction could destabilize multiple city blocks, not only the block from which a family was evicted but also the block to which it begrudgingly relocated. In this way, displacement contributed directly to what Jacobs called "perpetual slums," churning environments with high rates of turnover and even higher rates of resentment and disinvestment. "The key link in a perpetual slum is that too many people move out of it too fast—and in the meantime *dream* of getting out."[4] With Doreen's eviction, Thirty-Second Street lost a steadying presence—someone who loved and invested in the neighborhood, who contributed to making the block safer—but Wright Street didn't gain one.

RUBY, C.J., AND Mikey had kept on their school uniforms—oversized white T-shirts and black jeans—while they took turns at the front window, watching for the lunch truck. Three times a week, a local church delivered sack lunches to the neighborhood. This day, Ruby was the one to spot it. "Lunch truck!" she yelled, bounding outside with the others. The kids returned with a bag for everyone. They passed them out without peeking inside because that would ruin the game. Green apples were swapped for red ones, Fritos for SunChips, apple juice for fruit punch.

"I'll give you *two* juices," Natasha offered Ruby.

"For an Oreo cake?" Ruby asked. After thinking it over, she shook her head no.

"Ruby, you suck!"

Ruby flashed a white smile and started bouncing from leg to leg. Her Ritalin was wearing off. Some nights after its effects had dissipated completely, she and Mikey would land backflips off the mattress in the living room.

Natasha pouted. At nineteen, she was six years older than Ruby but acted more like the oldest child than the youngest adult. While Patrice had only just begun adolescence when she found herself a mother, Natasha balked at the thought of having kids. "They messy. They dirty!" she said. "And you don't know if they gonna be ugly or pretty—so hell no. . . . I'm living *free and independent!*" Natasha partied with the boys at Lamar's house and in the summertime sauntered around the neighborhood barefoot. She was light-skinned like Patrice—"redboned"—even though they had different fathers. Men in cars would slow down and crane their necks. Sometimes old ladies would slow down too and offer Natasha shoes with pity-filled eyes. That always made Patrice chuckle.

After reading aloud the prayers the church ladies had slipped inside the white sacks, the Hinkstons settled into their sack dinner and began a conversation about words they had a hard time pronouncing. "Royal." "Turquoise." Anything was a welcome distraction from the stench and state of the house. In the kitchen and bathroom, things had gotten so bad that Doreen was considering calling Sherrena and Quentin. She loathed calling them. The Hinkston family was slow to admit it, but their landlords intimidated them. "Quentin is a grouch," Patrice often complained. When Quentin was in the apartment, he made comments about how bad it smelled. If he brought workers over to fix a problem, he often left behind discarded materials, which Doreen and Patrice took as a sign of disrespect. "It's like you're his maid," said Patrice. Whether Quentin intentionally behaved this way to discourage tenants from calling him with housing problems was hard to say, but it had that effect.[5]

When Doreen phoned Sherrena to complain, she often found herself being complained about. "Every time we call about something," Doreen said, "she tries to blame it on us, and say we broke it. I'm tired of hearing it. . . . So, we just fix it every time it breaks."

"Fixing it" often meant getting on without it. The sink was the first thing to get stopped up. After it stayed that way for days, Ruby and Patrice took to washing dishes in the bathtub. But they weren't able to catch all the food scraps from going down the drain, and pretty soon concrete-colored water was collecting in the bathtub too. So the family began boiling water on the kitchen stove and taking sponge baths. Afterward, someone would dump the pot water down the toilet and grab the plunger, causing a small colony of roaches to scamper to another hiding spot. You had to plunge hard. It usually took a good five minutes before the toilet would flush. When the toilet quit working, the family began placing soiled tissue in a plastic bag to be tossed with the trash.

When Doreen finally did call Sherrena about the plumbing, she could not get ahold of her. After a week of voice messages, Sherrena called back, explaining that she and Quentin had been away in Florida. They had recently purchased a three-bedroom vacation condo there. In response to Doreen's complaint about the plumbing, Sherrena reminded her tenant that she was breaking the terms of her lease by allowing Patrice and her children to live with her.

To Patrice, it was déjà vu. Before moving upstairs, she had inspected the unit. It needed a lot of work—the lint-gray carpet was worn thin and filthy, the ceiling in the kids' bedroom was drooping, the balcony door was unhinged, and the balcony itself looked like it would collapse if you tossed a sack of flour on it—but Sherrena promised to attend to these things. Landlords were allowed to rent units with property code violations, and even units that did not meet "basic habitability requirements," as long as they were up front about the problems.[6]

Patrice took Sherrena at her word and handed her $1,100: the first month's rent and security deposit. But the repairs came slowly. Patrice's bathtub stopped draining, but Sherrena didn't return her calls. That time, she and Quentin were away on vacation. Patrice went two months without a working sink. When Patrice discovered a large hole in one of the walls, Sherrena gave her a pamphlet about how to keep her children safe from lead paint. When the door came off the hinges, "she sent her dope men over to our house to fix it," Patrice complained. Things came to a head.

"I'm gonna get an attorney and sue you!" Patrice shouted.

"Go ahead." Sherrena laughed. "But my money is longer than yours."

"If I'm giving you my money, why ain't my stuff fixed?"

The next month, Patrice tried a different approach. If Sherrena wouldn't respond when the rent was paid, maybe she would respond when it wasn't. Patrice gave Sherrena half the rent and said she would get the rest after she completed the promised repairs. As it was, the rent took 65 percent of Patrice's income. It was hard to give up such a big chunk of her paycheck to live in such conditions.

Patrice's plan backfired. Sherrena refused to work on Patrice's place unless she delivered her rent in full. To Patrice, it felt like a catch-22. If she was paid up, Sherrena often didn't answer the phone until the first of the month rolled around again. If she withheld rent, Sherrena refused to fix anything until she paid. "I'm not going to rush and bust my ass to take care of a bunch of issues, and you didn't pay me all my money," Sherrena said. Still, Patrice wanted to stay. She liked living above her momma and thought the apartment could be nice. Then Patrice's manager at Cousins Subs cut back her hours, and she lost what little leverage she had. After Sherrena served her the eviction notice, Patrice couldn't catch up. She promised to give Sherrena her

tax refund, but by that time it was too late. Belinda, the payee and
Sherrena's new best friend, had called asking for a place, and Sherrena
jumped at the opportunity. Patrice's place would be available in a few
weeks, Sherrena promised.

AFTER TWO MONTHS without a working bathtub or sink and with
a barely working toilet, Doreen decided to call a plumber herself. Having paid for a plumber the first time things got stopped up, Sherrena
was not keen to do so again. And after what had happened at Thirty-
Second Street, Doreen knew better than to call a building inspector.
The plumber charged $150 to snake out the pipes. He concluded that
the plumbing system was old and vulnerable and advised Doreen to
catch everything she could from going down the sink. The first thing
Doreen did after the man left was to run a hot bath and soak in it for
an hour.

Doreen decided to deduct the $150 from her rent. When Sherrena
responded by saying that would earn her an eviction notice, Doreen
went ahead and withheld all her rent. If she was going to get evicted,
she might as well save her money to put it toward the next move.[7] It
was a common strategy among cash-strapped renters. Because the rent
took almost all of their paycheck, families sometimes had to initiate a
necessary eviction that allowed them to save enough money to move
to another place. One landlord's loss was another's gain.[8]

If Doreen had to move, she knew she wouldn't be able to find a
much cheaper place, especially for three adults and five children. At
the time, median rent for a two-bedroom apartment in Milwaukee was
$600. Ten percent of units rented at or below $480, and 10 percent
rented at or above $750.[9] A mere $270 separated some of the cheapest
units in the city from some of the most expensive. That meant that rent
in some of the worst neighborhoods was not drastically cheaper than
rent in much better areas. For example, in the city's poorest neighborhoods, where at least 40 percent of families lived below the poverty

line, median rent for a two-bedroom apartment was only $50 less than the citywide median.[10] Sherrena put it like this: "A two bedroom is a two bedroom is a two bedroom."

This had long been the case. When tenements began appearing in New York City in the mid-1800s, rent in the worst slums was 30 percent higher than in uptown. In the 1920s and '30s, rent for dilapidated housing in the black ghettos of Milwaukee and Philadelphia and other northern cities exceeded that for better housing in white neighborhoods. As late as 1960, rent in major cities was higher for blacks than for whites in similar accommodations.[11] The poor did not crowd into slums because of cheap housing. They were there—and this was especially true of the black poor—simply because they were allowed to be.

Landlords at the bottom of the market generally did not lower rents to meet demand and avoid the costs of all those missed payments and evictions. There were costs to avoiding those costs too. For many landlords, it was cheaper to deal with the expense of eviction than to maintain their properties; it was possible to skimp on maintenance if tenants were perpetually behind; and many poor tenants would be perpetually behind because their rent was too high.

Tenants able to pay their rent in full each month could take advantage of legal protections designed to keep their housing safe and decent. Not only could they summon a building inspector without fear of eviction, but they also had the right to withhold rent until certain repairs were made.[12] But when tenants fell behind, these protections dissolved. Tenants in arrears were barred from withholding or escrowing rent; and they tempted eviction if they filed a report with a building inspector. It was not that low-income renters didn't know their rights. They just knew those rights would cost them.

"I think callin' a building inspector is only gonna cause more problems," Doreen told Patrice.

"It does," Patrice answered. "She can put us out if we call a building inspector." What Patrice meant was that Sherrena could evict them because Doreen had violated the terms of her lease—Patrice and her kids were "unauthorized boarders"—and that she likely would if DNS were phoned.

When tenants relinquished protections by falling behind in rent or otherwise breaking their rental agreement, landlords could respond by neglecting repairs. Or as Sherrena put it to tenants: "If I give you a break, you give me a break." Tenants could trade their dignity and children's health for a roof over their head.[13] Between 2009 and 2011, nearly half of all renters in Milwaukee experienced a serious and lasting housing problem.[14] More than 1 in 5 lived with a broken window; a busted appliance; or mice, cockroaches, or rats for more than three days. One-third experienced clogged plumbing that lasted more than a day. And 1 in 10 spent at least a day without heat. African American households were the most likely to have these problems—as were those where children slept. Yet the average rent was the same, whether an apartment had housing problems or did not.[15]

Tenants who fell behind either had to accept unpleasant, degrading, and sometimes dangerous housing conditions or be evicted. But from a business point of view, this arrangement could be lucrative. The four-family property that included Doreen's and Lamar's apartments was Sherrena's most profitable. Her second-most profitable property was Arleen's place on Thirteenth Street. In Sherrena's portfolio, her worst properties yielded her biggest returns.[16]

SHORTLY AFTER DOREEN told Sherrena she would be withholding her rent, Natasha discovered she was four months pregnant. When she told her momma, Doreen laughed and said, "I told you so!" She had noticed the changes Natasha had tried to ignore. Doreen was thrilled. "I'm about to be a proud grandmother again," she crowed. Natasha's boyfriend was thrilled. A new pregnancy, legitimate or otherwise, was something to celebrate—unless you were a young woman trying to live free and independent.[17] Natasha was devastated.

"It's probably a bigheaded boy!" Doreen teased.

"I don't see how in the *world* I got pregnant," Natasha whined. "I don't even like pregnant stomachs."

Natasha and Malik had been dating for about a year. They had met at Cousins Subs, where Malik worked with Patrice. He was shorter and darker than Natasha, with cornrows and a strong face. He had a gentle way about him, and although he was thirty-three, this would be his first child. Natasha liked him okay. But her heart still belonged to Taye, gunned down in a botched robbery two years earlier, when he was seventeen. In her purse, she still carried his funeral program, which listed Natasha as "a special lady friend" among his survivors. Ruby was crazy about that boy too, and sometimes with Natasha's prodding she would tell Taye stories. As Natasha listened quietly, she would smile like older people do when they've put some distance between themselves and the pain. In those moments it was as if some cruel force had wedged a vise between the sisters and sprung the crank, propelling Natasha beyond her years.[18]

Per Hinkston family tradition, Patrice would be the one to name the baby. Malik had other plans. When Natasha told Doreen and Patrice that Malik wanted the name to be Malik Jr. if it was a boy, they scoffed. "We don't do juniors," Doreen said. "We messed up once. I hate that I did that." C.J. was named after his father, but so the family wouldn't have to utter that man's name, they shortened Caleb Jr. to C.J.

If Natasha had to be a mother, she knew this much: she was not going to bring her baby into that house. Now that she was pregnant, she worried more about the apartment and about where they would go if Sherrena decided to evict them. But Doreen had carried the family on her back before, and Natasha believed she would do it again. "My momma, she strong," Natasha said. "And she's got us out of way worse situations than this. I mean, from shelters, livin' on the street, churches, cars. I got a lot of faith in my momma. Yeah, we've been on the street a few times, but my momma, she always had it." Only this time, Natasha didn't like her momma's plan. Ever since learning about an upcoming family reunion in Brownsville, Tennessee, Doreen had been thinking about moving the family down there. Patrice liked the idea; she was done with Milwaukee. "This a dead city," she said, "full of crackheads and prostitutes." But Natasha didn't want to take her baby away from its father.

Doreen and Patrice didn't think this was a legitimate concern. "He's not dependable," Doreen said. But Malik had been acting extra-dependable since learning he was going to be a dad, pulling double shifts, saving money, bringing Natasha food, and looking for an apartment for the three of them. The truth was that Doreen and Patrice didn't expect much from Malik, not because of anything he had done, but because of their own experiences with men. Patrice's and Natasha's fathers had left Doreen; Ruby and C.J.'s daddy was in prison. The fathers of Patrice's children played a negligible role in their lives, and her current boyfriend had recently put her through the dining-room table.[19] Doreen and Patrice did not see why a man needed to be involved in family decisions about where to raise a child, let alone what to name it. Said Doreen to Natasha, "There was no one around to rub my stomach when you were kicking me." Said Patrice, "We didn't have a daddy. My kids don't have no daddy. And your kids don't need no daddy."

Someone from the doctor's office called. "I gotta come back in for another ultrasound," Natasha told Doreen, getting off the phone. "They said they found somethin' hidin'."

"What do you mean they found somethin' hidin'?"

"Hidin'. Hidin', like behind the other baby."

Doreen gasped. "Natasha, are you going to have *twins*?"

"But I don't want no babies!" Natasha stomped her foot.

"Too late to say that now!" Doreen laughed.

"That's too much." Natasha slunk down on the couch and Coco jumped on her lap. "Coco, come here. Momma's havin' a bad day."

Doreen tried to cheer her up. "I'm gonna make sure you get a very big room when we move," she said. "Down the hall from me. Maybe downstairs. Yeah, I hope we get a house like we had on Thirty-Second."

"That would be a blessing," Natasha said, stroking Coco.

"Yes, it would." Doreen turned to Ruby, who had been sitting quietly on the floor, holding her knees to her chest. "What you think, Ruby girl, wanna move?"

"Of course," Ruby said. "I hate this house."

7.

THE SICK

Scott worked for cash here and there, but his main job was taking care of Teddy. He did the cooking, cleaning, and shopping. In the morning, he helped Teddy out of bed and the shower. Scott felt he had a calling for that sort of thing. It was why he had become a nurse. Thirty-eight and bald, with a ruddy complexion, dimples, and eyes that matched the blue flames of a gas-stove burner, Scott had a gentle, broken spirit. As for Teddy, he was a small man, bone thin, with scabbed-over arms displaying shriveled tattoos. He could hardly walk. Scott made him anyway, and Teddy would shuffle slowly around the trailer park, dragging his left leg behind him and looking much older than fifty-two.

Pam and Ned had left to go stay in a cheap motel for a few days, but Tobin was still moving forward with Teddy and Scott's eviction. They had fallen behind two months ago, when a neck X-ray and brain scan set Teddy back $507. Teddy's health problems began a year earlier, when he woke up in the hospital after tumbling down some steps around the Sixteenth Street Viaduct. The space beneath the viaduct was one of his favorite drinking spots, the cars zooming overhead and the valley floor below. He had gone there with a bottle and some men from the rescue mission. In the hospital, Teddy was told that he was partially paralyzed on his left side, that the doctors had had to fuse his neck back together, and that all the pins and screws were there to hold everything in place.

Scott put the eviction notice on their cluttered table, next to bills, beer cans, an old Polaroid camera, and a large ashtray. It was late morning, and the two men sat drinking cans of Milwaukee's Best. Teddy poked the eviction notice. "I suppose he wants to get a little more in his pot. His pot is a lot bigger than my pot."

Teddy had looked straight ahead when he said it, his back perfectly flat against the chair. Sometimes Scott would walk in and find Teddy sitting on the couch, motionless, arms limp at his sides, not watching television or flipping through a magazine, just sitting. The first couple times this happened, Scott leaned in to make sure Teddy wasn't dead.

"Maybe," Scott answered. "But what did Tobin do wrong?"

"He is purely an asshole. If you like him, that's your business. . . . If I was in the shape I used to be, I'd already have gone up there and punched him in the nose."

"That's effective," Scott said sarcastically.

"I'm a hillbilly. You can take the boy outta the country but you can't take the country outta the boy."

Teddy went on—he could talk when he wanted to—and Scott sat quietly listening. He didn't interrupt the old man when he launched into one of his monologues, drawn out long and syrupy, like his Tennessee accent. Scott stared into the living room. There was nothing on the wood-paneled walls except a large painting left behind by the previous tenants: Jesus and the two thieves hung on crosses, all reds and purples. A year ago, the men had moved in with little and had acquired little since. Teddy's prized possessions were his fishing rods and tackle. Scott's was a large plastic container filled with photographs, certifications, and mementos from his old life.

When Teddy had finished, Scott looked up from his beer and out the window. Across the way, he saw Ned and Pam's trailer, now abandoned, and Dawn's, where he sometimes bought morphine or, if he was in a pinch, Vicodin. Randy Shit-Pants, who thought his dead father was living in his trailer's heating vents, was filthy on his porch, smoking a clove cigarette and mumbling to himself. An airplane roared in low.

"I," Scott started. "I don't want to live here." He picked up the eviction notice. "You know what this is? The kick in the ass to get me out."

SCOTT HAD GROWN up on an Iowa dairy farm that later went to pigs. He once got a horse for Christmas. Scott never met his biological father, who, during a date, had forced himself on his mother. To save the family some embarrassment, Scott's mother, Joan, was made to marry the rapist. She was sixteen. But Scott's father soon made a clean break, never to be heard from again. The next husband was a mean cuss, a hitter; before they divorced, Joan had one child by him: a daughter, Clarissa. Then Scott's mother found Cam, a cowboy, and they had three more children. One of Scott's brothers became a firefighter; another delivered water for Culligan; and his youngest sister was a nurse. Clarissa was an alcoholic who lived in the worst apartment complex in Scott's hometown. Locals called it the Beehive because tenants buzzed in and out of it.

Scott never got on with Cowboy Cam. He was too sensitive a kid to please the grizzled ranch hand. Scott took the ACT, got into Winona State University, and left home for college at seventeen. He soon outgrew Winona, Minnesota, just as he had outgrown the soybean fields and water towers of rural Iowa. Scott had known he was gay from a young age. "I needed to find others like me," he remembered thinking before moving to Milwaukee. He finished at Milwaukee Area Technical College and later, at age thirty-one, received his nursing license.

Scott began his career in a nursing home. He checked vital signs, dispensed medication, monitored blood glucose levels, gave insulin injections, administered IV infusions, fed people through tubes, and cared for tracheotomies and wounds. He learned to make his hands light and quick, how not to puke, how to find the vein. Scott felt needed, and he was.

He rented nice apartments in up-and-coming neighborhoods: Bay View, the East Side. One year, his best, Scott took home $88,000. He sent money home to his mom.

After five years of hoisting limp women and men out of beds and bathtubs, Scott slipped a disk in his back. A doctor prescribed Percocet for the pain.[1] Around that time, two of Scott's best friends died of AIDS. "I fell off. I didn't cope well." The Percocet helped with that pain too.

Scott thought his pain would in time run its course, like any other illness. But when his doctor announced retirement, Scott found himself panicking. The doctor had become a treasure to Scott, like a bartender who pours to the rim; another might not be so forthcoming with the opioids. But there were other options. Scott began buying pills from fellow nurses and stealing them from work. His nursing-home patients too became regular suppliers, selling Vicodin pills at $3 a pop. Then they became regular suppliers without knowing it.

Several months after Scott started taking Percocet, he discovered fentanyl. That was when he fell in love. Fentanyl penetrated the central nervous system 100 times more effectively than morphine.[2] It offered Scott pure, calm happiness; it pulled him toward the sublime. "It was the best feeling of pleasure and contentment I have ever felt," he said.

In the nursing home, Scott would take a syringe and siphon fentanyl out of the Duragesic patches used for patients with chronic pain. He'd then swallow or inject the drug and reapply the empty patch, as his patients moaned softly in bed. "In your own heart, you convince yourself that you need it more than they do," Scott remembered. " 'If I do this, I'll be able to take care of thirty of you.' "

Like any other romance, Scott's relationship with fentanyl changed from something thrilling and magical into something deeper and more consuming. Soon, he was no longer chasing a high but running from withdrawal. "The sick," he called it. When he went without, he would shake and sweat, get diarrhea, and ache all over. "When you stop, it feels like you'd rather be dead." By this point, Scott needed opioids just to function. When he felt the sick right behind him, he did things he never thought he was capable of doing.

One day in August 2007, some of Scott's coworkers found him standing with his eyes closed, rocking back and forth. They sent him home and checked the patches, finding them drained. Scott's supervisor asked him to submit to a drug test, which came back positive for fentanyl. The same string of events repeated itself in November, but Scott was still allowed to keep his job because his supervisor, who had a drug history, gave him another chance. Then around Christmastime that year, patients complained that a male nurse had removed their patches. Scott was put in a cab and sent to a clinic for a third drug test. He shut the taxi's door and stood outside in the cold.

Behind the clinic's doors was a waiting room full of other junkies slumped in plastic chairs and gloved nurses with flat expressions, giving off neither pity nor disgust. Scott knew that Christmas music would be playing. He turned his back on the clinic and walked away.

Scared, Scott joined Narcotics Anonymous and tried to stop using. But it didn't take. "My life didn't get any better," he remembered. Four months later, Scott wore his best shirt to his disciplinary hearing in front of the Wisconsin Board of Nursing. The board ruled: "The license of [Scott W. Bunker], L.P.N., to practice as a nurse in the State of Wisconsin is suspended for an indefinite period."[3] That was the moment Scott decided to settle into a spot on the bottom and become a full-blown junkie. "I really cared about my nursing license," he remembered. "When they took it away, I was like, 'Fuck it.'"

AFTER SCOTT HAD lost his job and his upscale apartment, he sold most of his possessions and checked himself into the Lodge. At the shelter he met Teddy, who had recently been released from the hospital. He was drawn to Teddy for the obvious reason: Teddy was frail and sick and needed someone to help him climb steps and carry his food tray. Scott was still a nurse in heart and habit, even if he had lost his license.

Unlike Scott, homelessness was nothing new to Teddy. He had lived in shelters and under bridges since hitchhiking from Dayton, Tennessee, three years earlier. Teddy had grown up in a family with little money and fourteen kids. His father was an alcoholic who died young after slamming his truck into the back of an eighteen-wheeler. "Now, that's an experiment," Teddy liked to say when telling the story.

They made an unlikely pair: one a straight Southern man, who had lived for years on the street; the other younger, gay, and a new arrival at the bottom. But they became friends, and then decided to leave the homeless shelter together, as roommates.

Teddy's monthly income, from SSI, was $632, and Scott was only receiving food stamps. They needed a cheap apartment, but they also needed a landlord who wouldn't ask too many questions. College Mobile Home Park had a reputation for letting just about anyone in. When the two men visited the park, Office Susie showed them a small trailer without a stove. It was in a sorry state, but Tobin gave it to them and only charged $420 in lot rent. They moved in that week.

After leaving the nursing home, getting drugs had been a hassle. Scott would go to Woody's, the Harbor Room, or other gay bars and hope to run into someone. But in the trailer park, Scott met several neighbors with methadone prescriptions and others who sold drugs. Getting drugs was as easy as asking for a cup of sugar.

One morning Scott woke up and felt the sick coming. His pill suppliers had run dry. Scott asked Dawn for morphine, but she was out too. He downed several of Teddy's beers, but they didn't help. In the evening, Scott sat alone in his bedroom, shaking. He put on his baseball cap and, hands in pockets, began doing laps around the trailer park.

From a lawn chair outside her patio, Heroin Susie watched Scott pass by. She ashed her cigarette and went inside to tell Billy, her long-time boyfriend. When Scott walked by again, they called him over.

Susie and Billy had a small dog, a terrier mix, and a clean trailer stocked with newer furniture. Susie was middle-aged with long dirty-blond hair and dark rings underneath her eyes. Her mannerisms were silky, relaxed. She told people she had the gift of healing. Billy was a wiry man in a cutoff shirt who seemed to blink half as much as the average person. He had a gruff voice and faded prison tattoos. Susie and Billy had been together for years but still liked to hold hands.

Susie asked Scott if he was fiending. Yes, he nodded. She looked at Billy, who retrieved a small leather case. Inside was a package of new needles, alcohol swabs, sterilized water, tiny cotton balls, and black-tar heroin.

Never shoot it. It was the deal Scott had made with himself when opioids began taking over his life. He had promised he would never inject heroin, not after seeing what AIDS had done to his friends.

Billy held a spoon over a stove burner to cook the tar with water. Humming softly, he then soaked up the heroin into a cotton ball and pulled it into a syringe. It was dark, coffee-colored. Scott learned later that this meant it was strong. Scott took the needle behind his right knee. He closed his eyes, waited, and then came relief, weightlessness. He was a child floating back to the surface, the diving board bouncing.

They became friends, Scott, Susie, and Billy. Scott learned that Susie wrote poetry, liked telling stories of the days she dealt bricks of marijuana in the '70s, and had shot heroin for the last thirty-five years. Billy shot in his arms, and Susie in her legs, which were so scarred and discolored they made even Scott squeamish. It sometimes took Susie hours to find an opening. When she grew frustrated, Billy took the needle and forced it into her neck's jugular vein.

Billy and Scott sometimes scrapped metal or collected cans to raise dope money. (Black-tar heroin was cheap. A balloon holding about a tenth of a gram went for $15 or $20.) Other times, all three worked a hustle outside the mall. Billy would steal something of value from a department store, usually jewelry. Susie would then return the item, acting like a dissatisfied customer who had misplaced her receipt. Because Susie had no receipt, the store manager would give her a gift certificate in exchange for the item. Susie would then hand the gift certificate to Scott, who would hawk it in the parking lot, selling it below value. He might sell an $80 gift certificate for $40, taking the $40 straight to Chicago, where Susie's favorite supplier lived.

Lenny had approved Susie and Billy's application to live in the trailer park, just as he had approved Scott and Teddy's. Lenny did all of Tobin's screening. He never did credit checks, because there was a fee, and he didn't call previous landlords because he figured most applicants just listed their mothers or friends. Lenny's screening consisted mainly of typing names into CCAP.

CCAP stood for Consolidated Court Automation Programs. Like many other states, Wisconsin believed its citizens were entitled to view the affairs of its criminal and civil courts.[4] So, free of charge, it provided a website that catalogued all speeding tickets, child support disputes, divorces, evictions, felonies, and other legal business. Eviction records and misdemeanors were displayed for twenty years; felonies were displayed for at least fifty. CCAP also reported dismissed evictions and criminal charges. If someone was arrested but never convicted, CCAP displayed the violation with the disclaimer: "These charges were not proven and have no legal effect. [Name] is presumed innocent." Employers and landlords could come to their own conclusions. Among CCAP's "frequently asked questions" was this one: "I don't want my private information on Wisconsin Circuit Court Access. How can I get it removed?" An answer was provided: "You probably can't." Ask Lenny if he ever found incriminating records when reviewing applications, and he would grin at the question and say, "*Most* of the time I find stuff." And if you asked him what kinds of records prevented someone from being approved, he would tell you that he turned down everyone with a drug charge or domestic-violence offense. But both Susie and Billy had drug charges, and they weren't the only ones.

LENNY GOT UP early one Saturday morning. Office Susie met up with him, and Tobin picked them both up in the Cadillac. They were spending the day in Milwaukee's Landlord Training Program. None of them wanted to go, but they didn't have a choice. Attending the training was part of Tobin's agreement with Alderman Witkowski. Funded by the Department of Justice, the Landlord Training Program began in the 1990s with the goal of "keeping illegal and destructive activity out of rental property."[5]

Tobin, Lenny, and Office Susie joined sixty or so other landlords in a large classroom in the Milwaukee Safety Academy on Teutonia Avenue. At nine a.m. sharp, a tall woman with broad shoulders and a dark suit stood up and announced, "We start on time, and we end on time." Karen Long, the program coordinator, began talking at a fast clip, hands clasped behind her back. "What's the number one rule in real estate? Location, location, location," Karen said. "What's the number one rule for being a landlord? Screening, screening, screening. . . . You have to do a number of things to find out who's been naughty and who's been nice."

Karen told the room to collect an applicant's date of birth (to check his or her criminal record) and Social Security number (to check his or her credit) and to require two pieces of identification. "You need to require sufficient and *verifiable* income. If they say they are self-employed, well, drug dealers are self-employed." Karen brought up CCAP. The landlords also received an advertisement for ScreeningWorks, which promised to provide "the most comprehensive background information about your rental applicants." For $29.95, landlords could obtain a report listing an applicant's eviction and criminal record, credit evaluation, previous addresses, and other information. "ScreeningWorks is a service of RentGrow," the advertisement read. "RentGrow has 10+ years experience in multifamily resident screening, and serves over half a million rental units a year."[6]

"Look," Karen said, "if they have a recent court-ordered eviction or delinquency, you're not going to rent to them. If they have an eviction, what makes you think they're going to pay you?"[7] Herself a landlord, Karen paid attention to how someone looked at her unit. This point was repeated in the thick training manual landlords received at registration: "Do they check out each room? . . . Do they mentally visualize where the furniture will go, which room the children will sleep in, or how they'll make best use of the kitchen layout? Or do they barely walk in the front door before asking to rent, showing a surprising lack of interest in the details? People who make an honest living care about their home and often show it in the way they look at the unit. Some who rent for illegal operations forget to pretend they have the same interest."[8]

The small act of screening could have big consequences. From thousands of yes/no decisions emerged a geography of advantage and disadvantage that characterized the modern American city: good schools and failing ones, safe streets and dangerous ones.[9] Landlords were major players in distributing the spoils. They decided who got to live where. And their screening practices (or lack thereof) revealed why crime and gang activity or an area's civic engagement and its spirit of neighborliness could vary drastically from one block to the next. They also helped explain why on the same block in the same low-income neighborhood, one apartment complex but not another became familiar to the police.[10]

Screening practices that banned criminality and poverty in the same stroke drew poor families shoulder to shoulder with drug dealers, sex offenders, and other lawbreakers in places with lenient requirements. Neighborhoods marred by high poverty and crime were that way not only because poverty could incite crime, and crime could invite poverty, but also because the techniques landlords used to "keep illegal and destructive activity out of rental property" kept poverty out as well. This also meant that violence, drug activity, deep poverty, and other social problems coalesced at a much smaller, more acute level than the neighborhood. They gathered at the same address.

For people familiar with hunger and scarcity, addiction and prison, that often meant being isolated from job networks and exposed to vice and violence. But it also meant people could air problems; swap food, clothes, and information; and finish one another's sentences about lousy jobs or social workers or prison (*"They put gravy—"*... *"On everything!"*). It meant that, should they be in the early stages of opiate withdrawal, they could take a walk around their trailer park to calm the shakes and run into a fellow junkie who could give them what they needed.

Some landlords neglected to screen tenants for the same reason payday lenders offered unsecured, high-interest loans to families with unpaid debt or lousy credit; for the same reason that the subprime industry gave mortgages to people who could not afford them; for the same reason Rent-A-Center allowed you to take home a new Hisense air conditioner or Klaussner "Lazarus" reclining sofa without running a credit check. There was a business model at the bottom of every market.[11]

"Questions?" Karen's eyes panned the room.

"Should I do a short-term or long-term lease?"

"First, do a lease. Please. Put it in writing. Between sixty and seventy percent of rental agreements in this state are verbal."

A man in a camouflage hat raised his hand with a question about evictions: "Do you have to leave them there for three months or some foolish thing?"

"No. Nothing protects you from not paying the rent."

"Is there a maximum charge for a late fee?"

The room laughed nervously, and Karen frowned at the question.

"Can you go in any of the common areas, the hallways, the open basement, without any notice?"

Karen paused for effect. She smiled at the woman who had asked the question. She was a black woman, probably in her fifties, who had sat in the front row and taken notes throughout the day.

"What is the answer?" Karen asked the room.

"Yes," came the reply from several fellow landlords.

Karen nodded and looked back at the woman. "Okay, say this with me: This is my property."

"This is my property," the woman responded.

"This is my property." Karen said it louder and raised her hands, inviting the room to echo.

"This is my property," the landlords answered.

"*This is myyy property!*" Karen boomed, her finger pointing to the land below.

The voices in the room went up in unison, a proud and powerful chorus: "This is *my* property! *Myyyyy* property!"

AFTER RECEIVING THE eviction notice, it took Teddy a couple days to decide it was time to go home to Tennessee. He called one of his sisters, who told him that she'd be sending her husband up with the van. Teddy sent her a $500 money order. "I don't want to go to them broke," he told Scott, which also told him his money was gone.

Scott saw that he needed a plan. So he rang up Pito, an old Narcotics Anonymous buddy, and asked if he had any work. Pito connected Scott with Mira, a take-no-shit lesbian from Puerto Rico, who offered him a job cleaning out foreclosed homes. Mira paid Scott and the other crewmen in cash. The amounts varied widely; Scott didn't understand or ask why. They gave scrappers the metal and sold some valuables here and there, hauling the rest to the dump.

Scott was stunned by what people left behind. Sofas, computers, stainless-steel ranges. Children's clothes with the tags on them, tricycles, holiday decorations in basement bins, frozen pork chops, cans of green beans. Sheeted mattresses, file cabinets, framed posters and prayers and inspirational verses, curtains, blouses on hangers, lawn mowers, pictures. Sometimes the houses were humble and squat with cracked windows and grease on the ceiling. Sometimes they were cavernous, with thick carpet, master bathrooms, and back decks. To Scott, it felt like the whole city was being tossed out.

"Sometimes you walk into a house, and it's like, they just walk out with the clothes on their back," Scott was saying over another breakfast beer with Teddy. It had been roughly a week since they had received their eviction notice. "There's some profundity in it that I don't understand yet."

"I wish I could work," Teddy answered. "I wish I could be outside and work. But the shape that I'm in."

Scott wasn't interested in the work but the wreckage. "I can't figure out what happened to the people," he continued. "It's really—" He let the word float.

"Scott," Teddy said, slowly turning toward him. "You're just like my family. I hate to leave you, but I'm headed back home."

"I don't even like you," Scott responded with a grin.

"I know that's just a lie. I know you don't want to see me go. But I know you know it's got to be done."

Around sunrise Saturday morning, a white van pulled up to the trailer. Scott placed a bag of Teddy's clothes and his fishing gear in the back and helped his old friend into the passenger seat. Teddy's bendless arm raised in a quiet goodbye, as if by string, as the van pulled away under a Harley-Davidson–orange sky.

The following evening around dusk, while Scott was out with Mira's crew, people started raiding his trailer. Teddy was gone, and everyone in the trailer park knew that Scott would soon be too. They started small, taking shirts, movies, jackets, a backpack. Then they went for the larger items, carrying out the table, the couch, the crucifixion painting.

Larraine's brother-in-law, Lane, a skinny man with dark hair and a gold necklace, watched from his daisy-yellow trailer. "Buzzards," he said, shaking his head. "You'd better close your mouth when you sleep, or these people will steal the gold right out of your teeth."

When Scott got home that night and realized what had happened, he rushed to check if the plastic container in his room—the one stuffed with photographs, diplomas, and memories, hard evidence that he had once been someone else—was still there. It was. They had taken the bed but left the box. It felt like a gift. Scott then walked slowly from room to room, noticing what had been snatched and what was unwanted even by the desperate. No one took the books or the Polaroid camera, but they had collected the empty beer cans to recycle. Scott fingered the remainders like he sometimes did in the foreclosed homes, studying them as if they were dug-up artifacts or fossils.

He thought of the last home he had cleaned out that night. From the outside, it looked like any other house. But inside, he had found a stripper's pole attached to a homemade stage encircled by couches. Hard-core pornography was strewn about everywhere. There were three bedrooms upstairs. Two were covered in more smut. Scott opened the door to the third and stared down at a twin bed, toys, and half-finished homework. Most abandoned homes left him few clues about the people who had lived there. As he went about his work, Scott would fill in the rest, imagining laughter around the dinner table, sleeping faces in the morning, a man shaving in the bathroom. This last house told its own story. Thinking of that one bedroom, Scott sat down on his empty floor, in his gutted-out trailer, and wept.

8.

CHRISTMAS IN ROOM 400

Sherrena decided to evict Arleen. The funeral and subsequent welfare sanction had put Arleen too far behind: $870. Sherrena felt it was time to "let go and move on to the next tenant." Earlier in the month, she had filed the paperwork and received a court date of December 23, which would be the last eviction court before Christmas that year. Sherrena knew the courthouse would be packed. Many parents chose to take their chances with their landlords rather than face their children empty-handed on Christmas morning.[1] A new tenant had already asked Sherrena if a portion of her rent money could be returned so she could buy gifts. Sherrena told her, "You gotta have a house to put the Christmas tree and presents in. . . . You've been knowing Christmas was coming eleven months ago."

The night before Sherrena and Arleen's date in eviction court, snow began to fall. When Milwaukeeans woke up the following morning, they found their city buried in it. People in parkas and knit hats shuffled along the sidewalks. Mothers with bundled-up children huddled under bus-stop awnings, shifting their weight from one leg to the other. The city's smokestacks billowed cotton-thick clouds of steam into a pale sky. Holiday decorations dotted the North Side: a black Nativity, a snowman smiling from an abandoned lot.

Sherrena pulled up to the Milwaukee County Courthouse. The courthouse had been built in 1931 but made to look like it had always been there. Corinthian columns, taller and thicker than oak trunks, encircled the building, lifting its roof high above downtown. The building was enormous, with an imposing limestone façade on which the architects had etched in block letters: VOX POPULI VOX DEI. The voice of the people is the voice of God.

Sherrena wondered if Arleen would show. Most of the time, tenants didn't, and Sherrena preferred it that way. She had learned that it didn't matter how much kindness you had shown a tenant up to that point. "All that stuff goes out the window" in court. Sherrena had brought Arleen milk and groceries. She'd even had a worker deliver a stove that was sitting unused in one of her vacant units. But she knew that, once in front of the commissioner, Arleen was more likely to bring up the time the water heater went out or mention the hole in the window Quentin still hadn't fixed. Still, Sherrena had called Arleen that morning to remind her about court. She didn't have to, but she had a soft spot for Arleen. Plus, Sherrena worried more about the commissioners. She thought they were sympathetic to tenants and tried to block landlords with technicalities. Sherrena had had a couple cases thrown out on account of paperwork errors. When that happened, she had to start the eviction process all over again, which usually meant losing another month's rent on that unit. When things went her way, however, she could have the eviction squad physically remove tenants within ten days.

Once she was through security, Sherrena made her way to Room 400, Milwaukee County Small Claims Court, the busiest courtroom in the state.[2] Her footsteps clacked on the marble floors and echoed off the vaulted ceilings. She passed lawyers in trench coats, staring at the floor and talking on their cell phones, and young parents with children, gaping like tourists. The courtroom was full. Women and men were squeezed into long wooden pews and stood lining the walls, their bodies warming the chamber. Sherrena looked for a seat, waving at landlords she recognized.

At the back of the courtroom, landlords were talking tenants into stipulation agreements, offering to dismiss evictions if tenants caught up on the rent. One, a white man in a leather jacket who had been in the local paper a few months back for racking up hundreds of property violations, was joking with his young female assistant when a tenant approached. The tenant was a black woman, likely in her fifties. Her shoulders were uplifted under her worn overcoat. She reached into her purse and handed the landlord $700 in cash.

"I'm hoping—" she began.

The landlord cut her off. "Don't hope. Write the check."

"I can get you another six hundred in two weeks."

The landlord asked her to sign a stipulation, which included a $55 late fee. She reached for his pen.[3]

Toward the front of the room, in a reserved space with tables and plenty of empty chairs, sat lawyers in pinstripe suits and power ties. They had been hired by landlords. Some sat with manila folders stacked in front of them, reading the paper or filling in the crossword. Others joked with the bailiff, who periodically broke conversation to tell a tenant to remove his hat or lower her voice. Everyone in the reserved space, the lawyers and bailiff, was white.

In front of the lawyers, a large wooden desk faced the crowd. Two women sat on either side of the desk, calling out the day's cases and taking attendance. Most of the names flung into the air went unclaimed. Roughly 70 percent of tenants summoned to Milwaukee's eviction court didn't come. The same was true in other major cities. In some urban courts, only 1 tenant in 10 showed.[4] Some tenants couldn't miss work or couldn't find child care or were confused by the whole process or couldn't care less or would rather avoid the humiliation.[5] When tenants did not show up and their landlord or a representative did, the caller applied three quick stamps to the file—indicating that the tenant had received a default eviction judgment—and placed it on top of a growing pile. The sound of eviction court was a soft hum of dozens of people sighing, coughing, murmuring, and whispering to children interspersed with the cadence of a name, a pause, and three loud thumps of the stamp.

Behind the front desk, framed between two grand wooden columns, hung a large painting of Moses descending Mount Sinai with the Ten Commandments unbroken. He glared down at the Israelites in the desert, dancing around the golden calf. Doorways on either side of the callers' desk led to commissioners' offices, where the actual hearings took place. When their case was called, landlords and tenants walked through a side doorway, usually to emerge just a few minutes later.

A black woman whose hearing had just concluded stepped back into the room, holding her child's hand. Her head was wrapped, and she had kept on her heavy blue winter coat. She continued down the middle aisle of Room 400, walking by an anemic white man with homemade tattoos, a white woman in a wheelchair wearing pajama pants and Crocs, a blind black man with a limp hat on his lap, a Hispanic man wearing work boots and a shirt that read PRAY FOR US—all waiting for their eviction cases. Tenants in eviction court were generally poor, and almost all of them (92 percent) had missed rent payments. The majority spent at least half their household income on rent. One-third devoted at least 80 percent to it.[6] Of the tenants who did come to court and were evicted, only 1 in 6 had another place lined up: shelters or the apartments of friends or family. A few resigned themselves to the streets. Most simply did not know where they would go.[7]

The woman in the blue winter coat found the face of another black woman, sitting at the end of a pew. As she passed, she bent down and whispered, "Don't worry. It only takes a minute, honey." As usual, the courtroom was full of black women. In a typical month, 3 in 4 people in Milwaukee eviction court were black. Of those, 3 in 4 were women. The total number of black women in eviction court exceeded that of all other groups combined.[8] Children of all ages encircled these women. A girl with a full box of barrettes in her hair sat quietly, swinging her legs under the pew. A dark-skinned boy in a collared shirt two sizes too big sat up straight and wore a hard face. His sister next to him tried to sleep, folding one arm over her eyes and clutching a stuffed dog in the other.

In Milwaukee's poorest black neighborhoods, eviction had become commonplace—especially for women. In those neighborhoods, 1 female renter in 17 was evicted through the court system each year, which was twice as often as men from those neighborhoods and nine times as often as women from the city's poorest white areas. Women from black neighborhoods made up 9 percent of Milwaukee's population and 30 percent of its evicted tenants.[9]

If incarceration had come to define the lives of men from impoverished black neighborhoods, eviction was shaping the lives of women. Poor black men were locked up. Poor black women were locked out.[10]

A commissioner appeared from a side doorway and took a file from a caller. Sherrena tapped her foot, waiting her turn. At the beginning of the month, she had been in court for eight eviction cases, including Patrice's. Only one tenant made it: Ricky One Leg. He limped up to Sherrena in the hallway and complained, "Why you drag me down here?" Ricky had a high-pitched, sandpaper voice, beer on his breath, and a wooden leg he'd received after being shot four times on his twenty-second birthday.

"What? You want me to punch you in your other leg?" Sherrena shot back. She raised her fists, and Ricky pretended to stab her foot with his cane.

After they finished laughing, Sherrena said, "I love you, Ricky."

"I love you too, baby."

"You know, this is just a formality. You know, you can't go to the grocery store and say, 'Well, I'm gonna take that food, and I ain't paying you shit.'"

"I know, baby. If I had a business, I would feel the same way. . . . My daddy always told me you don't bite the hand that feeds you."

When it was time, Sherrena and Ricky approached the front bench. Since cases were grouped by plaintiffs (landlords), a caller made sure Sherrena's other tenants weren't there.

"Sissell Clement?" *Stamp, stamp, stamp.*

"Patrice Hinkston?" *Stamp, stamp, stamp.*

Patrice had gone to work at Cousins Subs instead of going to court. She couldn't find anyone who would swap hours, and she didn't want to lose this job. Her manager had looked past her Class A misdemeanor (writing bad checks). The only thing she liked about working at Cousins was her commute: a peaceful hour-long bus ride through streets lined with brick houses and mounted American flags.

"Eff her, and eff the court," Patrice later said. "My mom has been like through an eviction before, and the judge that she had was rude." Patrice would begin her rental career with an eviction record. She didn't give that much thought. "Everybody I know, except for my white friends, I swear they got an eviction on their record." Patrice knew that if she did come to court she not only would lose work hours and frustrate her manager but also would have to defend herself against someone who was more educated, more familiar with the law, and more comfortable in court. Other tenants had it worse, having to go toe to toe with their landlords' lawyer.

Plus, Patrice would have to set foot in that grand old courthouse. The nicest building in Patrice's life was Lena's Food Market off Fond Du Lac Avenue. It had shopping carts, bright fluorescent lights, and a buffed linoleum floor. Her white friends called it the ghetto grocery store, but it was one of the better markets on the North Side. And at Lena's, Patrice never felt her existence questioned. She tried not to go to parts of the city where she did. Patrice lived four miles away from the shore of Lake Michigan: an hour on foot, a half hour by bus, fifteen minutes by car. She had never been.

———

"SHERRENA," SOMEONE WHISPERED. Sherrena turned around and saw that Arleen had poked her head into Room 400.

Sherrena stepped into the hallway and walked up to Arleen, who was tucking her face underneath a red hoodie. "Girl," Sherrena said, "I got to get you up outta this house or get my money. Genuine. . . . I mean, 'cause I got bills. I got a bill to show you right now that's gonna take your eyes outta your head."

Sherrena reached in her files and handed Arleen a tax bill for a property the city had condemned. It listed delinquent storm water and sewer charges, fees for the board-up, and additional charges that totaled $11,465.67. Arleen stared blankly at the bill. It was more than her annual income.

Sherrena cocked her head and asked, "Do you see what I have to *go through*? . . . It might not've been your fault about what happened, but"—she pinched the bill between pointer and thumb and gave it a wiggle—"I got issues."

Sherrena reclaimed her seat in Room 400. She remembered her first eviction. Nervous and confused, she had gone over the paperwork a dozen times. Everything went her way. Soon after, she filed another eviction, then another. When filling out the court papers, Sherrena learned to put "et al." after a tenant's name so that the eviction judgment covered everyone in the house, even people she didn't know about. She learned that the correct answer on the documents asking her to estimate damages was "not over $5,000," the maximum amount allowed; learned that commissioners frowned on late fees in excess of $55; learned that dragging slow-paying tenants to court was usually worth the $89.50 processing fee because it spurred many to find a way to catch up. Plus she could add the processing fee to their bill.

This wasn't Arleen's first eviction either. That had happened sixteen years earlier, when she was twenty-two. Arleen figured she had rented twenty houses since turning eighteen, which meant she and her children had moved about once a year—multiple times because they were evicted. But Arleen's eviction record was not as extensive as it should have been. Through the years, she had given landlords different names; nothing exotic, just subtle alterations. Now "Arleen Beal" and "Erleen Belle" had eviction records. The frazzled court clerks, like many landlords, never stopped to ask for identification. Arleen remembered when they used to take a break from doing evictions around Christmastime in Milwaukee. But they did away with that in 1991, after a landlord convinced the American Civil Liberties Union to argue that the practice was an unfair religious celebration.[11] Some old-timers still observed the moratorium out of kindness or habit or ignorance. Sherrena was not one of them.

More time passed. The lawyers had gone home—their cases were called first—leaving only the bailiff and the callers up front. With no one to talk to, the bailiff, a white woman with a compact frame and overbite, began passing the time by snipping at tenants. "Silence your cell phone or it will be confiscated!" Both callers had stopped covering their yawns an hour ago. "You have to clear the doorway!" the bailiff announced. Children's shoes tapped the pews. "If you're going to talk, discuss your case outside."

Finally, Arleen looked up to see Sherrena step into the hallway and hold the courtroom door open. "We up," she said.

Sherrena had waited two hours for her cases to be called. She had drawn Commissioner Laura Gramling Perez, a white woman with military posture but a broad, open face. Gramling Perez, in a dark pantsuit and pearls, asked Arleen to wait in the front while she and Sherrena settled another matter. Sherrena followed the commissioner back to her office, a stately wood-paneled room lined with law books, framed certificates, and family photographs. The commissioner took her seat at the head of a large hardwood table and asked, "Any luck with that invoice?"

Sherrena had been in the office just the day before, asking the commissioner to approve a claim of $5,000 brought against another evicted tenant, the one whose building had been condemned. Each eviction case had two parts. The "first cause of action" dealt strictly with whether a tenant would be evicted. Next came "the second and third causes of action," which dealt with what was owed to a landlord: unpaid rent, court fees, and other damages.[12] Most tenants taken to eviction court were sued twice—once for the property and a second time for the debt—and so had two court dates. But even fewer tenants showed up for their second hearing than for their first, which meant landlords' claims about what was owed them usually went unchallenged. Suing a tenant for back rent and court fees was straightforward. Landlords were allowed to charge for unpaid rent, late fees the court found reasonable, and double rent for each day tenants remained in the home after their tenancy had been terminated. Things got murkier when tallying up property damages. Sometimes Sherrena guessed an amount on the ride over to eviction court. "How much should I put for the back door: One fifty? Two hundred?" Sometimes she added on an extermination fee even though Quentin would take care of it himself. When the charges didn't give them pause, callers approved landlords' second and third causes with a quick punch of the stamp. When they did, callers pushed the claim up to a commissioner like Gramling Perez, who was now asking Sherrena to provide evidence that would justify suing an ex-tenant for the maximum amount allowed in small claims court.

"What I'm trying to get from her doesn't even scratch the surface of what she did to the property," Sherrena replied, presenting photos of the trashed unit and the bill she had shown to Arleen.

Commissioner Gramling Perez looked everything over, then said, "I need something else."

Sherrena pushed back but got nowhere. "I'll never get that anyway," she finally said with a huff.

"And that's probably the case," the commissioner began. "So—"

"It's still not fair! Nobody ever does anything to these tenants. It's always the landlord. This system is flawed. . . . But whatever. I'll never see the money. These people are deadbeats."

Gramling Perez brought Sherrena's charges from $5,000 down to $1,285. That money judgment joined those of the eight other eviction cases Sherrena initiated earlier that month, which together totaled over $10,000. Sherrena knew that receiving a money judgment and actually receiving the money were different matters. After withholding tenants' security deposits, landlords had limited recourse when it came to collecting. Sherrena could try to garnish wages, but this was possible only for former tenants who were employed and living above the poverty line. She could garnish bank accounts. But many of her former tenants did not have bank accounts, and even if they did, state benefits and the first $1,000 were off limits.[13]

Even so, Sherrena and many other landlords filed for second and third causes. This carried consequences for tenants, since money judgments were listed on eviction records. An eviction record listing $200 of rental debt left a different impression than one listing $2,000. Money judgments could also suddenly reappear in tenants' lives several years after the eviction, particularly if landlords docketed them. Docketing a judgment slapped it on a tenant's credit report. If the tenant came to own any property in Milwaukee County in the next decade, the docketed judgment placed a lien on that property, severely limiting a new homeowner's ability to refinance or sell.[14] To landlords, docketing a judgment was a long-odds bet on a tenant's future. Who knows, maybe somewhere down the line a tenant would want to get her credit in order and would approach her old landlord, asking to repay the debt. "Debt with interest," the landlord could respond, since money judgments accrued interest at an annual rate that would be the envy of any financial portfolio: 12 percent. For the chronically and desperately poor whose credit was already wrecked, a docketed judgment was just another shove deeper into the pit. But for the tenant who went on to land a decent job or marry and then take another tentative step forward, applying for student loans or purchasing a first home—for that tenant, it was a real barrier on the already difficult road to self-reliance and security.

Sherrena had been thinking about hiring a company like Rent Recovery Service to collect on her second and third causes. The self-described "largest and most aggressive landlord collection agency in the country" reported delinquent tenants to three national credit bureaus and placed them on a nationwide tracking system that allowed the company to follow tenants' financial lives "without their knowledge." It saw when tenants attempted to get credit, apply for a job, or open a bank account. Like landlords docketing judgments, the company took the long view, waiting for tenants to "get back on their financial feet and begin to earn a living" before collection could begin. Rent Recovery Service "never closed an unpaid file."[15] Some of those files contained debt amounts calculated in a reasonable and well-documented way; others contained bloated second and third causes and unreasonably high interest rates. But since both had the court's approval, Rent Recovery Service did not distinguish between them.

WHEN HER TURN came, Arleen decided to sit right next to Sherrena at the commissioner's table. The two women looked for a moment like old friends or even sisters, with one reflecting life's favor. Sherrena was still stewing over being denied her $5,000 claim when the commissioner, without lifting her eyes from Arleen's file, said, "Your landlady is seeking to evict you for unpaid rent. Are you behind on rent, ma'am?"

"Yes," Arleen replied.

With that, she lost her case.[16]

The commissioner looked at Sherrena and asked, "Are you willing to work something out?"

"No," Sherrena answered. "Because the thing is, she's too far behind. See, I let her slide when the sister passed away or whatever. She didn't pay all her rent that month. And now it's another whole month has passed, and now she owes a total balance of about $870."

"Okay, okay," the commissioner cut in. She turned to Arleen. "So your landlady at this point wants you to move out."

"Okay."

"Do you have minor children at home?"

"Yup."

"How many?"

"Two."

Gramling Perez was one of the commissioners who sometimes subscribed to the court custom of giving tenants two extra days in the home for each dependent child.

"I'll be out before the first," Arleen said. "New Year's at the latest."

"But see, that goes into the beginning of rental period again," Sherrena interjected.

"So you're willing to do a stipulation if she's gone before the first?" the commissioner asked.

"*Well*," Sherrena began, her annoyance no longer even partially concealed. "I have people lined up that want to move in on the first."

But the commissioner had spotted an opening. She knew Arleen would have to leave, but she was trying to spare her the blemish of an eviction record. She tried again: "Would you be willing to offer something in return for her agreement to move out by the thirty-first, voluntarily?"

"What would I be proposing to offer?" Sherrena asked coldly.

"To dismiss."

"But what about the other money that she owes me?" A dismissed eviction judgment meant a dropped money judgment as well, and obtaining money judgments, even against single mothers on welfare, was one of the primary reasons Sherrena evicted tenants through the court system.

"Well, my point is that you maybe give up a couple hundred dollars so you don't lose these tenants who are coming in January." The commissioner knew Sherrena could pocket Arleen's security deposit, leaving an unpaid rent balance of around $320. "In exchange for an agreement that she won't go after you—"

Then Arleen interrupted the commissioner. "*I'm* not trying to be in her money," she said. She said it forcefully and looked offended. Arleen had gathered who was making the calls, and it wasn't the white lady with the pearl necklace.

Sherrena, who had been mulling things over, leaned forward in her chair. "I don't want to dismiss *anything*. I really don't. . . . I mean, I'm tired of losing out on *every single*—" She began slapping the table with each word.

Arleen looked at the commissioner. "I mean, I'm not trying to stay. I mean, I understand what she's saying. That's her place."

"I understand," said the commissioner.

"I'm not trying to be there."

"I understand."

The commissioner shuffled the papers and said nothing more.

In the pause, Arleen took another tack. She thought of the broken window, the sporadic hot water, the grimy carpet, and said, in a dismissive voice, "I would say something, but I'm not even gonna go there. I'm all right." That was her defense.[17]

The commissioner looked at Arleen and said, "Here's the deal. Ma'am, you're getting to move out voluntarily by January first. . . . If you don't do that, if you don't move out, then your landlord is entitled to come back here without further notice, and she can get a writ of eviction. And then the sheriff will come."

WHEN SHERRENA AND Arleen walked out of the courthouse, a gentle snow was still falling. Sherrena had agreed to give Arleen a ride home. In the car, Sherrena paused to rub her neck, and Arleen lowered her forehead into the palm of her hand. Both women had splitting headaches. Sherrena attributed hers to how court had gone. She was still fuming that Gramling Perez had reduced her money judgment. Arleen's was from hunger. She hadn't eaten all day.

"I don't want to be putting you and your babies out in the cold," Sherrena told Arleen as the car moved slowly through the slushy streets. "I wouldn't want nobody to do me like that. . . . Some of them landlords, they get away with murder down there. But there's some like me, who get in front of the commissioner, and she say whatever's on her mind, and that's the way it's gonna go. . . . She knows this system is screwed. It's all one-sided."[18]

Arleen stared out the window and watched the snow settle noiselessly on the black iron lampposts, the ornate dome of the Public Library, the Church of the Gesu's Gothic towers.

"And some of these tenants," Sherrena was saying, "they nasty as hell. They bring roaches with 'em. They bring mice with 'em. And who gotta pay for it? Oh, what about Doreen Hinkston? With her *ray-man noodles* down the sink, and they keep calling me about the sink being stopped up. . . . And *I* gotta call the plumber. Then you pouring grease down the sink from your fried chicken, you pouring the *grease* down the sink, and I gotta get a plumber out *again*."

The car turned down Center Street, passing a church where Arleen sometimes picked up gift baskets at Thanksgiving and Christmas. She had always aspired to have her own ministry like that, to be the one handing out food and clothing.

"So, Arleen"—Sherrena pulled in front of Arleen's place on Thirteenth Street—"if you ever thinking about becoming a landlord, don't. It's a bad deal. Get the short end of the stick every time."

Arleen stepped out of the car and turned back to Sherrena.

"Merry Christmas," she said.

PART TWO
OUT

9.

ORDER SOME CARRYOUT

Larraine was up before the sun, dashing cool water on her face. She usually rose before dawn, feeling her best in the morning. The day after her brush with Tobin was different. She had stayed in bed, trying to ignore the situation by burrowing under the covers. She only got up to let Digger out, looking through the cuts in the blinds for Tobin or Lenny before stepping out the door with the leash. Digger was her brother Beaker's dog, a small black mutt. Larraine had agreed to watch him while Beaker was in the hospital for his heart.

Larraine's trailer was spotless and uncluttered. When a visitor would comment on its cleanliness, she would smile and credit her handheld steamer or share tips, like slipping in an aspirin when washing whites. She had lived in her trailer for about a year and had come to like it, especially in the morning, before the gossips began congregating outside. She now had everything just-so. She had found white serving utensils to match the white cupboards in the kitchen and a small desk for her old computer. None of this made paying Tobin 77 percent of her income any easier.

The sun lifted higher and the trailer park began to stir with the sounds of children and car engines. Larraine studied her phone. She knew that there were two main programs in Milwaukee for people facing eviction. The first was Emergency Assistance for families at risk of "impending homelessness." You could apply for these funds once every year if you were a US citizen, in possession of an eviction notice, at or below 115 percent of the poverty level, and could prove with divorce papers, a crime report, a pink slip, or some other documentation that you had experienced a sudden loss of income. But to qualify you also had to have dependent children in your home; so Emergency Assistance was out.

The second program was the Homelessness Prevention Program, offered through Community Advocates and mainly federally funded. But to qualify for that benefit, you not only had to have experienced a loss of income, you also had to demonstrate that your current income could cover future rents. Plus, you needed landlord buy-in, which Larraine didn't have. Like Emergency Assistance, this service was reserved more for the unlucky—those who had been laid off or mugged—than the chronically rent burdened. Community Advocates was able to offer this benefit to only 950 families each year. It took Milwaukee less than six weeks to evict that many families.[1]

Larraine dialed a number by heart. "Yes. I was wondering. I was told that you help people with their rent? . . . Oh. Oh, no? . . . Okay." She hung up. Larraine dialed the Social Development Commission, an antipoverty organization. They couldn't help. Someone had told her that the YMCA on Twenty-Seventh made emergency loans. She called them. "Yes. I was instructed to call you because I was told you could help me with my rent. . . . My rent. . . . Rent. R-E-N-T." Nothing. Larraine did not dial the number to a tenants' union because Milwaukee, like most American cities, didn't have one.

By midmorning, Larraine had dialed all the nonprofit, city, and state agencies she could think of. None came through. On a lark, she dialed one more number. She lifted the phone and heard the indifferent throb through the speaker. Larraine shrugged. The line to the Marcia P. Coggs Human Services Center—the "welfare building"—was always busy.

THE MOVERS STARTED the trucks early in the morning, diesel engines grumbling as the men gathered with cigarettes and mugs of black coffee. The city was soggy from the previous night's rain. Some of the men were young and athletic with pierced ears. Others were barrel-chested and middle-aged, slapping their leather gloves on their jeans. The oldest among them was Tim, lean and sour-faced with reddish-brown skin, stubble, and a fresh pack of Salems in his front pocket. Almost all of the men were black and wore boots and work jackets with the name of their company—Eagle Moving and Storage—and various clever slogans: "Moving's for the Birds," "Service with a Grunt," "Order Some Carryout."

The Brittain brothers—Tom, Dave, and Jim—had taken over the company from their father. When he had started it back in 1958, there were only one or two eviction moves a week. He ran a two-truck operation out of his home and would pick up men from the rescue mission when he needed an extra hand. Fifty years later, the company employed thirty-five people, most of them full-time movers; owned a fleet of vans and eighteen-foot trucks; and operated out of a three-story, 108,000-square-foot building that had originally held a furniture factory. Forty percent of their business came from eviction moves.

Eagle's moving crew worked with two sheriff deputies. The deputies would knock on the door to announce the eviction; the movers would follow, clearing out the home. Landlords footed the bill. Before a landlord could activate the Sheriff's Office, he had to contract with a bonded moving company. There were four such companies in Milwaukee, Eagle being the largest. To hire one of Eagle's five-man crews, a landlord had to put down a $350 deposit, the average cost of an eviction job. Eagle then handed over a Letter of Authority, which the landlord would take to the Sheriff's Office, along with the necessary court documents and an additional $130 sheriff's fee. The sheriff had ten days to remove the tenants. A formal eviction that involved sheriffs and movers could run around $600, when you included the court filing charge and process-server fee. Landlords could add these costs to a judgment but often never got them back.

Dave Brittain, a white man with graying hair and a long stride, gave the men the signal, and they climbed into the trucks. Tim drove the van, and when Dave went out on moves, he sat in the passenger's seat.

The daily eviction route began with the northernmost address and pushed south. Eagle's trucks would lumber through the North Side ghetto in the morning and early afternoon. Then they would cross the Menominee River Valley and course through the predominantly Hispanic streets of the near South Side before ending their day in the trailer parks on the white far South Side.

The sheriffs met the moving crew outside an apartment complex on Silver Spring Drive. John, the older of the two deputies and the one who most looked the part—broad shoulders, thick jowls, sunglasses, cop mustache, gum—gave the door a knock. A small black woman answered, rubbing the sleep out of her eyes. When John looked around and saw a tidy house with dishes drying in the rack and not a box packed, he turned to his partner and asked, "Are we in the right house?" He placed a call back to the office.

When Sheriff John walked into a house and saw mattresses on the floor, grease on the ceiling, cockroaches on the walls, and clothes, hair extensions, and toys scattered about, he didn't double-check. Sometimes tenants had already abandoned the place, leaving behind dead animals and rotting food. Sometimes the movers puked. "The first rule of evictions," Sheriff John liked to say, "is *never* open the fridge." When things were especially bad, when an apartment was covered in trash or dog shit, or when one of the guys would find a needle, Dave would nod and say, "Junk in," leaving the mess for the landlord.

John hung up the phone and waved the movers in. At that moment, the house no longer belonged to the occupants, and the movers took it over. Grabbing dollies, hump straps, and boxes, the men began clearing every room. They worked quickly and without hesitation. There were no children in the house that morning, but there were toys and diapers. The woman who answered the door moved slowly, looking overcome. A sob broke through her blank face when she opened the refrigerator and saw that the movers had cleaned it out, even packing the ice trays.[2] She found her things piled in the back alley. Sheriff John looked to the sky as it began to rain and then looked back at Tim. "Snowstorm. Rainstorm. We don't give a shit," Tim said, lighting a Salem.

No one was home for the next eviction, a two-story baby-blue house. Half the time, the tenants weren't home. Some moved out before the sheriffs arrived. Others didn't realize their day had come. A rarefied bunch called the Sheriff's Office, asking if their address was on that day's eviction list. But many were unprepared and bewildered when the sheriff came knocking. Some claimed never to have received notice or pointed out, accurately, that the notice did not announce a date or even a range of dates when the eviction would take place. The deputies would shrug. They figured the tenants were just playing the system, staying as long as they could. Dave's assessment was subtler. He thought a kind of collective denial set in among tenants facing eviction, as if they were unable to accept or imagine that one day soon, two armed sheriff's deputies would show up, order them out, and usher in a team of movers who would make it look like they had never lived there. Psychologists might agree with him, citing research showing that under conditions of scarcity people prioritize the now and lose sight of the future, often at great cost. Or they might quote *How the Other Half Lives*, published over a century ago: "There is nothing in the prospect of a sharp, unceasing battle for the bare necessities of life to encourage looking ahead, everything to discourage the effort. . . . The evil day of reckoning is put off till a to-morrow that may never come. When it does come . . . it simply adds another hardship to a life measured from the cradle by such incidents."[3]

Then there were cases that didn't require any sort of psychological sophistication, cases where landlords purposefully conned or misled tenants.

Dave told Brontee, the rookie, to climb through a window of the baby-blue house and let them in. Inside, they found a Dell computer, a clean leather sofa, and new shoes lining the closets. Someone had left the television on. Dave pointed to the show playing on it and laughed. "Martha fucking Stewart!"

A few minutes later, an older-model Jaguar, forest green, pulled into the driveway. Four young black men hopped out.

"What is going on?" one asked.

"You've been foreclosed," John replied, holding up the paper.

"What? We just paid rent this month! Lord, have mercy."

One of the men marched straight into the house and quickly emerged cradling a shoebox. He held the box with both arms, the way a running back protects the football when the call is up the middle, then locked it in the Jaguar's trunk.

The sheriff deputies stepped away to confer. "These people got screwed," John told his partner. "The landlord took their rent but didn't pay the mortgage."

"Yeah, but John, this is a drug house," the other deputy replied.

John raised his eyebrows, and the sheriffs started for the kitchen. Tim was there, assembling boxes.

"Tim, this a drug house?" John whispered.

Without a word, Tim pulled out a kitchen drawer, as if he had been in the house before. Inside were small Ziploc bags and razor blades. The deputies looked at each other. Sometimes in situations like this, when a landlord foreclosure caught tenants completely unawares, John would refuse to carry out the judge's order that day, buying tenants more time. But he decided not to stop this one and not to ask to see what was in the shoebox.[4] Narcotics wasn't his beat, and he thought the faultless foreclosure was punishment enough.

The next stop was a "junk in." The one after that was quick. The old black man didn't have much. "Man, this makes no sense," he kept saying as one of the movers dumped the contents of his bedroom dresser into a box. As Dave headed to the van for the next job, he pointed to the man's pile of possessions, now slick with rain, and told John, "Some people paint on canvases. This is my art." The pile at the next eviction was even more impressive. It included a half-eaten birthday cake and a balloon still perky with helium.

LARRAINE HAD GROWN up with two brothers and two sisters in a squat, yellow-brick public housing complex across the street from a baseball field in South Milwaukee. Her mother was an invalid, her body swollen on account of her thyroid. Her father was a window washer. Larraine remembered him bringing home bags of Ziegler Giant Bars, when he washed the windows of the candy factory, or armloads of fresh bread, when the day's schedule took him to certain local restaurants. Larraine loved her childhood, especially her doting father. "We didn't know we were poor," she said.

Larraine had struggled in school. In tenth grade, she decided she'd had enough. "Everyone around me was making it but me." She dropped out and began working as a seamstress for $1.50 an hour. She went to work at Everbrite, which manufactured corporate signs. During a strike, she left and found work as a machinist at R-W Enterprises on Sherman Avenue. Her father constantly worried about his young daughter working with sheet metal and operating punch press machines. Maybe that's why, when a metal disk came down on her hand one day and pinched off the top half of her two middle fingers, all she remembered doing was crying out for her daddy.

At twenty-two, Larraine married a man named Jerry Lee. He asked that she leave R-W and stay home. So she did. When Larraine began studying for the driver's test, Jerry Lee asked her why she needed a license. She put away the manual. They had a daughter three years later, and another two years after that. Megan and Jayme. But soon the marriage began to unwind. It got to the point where Jerry Lee began bringing women back to their home. They divorced after eight years, and Larraine began life as a single mother. Those years were filled with poverty and double shifts and freedom and laughter. If you asked Larraine, she would tell you they were some of the best years of her life. That's when she began dancing on tables. She liked the money and feeling desired. She would bring the girls to her day job cleaning houses. They'd pitch in, and Larraine would split her paycheck.

One day, Larraine and the girls went to a Fourth of July barbecue. It was 1986. They had been invited because a friend wanted to set Larraine up with her brother, Glen. It worked. They fell for each other hard and fast. Glen was nothing like Jerry Lee. She didn't feel stupid around him. She felt beautiful. And useful. Glen was on parole for robbing a pharmacy. He had done prison time for that job; in fact, he had spent much of his life in and out of prison. Larraine tried to keep him out of trouble. She would rub his neck after a day of failed job searches. Glen encouraged Larraine to get a driver's license, and at thirty-eight, she did.

Glen was a romantic and a drinker. He and Larraine used to get into tumbling arguments. Sometimes, Glen would come after Larraine and she'd bloody his face with the phone. Once, their landlord evicted them for causing a racket. The morning after a fight, they would kiss softly and apologize. Theirs was a consuming, brutal kind of love.

Larraine still blamed herself for what happened next. Glen had come home from his sister's house, drunk and high and roughed up. He had been in a fight and was in one of his darker moods. Glen could slip into trenches of depression. Sometimes, Larraine remembered, he even heard voices. Glen snatched a container of prescription pills, and Larraine, thinking he might swallow the whole lot, grabbed his arm. They wrestled for the pills and Glen slipped against the refrigerator and crashed to the floor. Blood spilled from a head gash. Panicked, Larraine dialed 911. After the paramedics bandaged his head, the police officers cuffed him. He was sent back to prison for violating his parole by taking narcotics.

The last time Larraine visited Glen in prison, he didn't look right.

He was jumpy, and his eyes had a yellowish hue. Uncharacteristically, he asked to cut the visit short because he wasn't feeling well. The next morning, Larraine's phone rang. She remembered a woman's voice telling her: "There's just no way to say it, but Glen died." Overdose.

In the ensuing years, Larraine would come to believe that Glen had been poisoned by his cellmate. Whatever the case, after sixteen years together, Glen was gone. Larraine dropped the phone and screamed out his name. "I died right then and there," she said. "My heart fell apart. My body fell apart, my whole being. . . . When he died, it's like my whole life fell into a hole, and I haven't been able to get out ever since."

THE EAGLE MOVING trucks stopped outside a North Side duplex with cream siding. An older child answered the door: a girl, maybe seventeen with shorn hair, dark-brown skin, and unflinching gray eyes.

Dave and the crew hung back, waiting for John to give the okay. The deputies always went first and absorbed tenants' blowback if there was any. Things often got loud; they rarely got violent. Sheriffs used different diffusion strategies. John preferred meeting aggression with aggression. Once, he called the Sheriff's Office in front of a woman in a bathrobe and headwrap, saying into the phone, "If she doesn't shut her mouth and start talking like an adult, I'm going to throw her shit in the street!" The conversation with Gray Eyes was taking longer than usual. Dave watched a white man in a flannel shirt park his truck and approach the door. Landlord, he figured. After a few more minutes, John nodded at Dave, and the crew sprang up.

Inside the house, the movers found five children. Tim recognized one child as the daughter of a man who used to work on the crew. It wasn't uncommon to evict someone you knew. Most of the movers lived on the North Side and had at some point experienced the awkward moment of packing up someone from their church or block. Tim had evicted his own daughter. But this house felt strange. Dave asked what was going on, and John explained that the name on the eviction order belonged to the mother of several of the children. She had died two months earlier, and the children had simply gone on living in the house, by themselves.

As the movers swept through the rooms, Gray Eyes took charge, giving orders to the other children; the youngest was a boy of about eight or nine. Upstairs, the movers found ratty mattresses on the floor and empty liquor bottles displayed like trophies. In the damp basement, clothes were flung everywhere. The house and the yard were littered with trash. "Disgusting," Tim said to the roaches scaling the kitchen wall.

As the landlord changed the locks with a power drill and the movers pushed the contents of the house onto the wet curb, the children began to run around and laugh.

When the move was done, the crew gathered by the trucks, instinctively stomping the ground to shake loose any stowaway roaches. Those who smoked reached for their packs. They didn't know where the children would go, and they didn't ask.

With this job, you saw things. The guy with 10,000 audiocassette tapes of UFO activity who kept yelling, "Everything is in order! Everything is in order!" The woman with jars full of urine. The guy who lived in the basement while his pack of Chihuahuas overran the house. Just a week earlier, a man had told Sheriff John to give him a minute. Then he shut the door and shot himself in the head.[5] But the squalor was what got under your skin; its smells and sights were what you tried to drink away after your shift.

Gray Eyes leaned against the porch rail and took long drags of her own cigarette.

LARRAINE CONSIDERED ASKING her brothers and sisters for help. There was her eldest sister, Odessa, who lived a few miles away and spent her days in a nightgown on a corduroy recliner, watching talk shows next to a lampstand crowded with prescription medication containers. She was on SSI, and wouldn't be able to help even if she were willing, which she wasn't. Beaker was in worse shape than Odessa. A towering man with loose skin, Beaker was sixty-five and a heavy smoker who relied on a walker. The family, in the midwestern way, liked to poke fun at his failing health. *"We've got the funeral home on speed dial!"* Even if he wasn't in the hospital, Beaker's Social Security stipend was even less than Larraine's. He could afford the rent but little else, living hard in a filthy trailer covered in clothes, cigarette boxes and butts, food-encrusted plates, and stray dog shit.

Susan was better off. She lived with her husband, Lane, in one of the nicer trailers in the park. The couple were trying desperately to adopt their granddaughter, who had been born "glowing like a lightbulb," as Lane put it. (Their middle daughter—"our heartbreak"—was a heavy cocaine user.) And even if that situation weren't already demanding their resources and attention, Susan didn't trust Larraine with money. Susan had once gone weeks without speaking to her sister after learning Larraine had blown a few hundred dollars on a Luminess Air makeup application kit advertised on television.

Then there was Ruben, the blessed child. He was the only one who hadn't inherited their father's Croatian nose. And he didn't live in the trailer park, or even *a* trailer park, or even in Cudahy, like Odessa. He lived in Oak Creek, in his own home, which was big enough to host everyone for Thanksgiving dinner every year. Larraine could ask Ruben for the rent money, but she wasn't close with her baby brother. Plus, asking for help from better-off kin was complicated. Those ties were banked, saved for emergency situations or opportunities to get ahead. People were careful not to overdraw their account because when family members with money grew exhausted by repeated requests, they sometimes withheld support for long periods of time, pegging their relatives' misfortunes to individual failings. This was one reason why family members in the best position to help were often not asked to do so.[6]

Larraine thought her best bet was to approach her younger daughter, Jayme. Larraine found a ride to Arby's, where Jayme worked.

Before she left, she got dressed up, putting on a pale-blue shirt, clean dark pants, black low-heeled shoes, and lipstick.

"Can Jayme take our order?" Larraine asked another Arby's worker behind the counter.

"Jayme," the worker called out.

Jayme looked up from a pile of dirty dishes, rolled her eyes at her mother, and came walking to the front, her thick auburn curls tucked beneath an Arby's hat. She was not much taller than Larraine and wore wire glasses and a nun's expression: warm but distant. Staying behind the counter, Jayme whispered, "Mom, you're not supposed to be here."

"I know," Larraine said, dropping her smile to look deeply sad. "I know, honey. But I just got a twenty-four-hour eviction notice. They are going to throw me out if I don't pay the rent. And, um, I was wondering if there was any way you could help me?"

A line started to form. Jayme stepped away to take orders. Once Jayme had cleared the line, the manager appeared. A rail-thin white woman with straw hair and acne, she looked like a high school student.

"Mom, this is my *boss*." Jayme sounded embarrassed. Her manager looked to be ten years her junior.

"Did you come here to visit?" the manager asked.

"To order."

"Oh, okay." The manager put an arm around Jayme. "I just love your daughter. She is my very favorite worker."

Larraine ordered and pulled out her wallet to pay. But with a few snappy punches to the register, the manager cleared the charge. "This one's on me. Because Jayme is such a wonderful worker."

"Please don't fire her," Larraine replied.

The boss cocked her head at Larraine and skipped off to the drive-through window.

Alone again with Jayme, Larraine leaned in and whispered across the counter: "So what do you think about—"

"I can't."

"Okay."

"I can't."

Larraine looked at the floor.

Jayme gathered the apple turnovers. "I mean, I don't have anything now. But when I get my check, I can have it mailed to you. If you can get someone to help you out till I get paid. But right now there's nothing I can do. Can you find someone else?"

"I'll try. I'll pay you back. I promise."

"Mom, I don't *want* you to pay me back."

Larraine gathered up her food. "Well, okay," she said, turning to go.

"Mom, wait," Jayme said. "I want to give you a hug." She came around the counter, hugged her mom, and kissed her on the cheek.

Jayme didn't choose to work at Arby's. It was her work-release placement. She was in the final months of a two-and-a-half-year sentence. In the evenings, Jayme was transported back to the women's correctional facility on Keefe Avenue. It was her first time in prison, for her first arrest, and she had mainly kept her nose in her Bible. She'd had a baby in a toilet and left it there. No one in the family knew why; she was already a mother of a toddler at the time. Jayme had been a bookish child, with large round glasses and a mature-beyond-her-years way about her.

Now that her prison sentence was coming to an end, Jayme was focused on a single goal: saving enough for an apartment that could accommodate her son, now six, on overnight visits. The boy was staying with his father.

When Jayme went to prison, she gave Larraine her car and $500 to care for it. But not long after that, Larraine sold the car and used the $500 to pay a bill. Larraine had done a similar thing to Megan, her eldest daughter, borrowing money and failing to pay it back. This was the main reason Megan had not spoken to Larraine in years. Jayme couldn't hold that kind of grudge.

In the Arby's parking lot, Larraine stared out the windshield. Office Susie had told her to ask her family for rent. She often heard a similar line at the crisis centers. When the social workers behind the glass asked her, "Well, don't you have family that can help?" Larraine sometimes would reply, "Yes, I have family, and, no, they can't help."

THE MOVERS WERE standing in an empty kitchen, inspecting an open cupboard. "Old folks," Dave Brittain guessed by the style of the glassware. The house was nearly abandoned and show-ready. The tenants had mopped the floor on their way out. The crew was now on the South Side, and another pair of sheriff deputies had taken over.

At the next house, a Hispanic woman in her early forties answered the door holding a wooden spoon.

"Can I have until Wednesday?" she asked.

The deputies shook their heads no. She nodded with forced resolve or submission.

Dave stepped onto the porch. "Ma'am," he said, "we can place your things in our truck or on the curb. Which would you prefer?" She opted for the curb. "Curbside service, baby!" Dave hollered back to the crew.

Dave stepped into the house and tripped over a Dora the Explorer chair. He reached over an older man sitting at the table and flipped on more lights. The house was warm and smelled of garlic and spices. One of the deputies pointed to the built-in cabinets in the kitchen. "This is the kind of shit I like," he told his partner. "They don't make this stuff anymore. Tight."

The woman walked in circles, trying to think of where to begin. She told one of the deputies that she knew she was being foreclosed but that she didn't know when they were coming. Her attorney had told her that it could be a day, five days, a week, three weeks; she decided to ride it out. She and her three children had been in the house for five years. The year before, she had been talked into refinancing with a subprime loan. Her payments kept going up, jumping from $920 to

$1,250 a month, and her hours at Potawatomi Casino were cut back after her maternity leave.

Hispanic and African American neighborhoods had been targeted by the subprime lending industry: renters were lured into buying bad mortgages, and homeowners were encouraged to refinance under riskier terms. Then it all came crashing down. Between 2007 and 2010, the average white family experienced an 11 percent reduction in wealth, but the average black family lost 31 percent of its wealth. The average Hispanic family lost 44 percent.[7]

As the woman rushed away to frantically call people to come over and help, the movers exchanged tired glances and whispered curses. They hated doing a full house toward the end of the day but that was precisely what they had on their hands. A mover started in on a girl's bedroom, painted pink with a sign on the door announcing THE PRINCESS SLEEPS HERE. Another took on the disheveled office, packing *Resumes for Dummies* into a box with a chalkboard counting down the remaining days of school. The eldest child, a seventh-grade boy, tried to help by taking out the trash. His younger sister, the princess, held her two-year-old sister's hand on the porch. Upstairs, the movers were trying not to step on the toddler's toys, which when kicked would protest with beeping sounds and flashing lights.

As the move went on, the woman slowed down. At first, she had borne down on the emergency with focus and energy, almost running through the house with one hand grabbing something and the other holding up the phone. Now she was wandering through the halls aimlessly, almost drunkenly. Her face had that look. The movers and the deputies knew it well. It was the look of someone realizing that her family would be homeless in a matter of hours. It was something like denial giving way to the surrealism of the scene: the speed and violence of it all; sheriffs leaning against your wall, hands resting on holsters; all these strangers, these sweating men, piling your things outside, drinking water from your sink poured into your cups, using your bathroom. It was the look of being undone by a wave of questions. *What do I need for tonight, for this week? Who should I call? Where is the medication? Where will we go?* It was the face of a mother who climbs out of the cellar to find the tornado has leveled the house.

EVERY SUNDAY MORNING, Larraine stood on the seam that separated the linoleum in the kitchen from the thin green carpet in the living room, looking out the front window for Mr. Dabbs's truck. Mr. Dabbs, a member of her church, would drive into the trailer park, remove his hat, and knock softly on Larraine's door.

When they got to the Southside Church of Christ, a modest brick building with a high-pitched roof roughly a mile and a half northwest of the trailer park, Mr. Dabbs would hold the door open. Larraine would step gracefully in, walking past her photograph on the wall displaying members' portraits. In the sanctuary—a humble space, unadorned—sunlight from large back windows streamed onto the pews. The ceiling bowed up, resembling a great overturned boat. Larraine would take her seat in the second to last pew on the left, next to Susan and Lane. This was where her family had always sat. Susan usually ignored Larraine and pretended to read the bulletin as Pastor Daryl, a large man with red hair and beard, strolled the aisle, shaking hands and slapping backs.

This being a Church of Christ, there was no organ or piano; no acoustic guitar. When the congregation stood to sing "I Stand in Awe" or "O Worship the King," voices rose up a cappella. Larraine prayed with her palms resting gently on her thighs. When it was time to take the offering, she would let the basket pass. Susan would drop something in.

Recently, Pastor Daryl had been preaching on "The Cost of Discipleship." He would pace the front of the church, Bible in one hand, PowerPoint clicker in the other, and repeat Jesus's more impossible injunctions: "Anyone who does not carry his cross and follow me cannot be my disciple." "It is easier for a camel to go through the eye of a needle than for a rich man to enter the kingdom of God."

"I think one of the biggest shames of Christianity is people that halfway follow Jesus," Pastor Daryl observed one Sunday. "A partial commitment is a dangerous way to live. . . . You got neighbors around you that need help. You got people that need helping and that need loving and, as Christians, you can be demonstrating that love to them." During Pastor Daryl's sermons, Larraine would sit still with near-perfect posture, rapt from beginning to end. She loved going to church and had since she was a child.

When Larraine called Pastor Daryl to ask if the church could lend her money so that she might avoid eviction, he said he'd have to think about it. The last time Larraine called, she had said she'd been robbed at gunpoint. Pastor Daryl reached into the church's coffers and gave her a few hundred dollars for the rent. Larraine had been robbed, but not by a stranger with a gun. Susan and Lane's cokehead daughter had broken into her trailer when no one was home. Susan phoned Pastor Daryl to report Larraine's lie.

Pastor Daryl felt torn. On the one hand, he thought it was the job of the church, not the government, to care for the poor and hungry. That, to him, was "pure Christianity." When it came to Larraine, though, Pastor Daryl believed a lot of hardship was self-inflicted. "She made some stupid choices, spending her money foolishly. . . . Making her go without for a while may be the best thing for her, so that she can be reminded, 'Hey when I make foolish choices there are consequences.'" It was easy to go on about helping "the poor." Helping a poor person with a name, a face, a history, and many needs, a person whose mistakes and lapses of judgment you have recorded—that was a more trying matter.

Pastor Daryl called Susan and told her that Larraine had asked for money to stay her eviction. Susan replied by saying that she didn't think the church should give her sister anything. Pastor Daryl called Larraine back and told her that he wouldn't be helping this time.

IN THE TRAILER park office, Lenny was bent over his desk, filling in his rent rolls, when a woman named Britney Baker walked in. She was in her late twenties, wearing cheap sunglasses. Britney pulled her mail out of her box and then turned to Lenny.

"I'm going to pay it, you know," she said.

"Good," Lenny said.

"I'm going to pay this week. Don't give me a five-day. I mean, Tobin knows my situation."

And with that, Britney left. Lenny shook his head and looked back down at his rent rolls, which showed that Britney owed a balance of $2,156.

The relationship between nonpayment of rent and eviction was anything but straightforward. Every month in the trailer park, tenants who owed more than a thousand dollars were not evicted while some who owed far less were.[8] If you asked Tobin why, he would say, "You're loyal to the people who are loyal to you. Some people we work with. Some people I wouldn't give a single penny." Lenny put it like this: "Depends what their excuses are." With Larraine, Lenny and Tobin felt she was chronically behind. "Every month it's the same thing," Lenny said. "Ain't got no money." But every month it was the same thing with Britney Baker as well, and she would not be evicted.

Landlords and building managers weighed several factors when considering whether to evict a tenant. Tenants who could convince landlords that they had money coming down the pike, in the form of a tax refund, say, could avoid eviction. Tenants who fell too far behind without a clear way of getting caught up often could not. But evictions were not simply the consequence of tenants' misbehavior or landlords' financial accounting. Landlords showed considerable discretion over whether to move forward with an eviction, extending leniency to some and withdrawing it from others.[9] How a tenant responded to an eviction notice could make the difference. Women tended not to negotiate their eviction like men did, and they were more likely to avoid landlords when they fell behind. These responses did not serve them well.

Landlords and building managers generally hated it when tenants avoided them. "Ducking and dodging," they called it. When tenants hid from Lenny, it made him angry. "Fuck you!" he once yelled after a tenant peeked through the blinds and refused to answer her door. "You pissed me off now. You're out in five days!"

Like many women in her situation, Larraine was ducking and dodging Tobin and Lenny. She never once told them, or even Office Susie, how she was planning on getting caught up. She never asked for a little more time. Meanwhile, Larraine's neighbor, biker Jerry Warren, confronted Tobin and Lenny immediately, balling up his eviction notice and threatening to wreck Lenny's face. Belligerent as it was, Jerry's confrontational response aligned with Tobin's blunt and brusque way. Property management was a profession dominated by men and by a gruff, masculine way of doing business. That put men like Jerry at an advantage.[10]

Not only did Jerry confront Tobin immediately after being served, but he later offered to pick up litter and repair some trailers if Tobin cleared his debt. Jerry had done some work for Tobin in the past, painting trailer hitches and winterizing pipes. Having proved himself a reliable hand, he had established a "working off the rent" option should money run thin. Larraine rang up social services and begged family members. Jerry went straight to the man who had initiated the eviction. And it worked: Tobin later dismissed his eviction. Larraine's plan could work only if a local nonprofit organization, her family, or her church came through.

Men often avoided eviction by laying concrete, patching roofs, or painting rooms for landlords. But women almost never approached their landlord with a similar offer. Some women—already taxed by child care, welfare requirements, or work obligations—could not spare the time. But many others simply did not conceive of working off the rent as a possibility. When women did approach their landlords with such an offer, it sometimes involved trading sex for rent.[11]

The power to dictate who could stay and who must go; the power to expel or forgive: it was an old power, and it was not without caprice.[12] Tobin's decision to work with tenants could be arbitrary, his generosity unevenly dispensed. But at least you had a chance. In fact, one reason Larraine risked eviction and paid her gas bill was because other tenants had told her, speaking from experience, "Tobin's a nice guy. Just give him a little, and he'll work with you."

This was why, when Tobin complied with Alderman Witkowski's demand to hire an outside management company, the trailer park began to worry. New management would institute a new system—a cleaner, more professional, and fairer way of running the park. In other words, things were about to get much worse.

One day, a man showed up outside Lenny's office and drilled a sign into the cinder blocks that announced: PROFESSIONALLY MANAGED BY BIECK MANAGEMENT. When an older resident saw the sign, she stepped into the office and began sobbing. "They evicted me from my last place," she told Lenny. "They are so harsh."

"Yeah, I hear they are ruthless," Lenny said. "They put a whole lot of people on the streets. You know, if you can't work with people a little bit."

"What about you, Lenny?" the woman asked after collecting herself.

"They're looking for a way to get rid of me, I can see that." Lenny gestured toward the sign. "But it's not happening. You got to have somebody around here who knows the park," he told the woman, and himself.

WHEN EVERYONE ELSE had said no, Ruben had come through. Larraine's baby brother, who had found a way to lift himself into the middle class, who worked full-time for PPG Industries, had reluctantly agreed to pay Tobin. He brought the money to the trailer park himself. But Tobin refused to accept it, telling Larraine that he didn't want the money. Tobin walked away, leaving Larraine and Ruben standing, stunned, outside of the office. Ruben put his money back in his pocket and walked slowly with Larraine back to her trailer.[13]

A few hours later, Larraine answered a knock at her door and found two sheriff deputies standing on her small porch. Behind them, the Eagle Moving trucks were pulling into the trailer park. It was a tight pinch for the drivers, maneuvering through the narrow entrance, minding the unleashed dogs and children, and backing up to the designated spot; but Eagle had been in Tobin's park plenty of times. It was the last move of the day, and the crew was sore and eager to get home.[14]

The movers were hoping for a "junk in," but Larraine asked that her things be taken to storage. Ruben loaded her television and computer in his car and then left to pick up his kids. The movers began filling boxes with Larraine's things: the white utensils in the kitchen, a Christmas gift for her grandson, a necklace Glen had given her. A deputy taped an orange sign to her door.

NOTICE

You have been evicted from this property by virtue of a Court Order served by the Milwaukee County Sheriff's Office

YOUR PRESENCE ON THIS PROPERTY WITHOUT THE EXPRESS PERMISSION OF THE LANDLORD WILL BE CONSIDERED TRESPASSING AND MAY RESULT IN YOUR ARREST (STATUTE 943.14)

Larraine asked for more time to gather some belongings. The deputy said no. Then she asked if she could retrieve some items from the truck. A mover said no, citing the company's insurance policy.

Larraine stood outside, silently looking on. The movers carried out her chair, her washing machine, her refrigerator, stove, dining table. Next came the boxes with who knows what inside: perhaps winter jackets or shoes or shampoo. The neighbors began to gather. Some grabbed beers and positioned lawn chairs as if watching a NASCAR race.

It didn't take long. Larraine was cleaned out in less than an hour. She watched the truck lurch away. Her things were headed to

Eagle's storage warehouse, a dimly lit expanse with clear lightbulbs strung from a ceiling supported by large wood pillars. Inside, there were hundreds upon hundreds of piles, each representing an eviction or foreclosure. The piles were stacked to eye level and individually encircled in shrink-wrap like so many silken-wound insects on a spider's web. Up close, the contents were visible through the taut clear wrapping: scratched-up furniture, lamps, bathroom scales, and everywhere children's things—rocking horses, strollers, baby swings, bouncy seats. The Brittain brothers thought of the warehouse as a "giant stomach," digesting the city. They charged $25 per pallet per month. The average evicted family's possessions took up four pallets, or 400 cubic feet.

Larraine would have to find a way to pay her storage bill. If she fell ninety days behind, Eagle would get rid of her pile to make room for a new one. This was the fate of roughly 70 percent of lots confiscated in evictions or foreclosures. Years before, the Brittain brothers had approached Goodwill but were rebuffed; there was simply no way Goodwill could handle that kind of volume. The brothers searched elsewhere. They reached out to metal scrappers. They found someone who would buy the clothing by the bale, turning it into rags. They partnered with people who would rummage through the piles, looking for things to sell. They organized public sales twice a month, each involving ten to forty lots. But most of the stuff ended up in the dump.[15]

With the sheriff out of sight, Larraine ignored the orange sign and broke back into her trailer. The big items were gone, but the movers had left behind clothes, blankets, and miscellaneous smaller things. Larraine reached down and picked up her steamer.

There was only one option, Larraine thought: take what was left to Beaker's trailer. He was in the hospital. He couldn't say no. Larraine recruited a pair of boys to help, and the three of them made several trips between the two trailers, piling whatever they could carry in Beaker's living room.

When the work was done, Larraine gave each boy $5 and sat alone in Beaker's trailer, swatting away fruit flies. She swallowed pain pills, including 200 milligrams of Lyrica. In silence, she let the painkillers work. Once they had, she looked around at the clutter, the foulness, and the pile of things the movers had considered junk. Larraine let out a muffled scream and began punching the couch over and over and over again.

10.

HYPES FOR HIRE

Wright Street was covered in snow. An early December storm had arrived and was predicted to drop ten inches. It was that wet, slushy snow—the heavy kind you shovel in small doses so as to avoid throwing out your back. Lamar looked out the window as the snow continued to fall, drinking instant coffee and putting off the job he had to do.

Once he and the boys had finished painting Patrice's old unit, Lamar called Sherrena, who came straight over to inspect the work. After a swift march through the unit, she shook her head and offered an evaluation: "I tried to work with you, and you disrespecting me with this motherfucking shitty-ass job!"

"What I did is worth way more than two sixty," Lamar had yelled back. "I'm crawling around on my knees painting for you! And you gonna do me like this?"

Sherrena stormed off. A few hours later, Lamar dialed Sherrena's number. He begged her to let him finish the job, to cover the spots the boys had missed. "Please," he said, "I don't like being in nobody's pocket." Sherrena decided to give him another chance. It was his best hope of keeping his home.

Lamar finished his coffee and strapped on his legs. Grabbing his cane, he opened the door and stepped onto the porch, grimacing at the snow and clutching the stair rail to keep from falling. Patrice's son, Mikey, was outside, trying to shovel the sidewalk. He paused when he saw Lamar struggle on the porch steps, unsure of whether to offer his hand. He didn't, and Lamar managed fine. He even gave Mikey's shovel a few pushes. When Lamar said he was heading upstairs, Mikey asked if he could help.

"Come on, son," Lamar replied.

Inside, Mikey looked around the apartment he and his family had been evicted from.

"Why y'all didn't make it to school today?" Lamar asked. It was a Tuesday.

"I guess I fell asleep," Mikey answered. He was in the fourth grade.

"Ah, boy, Michael. You don't get no education like that, son."

Mikey put his head down. "We had art today," he said.

"Don't you know you can get rich off of art? Don't you know that you can have a—a *career* being an *artis*? An *architecter*?"

Mikey smiled a broad smile, and Lamar began sweeping a paintbrush through the pantry. To reach the lower sections, he unclipped his prosthetic legs and crawled on the floor. Mikey helped in any way he could. He passed Lamar rags and rollers with such quick eagerness you would think he was competing for the job. When Lamar got stuck on the floor, Mikey would fetch his cane.

"Where's your momma and them at, man?" Lamar asked.

"My momma? She went to get her QUEST Card from Dace," Mikey started, speaking of Patrice's food stamps and boyfriend. "And he took her cards, and she ain't have nothin' to eat. So. And her cards—"

"Michael, okay," Lamar interrupted, gently. "You could have just said she was gone. Don't tell nobody your momma's business, man. You know I'm a friend, but, but I didn't really want to know."

Mikey nodded slowly, pretending to understand.

Lamar scooted along the floor and, quietly resolved, lifted his brush. As the morning wore on, he began sweating and breathing heavily. He grunted and prayed for strength, "Jesus, get me through the day."

"It's ridiculous, Lamar," Mikey said, trying to console.

"No, it's people get outta you what they can get outta you. That's what it is, Michael."

When the job was complete, Lamar reaffixed his legs and headed back to his apartment. From there, he called Sherrena to tell her he had finished painting. Promising nothing, she said that she would come by later to have a look. Then she asked Lamar to mop the floor too.

Buck stopped by later in the afternoon. Noticing the paint on Lamar's skin and clothes, he asked, "I thought we was done up there, man?"

"Man, she made me go up there and take care of the pantry. People just don't be satisfied."

"That's money, pops!" Buck smiled, glad that Lamar and his boys would be able to stay.

Lamar sighed and massaged below his knees the way someone rubs an old, familiar injury. "They ain't gonna pay, man," he said.

"They gotta pay!"

"Man, they can get some hypes to do it for way less than that."

Lamar's labor was cheap, but he knew there were better deals to be had. When the plumbing broke, the roof leaked, or rooms needed painting, savvy inner-city landlords did not phone plumbers, roofers, or painters. They relied on two desperate and on-hand labor pools: tenants themselves and jobless men. New landlords would speak of "knowing a good plumber." Experienced landlords would say they "had a guy." Lamar knew that Sherrena "had people" and doubted that she would let him stay. He did the painting anyway, having no better option.

Buck frowned and stared at the snow. "Nah, pops," he said, disbelieving.

"Hypes!" Lamar shouted. "Hypes done messed up everything. It's hard to even sell a bus pass at the right price. . . . I had to argue with her to get *that* job for two sixty. She got guys that'll do it for a hundred. The *whoooole* thing. Drywall and all."

THE NEXT TUESDAY, Lamar woke up to a warm house. He had kept his stove burners on overnight to fend off winter's chill, a common trick used by those who inhabited the North Side's drafty duplexes with old furnaces. A week had passed without any word from Sherrena.

Most days, he had instant coffee and a cigarette for breakfast. But he had allowed Luke and Eddy to stay home from school; so he began frying eggs and boiling grits. The smell of bacon pulled the boys out of bed, and soon Buck stopped by, as if he had smelled Lamar's cooking from his house down the street.

A soft tap was heard at the back door, and one of the boys opened it. It was Kamala, the new upstairs neighbor—the third in five months. If you spotted her a block away, you might think she was in seventh or eighth grade. Kamala was petite with skin "blacker than purple," as the saying went. A white tank top clung to her thin frame. She wore no makeup or nail polish. Her only flourish was a locket that hung from a thin gold chain. Her eyes were heavy. Her whole spirit was heavy. She asked Lamar for a cigarette.

"Here you go, baby," Lamar said, handing her one. He was happy to see her.

Kamala thanked him and turned to leave. "Let me go check on these kids, make sure they not tearing up my house." Kamala had three daughters: ages three, two, and eight months.

"Well, come on down here and let 'em tear up my house. You don't play cards, do you?"

Kamala gave Lamar a small smile and started up the stairs only to be met by her two-year-old.

Lamar rolled his wheelchair up to the girl. "Lemme see who my little goddaughter's gonna be. Hey! How you doing?"

The child said something, but her words were woolly and half-formed. She had to repeat herself a few times before Lamar could understand that she was saying "Tummy hurt."

"You hungry?" Lamar asked. "We need to put some weight on her. You cook yesterday?" It was a pure question, untraced by incrimination.

"Yeah, but all's I got is a microwave up there," Kamala answered softly.

Like many inner-city landlords, Sherrena and Quentin tried to limit the number of appliances in their units. If you didn't include a stove or refrigerator, you didn't have to fix it when it broke.

"Huh. Okay." Lamar spun his chair and pushed himself into the pantry. When he rolled out, there was an electric hot plate on his lap. A few days earlier, after he had first met Kamala, Lamar had said that he "ain't getting too frien'ly" with her and her family. "It ain't gonna be no thing like, 'I need a cup of sugar,'" he had said. "We ain't doing that. . . . I keep to myself. It works out better." But there he was, giving Kamala something worth quite a bit more than a cup of sugar.[1]

"This was my mom's," Lamar said. "It cooks its ass off."

"Ain't gonna start no fire?" Kamala asked.

"It ain't start no fire."

"Okay. I'll take care of it. I thank you for it."

"You're welcome, honey. Y'all come down for dinner tonight."

Kamala took the hot plate and her daughter up the stairs.

The cards and blunts came out after breakfast. C.J., Patrice's young brother, came over and watched the game. He wasn't offered a hit and didn't ask for one. Luke's girlfriend showed up, and the two shut the bedroom door behind them. The morning passed slowly as milky smoke and the weed's sweaty pungency filled the house.

Just as Lamar and the boys were finishing a blunt, its pleasant effects setting in, someone knocked loudly and confidently on the front door. It sounded like a landlord's knock, or a sheriff's: four or five hard knuckle taps in quick succession. Everyone stopped talking and looked at one another.

After a moment had passed, Buck called out, "Who is it?"

"It's Colin, from the church."

"Shit!" Lamar said, at once relieved and annoyed. The boys muffled their laughter. Eddy threw open a window and everyone began frantically waving their hands through the air, pushing the smoke out, laughing harder. "Okay! Okay!" Lamar whispered, giving the sign to calm down and act normal. Then he had Eddy open the door.

If Colin smelled weed, he didn't say anything. He was in his late twenties and white, with ungelled hair, good posture, and a wedding band. In one hand, he carried a Bible and a workbook with the title *By Grace Alone*; in the other, cookies. After everyone had found a seat in the living room, everyone except Luke and his girl, Colin opened his Bible and dove in. He covered the basics. "For God so loved the world . . ." (John 3:16); "God made him who had no sin to be sin . . ." (2 Corinthians 5:21). The boys sat quietly, trying to hold on to their high. Then Colin asked them to read some passages. They smiled at one another and read with their fingers tracing the words. Lamar leaned into the scripture verses, nodding meditatively and finishing them by memory.

"For all have sinned—"

"—and fallen short of the glory of God," Lamar said.

"I been thinking like this, right," Buck started, reclining on a couch pillow.

"Then say it!" Lamar encouraged with closed eyes.

"I don't know why people don't believe in God."

"You believe in the devil too, right?" Lamar asked.

"I know they is one. But I don't want to know him," Buck responded.

"And Earth is hell," Lamar added.

"Well, not quite hell," Colin corrected.

Lamar opened his eyes and looked at the boy preacher. A silence hung in the air, and in that silence, adolescent moans and squeaks could be heard coming from Luke's room. Hearing this, the boys locked their eyes on the floor and focused on suppressing the laughter pushing its way up. After leading a closing prayer and handing Lamar a checklist of things he could pick up from the church—clothes, blankets—Colin left, and the house fell out laughing. When Luke joined the group in the kitchen, the boys erupted again. "We heard you getting it *in*," Buck teased, folding sideways from laughing. "The preacher here. You stupid, dude!"

Lamar shook his head and dealt the cards.

AT THE END of the month, Quentin parked outside of Arleen's apartment on Thirteenth Street and honked the horn. He wasn't there for Arleen this time; he was there for Chris, Trisha's new boyfriend. "Man, I'm hungover as shit," Chris said as he got into the truck. "My lady got me a six-pack of Heineken and a motherfuckin' fifth of Amsterdam."

Quentin put the truck in drive. His hair was parted in the middle and tied twice in the back, forming a pair of small afro puffs. Chris, who was in his late thirties, wore a large winter coat and covered his bald head with a knit cap. When Chris moved in with Trisha, after being released from prison, he called Quentin and said he was looking for work. Quentin was Chris's only source of income.

The Suburban pulled up next to an apartment and Chris jumped out to get Tiny, another worker. A few minutes later, he came back alone. "Man, dude said he don't feel like coming."

Quentin shrugged. "Dude playing games, man."

When Quentin called Sherrena to tell her that Tiny didn't want work, she replied, "We'll just slide someone else into his spot." Workers could be found and replaced just like that. There was Sherrena's brother, who had a crack habit, or Quentin's uncle, Verne, a gummy-faced alcoholic happy to log hours for beer money. Tenants often asked for work; even Ricky One Leg had been calling. Plus, Sherrena had on

call a crew of hypes—"jackleg crackheads," she called them—willing
to "work for peanuts." In a pinch, Quentin sometimes recruited men
right off the street. It wasn't hard to do with so many men in the
inner city out of work. Sherrena and Quentin provided tools, materials, and transportation. They paid workers by the task or the day. The
amounts typically ranged from $6 to $10 an hour, depending on the
job. "These people," Sherrena once said, "no matter how much money
it is, it's money. And they will work, and they will work for low prices."

Reported high rates of joblessness among black men with little education obscured the fact that many of these men did regularly work,
if not in the formal labor market. Some hustling in the underground
economy plied the illicit trades, but the biggest drug kingpin in the
city would have been envious of the massive cash-paid labor force
urban landlords had at their disposal.[2]

Quentin dropped Chris off at a newly acquired property he and
Sherrena were planning on renting to a woman with a housing voucher.
Quentin told Chris to steady the staircase railing and fix a door in anticipation of the Section 8 home inspection. "You know how rent assistance is," Quentin told Chris. "Everything gotta be perfect. . . . They
be coming with some ugly lists."

"All right, boy," Quentin said as he and Chris exchanged the Vice
Lords' handshake.

In high school, Quentin used to run with the Vice Lords, a street
gang that originated in Chicago. He was never very active in the gang,
and the two times he had been shot were not gang-related. Quentin
took his first bullet when he was nineteen. He and his friends were in a
heated confrontation with a group of guys when suddenly a van raced
up, and he heard the *pop-pop* of a 9mm. Quentin was shot in the leg.
The second time came a year later, during a mugging. That time, the
bullet lodged in his shoulder blade. The shootings left Quentin on
"super alert." A doctor later would diagnose him with stomach ulcers.
Over the years, he had learned to relax. When tenants threatened him,
he tried to let it slide. But every so often, something would happen,

and Quentin would put on his black hoodie and black jeans, and Sher-rena would shoot him a dirty look at the door but stay quiet because she had learned she couldn't say anything when it got to that point, and Quentin would climb in the Suburban and call his guys and go deal with something. The last time the black hoodie came out, a ten-ant had intentionally and severely damaged one of his properties, out of spite.

Around sunset, after running between Home Depot and Lowe's, where he was on a first-name basis with the cashiers, after transporting this worker and delivering that tool, Quentin popped his head into Patrice's old unit. His uncle Verne had spent the last two days there, gliding polyurethane over the hardwoods and covering up the white paint Lamar and his boys had dripped on the brown trim. Quentin was done negotiating with Lamar, even after he painted the pantry. He left Sherrena to deal with him. One thing was certain: if they were paying Uncle Verne, they weren't paying Lamar. He would have to come up with another plan, and fast.

Uncle Verne's greasy hair rebelled from all sides of his Baltimore Ravens cap. His pants and flannel shirt were covered in brown paint. His eyes were cloudy and bloodshot. Crumpled aluminum carcasses of drained tallboys—Steel Reserve 211, "crack in a can"—littered the stairwell.

"I need my juice," Uncle Verne told Quentin.

Quentin looked around. The work was shoddy but done. "It's good enough for a tenant to move in," he assessed.

"Huh. This ain't Brookfield!" Uncle Verne laughed, referencing the predominantly white and affluent suburb.

"You know," Quentin said, "it doesn't even matter, 'cause all they gonna do is tear shit up. Sliding furniture, sliding tables, kids, dogs with claws. . . . We don't need to take no time, trying to do no expensive-type stuff to it, 'cause they just gonna mess it up." Quentin reached for his wallet. "Boy, you racking up! That's gonna be like sev-enty by the time you done?"

"Seventy? Nah, 'cause this room thirty dollars." Uncle Verne motioned to the large living room.

"No. This room is twenty. 'Member we talked about this yesterday."

"No. *I* was charging twenty dollars, and *you* was charging ten a room." Uncle Verne laughed nervously.

"Well, then I'll just have Tiny do this, then!" This was Quentin and Sherrena's normal response when workers asked for more pay. They simply reminded them of their expendability.

Uncle Verne backed down. "Okay, okay!"

Quentin counted out the cash and gave his uncle a ride to the liquor store.

FROM THEIR DOWNSTAIRS unit, the Hinkstons had been listening to Quentin and Uncle Verne the whole time. When the men left, Patrice and Natasha snuck upstairs to have a look. Seeing the freshly painted walls and floors, the women sucked their teeth. The new tenant (or at least her payee, Belinda) seemed to know what Patrice did not: your leverage as a renter was strongest before you moved in.

"It looks so pretty," said Natasha. "I'm just, like, mad."

"Unreal," Patrice said.

"It's like a dream house up here. . . . And you in the rat hole!" Natasha laughed.

Patrice didn't join her. Thinking of Sherrena, she said, "She wouldn't survive a day in our house."

11.

THE 'HOOD IS GOOD

As her plane touched down, Sherrena looked out the window and sighed. That morning, she and Quentin had been in Jamaica. Milwaukee looked chilly and damp, like a left-out dishrag. Sherrena switched her phone back on and saw that she had forty voice messages.

Jamaica had been amazing. Sherrena and Quentin took long walks on warm, white beaches, chartered a glass-bottom boat, and zipped around the Caribbean on Jet Skis. Quentin bought a walking stick and had it engraved. Sherrena got her hair done in two thick braids that met in the back. They had stayed for eight days.

Sherrena and Quentin always planned their vacations so that they were back before the first of the month, when their days went long with eviction notices to pass out, new moves to manage, and rents to collect. Because most of their tenants didn't have bank accounts, collecting rent was a face-to-face affair.

A few of Sherrena's voice messages were from Tabatha, a social worker who made weekly visits to the Hinkstons' house. When Sherrena returned her call, Tabatha cited the plumbing situation at

Eighteenth and Wright and tried to advocate for some repairs. Not long after Doreen paid a plumber herself, the pipes backed up again. Sherrena was not hearing it. "I can't believe that you are on my phone complaining to *me* about the sink being stopped up when they're the ones doing it!" Sherrena said. "They pull hinges off doors . . . have clothes piled to the ceiling. The whiff of shit hits you in the face when you open the door. . . . I cannot *believe* that your organization is allowing her to have a house that looks like that."

Then Tabatha made a mistake, telling Sherrena that Doreen was looking for another place. Sherrena got off the phone and headed for the courthouse. If Doreen was withholding rent so the family could move, Sherrena would call her bluff. Sherrena paid the fee and scheduled a court date, giving Doreen an open eviction on CCAP. Now moving would be much harder. If the Hinkstons were going to go, Sherrena decided, they would go on her terms.

After Quentin delivered the pink papers, Doreen called Sherrena to clear things up. "We *do* need a bigger place," she said. "Natasha fittin' to have a baby, and we can't be stacked up in here like this. But I didn't mean immediately. I can't see myself trying to move in the middle of the winter. . . . She be delivering sometime in May. Maybe *then* we can try to find something bigger."

Sherrena told Doreen she wasn't calling off the eviction.

"I got you," Doreen said. "I got your money."

But Sherrena refused to accept it, citing the stress the family was putting on her unit. "What if the state come up in there?" she asked. "Then they shutting my place down, and we all gonna be in trouble. . . . I can't have all those people living in my apartment like that. Too much wear and tear." All Doreen could do was pray that Sherrena would change her mind before they met in eviction court.

ON THE FIRST of the month, Sherrena and Quentin flirted and giggled as they drove from one property to the next. They had brought some of Jamaica back with them. Their skin was sun-kissed and their spirits were buoyed. They caught Ricky One Leg outside, waiting for UPS to deliver a computer for his daughter.

"A computer?" Sherrena asked when Quentin climbed back in the Suburban.

"Yeah." Quentin smiled.

"See. See! He got money for a new computer but not for the rent. That's okay. 'Cause I got 'em. The rent's going up." Sherrena paused for effect. "Inflation!"[1]

Laughter filled the Suburban as it pulled onto the street. Quentin's seat was leaned so far back he was resting more on his hip than his rump. Air fresheners swayed from his rearview mirror and a large speaker in the back thumped bass whenever one of them was not on the phone, which was almost never.

As night fell, Quentin took a call from a rooming-house tenant, touching his Bluetooth earpiece. When the call ended, he said, "They money burning a hole in they pockets. You know, they got habits."

Quentin parked in front of the rooming house and went through a small ritual. He tucked his chains into his shirt, removed his pinky ring, and slid a sweatband over his thick bracelet. He had learned that "some people think you're out to take their rent money to buy, you know, fancy things." A tenant had recently pointed to Quentin's bling and said, "You just want to collect my rent to live your own life." When he relayed this story to Sherrena, she shrugged and said, "How else we supposed to do it?" To live, she meant.

The rooming-house tenants had smoked something but had not yet run through the rent money. The place was filled with music, laughter, and that carefreeness the benefits of the first of the month bring and the bills of the fifth of the month shoo away. The only tenant who appeared sober was an old man who had just moved in. He sat on his bed, shirt buttoned to the top. "Coming at night, huh?" he asked with a Mississippi drawl.

"When do you want to pay your rent?" Quentin replied.

"I'm ready. Always owing something."

Up walked another tenant with glazed-over eyes. "Hey, nigga!" he addressed Quentin, holding an unlit cigarette and leaning on the wall for support. "I, I be at the bar, man. They be fucking with me, man!"

"Straight up?" Quentin asked, sliding the old man's money in his pocket and heading for the door.

Back in the Suburban, Quentin presented Sherrena with a wad of cash. She had to admit it: "Those crackheads pay the rent!" They laughed.

It was almost nine p.m. when Sherrena asked Quentin to drive to the home of a new prospective tenant. Ladona invited Sherrena in and introduced her eight-year-old son, Nathaniel. A working single mother, Ladona was eager to move. "They shoot in broad daylight, right in the middle of the block," she said. "We got a hidin' place upstairs. And I'm getting tired of running up there."

"They need to get the National Guard up in here," Sherrena replied.

"Something. I'm leaving." Then Ladona handed Sherrena $500. "I want that house, and I'm not playin' with you. So Friday I'll give you another hundred. And then the following Friday, another hundred. And then the following week, another one seventy-five."

Sherrena climbed back in the Suburban, which Quentin had kept running. "She's crazy about that house." Then she went on: "There are so many rent-assistance people that have been calling me. You wouldn't believe it."

"Ah, they been calling me too," Quentin said.

"For single families?"

"For anything."

Ladona had a housing voucher. Sherrena and Quentin didn't accept rent assistance in most of their properties because they didn't want to deal with the program's picky inspectors. "Rent assistance is a pain in the ass," Sherrena said. Voucher holders made up a small share of the market anyway—only 6 percent of renter households in the city—and were not worth the headache. (The "SSI people," on the other hand, "now, *that* is an untapped market," Sherrena thought.)

But Sherrena had recently purchased the house that Ladona coveted, a two-story gem, and she was pretty sure it would pass inspection. If it did, the payout could be significant. With a housing voucher, Ladona would pay a small portion of the rent—30 percent of her income—and taxpayers would pick up the rest. Sherrena's rent would be virtually guaranteed. It would also be above market rate.

For each metropolitan area, the Department of Housing and Urban Development sets a Fair Market Rent (FMR): the most a landlord could charge a family in possession of a federal housing voucher.[2] FMRs were calculated at the municipal level, which often included near and outlying suburbs. This meant that both distressed and exclusive neighborhoods were thrown into the equation. New York City's FMR calculation included SoHo and the South Bronx. Chicago's included the Gold Coast and the South Side ghetto. This was by design, so that a family could take their voucher and find housing in safe and prosperous areas in the city or its surrounding suburbs. But the program did not bring about large gains in racial or economic integration. Voucher holders more or less stayed put, upgrading to slightly nicer trailer parks or moving to quieter ghetto streets. It could, however, bring about large gains for landlords.[3]

Because rents were higher in the suburbs than in the inner city, the FMR exceeded market rent in disadvantaged neighborhoods. When voucher holders lived in those neighborhoods, landlords could charge them more than what the apartment would fetch on the private market. In 2009, the year Ladona was hoping to move into Sherrena's new property, the FMR for a four-bedroom unit in Milwaukee County was $1,089. But the average four-bedroom apartment in the city rented for much less: $665.[4] When landlords were allowed to charge more, they did. Although Sherrena didn't think the Housing Authority would approve the maximum amount, she was planning on charging Ladona $775 a month, $100 more than the average rent for similar units but still well below the FMR limit. Ladona didn't mind. With a voucher, what she paid was a function of her income, not Sherrena's rent.[5] Her rental expense wasn't affected; the taxpayers' bill was.

In Milwaukee, renters with housing vouchers were charged an average of $55 more each month, compared to unassisted renters who lived in similar apartments in similar neighborhoods. Overcharging voucher holders cost taxpayers an additional $3.6 million each year in Milwaukee alone—the equivalent of supplying 588 more needy families with housing assistance.[6]

The idea of a "rent certificate program" was first proposed in the 1930s, not by some Washington bureaucrat or tenants' union representative but by the National Association of Real Estate Boards.[7] That group would later change its name to the National Association of Realtors and become the largest trade association for real estate agents, with more than a million members. A rent certificate program would be superior to public housing, they argued. Landlords and Realtors saw government-built and -managed buildings offered at cut-rate rents as a direct threat to their legitimacy and bottom line.[8] At first, federal policymakers disagreed and at midcentury decided to fund the construction of massive public housing complexes. But real estate interests kept lobbying for vouchers and were joined by numerous other groups of various political persuasions, including civil rights activists who thought vouchers would advance racial integration.[9] Eventually, after America's public housing experiment was defunded and declared a failure (in that order), they would have their day. As housing projects were demolished, the voucher program grew into the nation's largest housing subsidy program for low-income families. In policy circles, vouchers were known as a "public-private partnership." In real estate circles, they were known as "a win."

SHERRENA BOUGHT THE house she was going to rent to Ladona a few weeks before flying to Jamaica. It was a large, late colonial–style home with a round turret and generous porch. Someone had recently painted it black and white. The roof was new and so was the water heater and so were the wood-framed windows. The front door opened into a living room with a vaulted ceiling and an intricate mosaic fireplace. There was one bedroom downstairs and three upstairs, which you reached by mounting a long, bending staircase. Thick carpet lined the upstairs bedrooms, two of which, judging from the paint, used to belong to children. The house was in such fine shape that the inspector told Sherrena that he wanted to move in himself.

The black-and-white house was on a quiet street in the inner city. Sherrena judged the block stable "because it's been vacant one whole year and not one fucking window is broken" and because "the people lock it down. If you come over [to the house], they out on their porch like, 'Can I help you?' They have their eyes on the street." Sherrena's new pride and joy had cost her $16,900. She paid cash for it. She had purchased properties for less—$8,000, $5,000—but none were as stunning as this one. A few days before Ladona was scheduled to move in, Sherrena stopped by the house to check on the repairs. She walked through its rooms and smiled in disbelief. When the feeling welled up, she did a little dance.

Since the foreclosure crisis, Sherrena had been buying properties throughout the North Side at a rate of about one a month.[10] In some cities, as many as 1 in 2 foreclosures was renter-occupied. The crisis had provided landlords an almost magical opportunity. "This moment right now," Sherrena reflected, "it's going to create a lot of millionaires. You know, if you have money right now, you can profit from other people's failures. . . . I'm catching the properties. I'm *catching* 'em."

"If you have money right now"—that was the rub. The mortgage sector had shriveled up during the financial downturn: in 2007 alone, the number of loan organizations fell by 25 percent.[11] Fearing insolvency, banks still in operation turned into miserly lenders, instituting stricter lending standards, requiring pristine credit, and demanding large down payments. "If you want a loan this year," the *Washington Post* reported, "you're going to have to pay more—thousands of dollars more in some cases."[12] Landlords, naturally, were more succinct. "Banks went from stupid to stupid," their assessment went, meaning that banks had spun an about-face, going from being reckless to overly cautious. That was too bad for real estate investors not flush with cash because there were deals to be had: gorgeous, unprecedented deals. Rents had soared during the run-up to the crisis, in large part because the housing boom and aggressive property flipping left landlords with bloated mortgage payments and higher tax bills. After the crash, property values fell (and with them mortgage and tax bills)—but rents remained high. In January 2009, the Free Foreclosure List distributed to Milwaukee real estate investors displayed around 1,400 properties, each listing for "$30,000 or more below assessed value." The properties were ordered from least to most expensive, beginning with a two-bedroom unit listed at $2,750. Ten properties down, there was a three-bedroom going for $8,900. Ten more down: a four-bedroom for $11,900.[13]

If Sherrena couldn't buy a property outright, she financed the purchase in a number of ways. She took out conventional or even adjustable-rate mortgages. When she saw a deal but didn't have the down payment, Sherrena sought out "OPM" ("other people's money") or "hard money": shorthand for rich white guys from Brookfield or Shorewood who offered high-interest loans that didn't require any money down but instead placed a lien on the property. Sherrena put it this way: "Usually the banks say, 'We want twenty percent down.' Here's this private money guy saying, 'Hey, I'll give it to you, but your interest rate is going to be twelve percent, and you have to give me this money back within six months or a year.'" If Sherrena defaulted, she would lose the house to the private lender.

The same thing that made homeownership a bad investment in poor, black neighborhoods—depressed property values—made landlording there a potentially lucrative one. Property values for similar homes were double or triple in white, middle-class sections of the city; but rents in those neighborhoods were not. A landlord might have been able to fetch $750 for a two-bedroom unit in the suburb of Wauwatosa and only $550 for a similar unit in Milwaukee's poverty-stricken

53206 zip code. But the Wauwatosa property would have come with a much higher mortgage payment and tax bill, not to mention higher standards for the condition of the unit. When it came to return on investment, it was hard to beat owning property in the inner city. "You buy on the North Side because they 'cash flow' nicely," said one landlord with 114 central-city units. "In Brookfield, I lost money. But if you do low-income, you get a steady monthly income. You don't buy properties for their appreciative value. You're not in it for the future but for now."

Sherrena looked for properties that would give her a cash flow of at least $500 a month, after expenses. The house Ladona would rent easily cleared that bar. Sherrena owned it free and clear, the repairs only set her back $1,500, and the monthly rent would be $775. If the house inspired Sherrena to dance, it was because she knew she would recoup her total investment in about two years. She was used to this rate of return. Shortly after buying the black-and-white house, she bought a duplex off Keefe Avenue for $8,500, repairing it for $3,000. It would take only eight months to make that money back. After that, "it just cashed out."

Sherrena estimated her net worth at around $2 million, but equity was icing on the cake. The real money was made in rents. Every month Sherrena collected roughly $20,000 in rent. Her monthly mortgage bills rounded out to $8,500. After paying the water bill, Sherrena—who owned three dozen inner-city units, all filled with tenants around or below the poverty line—figured she netted roughly $10,000 a month, more than what Arleen, Lamar, and many of her other tenants took home in a year. As Sherrena liked to put it: "The 'hood is good. There's a lot of money there."

QUENTIN PULLED THE truck onto a dark and deserted street. There was one more stop to make: Terri on Cherry Street. This was Sherrena's most far-flung property, located on the West Side of Milwaukee, near Washington Park and a fifteen-minute walk to the colossal Miller Brewery. Sherrena pounded on Terri's door, loud the first time and even louder the second. The porch light flicked on and shone down on Sherrena. She was in the fur-lined Coach boots with matching purse she had bought in Jamaica.

"Who's that?" a gruff voice barked.

"It's the landlord."

"Oh," the voice said, resigned.

"That's right," Sherrena whispered to herself as the locks came undone.

Inside, the house was warm and smelled of dinner fried in grease. A single, small lamp was on, stingy with its light and leaving parts of the room veiled in shadow. Sherrena found Terri in the company of some elderly kin and older children. Terri was a plump and pretty woman, with dark skin, long braids, and an empty stare. She was mentally slow and received SSI for her condition. Her boyfriend, who had answered the door—Antoine, a bony man with slicked-back hair—leaned against the wall, just beyond the edge of the light.

"Um, what's going on?" Sherrena asked Terri.

"I ain't got any money with me and—" Terri's voice trailed off.

Sherrena leaned over Terri with her hands on her hips. "Terri," she began, using her stern-teacher voice.

"I know."

"Just give me the money. . . . I'll give you a receipt."

A moment passed, then Terri said, "All right," and reached into her pocket. Seeing this, several of the older children left the room.

Sherrena accepted a thick roll of cash. "Who did your hair?" she asked, reaching out and spinning one of Terri's braids. "You like her hair, Antoine?"

Antoine was bringing a cigarette to his mouth. The lighter's flame momentarily brought his face out of the darkness. It was a face creased with humiliation.

Lifting herself into the Suburban, Sherrena said to Quentin, "We got fourteen—fourteen hundred. . . . Why I can't get rid of her." Terri rented a four-bedroom apartment for $725 a month. She still owed $350 plus a late fee but said she'd have the rest of the money tomorrow.

"Well, all right!" Quentin congratulated his wife.

Sherrena felt accomplished if unsurprised. On multiple occasions she had taken a tenant's entire paycheck. Once, a young mother had offered Sherrena her debit card.

ON EIGHTEENTH AND Wright, Mikey was trying to do his homework at the kitchen table. Math. He wasn't confused, just distracted. There was so much noise. Ruby, who could fly through her homework before the bus pulled up to their stop, was practicing the Stanky Legg in front of the television. Patrice's middle child, Jada, was banging on different things with an empty Mountain Dew bottle. And Natasha was trying to comb Kayla Mae's hair, typically a three-hour war.

Natasha's belly was growing. The ultrasound had revealed only one baby, a bigheaded boy, just as Doreen had guessed.

Doreen and Patrice sat around the table, opposite from Mikey, and debated what to do about Sherrena's eviction notice. Doreen had had no luck finding another apartment. When she called one number listed in the *RedBook*, she heard a recorded message that listed prequalifications: "No evictions in the last three years. No money owing to a landlord. No criminal arrests in the last three years." Even though Doreen had withheld her rent after the incident with the plumber, they didn't expect Sherrena to start the court process so quickly. Patrice thought it was Social Worker Tabatha's fault. When Doreen told Patrice the reason Sherrena had given for the plumbing being neglected— Quentin had lent someone his truck for a month—Patrice rolled her eyes. "You're in Jamaica," she said, "and we can't even take baths. . . . All that money they got, she sound dumb. If I believe that, then slap me dead." Her hand fell hard on the kitchen table, and Mikey's head snapped up from his math problems.

Mikey took his papers to Jada and Kayla Mae's mattress. Before he got back to work, he pulled out a small American flag from its special hiding spot. His teacher had handed the flags out the day Obama was inaugurated. Before that, the North Side had been covered in political posters, those dark-blue signs planted firmly in lawns, taped to cracked windows, tacked up in people's bedrooms, and lining littered sidewalks. Wright Street had erupted in cheers the night Obama won. Neighbors had unbolted their doors and stepped out on their porches just to look at one another. Mikey stretched out on the mattress, holding the flag at attention and staring at the ceiling.

On the day of her eviction court hearing, January 27, Doreen limped out of her house and found the bus stop. She had wrapped her head and put on white Velcro sneakers. The shoes felt like they belonged to someone else. Doreen went barefoot when she was inside, which was almost always. She had become as much of a permanent fixture in the apartment as the floorboards and doorframes. She hated the idea of taking a bus downtown to eviction court. Plus her foot was throbbing. The night before, the back door had fallen on it. It first fell on Ruby when she had attempted to prop it back up, pinning her to the ground. When Doreen tried to free her daughter, she slipped and the heavy door came down on her foot. It had swollen up plump and watery. The doctor on the phone had advised going to the ER; but Doreen refused. "I'm just gonna end up waiting all night in that room," she said. Doreen didn't trust doctors any more than her father had.[14]

Doreen watched the icy city roll past her bus window. She didn't know how eviction court would go, so she allowed the new baby to occupy her mind. The thought of Natasha as a mother—fickle, youthful Natasha—made Doreen laugh. Doreen remembered when Patrice was born. They delivered her through a cesarean section because she was so big. Doreen had had to trade her baby clothes for bigger sizes. Natasha was big and C.J. too. So when Ruby came out weighing only six pounds, Doreen didn't know how to handle her. "She made me mad. I couldn't hold her." Natasha had recently applied for W-2, and Doreen worried that it would affect her benefits and cut into the family's food stamps. It would balance out if Natasha stayed in the house and helped pay the bills, but lately Malik had been asking Natasha if she wanted to move into his mother's place in Brown Deer. Natasha swore there was no way she would, but Doreen sensed that she was seriously considering it.

Sherrena left later, answering her phone as she drove downtown. A woman on the other end was saying that, during her break, she had walked out of her ten-dollar-an-hour temp job at Landmark Credit Union. "Chelsea!" Sherrena yelled, her voice thick with disappointment. "I don't think that was a good idea. . . . I'm gonna talk with you about it when I come out of eviction court, but you know I'm gonna fuss at you, right?"

"I know," Chelsea said.

"I'm on you. I'm *killing* you, Chelsea!"

Sherrena was trying to help Chelsea "get her credit together." For $150, Sherrena offered to examine her credit report and use a technique called "rapid rescore" to improve her score. Clients like Chelsea got their money's worth. Sherrena was a hard coach who worked for real results. She knew the value of a good credit score, especially when it came to selling her properties to her clients.

Sherrena had been dabbling in rent-to-own ventures. She would rent one of her more stable tenants a house for six months. During that time, Sherrena would attempt to rapid rescore the tenant's credit. If successful, she would then help that tenant secure a loan for the price Sherrena was asking for the property. The Federal Housing Administration often required only a 3.5 percent down payment, which most working tenants could cover with their tax refund. Sherrena had seen some of her properties double in value during the housing bubble, and she knew the inflated assessments wouldn't last forever. She was trying to sell a rent-to-own tenant one property for $90,000, a property she owned free and clear, having purchased it at a far lower price. Sherrena would reinvest the cash in more properties, and the new homeowner would inherit a massive debt. Sherrena would say that was better than not owning a house at all.

In years past, Sherrena had marketed her credit-repair-to-home-loan services to physically and mentally disabled people on SSI. "A whole bunch of those people came and bought houses. They ended up losing them, but the thing is they need to be policed a little bit more. . . . Wasn't nobody saying, 'Johnny, pay your mortgage!' They just may not have been mentally capable." They say the foreclosure crisis started on Wall Street, with men in power ties trading toxic assets and engineering credit default swaps. But in the ghetto, all you needed was a rapid rescore coach and a low-income tenant hungry for a shot at the American Dream.

When Doreen and Sherrena met in the courthouse, Sherrena was not in the best of moods. The conversation with Chelsea had annoyed her, and on top of that, the day before the city had pulled almost $20,000 in water bills and taxes from her bank account. The deduction was unexpected and left Sherrena with exactly $3.48 in her business account, $108.32 in her personal account, and a couple of uncashed checks in her pocket. Sherrena was not used to being broke, but the first of the month was a few days away.

In the hallway outside Room 400, Doreen explained that she wasn't trying to scam Sherrena by moving out quickly; she was looking for housing to plan for tomorrow. Sherrena was already savvy to the story. Unbeknownst to Doreen, Tabatha had called Sherrena that morning to plead her client's case. If she got the Hinkstons into this mess, she would try to get them out. When it looked like Sherrena would agree to a stipulation, Tabatha flattered her by saying, "You are a gangster when it comes to your money!" It made Sherrena laugh with pride.

Sherrena drew up a stipulation agreement. If Doreen wanted the eviction dismissed, she would have to pay $400 extra next month and an additional $50 the following three months. Doreen signed the papers. Saving for their move would have to wait.

12.

DISPOSABLE TIES

It was the day before Arleen had to be out, and she still hadn't received her welfare check. The family's caseworker at Wraparound had given the boys Christmas gifts. Arleen and their fathers did not. The boys didn't receive anything from their uncles or aunties either, not that they expected to. Arleen's three brothers and one sister had their own kids to worry about. One brother received SSI; another sold drugs and helped landlords repair properties; the other was out of work. Arleen's sister was trying to raise three kids on what she made as a school bus monitor.

Aunt Merva had money. She had held down steady jobs for as long as Arleen could remember and would bring her and her siblings food and gifts when they were children. "We wouldn't never see it," Arleen recalled. Her mother and stepfather got first pickings. But Arleen was not going to call her aunt Merva for something as frivolous as Christmas gifts or even rent. Over the years, she had learned to ask her favorite aunt for help only during true emergencies, and evictions didn't qualify. If Arleen asked too often or for too much, she would "hear about it." Merva might give her a lecture or, worse, stop returning her calls.

Sherrena assumed Arleen had "some sort of family to stay with." But none of Arleen's family members had gone to court with her. None had offered to help her make rent. None had opened their homes to her and her boys. None had offered to help her find another place to live. "They just funny like that," Arleen said. "My family don't help. I don't have no one to help me. I search around until I find somebody [who will]."

When Arleen answered the door, she found Sherrena standing on her porch with a woman in a tan winter coat. Sherrena, who had a habit of showing apartments before tenants had moved out, asked to come in.[1] She walked the prospective tenant through the apartment, stepping over Arleen's things. When the tour was over, Sherrena explained that Arleen had been evicted and would be gone by the next day.

The young woman asked where Arleen would go, and Arleen said she didn't know. The young woman took another look around, eyeing the tops of the walls as if judging the soundness of the foundation. She told Sherrena she'd take it. Then she looked at Arleen and told her that she and her boys could stay until they found a place. Arleen looked at Sherrena, who had raised her eyebrows at the woman. Sherrena said it was fine with her.

A hand had been extended, and Arleen needed to act quickly before anyone changed their mind. Arleen looked at the woman. She was well dressed in a full-length skirt and silk headwrap. Her face was warm, with saddle-brown skin that hued darker around her cheekbones. She spoke tenderly and wasn't "nasty," foul smelling, or in tattered clothes. She did look young, and Arleen had overheard her say this would be her first apartment. But Arleen had also gleaned that the woman had come from a Tuesday Bible study. Maybe she wasn't the wild type. Arleen had so many questions, but it was either this option or a shelter. She only had to say "thank you" and the stress that had been consuming her since Christmas would slide off.

"Thank you," Arleen said. She smiled, and the stranger smiled. She hugged the stranger, letting out a small cry. This made the stranger cry. Arleen was so relieved and grateful that she hugged Sherrena. Then she asked the stranger her name.[2]

CRYSTAL MAYBERRY MOVED into Thirteenth Street with only three garbage bags of clothes—no furniture, television, mattress, or microwave. Arleen didn't have much, but she had these things and suspected this was why Crystal had allowed her and the boys to stay. Arleen moved Jori and Jafaris into her bedroom. Crystal stored her things in the other bedroom and used it for privacy, but since she didn't have a bed, she slept on Arleen's love seat in the living room.

Arleen wasn't planning on staying long, so Crystal didn't ask her to split the rent. Instead, when her check arrived Arleen gave Crystal $150 and paid her phone and overdue electricity bill. She had enough left over to buy Jori a new pair of sneakers. That felt amazing.

Crystal was eighteen, younger than Arleen's oldest son. She had been born prematurely on a spring day in 1990 shortly after her pregnant mother was stabbed eleven times in the back during a robbery—the attack had induced labor. Both mother and daughter survived. It was not the first time Crystal's mother had been stabbed. For as far back as she could remember, Crystal's father had beat her mother. He smoked crack and so did her mother and so did her mother's mother.

Crystal was placed in foster care at age five and had bounced between dozens of homes. She lived with her aunt Rhoda for five years. Then Aunt Rhoda returned her. After that, the longest Crystal lived anywhere was eight months. When adolescence arrived, Crystal started getting into fights with other girls in the group homes. She picked up assault charges and a scar across her right cheek. People and their houses, pets, furniture, dishes—these came and went. Food was more stable, and Crystal began taking refuge in it.

When Crystal was sixteen, she stopped going to high school. When she turned seventeen, her caseworker began transitioning her out of the system. By that time, she had passed through more than twenty-five foster placements. Crystal was barred temporarily from low-income housing owing to her assault charge. But her caseworker arranged for her to move into an apartment subsidized by a child welfare agency. To keep the apartment, Crystal had to find a job. But she was not the least bit interested in pulling half-day shifts at Quad Graphics or dropping onion rings at Burger King. She submitted a single application. Plus, having been approved for SSI on account of bipolar disorder, Crystal thought that her $754 monthly check was more reliable than any job she could get. After eight months, the caseworker told Crystal she would have to leave the apartment. Crystal stepped out of foster care and into homelessness.[3] She slept at shelters and on the street. She lived briefly with her grandmother, then a woman from her church, then a cousin.

Arleen and Crystal met under peculiar circumstances, but they were engaging in a popular strategy poor people used to pay the bills and feed their children. Especially in the inner city, strangers brushed up against one another constantly—on the street, at job centers, in the welfare building—and found ways to ask for and offer help. Before she met Arleen, Crystal stayed a month with a woman she had met on a bus.[4]

In the 1960s and 1970s, destitute families often relied on extended kin networks to get by. Poor black families were "immersed in a domestic web of a large number of kin and friends whom they [could] count on," wrote the anthropologist Carol Stack in *All Our Kin*. Those entwined in such a web swapped goods and services on a daily basis. This did little to lift families out of poverty, but it was enough to keep them afloat.[5] But large-scale social transformations—the crack epidemic, the rise of the black middle class, and the prison boom among them—had frayed the family safety net in poor communities. So had state policies like Aid to Families with Dependent Children that sought to limit "kin dependence" by giving mothers who lived alone or with unrelated roommates a larger stipend than those who lived with relatives.[6]

The family was no longer a reliable source of support for poor people. Middle-class kin often did not know how to help or did not want to.[7] And poor kin were often too poor or troubled or addicted to lend much of a hand. Legal entanglements got in the way too. This was why Crystal believed her aunt Rhoda refused to open her door to her after she aged out of foster care. Rhoda had caught a case for her son, his dope found in her apartment, and was serving two years on probation. This meant that law enforcement officers could inspect her apartment. Knowing this, Crystal asked if she could sleep outside on her porch. Rhoda said no.

It was next to impossible for people to survive deep poverty on their own.[8] If you could not rely on your family, you could reach out to strangers, make disposable ties. But it was a lot to ask of someone you barely knew.[9]

A WEEK AFTER Crystal moved in, Arleen sat at the kitchen table, circling apartment listings in the newspaper and *RedBook*, skipping the addresses that included "background checks." Jafaris played with a caulk gun Quentin had left behind. Arleen's plan was to move by the first of the month. "I don't want to live in the inner city ever again," she said. That first meeting with Crystal had felt like a blessing; so Arleen decided to be picky. What she would love was a two-bedroom downtown apartment for under $525.

When Jori walked in the door, Arleen straightened her back. He dragged his backpack into the kitchen with his head bowed, wearing his new shoes. "You already know your teacher called me." Arleen's voice was sharp. Jori tried to explain himself, but Arleen cut him off. "I don't want to hear it, 'cause it's always a problem at every school you go to."

"Nah, 'cause he, he stepped on my shoes. I—I, I turned 'round, like, 'You done stepped on mine.' And teacher gonna say, 'What you say? What you say?' Everybody in that school, they say the teachers get slick with all the kids."

"I ain't trying to hear no excuses."

"Because you believing *nothing*," Jori snapped back. "That teacher already runnin' on people! Even the teacher cuss at the kids."

"All that what you doing, you can stop it," Arleen yelled.

Jori sniffed and tried to stop himself from crying. Arleen told him to start his homework, and he sulked back to their bedroom.

Grabbing the newspaper, Arleen left to look for apartments, leaving her boys with Crystal. She headed to Teutonia Avenue, a main thoroughfare that cuts diagonally through Milwaukee's North Side, and considered the snow. Arleen didn't remember seeing this much snow since she was a child. On Teutonia, she began calling on rent signs. Some landlords didn't answer; others wanted more rent than she could give.

Arleen found herself in the neighborhood where her brother Martin lived. She spotted rent signs but decided to move on. "Martin think he can eat off us any dang minute," she thought. Earlier, Arleen had looked in an area where Ger-Ger's father lived. She avoided that area too. "Those are just *too close* to him."[10]

Arleen was able to call on nine units before she answered her phone and heard Crystal screaming. "You gotta get the fuck out of my house tonight. *Tonight!* Get your shit and go *to-night!*"

Arleen stayed on the phone a few more seconds, then hung up. "This is too ridiculous," she said to herself. Crystal had said something about Jori being disrespectful, but Arleen sensed Crystal really was saying, *I'm hungry.* There was no food in the house, and Crystal had been complaining. Buying food was never part of the bargain, but Crystal was broke and her food stamps cut off.[11] "As long as we have food, she fine," Arleen thought. "But when we don't, it's like this."

Arleen stopped at a nearby corner store and ordered a $99 meat deal, an inner-city staple consisting of forty-five pounds of chicken wings and legs, pork chops, neck bones, salt pork, pig feet, turkey wings, bacon, and other cuts. The man behind the counter speaking in Arabic on the phone threw in two sacks of potatoes for free. Checking out, Arleen added soda and potato chips, paying in food stamps.

(She received $298 in stamps each month.) She paid for a pack of Newport 100s with cash.

When Arleen stepped back into the apartment, Jori immediately tried to explain his side of the story. "She talking about putting Jafaris out with no coat on, no shoes, no nothing!"

"Jafaris went outside on his own," Crystal snapped back. "But Jori like, '*Bitch*, I'm gonna punch you in your shit! *Bitch*, I'm gonna do this. *Bitch*, I'm gonna do that.'"

Arleen listened silently as a mother does when she comes upon fighting children. Jori was saying that he tried to stick up for Jafaris after Crystal threatened to put him outside. Crystal was saying that Jori exploded after she playfully locked them out of the house.

"Okay," Arleen said when she had heard enough. "You ain't gonna do nothing to her," she told Jori. Then she turned to Crystal. "And you're not gonna do anything to my child." When Jori tried to speak, Arleen snapped, "And you can shut your mouth."

"She not telling you the whole story!" Jori pleaded.

"Why would you call her bitches, Jori?" Arleen asked.

"She was callin' me out my name!"[12]

"You know what?" Crystal yelled. "Yeah, I'm a bitch. But remember I'm that *same bitch* that opened up my door and let you stay here even though I didn't know you from Adam and Eve. I was that *same bitch* that let you in! The landlord didn't care. She don't have to care."

"I don't know why you saying all this 'cause I know that," Arleen responded, her voice assertive and clear. She sent Jori out for the groceries.

Crystal waved her phone in the air. "Whatever my mom says I should do, I'm gonna do, because that's too much disrespect. *Too* much!" Crystal was putting Arleen's fate in the hands of her "spiritual mom," an older woman she met at a group home. She dialed the number, pressed the phone to her ear, and kept talking to Arleen. "If he'd just called me one bitch, that would've been fine. I'd have just chopped it off. But to be called a bitch for an hour straight?"

No one picked up. Crystal redialed.

Arleen walked to her room and began venting to the ceiling. "She always complaining there ain't no food. But it ain't my responsibility to feed nobody but my *kids*. Nobody!"

"I didn't ask you to buy *shit* for me," Crystal yelled back. "Because please believe it, *ple-ase*. 'Cause I'm gonna have whatever I need. Whatever. Whether I have to sell some ass, Crystal Sherella Sherrod Mayberry is gonna get whatever she needs! What-ev-er!"

Arleen looked at her boys. "I'm sick of y'all!" she yelled. "If I knew I'd be having to go through this, I would have left. What am I doing? I clean up. I just went and bought food for this house. What am I doing so wrong?"

Crystal dialed again, still no answer. Now it was her turn to talk to the ceiling. She began praying out loud. "God, I need an answer right now. God, please. I need to hear something from my momma, my bishop. God, I *prooooomise* you, I wish you wouldn't have let me learn to love the way I love. . . . I wish I would've been bitter for all the terrible things that happened in my life. *Whoa*, Lord!"

Crystal began singing a hymn. She walked around the apartment, humming and breathing in through her nose. Occasionally, she would pause and close her eyes. She was calming herself down.

Arleen looked at Jori. "You disrespecting, and she tell us, 'You gotta go!' Where is we going?"

"She—" Jori started.

"I said, *where* is we going?"

Jori went quiet and began to cry. Arleen had spent down her check and didn't know where she would take her boys if Crystal tossed them out. She looked at Jafaris, who during the fight had distracted himself by drawing in a notebook: two monsters in hats and shoes; one big, the other small.

"You know what," Crystal finally said. Her eyes were brimming with tears, and she was not yelling but purring in a new voice, hushed and soothing. "Let me say something. *Eww*, God, I wish you'd have never gave me the spirit of love. . . . My feelings are hurt from both of y'all. But, I can't, I can't put y'all out. . . . 'Cause, like I told you, I am filled with the Holy Ghost, and the Holy Ghost telling me not to make y'all leave."

"Filled with the Holy Ghost but does more cussing than a little bit," Arleen mumbled under her breath. To Arleen, it wasn't the Holy Ghost but the meat cuts and potato chips and love seat that had delivered the message. In the heat of the fight, she had made sure to tell Crystal, "I'm not leaving without taking my stuff out of here."

Jori sat on his mattress in the bedroom. He felt dejected, and Arleen knew it. Later on, after things were resolved, Arleen sat down next to Jori and tried to explain herself. "What kind of parent am I to just listen to her and not listen to you?" she said, softly. "But this is what comes when you lose your house. This is what comes."

13.

E-24

When Beaker found out that Larraine had moved into his trailer, he cussed from his hospital bed. Angry but helpless, he fingered the scar from his triple bypass, a nine-inch pink worm that puffed up from the middle of his chest. Larraine was breathing heavily when he got her on the phone. "Beaker," she said, "we're starting out fresh! I'm throwing everything out." She had spent the morning cleaning the kitchen, tossing the left-out black applesauce and fly-covered ribs before deciding that everything had to go, even the cans of food because bugs were crawling on them. Beaker suggested Larraine take the back bedroom, but she refused because it was filthy. She took out her steamer and worked it over the couch. She would sleep on its cushions, next to the mound of things she had rescued from her trailer.

When Beaker came home from the hospital, he planted himself at the kitchen table and dashed his cigarettes into a disposable plastic bowl, the kind you fill with olives at the deli. Beaker's real name was Robert, but everyone called him by his childhood nickname. A brooding and taciturn man, with slicked-back black-and-gray hair, Beaker had retired from driving a city bus a few years back, when his health began to deteriorate.

Beaker asked Larraine to split the rent, but Larraine said she couldn't because she had to make steady payments to Eagle Moving. They fought, and Beaker settled for Larraine covering the cable and phone bills. Then they fought over what to watch on television. Beaker preferred shows like *Ice Road Truckers*; Larraine demanded *So You Think You Can Dance*. Then they fought over Beaker's refusal to share his dinners from Meals on Wheels because he was still miffed that Larraine threw out his canned food. Larraine's food stamps had been cut off—in the turmoil of her eviction she had forgotten about a meeting at the welfare office—so she began asking neighbors for spare plates and visiting church pantries.

During her first visit to Eagle, Larraine gave her name to a black man behind the counter who was wearing a backwards cap and gold crucifix.

"And when I pay, can I go look at my stuff?" Larraine asked.

"No. This is a bonded storage, ma'am. I can't let you back there." Riffling through your things and pulling out, say, winter clothing was not allowed.

"All right."

"You got the in fee, the out fee, and the first month's storage," the man said. "That adds up to three seventy-five. Then each month after that, it goes up another hundred and twenty-five." The man suggested Larraine try to get her things out soon so she wouldn't have to pay on another month. But having just given him what amounted to over half her SSI check, Larraine knew this was impossible. It would take her several months to save for a new apartment while still paying Beaker and Eagle.

IN THE TRAILER park, Larraine tried to lie low and avoid Lenny and Office Susie. She knew that if they found out where she was staying, they would tell Tobin, who might throw her out, and Beaker along with her.

Lenny and Office Susie were crucial to Tobin—and to his tenants. They could get you evicted just as easily as they could get your toilet working again. Susie pushed for Pam and Scott to be kicked out, but she would also run down the Cadillac and yell at Tobin if she thought he was overcharging someone or moving too slow fixing a porch railing. Most important, Lenny and Susie were cultural brokers, bridging the gap between Tobin and his tenants and smoothing things over when he crossed the line: like the time he approached a tenant's kids, telling them their father owed rent. On numerous occasions, Lenny literally placed himself between Tobin and an enraged tenant. This was a common practice—outsider landlords hiring people from the community, usually their tenants, to manage property.[1]

The kids Tobin had approached about the rent belonged to Donny, a portly and unshaven man in his mid-thirties who was liked by almost everyone in the trailer park. Donny was already refusing to pay Tobin, not because he didn't have the money, but because he felt disrespected. He put his rent in escrow, citing his leaking roof and the black mold under the sink. Said Donny to his neighbor, Robbie, "You know what he tells me? 'You rented it as-is.' Tobin is just too ignorant to know that there are people in here that don't live off Social Security."

"Damn right!" Robbie spat. "He asked me if I had a job. I said, 'Motherfucker, I work for the union!'" Robbie was a deep-tunnel miner and a member of Local 113. "You gonna treat me like shit, I sure as hell ain't going to pay you. I don't care who you are. You're not gonna sit there and discriminate me. You know what I mean?"

"'Cause I'm a redneck."

"'Cause you live in a trailer court, period. You're still a fuckin' human."

Lenny was a redneck too, and understood where the men were coming from. He agreed that the old man was "losing it." But he also pushed back. "A lot of people say, 'Tobin, he's an asshole.' But why is he the asshole? You're the one who owes him." What Donny, Robbie, and the rest of the trailer park didn't know was that Lenny had a financial stake in them paying. Each month, he received a $100 bonus if he collected $50,000. He'd receive an additional $100 for every $2,000 collected after that.

SOME DAYS WOULD find Lenny walking alongside Roger from the Department of Neighborhood Services, finishing his sentences. Roger the Inspector glanced down at his clipboard, reviewing notes from his last visit. "Let's see, W-45 was—"

"The shed," Lenny cut in. "We got it out of here."

"Ah."

"Hey, Roger," a tenant called out from his porch. "See anything?"

"Do I *see* anything?"

Most park residents knew Roger, had his business card tucked away in a kitchen drawer. When they got fed up with some housing problem, they would not threaten to call DNS but Roger, specifically. A balding white man with a well-trimmed beard, Roger wore a white DNS polo shirt and 33/30 Levi's.

"Any violations?" the tenant clarified, trying to be helpful.

"Well, it's not country living, but if it's habitable inside, it looks good to me."

"So, there aren't any violations?"

Roger shrugged and kept walking. Of course there were. He had noticed the pile of trash behind the tenant's trailer and a plywood slab where a window should have been. There were trailers with several cracked windows, large steel barrels used for nighttime fires, and trash floating in standing puddles and overflowing from the two giant Dumpsters on either end of the park. Tobin had refused to pay for individual trash cans, but the Dumpsters would fill up days before they were emptied, attracting raccoons and possums. One resident had stabbed a possum dead a few nights before Roger's visit. Lenny had shot one once. When the garbage collectors came, residents whose trailers faced the Dumpsters would try to convince the truck driver to move them to another spot. They would point to a trailer, saying, sometimes truthfully, "That one's empty!"

Roger sighed. "Man, you gotta keep me from writing up so much shit."

"Well, don't let that hand go, then," Lenny replied, telling Roger not to record violations.

"Best of intentions, Lenny, best of intentions. Every time I walk through here, there's always something." And that was only from the outside. Roger's inspections usually did not take him inside trailers, where he would have seen sunken bathtubs propped up with car jacks or water heaters disconnected from ventilating pipes.

Roger stopped in front of a trailer. "These windows look like they're shot."

"Well," Lenny replied, "they don't have the money to buy new windows. So what do you want me to do? I don't want to buy 'em for 'em." The trailer was owner-occupied, meaning its residents were responsible for upkeep.

"I don't want you to have to either."

"So are we okay?"

"I'm okay with that."

Back in the office, Roger sighed and lowered his head into his palms.

Tobin hung up the phone. "Okay. What's the matter? What do we got?"

"Look," Roger began, "if you're going to let trailers that look this bad into your trailer park, you have to make it habitable." Roger began listing off some of the bigger problems: garbage, open storage sheds, broken windows.

Lenny cut in. "It's been a tough winter."

"I'm not going to write you up on that," Roger replied, speaking of the cracked windows. He knew cataloguing every code violation was neither feasible nor, he suspected, in the tenants' best interest.

Rufus the junk collector stepped into the office. "Are we safe?" he asked Roger. Although the city had renewed Tobin's license, many tenants still feared removal.

"Yes," Roger answered.

"Good. Now I don't have to move my giant cat house." When Rufus's mother died, she owned seventy-two cats. Rufus was down to three.

NOT LONG AFTER taking over the trailer park, Bieck Management fired Lenny and Susie. After reading his termination letter, Lenny began removing his things from the office in which he had worked for the past twelve years. He gathered his tools and unscrewed his deer antlers from the wall.

The door swung open and a man with sunglasses asked, "Can I get an extension?"

Lenny paused. "I don't know," he finally said. "I'm outta here."

What in the past had become routine was now far from certain. A worried look worked over the man's face. He left and told the first person he saw. As news spread, a tremor of fear whipped through the park. Would the new management company honor the deals struck over a handshake? Would rents go up? Would evictions? Some tenants hated Lenny and Office Susie, but at least they were known. "Ain't gonna get no leeway with this setup," Dawn said. "People that were working at the office worked with people because we're just making poverty over here." When the news reached Dawn's neighbor, Tam, a seven-months-pregnant drug addict, she walked into the office and gave Lenny a long hug.

On their last day, Office Susie erased her greeting from the voice-mail system, and Lenny laid his heavy ring of keys on the desk.

Bieck Management replaced Lenny with a recent graduate of the

University of Wisconsin at Eau Claire. At twenty-three, young enough to be Lenny's son, the replacement was clueless and patronizing, but he stuck it out. The new maintenance man quit after a week, saying, "I mean, ninety-nine percent of the houses in here are just too far gone. . . . I've been working on mobile houses for seven years, and I've never worked in a park like this."

With Lenny and Susie gone, Tobin had to take care of some matters himself. It didn't bother him; he had always been a hands-on landlord. In his twelve years at College Mobile Home Park, Tobin had learned to pull profit out of 131 dilapidated trailers. Most impressive was his ability to transform an utterly trashed trailer into a rent-generating machine in a matter of days—and for next to nothing.

After evicting a tenant named Theo and his girlfriend from E-24, Tobin needed to have the trailer cleaned out. Theo was known in the park as a "never sweat," a lazy slob who didn't work. His trailer was a disaster.

Tobin hired Mrs. Mytes to clean it out. Unlike some of the other older residents who seemed to be waiting to die, swallowing prescription pills and nodding off in front of the television, Mrs. Mytes still had plenty of fight left. She and her adult daughter, Meredith, would get into foulmouthed shouting matches first thing in the morning. While driving to or from their jobs, trailer park residents would sometimes spot Mrs. Mytes several miles away from home, pushing a shopping cart brimming over with aluminum cans. She was strong and knew how to work.

Mrs. Mytes was grateful for the extra money, even if it was E-24. She could smell the trailer standing ten feet away. Inside, the mess was pathological. There were ashtrays and cigarettes on the floor; the sink was piled high with food-encrusted dishes; black grime had overtaken the toilet; trash was everywhere; several spots in the carpet were damp with cat piss; and honey-colored strips of fly tape dangled from the ceiling. Theo and his girlfriend had moved in a hurry, leaving behind piles of stuff: a pair of roller skates, a motorcycle helmet, a couch, a full toolbox, a toy helicopter, a driver's license. Mrs. Mytes began hauling everything to the Dumpster. After a few loads, she asked Office Susie for a pair of rubber gloves.

Rufus the junk collector appeared at the door. "Whoa," he said, looking around. "I hate to say it, but even niggers are cleaner than this."

Mrs. Mytes let out a loud "Ha!" and kept working.

Rufus was there for the metal. He had been a full-time junk collector since 1984 and was proud that his life "didn't revolve around a mailbox" as it did for his neighbors who waited each month for their SSI checks. Tobin had asked Rufus to pull out the microwave, refrigerator, dryer, and any other larger items. He was yanking on the dishwasher when Tobin walked in. Wearing pressed khaki pants and a polo shirt, Tobin narrowed his eyes. He was unfazed, having seen this kind of mess before. "Okay, Rufus," Tobin said. "Let's get this shit out of here and see where we stand."

It took Rufus two hours to load everything into the bed of his old blue Chevy. Tobin didn't pay him anything, but he collected almost $60 from the scrap yard. It took Mrs. Mytes five straight hours. Tobin paid her $20.

Once the trailer was cleared out, Tobin placed an advertisement in the paper. Soon, couples were coming to look, and Tobin offered them the Handyman Special. He apologized for the condition of the trailer—it still smelled of cat urine and smoke, some windows were broken, and the black grime on the toilet was still there—but as consolation he threw in a couple months' free rent. A few weeks after Theo left, Tobin had a new pair of tenants in E-24. The couple began to use the money they were saving on rent to fix up their new home. Two months later, they began paying Tobin $500 a month in lot rent.

Office Susie thought Tobin had shortchanged Mrs. Mytes, but she didn't say anything. She called Tobin's other workers, who cut the grass or picked up trash for beer money, "regular trailer park tramps." Tobin fired the tramps after Alderman Witkowski stipulated he hire outside maintenance help, but some kept on working out of boredom or the hope that Tobin would still pay them something. Troy, a bony, out-of-work motorcycle mechanic, was one of them. He had even helped mop up the sewage spill that had made the news. For that, he got nothing but an earful from his common-law wife, Samantha.

"What are we supposed to do!" Samantha had yelled in her uniform from George Webb, a Wisconsin-based chain restaurant that served breakfast all day long. They were behind in rent and were hoping that Tobin would credit them something for Troy's eight hours of puke work, even if Tobin had not hired him for the job. "You cleaned up shit! Human shit!"

"I'll tell you," Troy said. "I've cleaned up horse shit, when I was shoveling stables. I've cleaned up chicken shit. But I ain't never had to clean up human shit. It was terrible."

"I know, 'cause you smelled *bad*!" Samantha took a breath. "I'm a bitch," she continued. "I'm a bitch. And, Troy, you don't got no *bitch* in you."

Troy dropped his head in quiet agreement, taking a sip of a milk shake that Samantha had brought home from work. "Tobin wants to whine and cry all the time," he said. "The guy's filthy rich, and he still wants money. He makes more than a million dollars on this park." He gestured toward the line of trailers. "Add it up."

Alderman Witkowski had quoted a similar number, estimating that Tobin's trailer park netted more than $900,000 a year. Both Troy and Witkowski arrived at that figure by multiplying Tobin's 131 trailers by the average monthly rent ($550). It was a sloppy calculation that assumed Tobin didn't have any expenses or vacancies—and that his tenants always paid their rent in full.

Tobin didn't have a mortgage: he had bought the trailer park for $2.1 million in 1995 and paid it off nine years later.[2] But he did have to pay property taxes, water bills, regular maintenance costs, Lenny's and Office Susie's annual salaries and rent reductions, advertising fees, and eviction costs. After accounting for these expenses, vacancies, and missing payments, Tobin took home roughly $447,000 each year, half of what the alderman had reported.[3] Still, Tobin belonged to the top 1 percent of income earners. Most of his tenants belonged to the bottom 10 percent.

Troy finished the milk shake. "Did that hit the spot, baby?" Samantha asked, rubbing his shoulder.

14.

HIGH TOLERANCE

Scott had no intention of fighting his eviction. He skipped his court date and never talked to Tobin about it. Instead, he focused his efforts on finding another place to live. After several calls, Pito from Narcotics Anonymous came through. Pito worked with landlords, repairing and filling their properties, and vouched for Scott to one he knew. The two-bedroom upper was on the near South Side. It was small and bare with a treacherous balcony and no shower. But the landlord was only asking $420 a month and didn't bother with a background check.

The apartment also came with Pito's nephew, who went by D.P. A baby-faced nineteen-year-old with several tattoos and earrings, D.P. had recently been released from prison, where he was serving time for weapons possession and tampering with a firearm. He had sawed off the barrel of a shotgun. D.P. ran with the Cobras and wanted a gun in case things heated up with the Kings. In prison, he got his GED and another tattoo that read BEGINNING.

One day, Pito learned from another landlord that an old man had died in a nearby trailer park and no one had come to claim his things. So he arranged for Scott and D.P. to clean out the trailer in exchange for them keeping whatever they wanted. In the dead man's closet, Scott had found a pressed suit in a zipped garment bag and a silk-lined suitcase. In the bathroom, he had learned the man's name from mailing stickers on *American Legion* magazines. But Scott found the cigarette burns next to the bed most revealing. They led him to speculate that the man was on morphine. In Scott's mind, drugs explained a lot about the world: why this man had died alone, why Pam and Ned got tossed from the trailer park, and why he was in a stranger's home, collecting shabby furniture for his apartment.

The new roommates loaded a dresser and sofa onto the oily bed of a Ford F-150. When the truck was full, D.P. started the engine and turned on loud rap music. Scott would have preferred something else—his favorite song was "Solsbury Hill" by Peter Gabriel—but he didn't say anything.

Scott was still on Mira's crew, but work had slowed. Mira had run through her jobs too quickly by working her men twelve hours a day, lugging washers and dryers, mattresses, sleeper sofas. When workers said they were exhausted or sore, Mira sold them painkillers. But Scott thought she charged too much. When he needed relief, he would ask Heroin Susie to meet him somewhere.

"I want to do what Pito's doing," D.P. said. "I want to come home clean and leave the house clean. I can't see myself at thirty doing this bullshit."

Scott couldn't either, years ago, when he was D.P.'s age.

After unloading the furniture, D.P. and Scott shared a beer on their front steps. The apartment was on Ward Street, on the west side of Kinnickinnic Avenue, which the locals shortened to "KK." It faced an undeveloped plot of land surrounding railroad tracks and was not far from an apartment Scott used to rent years ago, when he was still a nurse and living in Bay View, a thriving neighborhood that attracted young professionals, artists, and hipsters. From their stoop, Scott and

D.P. could see the crowning dome of the Basilica of St. Josaphat. One hundred years ago, Polish parishioners had emptied their savings accounts to fund the massive building project, "a scaled-down version of St. Peter's in Rome."[1] As Scott drank his beer, he joked about "taking his own vow of poverty. . . . All I'm going to do is buy some food and clothes and some drugs now and again."

D.P. said nothing.

"Damn," Scott said after the moment had passed. "My neck and back are killing me." His shifts with Mira were beginning to take a toll.

"Why don't you go to the doctor?" D.P. asked.

"Because I don't think there's anything they can do." Scott paused. "They could give me Percocet! Too bad I'd eat them all in one day."

SCOTT STILL BOUGHT his Vicodin at the trailer park. He thought Mrs. Mytes was the only adult there who didn't do drugs or have a history with them. Scott loved drugs. Being high was a "mini vacation" from his shame of a life. He took the trip whenever he could afford it.

Scott had gotten high with Pam and Ned shortly before they received their eviction notice and had moved in a hurry, leaving behind a couch, beds, dressers, and other large items. Scott figured Ned and Pam got what was coming to them. In his old life, before the fall, he might have been more sympathetic. But he had come to view sympathy as a kind of naïveté, a sentiment voiced from a certain distance by the callow middle classes. "They can be compassionate because it's not their only option," he said of liberals who didn't live in trailer parks. As for Ned and Pam, Scott thought their eviction came down to their crack habit, plain and simple. Heroin Susie agreed with him. "There's a common denominator for all evictions," she said. "I almost got evicted once. Used the money for other things."

Trailer park residents rarely raised a fuss about a neighbor's eviction, whether that person was a known drug addict or not. Evictions were deserved, understood to be the outcome of individual failure.

They "helped get rid of the riffraff," some said. No one thought the poor more undeserving than the poor themselves.[2]

In years past, renters opposed landlords and saw themselves as a "class" with shared interests and a unified purpose. During the early twentieth century, tenants organized against evictions and unsanitary conditions. When landlords raised rents too often or too steeply, tenants went so far as to stage rent strikes. Strikers joined together to withhold rent and form picket lines, risking eviction, arrest, and beatings by hired thugs. They were not an especially radical bunch, these strikers. Most were ordinary mothers and fathers who believed landlords were entitled to modest rent increases and fair profits, but not "price gouging." In New York City, the great rent wars of the Roaring Twenties forced a state legislature to impose rent controls that remain the country's strongest to this day.[3]

Petitions, picket lines, civil disobedience—this kind of political mobilization required a certain shift in vision. "For a protest movement to arise out of [the] traumas of daily life," the sociologists Frances Fox Piven and Richard Cloward have observed, "the social arrangements that are ordinarily perceived as just and immutable must come to seem both unjust and mutable."[4] This usually happened during extraordinary times, when large-scale social transformations or economic disturbances—the postwar housing shortage, say—profoundly upset the status quo. But it was not enough simply to perceive injustice. Mass resistance was possible only when people believed they had the collective capacity to change things. For poor people, this required identifying with the oppressed, and counting yourself among them— which was something most trailer park residents were absolutely unwilling to do.

During rent strikes, tenants believed they had a moral obligation to one another.[5] If tenants resisted excessive rent hikes or unwarranted evictions, it was because they invested in their homes and neighborhoods. They felt they belonged there. In the trailer park, that sentiment was almost dead. For most residents, Scott among them, the goal was to leave, not to plant roots and change things. Some residents described themselves as "just passing through," even if they had been passing through nearly all their life. One, an out-of-work father of three who powered his trailer with stolen electricity, said, "We don't let family come here. It's not us. It's lower-class living, and I didn't come from this." Lenny's ex-wife, who being Lenny's ex-wife was virtually married to the trailer park at one time, liked to tell people, "You forget that I'm the one that used to go to the opera." Tam, the pregnant drug addict, thought of the trailer park "as a hotel."

Poor neighborhoods provided their residents with quite a lot. In the trailer park, residents met people who knew how to pirate cable, when the best food pantries were open, and how to apply for SSI. All over the city, people who lived in distressed neighborhoods were more likely to help their neighbors pay bills, buy groceries, fix their car, or lend a hand in other ways, compared to their peers in better-off areas.[6] These exchanges helped people on the receiving end meet basic material needs; and they helped those on the delivering end feel more fully human.

But for such vital exchanges to take place, residents had to make their needs known and acknowledge their failures. For Larraine to ask her neighbor if she could use her shower, she needed to explain that her gas had been shut off. That fact became public when she walked back to her trailer with wet hair. On another occasion, a tenant named Rose had her children taken by Child Protective Services. Trailer park residents sat beside her as she wailed. They comforted her and made sure she didn't hurt herself, but because they saw what had happened, they also judged her. "It ain't nothing to be proud of," Dawn told her. "But the Lord took 'em for some reason."[7]

When people began to view their neighborhood as brimming with deprivation and vice, full of "all sorts of shipwrecked humanity," they lost confidence in its political capacity.[8] Milwaukee renters who perceived higher levels of neighborhood trauma—believing that their neighbors had experienced incarceration, abuse, addiction, and other harrowing events—were far less likely to believe that people in their community could come together to improve their lives.[9] This lack of faith had less to do with their neighborhood's actual poverty and crime rates than with the level of concentrated suffering they perceived around them. A community that saw so clearly its own pain had a difficult time also sensing its potential.

Every so often, Tobin's tenants would air a passing remark about their landlord's profits or call him a greedy Jew. *"That Cadillac got some shiny rims. I know that didn't cost no ten dollars." "He just wants to butter his pockets."* But for the most part, tenants had a high tolerance for inequality. They spent little time questioning the wide gulf separating their poverty from Tobin's wealth or asking why rent for a worn-out aluminum-wrapped trailer took such a large chunk of their income. Their focus was on smaller, more tangible problems. When Witkowski reported Tobin's annual income to be close to $1 million, a man who lived on the same side of the park as Scott said, "I'd give two shits. . . . As long as he keeps things the way he's supposed to here, and I don't have to worry about the freaking ceiling caving in, I don't care."

Most renters in Milwaukee thought highly of their landlord.[10] Who had time to protest inequality when you were trying to get the rotten spot in your floorboard patched before your daughter put her foot through it again? Who cared what the landlord was making as long as he was willing to work with you until you got back on your feet? There was always something worse than the trailer park, always room to drop lower. Residents were reminded of this when the whole park was threatened with eviction, and they felt it again when men from Bieck Management began collecting rents.[11]

IT HAD BEEN a bad week. First Scott lost his keys and decided to break into his apartment by putting a fist through the front window. Then his electricity went out. Then Mira fired him. Nothing personal: she had found a crew of hypes willing to work for $25 a day. In NA, Scott had learned that addiction tightened its grip when you were hungry, angry, lonely, or tired—"HALT"—and Scott was all four.

After Mira fired him, he used part of his last paycheck to get drunk and high at a friend's house. That's when he called his mom, a hospital housekeeper in rural Iowa. On the phone, Scott told his mother about his drinking (but not the heroin) and about losing his nursing license after getting hooked on painkillers. She knew none of it. Scott hadn't spoken to his mother in over a year.

"Mom," Scott was crying. "I'm sorry. I'm a mess. I'm a fucking mess."

Before Scott could finish, his mother cut him off, failing to realize that it took everything he had in him (and a twelve-pack) to dial all ten numbers and not hang up when he got to the seventh or ninth, like he usually did. She explained that she was in a van full of relatives and unable to talk at the moment. They were all going to Branson, Missouri, for the weekend. "But, Scott," she said, "you know that you can always come home."

Scott thought about her offer. How could he get to Iowa with no car and no money for a train ticket? And how could he find heroin there? After a day, the sick would start working its way through his body. Then there was the part about being an object of pity. Scott thought about this as he walked through Pick 'n Save the day after the call. He had offered to buy Heroin Susie lunch with his food stamps if she'd give him a hit. "I mean, I could go back home, but, damn, I'm forty fucking years old . . . I'd have to go back and tell them, you know, that I fucked my whole fucking life up." Scott had never reached out to his family for help. He considered their lawns and jobs and children and normal problems and concluded, "They wouldn't know what to do. . . . How much help could they possibly be?" Middle-class relatives could be useless that way.

Scott joined the checkout line and noticed the man in front of him was buying Robitussin.

"You got a cold?" Scott asked.

"Yeah," the man said. "Can't seem to shake it." He coughed as if to prove his point.

"Here," Scott said. He took out a pen and scrap of paper and wrote, "*Vitamin C, Zinc, and Echinacea.*" "That's what I would recommend," he said.

Scott didn't go back to Iowa. Instead, he decided to go to rehab. On the morning he planned to check himself in, Scott woke up while it was still dark, trimmed his beard, and tucked in his T-shirt. He wanted to climb back out. He felt nervous but ready.

When Scott stepped out of the elevator at seven a.m., an hour before the clinic's doors opened, he saw that he was late. Fifteen people were already in line. There were older black men who had dressed up for the occasion; a foulmouthed white woman, fifty perhaps, in cowboy boots; a pair of young Mexican men sitting on their feet and whispering in Spanish; a twenty-something black man whose pants were falling down; a brooding, white teenager who had pulled her bangs over her eyes and her sleeves over her hands. Scott slumped against the wall at the end of the line.

After a few minutes, the elevator opened again and an older Mexican woman stepped out. Her hair was long and black except for a streak of gray down the middle. She wore a walking cast and looked over her large glasses with eyes the color of floodwater. She resigned herself to a spot on the floor next to Scott.

The woman told Scott she had been there the day before, but they only took four people. When social workers began appearing at desks behind the glass, she observed, "They are calling the county to see how many spots are available."

"For what?" Scott asked sardonically.

"For *you*. You're here to get treatment, right?"

Scott looked up at the ceiling's fluorescent lights and inhaled slowly, purposefully. He was trying to endure. "Yes."

"Look at that girl," the woman motioned to the white teenager. "She looks suicidal. I'll bet they take her in. You have to camp out to get a spot."

Scott began to tap his foot.

At 8:10 a.m., a woman wearing gold earrings and a silk blouse opened the door and announced that they could take five people today. A man emerged with a clipboard. "Number 1. Number 2," he began counting. The line stood and tightened. Scott stepped toward the elevator and pushed the Down button. He could have tried again the next day, but he went on a three-day bender instead.

15.

A NUISANCE

The day after Crystal and Arleen's argument, Trisha came down-stairs from her apartment after Chris had gone to work with Quentin. Trisha liked Crystal. She was much more youthful and silly than Arleen. That morning, the two women passed the time fooling around and playing pattycake. Their palms slapped together as they sang:

Shame, shame, shame.
I don't wanna go to Mexico
No more, more, more.

There's a big fat policeman
At my door, door, door.

He grab me by my collar.
He made me pay a dime.

I don't want to go to Mexico
No more, more, more.

Arleen watched unamused. She was reviewing apartment listings and making notes on a notepad with HOUSE written in block letters at the top. She regretted not going to a shelter after eviction court. But she hated shelters; mostly she hated the other residents. Collecting her papers, Arleen nodded at Crystal and left to find a new place to live.

Arleen was able to call on two dozen places before heading back to Thirteenth Street. She had no leads but was undefeated. "If I keep being persistent, I'll find me a house," she told herself. She also believed that Sherrena had dismissed her eviction. She had not.

When Arleen came back, the apartment was quiet, and Crystal looked troubled. After Chris had gotten home from work and Trisha went back upstairs, Crystal had heard him yelling at her for smoking his cigarettes and drinking his beer. She had heard other noises too.

"The lady upstairs getting beat," Crystal told Arleen.

"Who cares? I don't," Arleen answered. She had painful menstrual cramps and just wanted to lie down. "I kind of figured that was going to happen when he got here." Arleen didn't feel she had enough space in her head or her heart to consider Trisha's problems. Her own problems were enough.[1]

After night fell, more sounds came through the ceiling. There were blunt and muffled thuds, interspersed with loud pounds when Trisha slammed into the floor. Arleen covered her head with a pillow, but Crystal stewed. "I ain't fixing to see no woman getting beat up by no man," she said. She wanted to help Trisha, but she also couldn't help feeling repulsed by her weakness. She pitied Trisha and found her pathetic. "If a man hits you like that and you let him back in, you like it," Crystal mused. At one point, she had had enough. Crystal climbed the steps to the upper unit and yelled through the locked door, "I'm gonna dot your eyes, you scary ho! And I want Chris to hear me too, 'cause I dare him to put his hands on me!"[2] Arleen had to pull Crystal back downstairs.

Crystal called Sherrena, who didn't answer. Then she called 911 three separate times. The police finally showed up and took Chris away. When they left, Arleen looked at Crystal. "You must want to lose your house," she said.

The next day, the police called Sherrena. The officer, a woman, sounded stern, but Sherrena had been through this before. Last year, she had received a letter from the Milwaukee Police Department regarding the same apartment on Thirteenth Street. "Pursuant to Section 80-10 Milwaukee Code of Ordinances (MCO)," the letter began, "I am informing you that the Milwaukee Police Department has responded to nuisance activity at your property . . . on at least three occasions within a thirty-day period." It then listed the nuisance activities, which included a fight and a woman being sliced with a razor blade. The letter went on to inform Sherrena that she would be "subject to a special charge for any future enforcement costs for any of the listed violations" that occurred at her property. The city had itemized all police services, down to $4 per 911 call. Sherrena was to respond in writing with a plan to "abate the nuisance activities" occurring at her property. Should those activities continue, the letter concluded, she could be subject to a fine between $1,000 and $5,000 or thrown in jail.

Sherrena wrote back to the Milwaukee PD, explaining that the 911 calls that had generated the letter were attributed to a domestic-violence situation. "If these problems continue," she wrote, "I will ask her to vacate the premises." When the district captain read Sherrena's reply, he underlined the word "ask" and drew a question mark in the margin. "Not accepted," he scribbled on her reply.

After she was notified that her abatement plan was rejected, Sherrena stapled a copy of an eviction notice to her next letter to the police. The district captain wrote back, "This notice serves to inform you that your written course of action is *accepted*."

Now Thirteenth Street was a nuisance again, with issues upstairs and down. Most of Crystal's 911 calls were on Trisha's behalf, but once she had also called after getting into a roaring argument with Arleen. The police officer on the phone was asking Sherrena to explain why her former and current tenants were living together. Sherrena told the officer how Crystal and Arleen had met. When the officer asked Sherrena why she had allowed such an arrangement, Sherrena replied by saying that she had felt sorry for Arleen. "But neither of them have a pot to piss in," she said. "And they don't have a window to dash it out of."

The officer laughed.

"She did wrong for trying to sublease my place," Sherrena said. "You know, Crystal doesn't quite understand that it's her place, but it's not her place."

The call had embarrassed Sherrena. "I'm steady trying to work with these low-quality people," she said after hanging up. She had been content to "turn a blind eye to Arleen still being there," but now the police were involved. The officer advised Sherrena to toss them both out. Sherrena decided to start with Arleen. She called her and began yelling into the phone. "I'm sick of the bullshit," Sherrena said, "sick of this motherfucking shit. . . . Tired of you throwing your fucking weight around when you're the one who owes. When your kids didn't have nothing to eat who was it that went to the church and got a big box of food, milk and stuff like that for them, when you first got there, who had spent her money and she didn't ask for it back, and you know—hello? Hello?"

THE POLICE HAD called Sherrena on a Saturday. She had told Arleen to be out by Monday. Sunday morning found Arleen sweeping the carpet as Trisha looked on. On the kitchen counter, cornbread was still caked in the pan, the brown edges giving way to the spongy yellow middle. The night before, Arleen had made muffins too, and boiled pinto beans and neck bones. Her brothers had come over to eat, smoke, and throw spades upstairs at Trisha's. They drank but knew not to offer Arleen a cup. She almost never drank alcohol, didn't like the feeling. "Thing I hate about Milwaukee," Arleen said, "is that the rent is so high."

"High!" Trisha agreed, clicking her tongue. "I pay upstairs four hundred and fifty for a one bedroom?"

The house was quiet with Crystal and Jori at church. Jori had gone with his dad. Jafaris sat silently on the floor, coloring. Arleen tried to calculate how much time she had. If Sherrena served the writ the next day "that's still another five days to get my stuff outta here before the sheriff come."

Trisha nodded.

Arleen sat down at the table and looked at Jafaris while talking to Trisha. "We in this house. So I didn't think about moving. I didn't have to think about my kids changing schools. I didn't have to think about none of that. No sense in crying," she said, straightening up. "I might as well wipe my tears and do what I got to do."

She called Sherrena. Arleen started and stopped. Her words caught at the bottom of her throat. But she managed to ask Sherrena if she could stay until Thursday. Sherrena said no, and Arleen protested. "That's Crystal! Ain't no police been called 'sides Chris beating up Trisha. It's been her!"

IN THE LAST decades of the twentieth century, as the justice system was adopting a set of abrasive policies that would swell police forces and fuel the prison boom, it was also leaving more and more policing responsibilities to citizens without a badge and a gun.[3] What about the pawnshop owner who sold the gun? Isn't he partially responsible for the homicide? Or the absentee landlord who failed to screen his tenants? Didn't he play a role in creating the drug house? The police and courts increasingly answered yes.[4] It was in this context that the nuisance property ordinance was born, allowing police departments to penalize landlords for the behavior of their tenants.[5] Most properties were desig-nated "nuisances" because an excessive number of 911 calls were made within a certain timeframe. In Milwaukee, the threshold was three or more calls within a thirty-day period. The ordinances pushed prop-erty owners to "abate the nuisance" or face fines, license revocation, property forfeiture, or even incarceration. Proponents argued that these new laws would save money and conserve valuable resources by enabling police departments to direct manpower to high-priority crimes.

In 2008 and 2009, the Milwaukee PD issued a nuisance property citation to residential property owners every thirty-three hours.[6] The most popular nuisance activity was "Trouble with Subjects," a catchall designation applied to a wide variety of incidents, including people refusing to leave a residence and loud arguments. Noise complaints came second. The third most common nuisance activity was domestic violence. The number of domestic violence incidents—most of which involved physical abuse or a weapon—exceeded the total number of all other kinds of assaults, disorderly conduct charges, and drug-related crimes combined. One incident involved a woman having bleach thrown in her face. In another, a woman was "hit [on the] head with a can of food." Two involved the battering of pregnant women. Box cutters, knives, and guns were used. In one incident, "the caller stated that [her boyfriend] just sprayed her with lighter fluid and also set a piece of paper on fire."

Most nuisance citations were addressed to properties on the North Side. In white neighborhoods, only 1 in 41 properties that could have received a nuisance citation actually did receive one. In black neighborhoods, 1 in 16 eligible properties received a citation. A woman reporting domestic violence was far more likely to land her landlord a nuisance citation if she lived in the inner city.[7]

In the vast majority of cases (83 percent), landlords who received a nuisance citation for domestic violence responded by either evicting the tenants or by threatening to evict them for future police calls. Sometimes, this meant evicting a couple, but most of the time landlords evicted women abused by men who did not live with them.[8]

One landlord wrote to the Milwaukee PD: "This is one girl in one apartment who is having trouble with her boyfriend. She was a good tenant for a long time—until her boyfriend came around. Probably things are not going to change, so enclosed please find a copy of a notice terminating her tenancy served today." Another wrote: "I discussed the report with [my tenant]. . . . Her boyfriend had threatened her with bodily harm and was the reason for the [911] call. We agreed that he would not be allowed in the building, and she would be responsible for any damage to the building property and evicted if he returned to the property." Another wrote: "First, we are evicting Sheila M, the caller for help from police. She has been beaten by her 'man' who kicks in doors and goes to jail for 1 or 2 days. (Catch and release does not work.) We suggested she obtain a gun and kill him in self defense, but evidently she hasn't. Therefore, we are evicting her."

Each of these landlords received the same form letter from the Milwaukee PD: "This notice serves to inform you that your written course of action is *accepted*."[9]

The year the police called Sherrena, Wisconsin saw more than one victim per week murdered by a current or former romantic partner or relative.[10] After the numbers were released, Milwaukee's chief of police appeared on the local news and puzzled over the fact that many victims had never contacted the police for help. A nightly news reporter summed up the chief's views: "He believes that if police were contacted more often, that victims would have the tools to prevent fatal situations from occurring in the future." What the chief failed to realize, or failed to reveal, was that his department's own rules presented battered women with a devil's bargain: keep quiet and face abuse or call the police and face eviction.[11]

CRYSTAL BLEW THROUGH the door along with the cold air, and the house tightened up. Church had taken a lot out of her, and "her stomach was touching her back," as the saying went. She poured herself a bowl of Cap'n Crunch and planted herself on the love seat. She was wearing a black-and-gold silk blouse, a calf-length skirt, and a red headwrap. Crystal was aware of Arleen's situation, having returned

Sherrena's call on her bus ride home. Sherrena had given some ground. Arleen could stay until Thursday if Crystal agreed to move into one of Sherrena's other properties. If Crystal said no, Arleen had to be out the next day.

Her cereal gone, Crystal was still hungry. She put some of Arleen's biscuits in the oven. "You want some of these, baby?" she asked Jafaris.

"He don't want none of that," Arleen snapped.

"You can't get mad at me. You can take it out on Sherrena."

"I'm pissed off at you, and I'm pissed off at Sherrena!"

"I have no control over what my landlord say!" Crystal interrupted, pleading. "I told y'all you can stay until February, because that's what you paid me for. But Sherrena . . . said that you got to go. I have no say-so over that because I'm not fitting to be out on the street because somebody gave me a hundred and fifty dollars." Crystal breathed in deep and continued. "I'm not fittin' to get irritated. I'm not fittin' to get agitated. I'm not fittin' to get frustrated. I'm not fittin' to call Momma and tell her I ain't got no peace, 'cause I got peace right now. And I'm keeping it. I'm keeping it. I'm keeping it."

"You got peace, and me and my kids got to go."

Crystal bit her lip and looked to the ceiling.

"I can be out tomorrow. It don't matter! You can put my biscuits back in the refrigerator where you got 'em from." Arleen was yelling now.

Crystal shook her head and called Sherrena. "Which day did you say you want Arleen out? . . . Monday? You said Monday?"

Arleen began pacing around, talking to the room. "I really truly hate that I got into this situation. . . . That's bogus, that is bogus as ever. I swear to God! That is bogus!"

"I called the police," Crystal was telling Sherrena. "Chris and them was making a lot of noise upstairs, and he was up there beating on that girl."

Arleen asked for the phone and Crystal ignored her.

Arleen began to shake. "Now look! Now my kids homeless! Nowhere to go and ain't got no money! . . . Fuck me and my kids. Just fuck it! Fuck it!"

Crystal had never seen Arleen like this, so unraveled. She handed her the phone.

"I mean," Arleen said to Sherrena, "they just *throw* me and my kids out on the street! After I got my money, after we ain't got nothing no more! . . . It was okay that we was here up until last time when the police got called. . . . All I can say is thank you for what you done for me and my kids. Before Thursday, me and my kids will be gone. That's my promise. I *can't give you* nothing else!"

Arleen listened for a few seconds before shutting the phone while Sherrena was midsentence. "I feel that we getting used. Me and my kids getting used!" She looked at Crystal, who that morning carried an old and calm spirit. "I'm frustrated," she apologized. "If I took my anger out on you, I'm pissed. . . . Arrangements was *made*." She slapped her palm with the back of her hand.

"But the reason I know what you feel is that my family did this to me. . . . The issues you got? Can't nobody fix 'em but God."

"I don't have nothing but a trust issue, and I'ma always have a trust issue." Arleen sat down.

"But you shouldn't speak that over yourself, 'cause everybody's not out to get you."

"Everybody they *is*, though. . . . You don't know what it's like. You don't know what I been through. You don't know what it's like to have your father molest you and your mother not care about it!" It was her stepfather, the minister. She was ten when it started and sixteen when it stopped.

"Oh, yes I do," Crystal said. "Yes, I do! I know *exactly* what that's like 'cause my stepfather molested me when I was just a little girl, and that's why they sent me to the foster care. I swear to God I know exactly what you been through! I swear to *God*."

Arleen took it in. Jori had led Jafaris into their bedroom and turned on some music, which drifted into the living room as the women let a moment of shared comprehension pass in silence. Each knew something of the other's pain. The boys were sitting on a mattress, playing with Little. Arleen dropped her head, saying, "I'm sick of getting hurt."

"Okay, you know what?" Crystal said. "I remember this like it was yesterday. I had been going to church for a month or so, and the spirit moved on me, and I told God: 'I'm tired of hurting. I'm tired of crying. I'm tired of suffering. I'm tired of people hurting me.' . . . But it's just to build and make you. Because me being hurt, me being lied on, me being talked about, me being abused. Everything. Me being in foster care, me not having no momma, me not having no daddy, siblings don't care, aunties don't care, uncles don't care—*made me*. . . . If you want me to love you, how can I love you if you don't trust me? How can I comfort you? . . . Can't nobody help you unless you allow them to do it. You've been molested? I've been molested too. . . . At ten, I had a flashback, and I was five years old. I looked at my mother, and my mother was still doing drugs. My mother stayed with this man. . . . My mom did the crack pipe. She was pregnant with me. My dad beat my mom, and my mom got stabbed in her back eleven times. So, I know God got a *calling* on my life, but if I don't allow him to use me to do that calling, how can he do it? . . . Church was awesome. I could see the Spirit of God. I can feel the Spirit of God. I know when the Spirit moving in church because it be real smoky. And people might think I'm crazy for believing like that, but, I mean, that's how I believe. . . . My pastor treats me more like a daughter than my mother. I can say that much. And once again I can't say how you feel because you don't have a mother, but once again I can. . . . Everybody goes through stuff in life. And you're going to continue to go through. Your situation, it's to make you. It's to *build you*. . . . I went through it all summer. All summer. Felt like I didn't have nobody. Was ready to do crack this summer. But I prayed a prayer that my pastor prayed over me two years ago, and I firmly stand on that word and believe in it. I didn't even tell my pastor that my momma did crack at this time, and my pastor walked in the aisles, laid her hands on me and said, 'Momma did crack. You ain't gonna do crack.' All I could do was cry."

Crystal's last word lingered in the air until it dissolved in the chattering of the television. Arleen sat there, stunned. Her phone rang and snapped her back. A friend had a lead on an apartment. "Does he do background checks and stuff?"

"Come here," Crystal said once Arleen was off the phone. Arleen obeyed and Crystal held her. "What's the rent at that place?"

"You know what, I didn't even ask him." Arleen called back, learned it was $600 a month, and hung up. "Nope."

Crystal left to inspect Sherrena's other apartment. "It's gonna be all right," she told Arleen. "If I can't promise you nothing else, it'll be all right. That much I can say."

16.

ASHES ON SNOW

When the first of the month came, commas once again returned to Sherrena's bank account. It wasn't any ordinary month either; it was February, when tenants received tax credits and wrote big rent checks. One had cashed her tax return and paid Sherrena $2,375. Doreen came up with $950, as her stipulation dictated. Lamar paid $550 but, since his painting job had earned him nothing, was still behind as far as Sherrena was concerned. He would have to be evicted.

Maybe to fully efface the recent memory of being broke, or maybe just for the hell of it, Sherrena and Quentin took themselves to the casino on a Wednesday night. Sherrena put on a Rocawear sweatsuit, maroon and gold. Quentin sported a G-Unit leather jacket, a straight-billed black cap, and a large pinky ring. He found a handicapped parking spot near the main entrance of Potawatomi Casino and hung from his rearview mirror the necessary permit, a gift from a handicapped tenant.

As they made their way to the bar and grill, past the robotic jungle sounds from all the machines, Sherrena smiled impishly and said, "I hope you don't have nothing planned for the morning." She could pass entire nights at the casino, staying until three or four a.m., long after Quentin had gone home to sleep.

After dinner, where they discussed Sherrena's upcoming presentation on "The Art of the Double Closure" over burgers and Long Island iced teas, they headed to the blackjack section. Sherrena walked slowly through the tables and decided on the one with two white men, one alone and smoking, the other jittery with a high-fiving blonde on his shoulder. Sherrena placed $100 on the table—the minimum bet was $25; she rarely played for less—and pulled up a stool. She stayed quiet at the table, tapping her finger for a hit and slicing two through the air to pass.

Across town, at Eighteenth and Wright, Lamar dealt the cards as Luke, Eddy, Buck, and some of the other neighborhood boys gathered around the table. It was a bitterly cold night, and the warmth of their bodies was fogging up the kitchen windows. The game had a different rhythm, slower and less boisterous, because Kamala was there. Lamar had been asking Kamala to join him at spades ever since she moved upstairs, and she finally said yes, arranging for her father to stay with her daughters as they slept. Kamala had a man, Devon, the father of her children, but Lamar flirted softly with her all the same. The presence of a woman had a way of altering the house's chemistry. Before she was pregnant, Natasha once had caused so much tension at the spades table, solely by being beautiful and desired, that Lamar cut the game short and kicked everyone out. But the boys were on their best behavior around Kamala. They didn't talk much about girls and refrained from calling Lamar a "monkey's ass" as they had been doing since he shaved his mustache. Kamala was only a few years older than Natasha but seemed much more of a woman to them, encased as she was in a hard shell of dignity and world-weariness.[1]

Lamar's New Year's resolution was "to honor God, stay clean, and find a new place." Sherrena had been ignoring his requests for repairs: the kitchen sink had been leaking for the better part of a week and was now running onto the floor. Lamar figured Sherrena would not let him stay much longer anyway. Maybe it was for the best, he thought. Maybe his next place could also be a safe haven for all his boys. Lamar didn't understand why Sherrena treated him like she did. "Why would you fuck someone that's not trying to fuck you?" he wondered. Sherrena wondered the same thing. Lamar said the sink was broken. Sherrena said he broke the sink.

Quentin didn't join Sherrena at the blackjack table. He never did. Instead, he watched from a distance and made sure nobody got angry or fresh with his wife. Whatever pleasure he took from being at the casino had to do with seeing Sherrena happy. Quentin hated gambling. "Bam, there goes fifty dollars right there," he murmured after Sherrena lost another hand.

Cards fell. The night unfurled. Quentin took a phone call, hung up, and approached the blackjack table. He brought his face next to Sherrena's and whispered that Eighteenth and Wright was on fire. She immediately collected her chips and followed Quentin out the door.

"Doreen's?" Sherrena asked when she caught up to Quentin.

"No. The back unit."

"Lamar's?"

"No. The upstairs. Kamala's."

Quentin sped away from the casino. "*Lord, please, please let this be something minor,*" Sherrena prayed, holding on to the door handle as the Suburban careered through the back roads that lead to Eighteenth Street. Lifting her head, she fretted, "Shame on them. . . . I hope my shit ain't burnt to a crisp."

When Quentin tried turning down Eighteenth Street, he met a roadblock. "Already that motherfucker lit up like Christmas down here," he said. He could see fire trucks in front of the property, their red and white lights shooting out in every direction, but not the house itself. Quentin tried another route, then another, but fire trucks and ambulances had blocked off the surrounding streets and alleyways. As he maneuvered the Suburban, Sherrena caught brief glimpses of the scene as it flashed up through breaks in the neighboring houses. Finally, Quentin tried a back alley a block behind Eighteenth Street. Through the Suburban's window, the shadowed rear of a garage gave way to a snow-covered abandoned lot, and the property showed itself in full view.

Sherrena lost her breath.

"Damn! That's real bad, Sher," Quentin let out.

The house was engulfed. Flames were leaping from the roof and disappearing into a milky column of smoke and steam towering into the winter sky. Quentin and Sherrena watched firefighters' silhouettes dash around what had been Kamala's apartment, now a gutted, charcoaled shell. What was not burning was slicked in ice from frozen hose water.

Quentin headed toward the house. Sherrena stayed put. The fire reminded her of the time a disgruntled mortgage customer tossed a homemade bomb through her office window. Since then, the sight of fire disturbed and reduced her.

Quentin recognized Luke as Lamar's eldest son, even as he was crying with his head between his knees. A teenage girl consoled him on Doreen's steps. It was hard to hear over the noise: the grumble of diesel engines, the jackhammer whirring of the water pumps, the sizzle of water meeting heat, the splitting of wood under axes. Patrice was outside too, shivering in only a T-shirt and jeans. She motioned to Quentin and, lifting her voice, hollered in the direction of a firefighter, "He the landlord!" The firefighter nodded and approached Quentin. Bystanders' faces glowed orange out of the darkness when the flames burst upward. Patrice allowed herself one more look at the paramedics gathered at the rear of an ambulance and went inside.

The Hinkstons' house, separated from the back house where Lamar and Kamala lived by only a small patch of mud and weeds, was crammed with people. Doreen was sitting near the front door, cradling her youngest granddaughter, Kayla Mae. Natasha was on the floor next to Ruby, draped in a blanket. The rest of the Hinkston kids sat in a row on a mattress, wide-eyed at the weight of the moment. Lamar was slumped in his wheelchair, rubbing his head and drying his eyes. Eddy and Buck stood by his side. White people in hard hats milled through the crowd, apologizing and collecting information. "I'm sorry. Can I get your name?"

Patrice, who had seen a firefighter carry something to the ambulance under a white sheet, looked to Kamala. She was writhing on the floor, screaming, *"My baby! My baby!"* Her hair had been burnt off on one side. She arched her back and pressed her face into the ground. An older woman nobody recognized tried to hold her. "Whoa!" she would say as Kamala lurched. "Whoa." When the old woman grew tired, she let go, and Kamala collapsed onto the floor, wailing.

Devon walked into the house, carrying two of his daughters, both toddlers. He pushed the scared girls past the crescent of police officers who were surrounding their mother. Kamala sat up and pulled the girls in. She clung to them, kissed their faces all over, and pressing her head into theirs, spilled her tears onto their hair.

An older firefighter stepped into the Hinkstons' house. He knelt down beside Kamala and told her what she already knew. Her youngest daughter, eight months old, was dead. Kamala fell back and let out a trembling, otherworldly groan.

"He killed my baby!" Kamala screamed, convulsing. "I'ma kill him! *I'ma kill him!*"

Devon began pacing the room with clenched fists. Over and over, he whispered, "That's the second one. That's the second one." At one point, he stopped and stood over Kamala. The room hushed and looked on. Devon looked to be on the verge of violence. But the moment passed, and he resumed his pacing and mad chant. "That's the second one." They had lost a baby just a year earlier, a daughter who was stillborn. Kamala and Devon wore her ashes around their necks in matching lockets.

"Oh, God," Sherrena said when Quentin told her. "I hope they didn't leave that baby at home by herself." Sherrena's mind drifted back to earlier years, when she was a fourth-grade teacher and Kamala her student. "She was always a good girl in school," she said.

Back at home, Quentin and Sherrena tried putting the pieces together. "Devon and Kamala—" Quentin began.

"Was downstairs," Sherrena followed.

"Playing cards with Lamar. And maybe left something on. . . . And by the time they realized it was a fire, they tried to run upstairs, but it was too late."

Quentin keyed the computer to see if the fire had made the news. It had. "Firefighters did not hear smoke detectors when they arrived," he read. "There is a smoke detector in the kitchen," he said.

"There's supposed to be one in each sleeping area," Sherrena replied. "I thought we had put some smoke detectors up there. I can't remember right now."[2]

THE FOLLOWING DAY, Sherrena heard from the fire inspector. He said the fire had started when one of Kamala's daughters climbed out of bed and knocked over a lamp. Kamala's father had either fled without grabbing the baby or, more likely, left the girls alone earlier in the evening. Both Kamala and Luke had tried to rescue the child, but the fire was all-consuming. Kamala's other two daughters walked out themselves, before the fire got out of control. Nobody had heard a smoke detector go off.

The fire inspector told Sherrena she "didn't have anything to worry about." She wasn't liable for anything that had happened. Sherrena then asked if she was obligated to return Kamala's and Lamar's rent, since the fire happened a few days after the first of the month. The fire inspector said no, and that settled it in Sherrena's mind. "They are not getting any money back from me," she said. Sherrena figured both Kamala and Lamar would ask for their rent to be returned, and she was right.

Sherrena planned to tear the place down and pocket the insurance payout. "The only positive thing I can say is happening out of all of this is that I may get a huge chunk of money," she said. That—and "getting rid of Lamar." The Red Cross would find Lamar and his sons a new place to live, giving Sherrena one less eviction to worry about.

Earlier that morning, loud knocking had pulled Doreen out of bed. She opened the front door in her nightgown to find reporters with cameras and microphones. After a few questions, Doreen shut the door and told herself not to answer it for the rest of the day. She walked through the kitchen and looked out a back window. Kamala's second-floor apartment looked like a dark cave. The windows had been broken out and a large section of the roof was gone, leaving only support beams. Runoff had left the siding streaked with gray grime. The snowy ground was blackened with ash. Scattered about were roof shingles, long pieces of wood, the skeletons of furniture and other household items—a gnarled junk heap all charred and coated with hardened foam from the fire hoses. Water had frozen into thousands of icy bulbs that appeared to drip off the tips of surrounding tree branches. Doreen lowered her eyes and saw, on the house's front porch, six white lilies tied with a cream ribbon. Spring in the dead of winter.

PART THREE

AFTER

17.

THIS IS AMERICA

Arleen was in the living room at Thirteenth Street, shivering. She didn't have a winter coat, so she pulled on another T-shirt and an oversized hoodie. The Milwaukee weathermen had been working themselves up. They said it was going to be the coldest week in a decade, that the temperature could bottom out at forty below with the wind chill. The local news kept flashing a warning: FROSTBITE TIME: 10 MINUTES. People were urged to stay inside. Arleen had three days to find another apartment.

Sherrena was done with both Arleen and Crystal. The conversation with the Milwaukee PD had spooked her; she decided to have the sheriffs remove Arleen and deliver Crystal an eviction notice. "I'm not gonna be *arrested* because of those people over there," Sherrena said. "I'm not gonna have them take my *property* because of them. I'm tired of this shit. . . . Arleen is being real selfish. She doesn't care about anybody else but her and her kids. She doesn't care about me." Sherrena faxed a copy of Crystal's eviction notice to the Milwaukee

PD. A few days later, she received a letter back: "Your written course of action is *accepted*."

Arleen had made an appointment with a landlord and was waiting outside her apartment complex when the woman pulled up in a Subaru, thirty minutes late. Tall and white in a North Face fleece and new tennis shoes, she rushed through an apology and introduced herself as Carol.

Carol's apartment was a small and plain one-bedroom unit renting at $525 on the northern edge of the North Side. It took Arleen all of thirty seconds to scan the place and say that she'd take it. She didn't like the apartment or the neighborhood or the fact that the boys would have to switch schools again if they moved there. But all that was secondary. "It don't matter," she thought. "A house is a house for now."

Carol decided to screen Arleen on the spot. She sat down on the floor in the empty living room and asked Arleen to spell her name and provide her date of birth and Social Security number. Carol's first substantive question was, "Have you been evicted in the last three years? . . . I'm going to check CCAP, so you might as well get it out in the open." Arleen had given Carol her real name and wasn't sure which evictions were attached to it. So she decided to tell Carol what she had been through since being forced to move from the condemned house with no water. She told her about the drug dealers on Atkinson and her sister dying. This took a while. There were so many moves and so many details, and soon Carol's confusion turned to annoyance. She cut Arleen off and asked about her income: "How long have you been on W-2, and what's the reason?"

"They actually had me on W-2 T because, um, I go to counseling for depression. . . . I go see my therapist once a week. And they have me doing a job search. They're trying to get me job-ready, but they're also trying to get me to apply for SSI."

"Better to not live on either," Carol said, telling Arleen to get a job.

"I know," Arleen said.

Arleen fudged her income, telling Carol she actually received child support. And after Carol said, "We don't have any kids in this building," Arleen lied about her kids too, mentioning only Jafaris. "I need to come see where you live now," Carol told Arleen. She said she'd stop by Thirteenth Street in a couple of hours.

Back in her apartment, Arleen took out the trash and swept the carpet and hid all of Jori's clothes. There was little she could do about the bathroom—there was standing water in the clogged tub, and the sink didn't work—but the light was also out, so maybe Carol wouldn't notice. In the kitchen, Arleen stood over the sink, staring at a pile of dishes. Little rubbed himself against her legs and meowed for food. They were out of dish soap, so Crystal's laundry detergent would have to do. As the water ran, Arleen placed both hands on either side of the sink. She scrubbed the pots. Her phone rang. "It's nothing," she said to the person on the other line. "Nothing. Nothing." Then she allowed herself a hard cry.

Crystal, who had stayed on the couch and watched Arleen frantically scurry around, got up and embraced Arleen. Arleen cried into Crystal's shoulder, and Crystal did not pull away. When Arleen stepped back, Crystal said, "I promise you, if you believe, you will have a house."

The apartment looked decent when Carol showed up. Arleen had even sprayed Febreze. After a brisk walk-through, Carol sat down at the glass dining table. "This just, honestly, does not look good," she began. "And, yeah, I understand your sister died and everything, but how is that your landlord's problem?"

"I understand what you're saying." Arleen thought that white people liked it when she said "I understand what you're saying," and "I'm trying to get my stuff together and stop making dumb choices," and "I'm going to start going back to school for my GED." And eye contact, lots of eye contact.

"I'm not saying it isn't terrible," Carol continued. "But I mean, we actually have an employee whose mother died. And she had no insurance or anything. The county paid. You know, they give you three hundred dollars or whatever for the funeral. And that's the funeral she got."

Eye contact.

"So what changes are you going to make so that I'm not throwing you out in a month?" Carol tapped her pen.

At this point, Arleen had applied for or called on twenty-five apartments, and Carol was her only hope. Sensing that hope pulling away, Arleen played the only card left in her hand. She offered Carol the option of arranging a "vendor payment" with W-2, which would automatically deduct rent from each month's check. "So that by the time I get my check you already have your payment."

"I like that!" Carol responded, surprising herself. "That sounds like a good compromise." Then she added, "The cat can't come."

"Okay."

"I was going to say, you got to worry about feeding you and your kid."

"I want to give you a hug because, let me just." Arleen hugged Carol, who blushed and dashed out the door. Arleen hugged Crystal and ran around and danced. "I got a house! I can't believe it! I got a *hoooooouse*!"

CAROL TOLD ARLEEN that she could move in the first of the month. Until then, Arleen planned to take her boys to a shelter and lock her things in storage. As a shelter resident, she would be eligible for Red Cross funds that would cover her security deposit. It was the only way she could give Carol all her money.[1] Arleen collected cardboard boxes from neighborhood liquor stores and began packing her things.

"Don't cry when I leave," Arleen told Crystal as she placed dishes in a box.

"Bitch, you act like you gonna be gone forever. You gonna come around. 'Cause you can't live without me now."

"And you can't live without me either." Arleen smiled.

Crystal began clapping her hands and singing, "*I ain't going. I ain't going.*" Then she slapped Arleen on the back.

"Ow, Crystal!" Arleen said, and the two women wrestled a bit, laughing.

As Arleen resumed packing, Crystal asked, "Could you leave me some dishes?" Arleen set a few aside.

At sunrise on Thursday, the sky was the color of flat beer. By midmorning, it was the color of a robin's egg. The still and leafless tree branches looked like cracks in the sky's shell. Cars rolled slowly through the streets, caked with salt and winter's grime. Milwaukee Public Schools canceled classes because of the cold advisory. Arleen's boys weren't going anyway. She needed them to help her move. Jori loaded a U-Haul truck that a family friend had rented for them. The cold gripped him. His fingers and ears began to sting. Icy air filled his mouth, and it felt like his gums were hardening into one of those plastic molds of teeth in the school nurse's office. His breath was a thick white gauze circling his face. He smiled through it, happy to be useful.

After a few trips, Jori ate his pride and put on Crystal's sand-colored coat. Crystal herself sat on the floor, covered in church-donated blankets, eating banana pudding and watching talk shows.

The night before the move, Arleen had glued on a new wig and cleaned her shoes. She wanted to look younger than she was because who knew whom she might meet at the shelter or Public Storage. No shelters had called back, and Arleen didn't know where she and her boys would sleep that night. She would have to worry about that later. For now, she was focused on taking what she could to a storage unit.

The man behind the counter at Public Storage wore a pinky ring. His hair was slicked back, and he smelled of liquor and cheap aftershave. Arleen's storage unit would be C-33, a ten-by-ten-footer. "It's the same size as the truck you got," the man said with a Texas drawl. "All you got to do is be creative." Everything fit easily. Arleen had scraped together $21 for the discounted fee by selling some food stamps and a space heater. (Next month's fee would be $41.) But she didn't realize she had to buy a lock and $8 worth of insurance too. She didn't have it. The Texan, whose weatherworn face told her that he had seen hard times too, found Arleen a lock and let her slide on the insurance. She thanked him before shuffling through the cold concrete lot to close the orange aluminum door to C-33. At least her stuff had a home.

THEY SPENT THE night, then the weekend, back at Thirteenth Street with Crystal, sleeping on the floor.

Arleen called the Lodge and other shelters, but they were full as usual. On Monday morning, she tried domestic-violence shelters and secured a room at one she had stayed at years ago, when fleeing Jafaris's father. When Arleen called Carol to tell her the name of the shelter for Red Cross money purposes, she learned that Carol had rented the apartment to someone else. Arleen didn't ask why, but she figured Carol had found a better tenant, someone with more income or no kids. Arleen let out a long, emptied-out sigh and balled herself up in a chair. "I'm back to square one," she said.

Soured, Arleen gathered their last remaining things in the apartment. She took down her curtains and remembered some dirty clothes that were in Crystal's closet. She and Jafaris brought Little upstairs to Trisha.

"Take care of kitten," Jafaris asked.

"I am, baby, I promise," Trisha answered.

He thought and said, "Give him some food."

Arleen planned on leaving behind her love seat, which had collapsed since Crystal began sleeping on it. Besides that and a scattering of clothes, blankets, and broken lamps, the place was barren. Then Arleen remembered that she had bought a $5 adapter that connected the stove to the gas line. She told Jori to remove the part, which would have rendered the stove useless.

Seeing this, Crystal screamed, *"Get out of my house!"* She began picking up Arleen's things and throwing them out the front door. "I don't need none of your shit! . . . Got me fucked up!"

"Stankin' ass bitch!" Arleen yelled, getting in Crystal's face.

"You call me stankin', but whose clothes you got on? Mines. *My shirt!* . . . Three days in a row, you nasty bitch!"

"I'll hit you in yo' mouth!" Jori yelled at Crystal, running up. He put his nose inches away from Crystal's face and cocked his fist back. "I'm fittin' to scrap you!" he yelled. "I don't give a fuck about no fucking police!"

Suddenly, Quentin was in the room. He had been showing prospective tenants the rear apartment when he overheard the commotion. Quentin walked in the open door and grabbed Jori by the shirt collar. "Hey! Hey!" he barked.

Jori lunged at Crystal. "Come on!" he yelled, his fists flailing. Quentin tugged him back. Crystal only stepped closer. "Look, boy," she said, chuckling. "You are not hard as you think."

"No! No!" Jafaris cried. Trying to be helpful, he had found a broken shower rod and was hitting Crystal with it. Arleen grabbed Jafaris and pulled him out the door. At Quentin's prodding, Jori moved in that direction, stopping to kick in Crystal's floor-model television.

As the family left, Crystal stepped onto the front porch and continued throwing their things everywhere. The front lawn was soon littered with random stuff: schoolbooks, a Precious Moments doll, a bottle of cologne. "Y'all ain't untouchable," Crystal was screaming. "This is America! *This is America!*"

If Arleen hadn't been under so much pressure, she might have realized that removing the adapter was throwing Crystal's desperation in her face. Maybe she would have been able to defuse the situation. Under better circumstances, they could have been friends. They got on when there was food in their bellies and some certainty about the next day. But Arleen was in the press of the city, depleted. So when Crystal exploded, Arleen exploded right alongside her.[2]

Crystal could quickly turn violent. The year before she met Arleen, Crystal had been examined by a clinical psychologist who diagnosed her with Bipolar Disorder, Posttraumatic Stress Disorder, Reactive

Attachment Disorder, Borderline Intellectual Functioning, Neglect of a Child, Sexual Abuse of a Child as Victim, and Emerging Personality Disorder Dynamics with Borderline Features. Her childhood had left a mark. "Crystal is highly sensitive to anticipated rejection, abandonment, and harm in her relationships," the psychologist wrote in his report. "She has immense underlying rage at significant others for their perceived unwillingness and/or inability to respond to her needs for nurturance, security, and esteem. . . . She has limited ability to tolerate much in the way of frustration or anxiety and a proneness to act out her tensions without much . . . forethought or deliberation. . . . She is still seen as being fragilely integrated." The report surmised that Crystal had an IQ of about 70 and anticipated that she would need "long-term mental health treatment and supportive assistance if she [was] to be maintained in the community as an adult."

And yet there she stood alone, in an empty apartment. Crystal picked through the things Arleen had left behind. When she wandered into the kitchen, she discovered that Jori hadn't been able to remove the stove piece, but he did cut the electrical cord. Crystal told herself she wasn't planning on eating that day anyhow. Pastor had called a fast.

18.

LOBSTER ON FOOD STAMPS

The line around the welfare building spanned the length of Vliet Street and wrapped around the corner. Barricades had been erected and extra police officers summoned. The governor had announced that food vouchers would be given to households affected by storms that had flooded parts of the state, including Milwaukee County, and by seven a.m., thousands of people had lined up, jostling for position and even trying to get inside by taking a door off its hinges.

The Marcia P. Coggs Human Services Center was massive. Three stories of cream brick, it had 170,000 square feet and 232 large windows. The building had originally held a Schuster's department store. But the store, along with the surrounding neighborhood and city, had fallen on hard times around midcentury. It was finally shuttered in 1961 and the building sold to the county. When the building was renovated in the early 2000s, it consolidated 450 county employees under one roof. A California-based artist was commissioned to install bright, multicolored ceramic tiles above the windows that displayed words like "contemplation" and "dance." She called her installation "Community Key."[1]

A little past eight a.m., Larraine walked past the crowd and made her way inside, hardly looking up to notice the strolling security guards or escalators transporting people between floors to fill out forms and meet with caseworkers. She took a number (4023) and waited. Larraine was there to get her food stamps reinstated. Soon, not a seat was empty, and Room 102 filled with the sounds of children and chatter. An older woman leaned on her umbrella and tried to sleep. A mother spanked a toddler. Another was engrossed in *Women Who Love Too Much*. After one hour and forty minutes, Larraine's number was called. Not bad, she thought, having spent entire days in the welfare building.[2]

"I had an appointment on the twentieth of this month," Larraine explained to the multitasking and manicured woman behind the glass. "But I got, between the time of my scheduled phone call, I had gotten evicted."

"You have to reschedule your appointment," the woman replied. It was another missed meeting and another canceled benefit, both the result of an eviction that threw everything off course. The woman handed Larraine some papers. "Here is a list of things you need to bring with you."

"I don't have anything with me," Larraine replied, reading the list. Most of the necessary paperwork was in storage.

"Well, if you don't have anything, then you can't bring anything." The woman smiled.

Larraine looked confused. "But will I still get my benefits?"

"That's why you have to come in for the appointment. . . . I can give you a food pantry referral. Would you like to go to the food pantry?"

Larraine took an escalator downstairs to the food pantry, walking out with two grocery bags filled with canned beef and kidney beans and other things she hated. Sometimes, family members who didn't know any better would ask Larraine why she didn't just call to schedule her appointments. Larraine would laugh and ask, "Oh, *you* want to try the number?" She had never once gotten anything but a busy signal.

At her follow-up appointment, Larraine managed to get her $80-a-month food-stamp allowance reinstated even without all the necessary paperwork. Leaving the welfare building, she shuffled past throngs of bored, tired people and street alcoholics congregating outside and into a nearby furniture store with bars over the windows. Inside, experimental jazz was playing over an organized clutter of plump recliners, dark wood dining-room sets, and brass lamps.

A salesman with a Middle Eastern accent approached Larraine, who asked to see the armoires. She inspected a seven-piece bedroom set. She gawked at a sixty-two-inch television.

"I have TVs smaller than this," the salesman said.

"No, but I want this one!" Larraine smiled.

"Why don't you do it layaway, then?"

"You have layaway? I love layaway!"

Larraine was participating in a kind of cleansing ritual, swapping the welfare building's miasma of unwashed bodies and dirt with the smell of a new leather sofa. She was also entertaining a fantasy of making a good home for herself and her daughters. Jayme was finally out of prison and staying with Larraine and Beaker until she found an apartment; and maybe Megan would come around. She used to put the girls' clothes, new clothes, on layaway.

To Larraine, putting something on layaway was saving. "I can't leave money in my bank," she said. "When you're on SSI you can only have so much money in the bank, and it's got to be less than a thousand dollars. Because if it's more . . . they cut your payments until that money is spent." Larraine was talking about SSI's "resource limit." She was allowed to have up to $2,000 in the bank, not $1,000 like she thought, but anything more than that could result in her losing benefits.[3] Larraine saw this rule as a clear disincentive to save. "If I can't keep my money in the bank, then I might as well buy something worthwhile . . . because I know once I pay on it, it's mine, and no one can take it from me, just like my jewelry." Well, no one except Eagle Moving.

Before her eviction, Beaker had asked Larraine why she didn't just sell her jewelry and pay Tobin. "Of course I'm not going to do that," she said. "I worked way too hard for me to sell my jewelry. . . . I'm not going to sell my life savings because I'm homeless or I got evicted." It wasn't like she had just stumbled into a pit and would soon climb out. Larraine imagined she would be poor and rent-strapped forever. And if that was to be her lot in life, she might as well have a little jewelry to show for it. She wanted a new television, not some worn and boxy thing inherited from Lane and Susan. She wanted a bed no one else had slept in. She loved perfume and could tell you what a woman was wearing after passing her on the sidewalk. "Even people like myself," Larraine said, "we deserve, too, something brand-new."[4]

Larraine didn't put anything on layaway that day. But when her food stamps kicked in, she went to the grocery store and bought two lobster tails, shrimp, king crab legs, salad, and lemon meringue pie. Bringing it all back to Beaker's trailer, she added Cajun seasoning to the crab legs and cooked the lobster tails in lemon butter at 350 degrees. She ate everything alone, in a single sitting, washing it down with Pepsi. The meal consumed her entire monthly allocation of food stamps. It was her and Glen's anniversary, and she wanted to do something special. "I know our relationship may not have been good, but it was our relationship," she said. "Some things I will not ever get over." But the lobster helped.

WHEN LARRAINE SPENT money or food stamps on nonessentials, it baffled and frustrated people around her, including her niece, Sammy, Susan and Lane's daughter.[5] "My aunt Larraine is one of those people who will see some two-hundred-dollar beauty cream that removes her wrinkles and will go and buy it instead of paying the rent," said Sammy, a hairstylist with her own shop in Cudahy. "I don't know why she just doesn't stick to a budget." Pastor Daryl felt the same way, saying that Larraine was careless with her money because she operated under a "poverty mentality."

To Sammy, Pastor Daryl, and others, Larraine was poor because she threw money away. But the reverse was more true. Larraine threw money away because she was poor.

Before she was evicted, Larraine had $164 left over after paying the rent. She could have put some of that away, shunning cable and Walmart. If Larraine somehow managed to save $50 a month, nearly one-third of her after-rent income, by the end of the year she would have $600 to show for it—enough to cover a single month's rent. And that would have come at considerable sacrifice, since she would sometimes have had to forgo things like hot water and clothes. Larraine could have at least saved what she spent on cable. But to an older woman who lived in a trailer park isolated from the rest of the city, who had no car, who didn't know how to use the Internet, who only sometimes had a phone, who no longer worked, and who sometimes was seized with fibromyalgia attacks and cluster migraines—cable was a valued friend.

People like Larraine lived with so many compounded limitations that it was difficult to imagine the amount of good behavior or self-control that would allow them to lift themselves out of poverty. The distance between grinding poverty and even stable poverty could be so vast that those at the bottom had little hope of climbing out even if they pinched every penny. So they chose not to. Instead, they tried to survive in color, to season the suffering with pleasure. They would get a little high or have a drink or do a bit of gambling or acquire a television. They might buy lobster on food stamps.[6]

If Larraine spent her money unwisely, it was not because her benefits left her with so much but because they left her with so little. She paid the price for her lobster dinner. She had to eat pantry food the rest of the month. Some days, she simply went hungry. It was worth it. "I'm satisfied with what I had," she said. "And I'm willing to eat noodles for the rest of the month because of it."

Larraine learned a long time ago not to apologize for her existence. "People will begrudge you for anything," she said. She didn't care that the checkout clerk looked at her funny. She got the same looks when she bought the $14 tart balsamic vinegar or ribs or on-sale steak or chicken. Larraine loved to cook. "I have a right to live, and I have a right to live like I want to live," she said. "People don't realize that even poor people get tired of the same old taste. Like, I literally hate hot dogs, but I was brought up on them. So you think, 'When I get older, I will have steak.' So now I'm older. And I do."

THE NEXT MONTH was August, and Larraine used some of her food stamps to buy instant mashed potatoes, ham, and creamed corn for a hard-luck family that had moved into the trailer next to Beaker's. The family of six had recently lost many of their things in an eviction and were sleeping on the floor. Once dinner was ready, Larraine led a prayer. "*Dear God in Heaven, thank you so much for this food. And thanks for all the people in my life who have blessed me. Thank you for Jayme. And thank you for my brother, Beaker. Even though he makes me so angry sometimes, I still love him, Lord. Please take care of my brother. Amen.*"

Two days later, someone knocked on the door. It was a tall white man with a mustache and a tucked-in collared shirt. He was holding a bright-yellow piece of paper.

"Good morning. We are going to have to shut your gas off this morning," he said.

Larraine took the paper. "Oh, okay," she said sheepishly.

"There's payment information on the back there. Have a nice day." The man went behind the trailer with his toolbox.

"So Uncle Beaker hasn't been paying the gas?" Jayme asked, working her mascara brush.

"I guess not," Larraine said, looking down at the yellow paper reporting a debt of $2,748.60.

"When do you finally grow up and start paying your bills? Uncle

Beaker needs to grow up and stop living like a child. You too, Mom. You have a real problem with living above your means. You need to really, just, not do that."

Larraine looked at her daughter. "I don't know when you got so cute," she said.

As fall bled into winter, warmth began seeping out of the trailer. The thin walls and countertops and water and silverware in the drawer grew cold. Larraine and Beaker burrowed under blankets, doubled up on sweaters, and plugged in two small space heaters. They both slept more to keep warm. If Larraine fell asleep on the couch, Beaker would put an extra blanket over her. Early morning was the worst. Beaker would put on his heavy coat, but Larraine's winter clothes were sitting in Eagle Moving's bonded storage facility. They were not the only tenants in the trailer park who couldn't afford to reinstate their gas before the first snow fell. As for Tobin, he hated the snow. He traveled to warmer climates during the winter.

ONE FALL DAY, Beaker told Larraine he was moving to a federally subsidized assisted-living facility for the elderly and disabled. The following morning, he did. This caught Larraine by surprise. They had never really learned to talk to each other.

After Beaker left, Larraine knew she had to come out of hiding and make new arrangements, if not with Tobin, then at least with the new management company. She worked up the courage and walked down to the office in sweatpants and a stained black fleece.

"I need to get emergency assistance as soon as possible," Larraine told the college kid who had replaced Lenny. "I'm so cold. . . . The heat. All I know is I need the heat on."

"Oh my goodness," the college kid said without looking up. He was nonplussed. He was learning. The college kid dialed the number to Bieck Management and put Larraine on the phone with Geraldine, the office manager. Geraldine told Larraine that Beaker owed almost $1,000 in back rent. The gas bill was not the only one he hadn't paid.

Larraine sat in the office chair, resting her forehead on her palm. "Please, Geraldine, I need your help. I need your understanding." After a few more minutes, Larraine hung up the phone. Her best hope of staying, she believed, was to convince Beaker to pay his back rent.

Beaker's new place was in the Woods Apartments, on College Avenue and Thirty-Fifth Street, across the street from Mud Lake. It was white-wall clean and new-smelling and warm. Larraine asked Beaker to settle his debt with Bieck. He said he could not pay two rents. Larraine said she couldn't pay last month's rent because her money had already gone to storage. At this point, Larraine had paid Eagle Moving $1,000.[7] Ruben had room to store Larraine's things, and Lane had a truck. But both said no when Larraine asked them for help.

"Well, I hope you go live with your storage because that's all—"

Beaker stopped himself. Larraine looked pitiful. She had heavy bags under her eyes, and her hair was a mess. It had been days since she last showered. She refused to ask Lane and Susan to use theirs. Beaker knew his trailer might just as well have been an abandoned shed: the heat, hot water, phone, and cable had been cut off. A helpless, dull silence hung between brother and sister.

Then Beaker said, "Take one of those sweaters."

LARRAINE HAD SIX days to be out of Beaker's trailer. Beaker had written Bieck Management a letter that read, "I'm moving and will be leaving my trailer to Bieck Management for the money I owe them. I'll be out . . . and so will my sister." Larraine learned about Beaker's betrayal—that's what it felt like, anyway—when one of Bieck's property managers got her on the office phone three days after she had visited her brother in the Woods Apartments. The manager told Larraine to be out by the first of the month. She had pleaded, "Please, I have no place to go," and "I'm not this bad person," but in the end she just said, "I see. I see. Thank you for your time, and God bless you." Larraine sat down. "I don't know what to do or where to go anymore," she said. "I have no idea."

Larraine began looking for a new place to live in the streets surrounding her church. It was the centerpiece of her life; it might as well be the centerpiece of her housing search too. She shuffled gingerly along the icy sidewalks, calling landlords. Then she decided to stop by the housing projects in South Milwaukee, where she grew up. The woman in the office told Larraine they were full and not accepting applications, but she gave Larraine the address to HUD's offices.

The Milwaukee branch of the Department of Housing and Urban Development was located downtown, on a top floor of The Blue, a grand modern tower with a mirrored façade interspersed with rows of candy-blue glass. Larraine's wet shoes squeaked on the lobby's terrazzo floors. The HUD receptionist handed Larraine the Multifamily Housing Inventory Report, thirteen legal-size pages listing all federally assisted rental housing in the metropolitan area. "I have no idea where half of these places are," Larraine muttered at the long list of addresses and phone numbers. It hardly mattered, since most of the properties were reserved for the physically disabled or elderly. In fact, for years Larraine had assumed that most public housing was exclusively for senior citizens. "And even they, a lot of them, couldn't get low-income housing," she remembered. "So I thought, if they can't, neither can I." It was why Larraine had never before thought to apply for public housing.

Politicians had learned that their constituents hated the idea of senior housing a lot less than public housing for poor families. Grandma and Grandpa made for a much more sympathetic case, and elderly housing provided adult children with an alternative to nursing homes. When public housing construction for low-income households ceased, it continued for the aged; and high-rises originally built for families were converted for elderly use.[8]

Larraine found two addresses on HUD's Housing Inventory that accepted applications for people who were neither elderly nor handicapped and that were located on the far South Side of the city. Larraine did not consider the near South Side to be an option, let alone the North Side. The application asked if she had ever been evicted.

Larraine circled yes and wrote: "I had some complications with the landlord, and he evicted me."

ON THE DAY Larraine had to be out of Beaker's trailer, ice spread over the city. An early December snow had fallen, melted, and, when the temperature dropped, froze. Larraine stood in her kitchen listening to the sawing sounds of people scraping their car windows and chipping the ice from their doors. There was a pile of trash on the floor, mainly Beaker's empty Maverick cigarette boxes and chocolate-milk bottles, and dirty dishes were piled in the kitchen sink. The cold had immobilized Larraine under blankets on the couch—the cold and the question of what to do next. Little had been cleaned since winter had arrived. "I don't care anymore," she said, swallowing pain relievers and antidepressants.

Larraine had applied to or called on forty apartments. She had had no luck on the private market, and her applications to public housing were still being processed. Larraine didn't know where she was going to go. She was considering approaching Thomas, a man her age who lived alone in the trailer park, or Ms. Betty, whom Larraine knew only as an "old lady who lives across the road." Larraine packed up her remaining things. Her plan was to pay Public Storage $50 to keep them.

Late in the day, Larraine knocked on Ms. Betty's door. She was a small white woman with crystal eyes and silvering blond hair falling past her shoulders in double braids. Ms. Betty looked younger when seated and enjoying a slow cigarette, but she walked like an old woman, hunched with one arm held close. What the women knew of each other came from passing hellos and rumors. But when Larraine asked Betty if she could stay with her, Betty said yes.

"Sure you can stay with me, until after the winter." Ms. Betty raised an eyebrow. "I know you're not as big of a problem as they say you are."

Larraine smiled. "I'll be able to take a shower and everything," she said.

Betty's trailer might have been the most cluttered in the whole park. There was room for Larraine but little else. Ms. Betty had piled her tables with magazines and old mail and canned food and bottles of soy sauce and candy. In the living room, a tree bent toward the window, shedding its leaves on the floor, and keepsakes were clustered together on shelves next to a picture of Jesus. There was an order to the mess. The bathroom drawers bore a resemblance to the nuts-and-bolts aisle at the hardware store, with all the travel-sized tubes of toothpaste and bobby pins and hair ties and nail clippers grouped together in their own respective compartments. In the kitchen, Betty had hung a sign: SELF-CONTROL IS DEFINED AS REFRAINING FROM CHOKING THE SHIT OUT OF SOMEONE WHO IS DESPERATELY DESERVING OF IT. Larraine agreed to pay Betty $100 a month.

A few days after moving in with Ms. Betty, Larraine heard back on her applications to public housing in the form of two rejection letters. Each letter listed a pair of reasons Larraine's applications were turned away: "Collections from the State of Wisconsin" and "Eviction History."

Larraine understood "Eviction History," but not "Collections from the State of Wisconsin." When she called to find out more, she was told she owed property taxes. "Property!" She laughed after getting off the phone. "I'd love to know how I owe property taxes."[9]

Betty thought Larraine should appeal. She looked over the top of her large glasses and said, "You have to fight, Larraine. I had to fight for my Medicaid."

"I don't have the energy," Larraine answered. "And I don't feel like getting rejected again."[10]

Betty nodded. She understood.

A few days later found Larraine in an especially religious mood, her church's Truth Class fresh in her mind.

"When you look at Jesus, what do you see?" Larraine asked Betty.

"A hottie," Betty replied without missing a beat. A long, unlit cigarette shot out of her lips like a plank from a ship.

"Oh, Betty!" Larraine giggled.

Betty sauntered over and tapped the Jesus picture. "Hottie," she repeated. "I've always liked men with facial hair."

"Naughty, Betty," Larraine cooed.

The new friends talked and laughed into the night. On the couch, they fell asleep at the same time.[11]

19.

LITTLE

The cheapest motel Pam could find charged $50 a night. They checked in and started calling friends and relatives, hoping someone would take them in. Two days passed without any luck, and Pam began to worry. "Everybody we knew weren't answering our phone because they knew we needed a place to stay," she said.

Then Ned lost his part-time construction job. He was fired for the two days of work he missed when helping his family move from the trailer park. Job loss could lead to eviction, but the reverse was also true.[1] An eviction not only consumed renters' time, causing them to miss work, it also weighed heavily on their minds, often triggering mistakes on the job. It overwhelmed workers with stress, leading them to act unprofessionally, and commonly resulted in their relocating farther away from their worksite, increasing their likelihood of being late or missing days.[2] Ned's firing wasn't out of the ordinary, but that was little consolation for Pam. Their money was running out.

Even so, Ned refused to call his family. Typical, thought Pam. Ned called home to brag but rarely to ask. So Pam worked her phone, calling almost everyone she knew and even churches. Nothing. Finally, a friend agreed to take the girls until Pam and Ned got back on their feet. They dropped off the three oldest girls and kept two-year-old Kristin with them. Then Ned's phone rang around ten p.m. It was Travis, a buddy they used to party with in the trailer park and who had since moved into a nearby apartment complex. Travis offered his couch. Pam breathed a sigh of relief. At least she wouldn't have to bring her new baby back to a cheap motel.

Travis was their first godsend; Dirky was their second. A muscular, white-haired man with a professional-grade mechanic's shop in his garage, Dirky gave Ned an off-the-books job customizing motorcycles. Ned had met him through a mechanic buddy.

After a month at Travis's, Pam and Ned sensed he was about done with them. When Kristin got fussy, Travis would tighten his jaw and shut his bedroom door, and not only because he had to be up at four thirty the next morning for work. The last time Travis let someone stay with him, it was his brother and nephew, and those two drunks got him evicted. Ned would tell Pam to hush her kid, and Pam would tell him that she was his goddamn kid too.

One morning, they drove to Dirky's garage, Kristin and her Care Bear buckled up in the backseat. Pam was due in nine days; they were no closer to a new home than they were the day Tobin kicked them out of the trailer park; they might have to live on the near South Side, with the Mexicans; Ned was out of cigarettes because Pam was smoking more to offset stress and hunger pains; Kristin was throwing a fit because her lovey teddy got thrown in storage after the eviction; Dirky wanted Ned to do a transmission, which would probably mean working deep into the night; and he hated that his family had to rely on Travis. When he turned toward the booming music and saw a car with two young black men in the lane next to him, he hated them too. "Fucking niggers," Ned bit.

A few minutes later, Ned spotted a rent sign in white, working-class West Allis and told Pam to write down the phone number. She missed it.

"I told you," Ned said. "I told you the fucking number, and you just can't write it down?"

"Not when you say it so fast!"

"*I'm* not the one with the fucking problem!"

They circled back and got the number. "Hi, I was calling about your place on Seventy-Sixth and Lincoln? . . . What's that, a two-bedroom?"

"Yep," a man's voice said. "It's six hundred and ninety-five a month with heat."

Pam didn't hang up. Maybe he was flexible. "Okay. When is it available?"

"Now."

"It is? Okay."

"And who would be living with you?"

"My family." Pam paused and then decided to tell him about most of the kids. "I've got three children and one on the way. But they're all girls!"

"Oh, no, no, no. We're trying to keep it to all adults."

"Oh, okay. Thank you." Pam brought the phone down. "They don't want kids."

Ned was wearing a black Ozzy Osbourne cutoff T-shirt and a Harley-Davidson cap turned backward. He whistled through his teeth. "I know. As soon as you say you've got four fucking kids, we're fucked."

Pam knew it didn't even take that. When house hunting a few days earlier, two landlords had turned her away on account of her kids. One had said, "We're pretty strict here. We don't allow no loud nothing." The other had told Pam it was against the law for him to put so many children in a two-bedroom apartment, which was the most Pam and Ned could afford. When talking to landlords, Pam had begun subtracting children from her family. She was beginning to wonder what was most responsible for keeping them homeless: her drug conviction from several years back, the fact that Ned was on the run and had no proof of income, their eviction record, their poverty, or their children.

Children caused landlords headache. Fearing street violence, many parents in crime-ridden neighborhoods kept their children locked inside. Children cooped up in small apartments used the curtains for superhero capes; flushed toys down the toilet; and drove up the water bill. They could test positive for lead poisoning, which could bring a pricey abatement order. They could come under the supervision of Child Protective Services, whose caseworkers inspected families' apartments for unsanitary or dangerous code violations. Teenagers could attract the attention of the police.

It was an old tradition: landlords barring children from their properties. In the competitive postwar housing market of the late 1940s, landlords regularly turned away families with children and evicted tenants who got pregnant.[3] This was evident in letters mothers wrote when applying for public housing. "At present," one wrote, "I am living in an unheated attic room with a one-year-old baby. . . . Everywhere I go the landlords don't want children. I also have a ten-year-old boy. . . . I can't keep him with me because the landlady objects to children. Is there any way that you can help me to get an unfurnished room, apartment, or even an old barn? . . . I can't go on living like this because I am on the verge of doing something desperate." Another mother wrote, "My children are now sick and losing weight. . . . I have tried, begged, and pleaded for a place but [it's] always 'too late' or 'sorry, no children.'" Another wrote, "The lady where I am rooming put two of my children out about three weeks ago and don't want me to let them come back. . . . If I could get a garage I would take it."[4]

When Congress passed the Fair Housing Act in 1968, it did not consider families with children a protected class, allowing landlords to continue openly turning them away or evicting them. Some placed costly restrictions on large families, charging "children-damage deposits" in addition to standard rental fees. One Washington, DC, development required tenants with no children to put down a $150 security deposit but charged families with children a $450 deposit plus a monthly surcharge of $50 per child.[5] In 1980, HUD commissioned a nationwide study to assess the magnitude of the problem and found that only 1 in 4 rental units was available to families without restrictions.[6] Eight years later, Congress finally outlawed housing discrimination against children and families, but as Pam found out, the practice remained widespread.[7] Families with children were turned away in as many as 7 in 10 housing searches.[8]

Ned got out of the car and gave Kristin the rest of his McDonald's breakfast sandwich. "Give Daddy a kiss. I'll be working. Love you." He kissed Pam too.

Pam put her hand to her forehead. "I'm ready to pop."

"Momma? Playground. Play!" Kristin asked from the backseat.

"No, Kristin. Momma's busy looking for a place for us to live."

"How old is the child?" the landlord asked.

"Six."

"Call back next month."

Arleen hung up. She had called on or applied for eighty-two apartments. She had been accepted to none. Even in the inner city, most were out of her reach. And the landlords of the places she could afford if she handed over everything weren't calling back.

Arleen started again, dialing three more numbers. Too expensive. Automated message. "Call back Monday." Arleen was exhausted from rushing to the hospital the night before. She had run out of prednisone, and Jafaris had had an asthma attack. It was hard for Arleen to stay on top of his asthma with so many other things to worry about. Once, she ended a long and fruitless day of apartment hunting with the awful realization that she had left a backpack with Jafaris's breathing equipment at a bus stop. After a day without treatment, Jafaris seemed fine. But two days later, he woke up and told Arleen, "Mommy, I don't feel good." She heard him wheezing and called an ambulance. That time, they had transferred him to Children's Hospital, near the zoo, and kept him overnight. This time, they were able to make it back to the shelter by ten thirty p.m. And the on-call social worker was nice enough to pay for a cab to and from the hospital.

When Number 85 answered the phone, Arleen replied, "Hi! *How* you doing?" instead of "Hi, how *you* doing?" or "Hi, I'm calling about your property." She had been trying different pitches and bending her voice in different directions. She would tell one landlord one thing and another something else. Sometimes she was in a shelter; sometimes she wasn't. Sometimes she had two children; sometimes one. Sometimes they were in child care; sometimes they weren't. Sometimes she received child support; sometimes she didn't. She was grasping, experimenting, trying out altered stories at random. Arleen wouldn't know how to game the system if she wanted to.

"Is there a man in the picture?" Number 85 asked.

"There won't be no man."

"Are you going to have men coming over once in a while?"

"No. It's just me and my son."

"How old is your son?"

Number 86 had wanted $825 a month plus another additional $25 for Jori, but Number 88 had left her with a good feeling.

Number 88 was a large three-story brick building at the end of a dead-end road on Milwaukee's North Side. "I think that at one time it was an institution," the building manager told Arleen. "Could have been an old people's house or something."

Mental ward, Arleen guessed. Inside was clean and quiet. The walls were not off-white or beige but hospital-white, rich-people's-teeth white. Dark wood doors with brass numbers opened into long and low-ceilinged hallways. Arleen and the boys followed the building manager and listened to the squeaks of their shoes. Behind the manager's back, Jori lunged at Jafaris, making him jump, and the boys let out a muffled laugh, which helped shake away the creeps.

"My name is Ali," the building manager said. "It means 'of noble descent.'" A straight-backed black man with a brown kufi, Ali wore beige pants and a matching beige shirt, buttoned to the top. He showed Arleen into the first unit. "I got one or two problem tenants," he said, "but that's it. It's just that some people, they can't get with that Huxtable culture. They more South Central in they culture. And I don't like that culture."

Arleen looked around the apartment, which was decorated with sparse furniture that probably pre-dated *The Cosby Show*.

"You know," Ali continued, "doing life like you supposed to be doing. Paying your bills." He was clearing his throat and speaking stronger now. "In a committed relationship. That's a big one right there. I be on black women. You know, not having no committed relationships, and be Ms. Independent. . . . Let's *bring back* family. If you ain't trying to be about family, then I don't care about sister here, in helping you any sort of way. . . . I'm about family. About what's right and good."

Arleen had been smiling at Ali, and he'd just noticed. He was funny.

"Um, you like this one or you want to see another one?"

"Doesn't even matter. I just need a place."

The rent was $500 for a one-bedroom; the light bill would be in Arleen's name. On the application, next to "Previous landlord?" Arleen wrote, "Sherrena Tarver." Next to "Reasons for moving?" she decided on "Slumlord." Arleen hesitated, then went ahead and asked if cats were allowed.

"They say no pets, but I myself I do like cats. Can't stand dogs. So I might be willing to negotiate on that."

"Well, I'd appreciate it. Um, and we, um." Arleen looked at Jori. She was mostly doing this for him. He understood that, and it showed in his big brown eyes. "Don't cry, Jori, 'cause you about to make me cry!" Jori quickly turned away and walked to the window.

ARLEEN DECIDED TO stop to see her cousin, J.P. She adored J.P.,
with his wide face and easy demeanor. "Let's see if his landlord have
anything," she said. Ali was nice, but he wasn't the one who approved
applications. Arleen also wanted to check in on her son, Boosie, who
had been sleeping at J.P.'s place on Twenty-Sixth Street and Chambers,
which might have been the exact middle of the ghetto.

Not long after Larry walked out, Child Protective Services removed Ger-Ger, Boosie, and Arleen's three other children from her
care. "I just gave up responsibility," Arleen remembered. "That really,
really hurted me when he did that. I wish I was stronger." In the years
that followed, Arleen's children grew up in and out of foster care. "But
Boosie never wanted to come back home," Arleen said. She remembered Boosie calling CPS when he was fifteen, telling a caseworker
that the children had been left alone. "So they came to take my kids
again." She had Jafaris by then. He was two at the time, and Jori was
ten. Both boys would later rejoin Arleen, but Boosie and Arleen's other
two children from Larry remained in the system. Arleen didn't know
why. She did know that their foster families had more money than
she did. They could buy her children new clothes, feed them every
night, and provide them with their own beds to sleep in. But unlike
his younger brother and sister, Boosie didn't stay in the system for
long. When he was seventeen, he left his foster family, dropped out of
high school, and started selling crack.

A dark stairwell opened into the bright apartment. The house
was warm and smelled of eggs and sausage. Boosie was on the couch,
skinny with a backwards cap. After noticing Arleen and the boys, he
grabbed a pellet gun made to look like a .45 and charged toward Jafaris. Boosie stuck the gun in Jafaris's back and tackled him onto a
mattress in an adjoining bedroom, causing someone's copy of *Bastard
Out of Carolina*, folded down to keep a place, to flop on the floor. Jafaris wiggled and laughed but couldn't escape.

"*Man*, have you ever seen a six-year-old more gangsta?" Boosie
laughed, releasing Jafaris and handing him the gun.

Jafaris smiled and inspected the piece.

"A'ight little nigga, gimme back my gun."

Arleen shook her head, and Boosie nodded back at his mother.

Arleen asked J.P. to call his landlord, and he did. The landlord said that the downstairs unit was available. Before leaving, Arleen made an appointment to see it the next day.

"Boosie bogus!" she vented to Jori when they got outside. "As skinny as he is! He either tweakin' or they ain't feeding him." Her face was heavy with a mother's concern. She shook it off. "I can't worry about that now."

"You gonna take it?" Jori asked, hopeful.

Arleen considered the lower unit. "I don't know. There's too much drama over here," she said, thinking about cops and drugs.

Arleen pushed on, staying on the North Side. She passed the simple blue house where her mother had died and the apartments on Atkinson she called "Crackhead City." She stopped by her old condemned house, on Nineteenth and Hampton, squat, quiet, and still half-painted. On the front door a sign was posted: THIS BUILDING IS ILLEGALLY OCCUPIED OR UNFIT FOR HUMAN HABITATION AND SHALL BE VACATED.

"God, I miss living at this house," Arleen said. Jafaris volunteered to check the mail, and Arleen smiled at him. "We ain't got no mail, boo." What forced her to finally call the city was not the water problem. When it didn't work they made do, fetching gallons from a nearby store. But when the landlord finally came over with his toolbox, he sawed holes all over the bathroom walls and did something to the pipes that caused water to leak in. When Arleen called to complain, she remembered him saying, "Well, I've got over fifty properties. If you can't wait, move." That's when Arleen called the building inspector. "Stupid of me."

NED SPENT ALL day on the transmission, and Pam spent all day looking for housing. She called so many numbers that she lost track and phoned landlords who had already told her no. In the fuzz of the afternoon, she dialed the number of the West Allis landlord again. "We don't want your kids, ma'am," he said, annoyed.

Pam decided to try an apartment complex her friend told her was full of "crack and hookers," figuring the landlord didn't do background checks. But the landlord wanted $895 for a three-bedroom unit. Pam couldn't believe it: "To live in this shithole?" It was then that she began looking on the Hispanic South Side. She sighed, "Well, I guess I don't have a choice."

After calling on thirty-eight apartments, Pam had only two appointments to show for it: one in Cudahy, a working-class white suburb whose western border ended at the airport, and another on the South Side. The Cudahy apartment was a two-bedroom place on Packard Avenue. The rent was $640 with heat. Early on in her housing search, Pam had fantasized about finding something for only $500, "in case me and Ned, I mean, who knows what'll happen." But that was close to impossible.[9] Pam would rather have given a landlord everything she had than live on a block where most of her neighbors weren't white.

Ned and Pam waited anxiously outside the Packard Avenue apartment. Ned told Pam to keep her mouth shut and let him do the talking. That was fine with Pam, who was due any day and just wanted to crawl into bed.

"Pray and pray and pray," Pam whispered.

"There ain't no need to pray because there ain't no God up there anyway," Ned said, spitting.

When the landlord arrived, Ned started jawing with him. "I've been in construction for damn near twenty years. . . . You need work doing around here?" The apartment was clean and new, with a huge bedroom in which all the girls could fit. Things seemed to be going well until the landlord asked them to fill out an application. Ned offered cash, but the landlord insisted Ned fill out the form.

"Is it hard to get in?" Ned asked.

"We do a credit check and stuff," the landlord said.

"Well, our credit ain't the greatest."

"That's okay as long as you don't have any *con*-victions or *e*-victions."

The second appointment was on Thirty-Fifth and Becher, on a quiet street in a predominantly Hispanic neighborhood. The landlord was asking $630 for a three-bedroom unit.

"That's okay," Ned said, looking up and down the block. "I can live with the Mexicans. But not with the niggers. They're pigs." He grinned, remembering. "Eh, Pam, what's a name you never want to call a black person? I'll give you a hint, it starts with an *n* and ends with an *r*. . . . Neighbor!"[10]

Ned cackled, and Pam forced a smile. She sometimes bristled at Ned, especially when he said things like this in front of Bliss and Sandra or told them that their curly black hair looked ugly. But it wasn't like Pam felt differently, at least as far as neighborhoods were concerned. "I would rather live in a motel room than live in the ghetto," she said. "At least at the trailer park everybody there was pretty much white. They were trashy white, but still." There were no variations in the ghetto as far as she was concerned. It was one big "black village."

The landlord arrived—a silver-haired man with a large belt buckle—and showed Pam and Ned in. The apartment was gorgeous with polished wood floors, new windows, fresh paint, and spacious bedrooms. Pam looked out the back window to see white children playing in a well-kept backyard. The landlord even offered to "throw in some appliances."

Ned and Pam laughed at Belt Buckle's jokes and started ingratiating themselves to him. "I see you need some concrete work done," Ned said. "I do good work at reasonable prices." Pam joined in, saying she'd be ready in a couple weeks if he was in the market for a cleaning lady.

When it was time to fill out the application, Ned took a different approach. "What's this, credit references?" he asked.

"Just leave them blank," the landlord responded.

"What if we don't have a bank here. We just moved from Green Bay."

"Just leave it blank, then."

After waving goodbye, Pam turned to Ned. "Even if the area's a shithole, at least it's nice, a nice place. We'd be living in an upgrade of a ghetto."

"Maybe I'll get a concrete job outta it?" Ned wondered.

"Maybe I'll get a cleaning job outta it?"

Ned lit a Marlboro Red.

"It really looks like something we could get into," Pam added.

Ned felt the same way. He told Pam to stop copying numbers off rent signs. "Don't worry about it, Pam. We've got a place."

That evening, Travis told Ned and Pam they had to leave. They checked into a cheap motel. Sitting on a scratchy, overwashed comforter on the edge of the bed, Pam breathed slowly and talked to her baby. "Hold off. Until we sign that lease, just hold off." The baby didn't listen. Pam's water broke, and an older woman staying at the motel gave her, Ned, and Kristin a ride to the hospital. The baby weighed seven pounds, ten ounces. Ned thought she was big for a girl. "That's proof that cigarette smoking doesn't cause low birth weight." He laughed. They stayed in the hospital for two nights, on doctor's orders, being charged for a motel room they were using only to hold their things.

Four days after the baby came, Belt Buckle called and told Pam and Ned that their application had been approved. Pam had two evictions on her record, was a convicted felon, and received welfare. Ned had an outstanding warrant, no verifiable income, and a long record that included three evictions, felony drug convictions, and several misdemeanors like reckless driving and carrying a concealed weapon. They had five daughters. But they were white.

Pam would have preferred the Packard Avenue apartment. Even if it was smaller, it was in Cudahy. But that landlord had said no. Their eviction and conviction records pushed them out of white neighborhoods and into an area that families living on the North Side dreamed of moving to.

Ned squandered it. Three days after moving in, he got into a drunken altercation with the upstairs neighbors. The landlord gave them a week to find a new place. That was all the time they needed. Ned found a clean two-bedroom apartment in a working-class white area near Dirky's garage, going for $645. It had a pear tree out front. Ned applied by himself, leaving Pam and her two black daughters off the lease. "People like single dads," he told Pam. The landlord approved him.

"The landlord doesn't know about me or the two girls?" Pam asked.

"Nope, but give it some time. I had to get a house, and I got us this place in a week." Ned raised his hands as if accepting applause. "See, good things happen to good people."

Soon after moving in, a neighbor hooked Ned up with a construction job and Pam began working as a medical assistant. Ned told Bliss and Sandra to tell the landlord they didn't live there, if she ever asked. He told them a lot of things, like: "You're as stupid as your father" and "You're a half-nigger snitch." One day he got a kick out of getting all the girls to march around the house chanting, "White power!"

It emptied Pam out. She prayed it wouldn't hurt the girls in the long run. She prayed for forgiveness, for being a failure of a mother. But she felt that circumstances bound her to Ned. "This is a bad life," she told herself. "We aren't doing crack, but we are still dealing with the same fucking shit. . . . I've never been in a position to leave." The best she could do was to tell her girls, when they were alone, that Ned was the devil. Some nights, before she fell asleep, Pam wondered if she should take her girls to a homeless shelter or under the viaduct. "As long as we're together and we're happy and positive things are said. And I just want to tell them that they're beautiful, 'cause my girls are the strongest little women in the world."

ARLEEN TRIED A large apartment complex on Silver Spring Drive. (Ali, Number 88, never called back.) She dialed the number, and the building manager agreed to show her a unit on the spot.

"We home Jafaris!" Jori yelled, smiling.

"Don't tell him that," Arleen said.

"This is our *home*, man!" Jori joked again, elbowing his brother.

"Stop sayin' that!" This time, Arleen yelled it imploringly.

After another showing, another application, they were back on the sidewalk.

"I'm hungry," Jafaris said.

"Shut up, Jafaris!" Arleen snapped.

After a few minutes, Arleen dug in her pocket, found enough change, and stopped by McDonald's to buy Jafaris some fries.

Near the end of the day, Arleen and the boys made their way to their old place on Thirteenth Street. Arleen had left a pair of shoes there. As they approached the house, they saw Little outside in the snow, pawing at the door. Jori and Jafaris ran to him. Jori picked up Little and handed him to Jafaris, who pulled him in and kissed him.

"Put it down, dang!" Arleen yelled. She jerked Jafaris's arm back, and Little fell to the ground.

When Arleen was alone, she sometimes cried for Little. But she was teaching her sons to love small, to reject what they could not have. Arleen was protecting them, and herself. What other self-defense was there for a single mother who could not consistently provide for her children? If a poor father failed his family, he could leave the way Larry did, try again at some point down the road.[11] Poor mothers—most of them, anyway—had to embrace this failure, to live with it.

Arleen's children did not always have a home. They did not always have food. Arleen was not always able to offer them stability; stability cost too much. She was not always able to protect them from dangerous streets; those streets were her streets. Arleen sacrificed for her boys, fed them as best she could, clothed them with what she had. But when they wanted more than she could give, she had ways, some subtle, others not, of telling them they didn't deserve it. When Jori wanted something most teenagers want, new shoes or a hair product, she would tell him he was selfish, or just bad. When Jafaris cried, Arleen sometimes yelled, "Damn, you hardheaded. Dry yo' face up!" or "Stop it, Jafaris, before I beat yo' ass! I'm tired of your bitch ass." Sometimes, when he was hungry, Arleen would say, "Don't be getting in the kitchen because I know you not hungry"; or would tell him to stay out of the barren cupboards because he was getting too fat.

You could only say "I'm sorry, I can't" so many times before you began to feel worthless, edging closer to a breaking point. So you protected yourself, in a reflexive way, by finding ways to say "No, I won't." I cannot help you. So, I will find you unworthy of help.[12]

Ministers and church ladies, social workers and politicians, teachers and neighbors, police and parole officers throughout the black community would tell you that what you were doing was right, that what these young black boys and girls needed was a stern hand. Do not spare the rod. What began as survival carried forward in the name of culture.[13]

As they walked away from Thirteenth Street and Little and the detritus of their things still scattered in the snow, Jafaris opened his hand to reveal a pair of earrings.

"Where'd you get these from, Jafaris?" Arleen asked.

"Stole 'em from Crystal."

"Oh, wow." A pause, then: "That's not funny, and it's not nice, Jafaris. You hear what I'm saying?" Jafaris's face fell. He just wanted to do something sweet for his momma. Arleen knew this and was touched. She would return the earrings later, but for the moment, she put them on. Jafaris smiled.

They had one more stop to make. As the sky grew inky blue and temperatures fell, Arleen met a white landlord in a flannel shirt and tool belt, fixing up a two-bedroom apartment with such haste and stress Arleen wondered if the inspector was coming the next day. She filled out an application, and Jafaris used the bathroom. It was too late when he discovered the toilet didn't flush. Arleen thanked the landlord and, taking Jafaris by the hand, rushed out.

A few minutes later, her phone rang. "That was very rude!" the landlord was yelling. "And I don't like children like that."

Arleen and her boys could stay in the shelter for twenty-nine more days.

20

NOBODY WANTS THE

NORTH SIDE

The Lodge sat on the corner of Seventh and Vine Streets, near downtown. On most days, residents gathered near the entrance, talking, smoking, and running after their children. That was where Crystal had been spending most of her time since the final days of February. On Crystal's eviction court papers, Sherrena had checked the box next to "the LANDLORD desires the premises for the following reason(s)," writing in: "Causing substantial disturbances with upper and lower tenants (with police involvement). Also, unauthorized subleasing to an evicted tenant." Crystal was confused by the whole process. Could Sherrena call Arleen "unauthorized" when she knew about their arrangement from the start? She packed her things into two clear garbage bags and left without going to court, wrongly assuming that doing so would keep her name clean.

Crystal hated the food at the Lodge, and some of the maintenance men propositioned the residents for sex, offering fresh sheets, snacks, or extra shampoo.[1] But she liked her room. It was warm, clean, and free. Said Crystal, "I ain't paying no five fifty and feel like I'm getting nothing." Plus, she was on the hunt for a new friend, and the Lodge was a great place to find one. It collected under a single roof dozens of people who had found themselves in especially desperate situations, who were all "going through a thing," as shelter residents put it.[2]

People were attracted to Crystal. She was gregarious and funny with an enduring habit of slapping her hands together and laughing at herself. She would saunter out the doors of the Lodge, singing gospel, her hands raised in praise. Crystal had some suitors, but what she wanted most of all from her new friends, and what she had wanted from Arleen, was a mother figure. She found one in Vanetta.

Vanetta Evans had been staying at the Lodge since January. At twenty, she was not much older than Crystal, but she'd grown up fast. Vanetta had her first child, Kendal Jr., when she was sixteen; then a daughter, Tembi, the next year; and a third the year after that: a boy named Bo-Bo. You might say Vanetta was raised in the Robert Taylor Homes, Chicago's infamous public housing towers, or you might say that her mentally challenged mother, whom Vanetta and her siblings unaffectionately called Shortcake, raised her "in almost every homeless shelter in Illinois and Wisconsin." Crystal liked the way Vanetta carried herself. She was always put-together, with her hair pulled back tight in a small ponytail. She even wore her cell phone on a belt holder, like a landlord. Vanetta's dark-brown skin matched Crystal's, and she had a smoky, lounge-singer voice that she almost never raised at her kids. She could snap them in line by giving them the Look. When Kendal Jr. acted up, Vanetta pretended to call Big Kendal, his father, on the phone. The boy knew she was faking but would calm down anyway. When Bo-Bo had seizures, she rushed him to the hospital.[3]

The two women began swapping cigarettes, each keeping mental note of the number of Newports given and received. Soon they upped the ante, taking incremental but expedited steps toward establishing a relationship of reciprocity. They exchanged snacks, then small bills, then meals purchased at fast-food restaurants. Through passing references, they began learning about the other's resources—Vanetta received $673 a month from welfare and $380 in food stamps—as well as their character and temperament. Crystal and Vanetta began calling each other "sister."[4] After a week, they decided to look for housing together. Roommates inside the homeless shelter would become roommates outside of it.

Crystal didn't think she needed to worry about Vanetta's upcoming sentencing hearing. "Prayer is a powerful thing," she said. Vanetta thought her chances of avoiding prison were decent even without Jesus. It was her first offense.

The trouble had started when Old Country Buffet slashed Vanetta's hours. Instead of working five days a week, she would now only work one. Her manager blamed the recession. After that, Vanetta couldn't pay her electricity bill. We Energies threatened disconnection unless she paid $705. There was no way she could pay that and the rent. But she worried that Child Protective Services would take her kids away if her lights and gas were shut off. The thought of losing her children made Vanetta sick to her stomach. Then she fell behind in rent and received an eviction notice. She felt helpless and terrified. Her friend, who had also received the pink papers, felt the same way. One day with Vanetta's boyfriend, the two women sat in a van and watched another pair of women walk into a Blockbuster carrying purses. Someone suggested robbing the women and splitting the money; then all of a sudden, that's what they were doing. Vanetta's boyfriend unloaded his gun and handed it to her friend. The friend ran from the van and pointed the pistol at the women. Vanetta followed, collecting their purses. The cops picked them up a few hours later.[5]

In her confession, Vanetta had said, "I was desperate to pay my bills, and I was nervous and scared and did not want to see my kids in the dark or out on the street." When she turned eighteen, Vanetta had put her name on the list for public housing. Becoming a convicted felon meant that her chances of ever being approved were almost zero.[6]

At her plea hearing, the judge told Vanetta that she could be "subject to a fine of up to a hundred thousand dollars, forty years of imprisonment, or both." Vanetta tried not to think about that. After her hearing, she was fired and then evicted, which was when she took her kids to the Lodge.

CRYSTAL AND VANETTA agreed to look for an apartment exclusively on the Hispanic South Side. When they felt God smiling on them, they even looked in white neighborhoods. They refused to consider the North Side. "It would be nice to get away from these black motherfuckers," Crystal said.[7] They began making daily bus trips to the South Side and calling on rent signs. Even in the age of online apartment listing sites, the humble rent sign remained a visible and effective beacon, especially in minority neighborhoods. Only 15 percent of black renters looking for housing relied on the Internet. By not consulting print or online listings, Crystal and Vanetta constricted their options to what they could see with their own eyes, often from a foggy bus window.[8]

The new friends looked at a small two-bedroom unit but turned down an application when they learned the landlord didn't allow smoking. They hung up when a landlord answered in Spanish. "You want six fifty for a two-bedroom? You outta your mind," Crystal told one landlord. After calling a dozen apartments, Vanetta suggested they try Affordable Rentals. You wouldn't know it from its tiny, storefront office on National Avenue, one of the South Side's main motorways, but Affordable Rentals was a giant in Milwaukee's low-income rental market. The company owned over three hundred rental units and managed almost five hundred more.[9]

"Don't get ghetto in there," Vanetta reminded Crystal as they walked toward the door.

Inside, they put down a deposit and the receptionist behind thick glass handed them a master key so they could inspect the units on their own. The places were small but clean, except for the one with diapers and tires in the backyard. The gem of the bunch was a two-bedroom apartment—with a tub—renting for $445. Vanetta wanted a tub so her kids could take baths. The women rushed back and filled out an application. A paper taped to the wall announced Affordable Rentals' screening criteria:

WE REJECT APPLICANTS FOR THE FOLLOWING REASONS:

1. First time tenants without a cosigner
2. Any evictions within the last 3 years
3. Felony drug or violent crime conviction within the last 7 years
4. Misdemeanor drug or disorderly conduct crime charges within the last 3 years
5. Non-verifiable income or insufficient income
6. Non-verifiable rental history or any bad reference from a previous landlord

Crystal and Vanetta paid no mind to the sign. On their rental application, Vanetta listed her twin brother as a reference. Crystal listed her spiritual mom.

As she waited to hear back from Affordable Rentals, Vanetta wondered if they needed to look at units priced over their $550 limit. But she didn't want to go higher, mainly because she didn't know if Crystal was able to hold on to her money. At the Lodge, Vanetta had watched Crystal spend down her check on clothes, fast food, and even slot machines at the casino. "Girl, I'm gonna punch you in the mouth," Vanetta would vent. A healthy chunk of Crystal's money also went into the offering basket the first Sunday of every month.

"I'm sowing seeds," Crystal said as the women sat down at George Webb. It was Crystal's treat. She had won $450 at Potawatomi Casino the night before, using a $40 birthday present from her foster care agency to play the slots. The waitress brought Crystal the cup of hot water she requested. She slid her silverware in the cup to clean it. "Remember how I explained to you last time? If you a farmer and you plant your seeds for your corn and your vegetables and all that, and you water and take care of it, your crops gonna come. That's how I look at it when I sow seeds in the church. I need something from God. So I sow a seed. . . . I need a house. I need financial breakthrough. I need healing from stuff. I need to be made *whole*. That's how I'm gonna put it."

Vanetta held her chilled look. "That's why I don't creep with your church, 'cause they don't have nothing to offer you, but they got a lot to say. And I don't like that. And then you go to them and tell them the situation that's going on, and it's like they don't care."

Crystal looked at her food. "I dunno," she said. "It's, I'm just waiting to move." She tried to change the subject. "That cheesecake bangin'."

But Vanetta was not through. "Don't ball up your face," she said. "Motherfuckers smile in your face when you tithe."

"Nuh-uh!" Crystal shook her head.

"You be throwing all that money in they basket! Don't say 'nuh-uh' 'cause I seen it when I went Sunday."

Vanetta knew how much Crystal's church meant to her. She had heard Crystal run on about Minister Barber and the bishops and the Holy Ghost and all that. She had watched Crystal take herself to church on Sundays, Tuesdays, Fridays, and sometimes Saturdays for special services. If the congregation at Mt. Calvary Pentecostal wasn't Crystal's family, who was? But Crystal's church was Vanetta's biggest competition. Every seed Crystal sowed in the offering basket left Vanetta with less money for their budding household. Vanetta didn't know if what she'd said had penetrated until later that day, when she came upon Crystal crying into her phone and praying in tongues: "*Eeh Shanta. Eeh Shanta.*"

When late afternoon arrived, Vanetta had to be back for her GED class. "Don't go," said Crystal.

"I can't miss. I want that diploma," Vanetta answered.

"You can't miss?"

"Only in a real emergency."

"Bitch, you looking for housing. This *is* a real emergency."

Vanetta smiled and left.

Crystal was supposed to continue the housing search, but she decided to stop by her church instead. Mt. Calvary Pentecostal Church was on Sixtieth and National, on the far Southwest Side of the city but still accessible by bus. It was a handsome brick building with stained-glass windows and rain gutters painted fire-engine red. It was Monday night, so the church's food pantry was open.

Crystal picked up a bag of groceries and accepted a hot dog from her minister. Bishop Dixon teased Crystal about texting during the service, and Crystal countered by asking the old man if his teeth ever fell out when he was giving the blessing. She told Sister Atalya to bring her dog to church. "Why not? Maybe she can get the Word too." They laughed. Elder Johnson was there, in a preachy mood. "If we really got Jesus in our souls," he said, "I'm supposed to be able to feel your pain, and you're supposed to be able to feel my pain."

Elder Johnson didn't feel Crystal's pain. It wasn't that he didn't care, like Vanetta thought; it was that he didn't know. Elder Johnson, Bishop Dixon, Sister Atalya—none of them knew Crystal was staying at the Lodge. Only Minister Barber knew. Crystal didn't want members of her church to reduce her, to see her as an object of pity, a member of "the poor and the orphaned." She wanted to be seen as Sister Crystal, part of the Body, the Beloved. Crystal received a bag of food once in a while; and congregants had opened their homes to her for a night or two. But her church was in no way equipped to meet Crystal's high-piled needs.[10] What her church could offer was *the peace*.

"What's your favorite verse, Sister?" Elder Johnson asked. He had seen Crystal lift one of the nearby Bibles.

"Don't be trying to put me on the spot." She smiled. Then she said, " 'Though He slay me, yet will I trust Him.' "

CRYSTAL AND VANETTA kept looking for a place to live. Sometimes Vanetta took her kids with her; sometimes she took them to the day care or to stay with her older sister, Ebony. Vanetta had them with her when she and Crystal visited their thirty-second apartment, on

Fifteenth Street and Madison. The landlord stepped out of his Saab and opened the door to a small two-bedroom unit. The showing was scheduled in the evening because the landlord had a government day job in Madison. He was a well-fed Puerto Rican man in pleated slacks and a dress shirt.

The place was small, dumpy, and without a bathtub. After a walk-through, Vanetta asked the landlord if he had any other units with tubs. He said he did and began describing another apartment. It was bigger and somewhat nicer than the place he was showing Vanetta and Crystal, but the rent was the same. Then, suddenly, as if forgetting something, the man stopped himself. His hand went for his pocket, and he answered his cell phone. It was obvious to Vanetta and Crystal that no one had called, but he pretended to have a conversation. Hanging up, the landlord said that it had been his partner on the other line and that he had just rented out the bigger and nicer unit.

The women stood outside and watched the Saab pull away. Crystal reached for her old MP3 player and put in headphones. Vanetta was shaking. "I'm so angry," she whispered.

"*Get it together, you have to heal your heart,*" Crystal sang, eyes closed, swaying back and forth.

"He just like, 'Oh, they black. They trash the place anyways.'" Vanetta wiped a tear away with a quick swipe and sucked in her quivering bottom lip. Her kids looked up at her, confused.

"*Get it together, you can fly, fly,*" Crystal lifted her voice.

Most Milwaukeeans believed their city was racially segregated because people preferred it that way. But the ghetto had always been more a product of social design than desire.[11] It was never a by-product of the modern city, a sad accident of industrialization and urbanization, something no one benefited from nor intended. The ghetto had always been a main feature of landed capital, a prime moneymaker for those who saw ripe opportunity in land scarcity, housing dilapidation, and racial segregation.

Maybe it began in the late fifteenth century, the weaponry of war to blame. With the invention of the iron cannonball, cities could no longer rely on moats and modest ramparts to fend off attack. Complicated systems of defense had to be constructed and cities had to grow vertically behind high walls. Old Geneva and Paris saw tenements climb six stories. Edinburgh boasted of tenements twice as high. While agrarian families were driven from the land to increasingly congested cities, the competition for space drove up land values and rents. Urban landlords quickly realized that piles of money could be made by creating slums: "maximum profits came, not from providing first-class accommodations for those who could well afford them . . . but from crowded slum accommodations, for those whose pennies were scarcer than the rich man's pounds."[12] Beginning in the sixteenth century, slum housing would be reserved not only for outcasts, beggars, and thieves but for a large segment of the population.

During its rapid period of urbanization, America imported this model. Colonial proprietors adopted the institutions and laws of England's landed gentry, including the doctrine of absolute liability for rent, which held tenants unequivocally responsible for payments even in the event of fire or flood. Throughout the eighteenth and nineteenth centuries, America's poor lived in cellars, attics, cattle sheds, and windowless rooms that held multiple families.[13] Some slums were cut off from basic municipal services and local wells; so families begged for water in other parts of town.[14] Rents continued to rise as living conditions deteriorated. Soon, many families could not afford their housing. When this happened, landlords could summon the "privilege of distress," which entitled them to seize and sell tenants' property to recover lost profit, a practice that persisted well into the twentieth century.[15]

Racial oppression enabled land exploitation on a massive scale. During slavery, black slaves pulled profit from the dirt but had no claim to the land. After the Civil War, freed slaves saw in landownership the possibility of true liberation, but during Reconstruction wealthy whites maintained a virtual monopoly on the soil as lands seized from or abandoned by Confederates were restored to their original owners. Returning to plantations as sharecroppers, black families descended into a cycle of subsistence farming and debt, while white planters continued to grow rich.[16] The slave shacks stood, and so did the plantation mansions.

In the early decades of the twentieth century, African-American families seeking freedom and good jobs participated in the Great Migration, moving en masse from the rural South to cities like Chicago, Philadelphia, and Milwaukee. When they arrived in those cities, they were crowded into urban ghettos, and the vast majority depended on landlords for housing.[17] Ghetto landlords had a segregated and captive tenant base and had nothing to gain by improving their run-down houses. They began dividing their properties into small "kitchenette" units, throwing up so many plywood walls their apartments resembled "rabbit warrens." Many houses lacked heating and complete plumbing. So black families cooked and ate in winter coats and relieved themselves in outhouses or homemade toilets.[18] They came to know well the sound of the tuberculosis cough. In 1930, the death rate for Milwaukee's blacks was nearly 60 percent higher than the citywide rate, due in large part to poor housing conditions.[19] For the first time in the history of America, New Deal policies made homeownership a real possibility for white families, but black families were denied these benefits when the federal government deemed their neighborhoods too risky for insured mortgages and officials loyal to Jim Crow blocked black veterans from using GI mortgages.[20] Over three centuries of systematic dispossession from the land created a semipermanent black rental class and an artificially high demand for inner-city apartments.[21]

In the 1950s, white real estate brokers developed an advanced technique of exploitation, one that targeted black families shut out of the private housing market. After buying houses on the cheap from nervous white homeowners in transitioning neighborhoods, private investors would sell these houses "on contract" to black families for double or triple their assessed value. Black buyers had to come up with sizeable down payments, often upwards of 25 percent of the property's

inflated value. Once they moved in, black families had all the responsibilities of home ownership without any of the rights. When families
missed payments, which many did after monthly installments were
increased or necessary housing upkeep set them back, they could be
evicted as their homes were foreclosed and down payments pocketed.
The profits were staggering. In 1966, a Chicago landlord told a court
that on a single property he had made $42,500 in rent but paid only
$2,400 in maintenance. When accused of making excessive profits,
the landlord simply replied, "That's why I bought the building."[22]

The 1968 Civil Rights Act made housing discrimination illegal,
but subtler forms prevailed. Crystal and Vanetta wanted to leave the
ghetto, but landlords like the one on Fifteenth Street turned them
away. Other landlords and property management companies—like
Affordable Rentals—tried to avoid discriminating by setting clear cri-
teria and holding all applicants to the same standards. But equal treatment in an unequal society could still foster inequality. Because black
men were disproportionately incarcerated and black women disproportionately evicted, uniformly denying housing to applicants with recent criminal or eviction records still had an incommensurate impact
on African Americans. When Crystal and Vanetta heard back from
Affordable Rentals, they learned their application had been rejected on
account of their arrest and eviction history.

Eviction itself often explained why some families lived on safe
streets and others on dangerous ones, why some children attended
good schools and others failing ones. The trauma of being forced from
your home, the blemish of an eviction record, and the taxing rush to
locate a new place to live pushed evicted renters into more depressed
and dangerous areas of the city.[23] This reality had not yet set in for
Vanetta and Crystal. They were just coming out of the first, fresh-
feeling phase of house hunting. It was only after they had tried for over
fifty apartments that Crystal and Vanetta began reluctantly scouting
in the inner city. The new friends were circling back to the ghetto but
not fully committing to it.

CRYSTAL HAD BEEN working to keep her emotions in check. It was why she chose to stop by church Monday night instead of looking for housing. It was why she grabbed her music and sang after the incident with the landlord on Fifteenth Street. "This is too much, too much stress. But I'm not gonna make myself sick," she said. When Crystal finally did blow up, it was at one of the shelter's maintenance men, over clean linens he refused to supply. She was already in trouble for sleeping through a mandatory job training. Crystal blamed her sleep apnea. After the altercation with the maintenance man, Crystal was told to be out by breakfast the next morning.

Crystal spent the following day on the phone, trying to find someone who would open their doors to her. With no luck and night coming on, she sighed and called Minister Barber, who found an older couple in the congregation who agreed to help. Crystal spent the night in their La-Z-Boy recliner.

The following evening, after Bible study at Mt. Calvary, Crystal returned to the elderly couple's house. Rain was falling hard onto dark, empty streets. It was that icy, bitter rain that comes when winter first begins to thaw into spring. Crystal knocked, and the husband cracked the door without unlatching the chain. The house was on Fourteenth and Burleigh, in one of the most crime-ridden areas of the city. Seeing Crystal, the man kept the chain taut, handed over a small bag of Crystal's things, and shut the door.

Crystal figured it was because she didn't "hit their hand." But she didn't have any money to give, having lent one of her cousins $400, mostly from her casino winnings. Her cousin needed rent money. When Vanetta heard about that, she said, "Crystal, if I was there I would have smacked the *mess* outta you! You don't have a place to stay yourself. I don't care if they your family or not, you been homeless for a grip, and you need a roof over your own head."

Sometimes Crystal couldn't help herself, like the time she and

Vanetta were eating lunch at McDonald's, and a boy walked in. He was maybe nine or ten in dirty clothes and with unkempt hair. One side of his face was swollen. The boy didn't approach the counter. Instead, he wandered slowly through the tables, looking for scraps.

Crystal and Vanetta noticed him. "What you got?" Crystal asked, riffling through her pockets. The women pooled what they had to buy the boy dinner. Staring up at the menu, Crystal wrapped her arm around the boy like she was his big sister. She made sure he was okay, handed him the food, and sent him away with a hug.

"Reminds me of when we was kids," Vanetta said, shaken.

Crystal watched the boy dash across the street. "I wish I had me a house. I would take him in."

On Burleigh Street, the wind-pushed rain fell sideways in sheets. In the yellow beam of the streetlight, it looked like an unending school of silvery fish darting through the light before disappearing into the surrounding pool of darkness. Crystal considered her phone. It was almost eleven o'clock at night. She dialed a number. Her cousin who owed her didn't pick up. She dialed a number. Her foster-care mother said her house was full. She dialed a number. She dialed and dialed and dialed and dialed.

21.

BIGHEADED BOY

Sherrena had Lamar and Kamala's torched building bulldozed. She used the insurance money to buy two new duplexes, doubling the units she had lost to the fire. When the Hinkstons looked out their back window, all they saw was a vacant lot. The only remaining visible reminder of that night was a makeshift memorial Kamala and her family set up: stuffed animals and photographs tied to a tree with a cotton sash cord. The most prominent photograph showed the baby in an Easter dress, her calm eyes large in her small face. For the animals, they had selected rabbits, bears, a goose, a raccoon, and a hippopotamus. Candles in glass vases and Coke cans circled the base of the tree.

Natasha was sorting through a garbage bag of baby clothes a friend had picked up at a church pantry. She moved her hands tenderly and smiled at each miniature item. The idea of becoming a mother was growing on her.

"I want my baby to have my looks," Natasha said. "I don't want my baby lookin' like Malik. He got some big ol' buck eyes."

"You so mean!" Doreen said.

"He all *black*."

Overhearing, Patrice came into the dining room, wearing her Cousins Subs uniform. "Your baby gonna come out lookin' like a whole lotta folks," she teased.

"No!" Natasha laughed.

Patrice sighed and changed the subject. "We got to do something about this toilet, fam." The toilet was stopped up again. So was the kitchen sink, brimming with gray water lined with a rust-orange film. Periodically, someone would bucket it out. This made washing difficult, and dirty pots and plates began accumulating on the counter. So did more roaches and other bugs.

Doreen didn't call Sherrena about the plumbing. She didn't want a lecture and figured she wouldn't help anyway, since they were still behind. She didn't call a plumber either. Even if she could come up with the money, that would feel too much like helping Sherrena, and nobody was interested in doing that, especially after the courthouse letter Patrice had received a few days back. It said she owed $2,494.50—the result of her second and third causes hearing.[1]

"I live in that house for four months," Patrice had said. "She said I owe her twenty-four hundred dollars!"

"That means you didn't pay any rent at all," Doreen said.

"Nah! Now you just making up stuff." Patrice stared at the bill. She thought she owed more like $900.

"What are you gonna do?"

"I don't know what I *can* do."

The Hinkstons expected more of their landlord for the money they were paying her. Rent was their biggest expense by far, and they wanted a decent and functional home in return. They wanted things to be fixed when they broke. But if Sherrena wasn't going to repair her own property, neither were they. The house failed the tenants, and the tenants failed the house.[2]

The worse the Hinkstons' house got, the more everyone seemed to become withdrawn and lethargic, which only deepened the problem.

Natasha started spending more time at Malik's. Doreen stopped cooking, and the children ate cereal for dinner. Patrice slept more. The children's grades dropped, and Mikey's teacher called saying he might have to repeat, mainly because of so many missed homework assignments. Everyone had stopped cleaning up, and trash spread over the kitchen floor. Substandard housing was a blow to your psychological health: not only because things like dampness, mold, and overcrowding could bring about depression but also because of what living in awful conditions told you about yourself.

It was once said that the poor are "constantly exposed to evidence of their own irrelevance."[3] Especially for poor African American families—who live in neighborhoods with rates of violence and concentrated poverty so extreme that even the worst white neighborhoods bear little resemblance—living in degrading housing in dangerous neighborhoods sent a clear message about where the wider society thought they belonged.[4] "Honestly, this place is a shack," Doreen once said. Not long after that, Ruby came through the door and announced that "a man just got killed right in front of the store." Growing up in a shack in the ghetto meant learning how to endure such an environment while also learning that some people never had to. People who were repulsed by their home, who felt they had no control over it, and yet had to give most of their income to it—they thought less of themselves.[5]

The older children found some reprieve from the apartment in the public library on Center Street. C.J., Ruby, and Mikey liked playing on the computer best. Ruby would begin her time there by checking in on "her house," which she had gradually built up and improved through a free online game called Millsberry, a marketing tool created by General Mills. Her house was located on Bounty Drive in Golden Valley. It had clean, light-reflecting floors, a bed with sheets *and* pillowcases, and a desk for doing schoolwork. Doreen or Patrice could have walked to the library and searched for new housing on the Internet. But they never did. This was partially because paying Sherrena back meant they didn't have enough money to move; partially because like most black renters they didn't search for housing online; and partially because the family had sunk into a hazy depression.

Patrice could feel the house sucking their energy. "We just hit a mud hole with this house," she said. "No one's trying to get better. Makes me not want to get better. If you're around people every day that doesn't want to do anything, eventually you will feel like doing nothing." Tennessee was sounding better to her by the day.

WHEN IT WAS time, Malik rushed from work to meet Natasha at the hospital: Wheaton Franciscan–St. Joseph Campus, on Chambers and Forty-Ninth Street. She looked ready and scared. She clutched the bed railing with one hand and Malik's hand with the other. When Malik would try to stand up, Natasha would pull him back down. He would smile and rub her back. She focused on her breathing, just like they had practiced in birthing class. Doreen watched knowingly from the rocking chair, arms folded over her stomach.

The baby came at 11:10 p.m., weighing eight pounds, three ounces. He was round-faced with a full shock of hair, pinkish-brown skin, and a broad Hinkston nose.

As she lay sleeping the next morning, Natasha heard Patrice whisper "Hey, Momma" in her ear. She smiled before opening her eyes.

When the baby stirred, he was passed around, though Natasha had a hard time letting him go. All day long, she lifted him to her and kissed him softly on the nose and forehead. Patrice noticed Malik's proud face and decided then and there to name the baby Malik Jr.

The next day, Natasha swaddled her tiny, cherished boy and took him back to the rat hole.

22.

IF THEY GIVE MOMMA

THE PUNISHMENT

In April, Vanetta hid candy Easter eggs around the Lodge for her children to find. Kendal let Tembi and Bo-Bo collect them. Sometimes, the boy already seemed finished with childhood. At four years old, he refused to hold Vanetta's hand and didn't like singing in his preschool class. A handsome boy, with pinched lips and espresso-colored eyes, he intuited that his momma had enough to worry about. This, of course, made Vanetta worry.

A few days before Easter, Tembi pulled the fire alarm. When management found out who was responsible, they told Vanetta she had to be out the next day. Vanetta didn't waste much time protesting. She headed straight for the heart of the ghetto and began calling on apartments. She called on every rent sign she saw, regardless of the condition of the house or the neighborhood. She toured a dirty apartment with cracks down the walls and grease on the ceiling on a block with abandoned homes and gang graffiti. She hated it and filled out an application.

"Girl, you got put out because of yo' kids?" Crystal asked. That cold night on the porch, Crystal had finally gotten ahold of a cousin, who allowed her to spend the night. After that, Crystal began sleeping in the waiting room of Wheaton Franciscan, which she called "St. Joseph's Hospital," and the newly remodeled Amtrak station, downtown, where she tried blending in with waiting passengers. One day at a bus stop, she met a woman named Patricia. They were roommates by day's end. Crystal needed a place to stay, and Patricia, who had been plotting to toss her abusive husband, needed an income to replace his. Patricia was twice Crystal's age, with a teenage daughter and a single-family home in one of the quieter sections of the North Side. Crystal began calling Patricia "Mom."[1]

The next day, Vanetta checked out of the Lodge and took her things to her older sister's apartment. Ebony lived on Orchard Street, a residential street near the Hispanic Mission, in a small three-bedroom upper with her husband, three kids, and Vanetta's younger sister. The place was cluttered and worn, with a stained beige carpet, mattresses in almost every room, and a small kitchen tucked in the back. Vanetta wasn't planning on staying long. She gave her sister $50, moved her kids into one of the small bedrooms, and headed downtown to the courthouse for D'Sean's re-confinement hearing.

D'Sean was Bo-Bo's father, and Vanetta thought she loved him. He was a good dad when he wasn't drinking. The police had picked him up six months earlier for a parole violation linked to a drug-possession charge. As the judge weighed the facts of the case, he cited several 911 calls Vanetta had made when D'Sean got rough. "And then on October 10, a call from Vanetta Evans. And then on October 19, another call from Ms. Evans." Mortified, Vanetta put her hands in her face and cried. She remembered those calls and what had happened after she kicked D'Sean out. He returned later, drunk, smashed the door down, and beat her. After that incident, Vanetta remembered the landlord taking her rent money with one hand and handing her a twenty-eight-day "no cause" eviction notice with the other. At the re-confinement hearing, the judge gave D'Sean eighteen months. Vanetta almost never drank, but that night she bought a bottle of New Amsterdam gin and passed out next to her children.

She slept through Crystal's phone call. So Crystal hung up and dialed her cousins and foster sisters. Her arrangement with Patricia had come undone. Patricia's fourteen-year-old daughter had taken Crystal's cell phone to school and either lost or sold it. Crystal demanded compensation, but Patricia refused to pay. "I'm gonna get you out of my house!" Patricia yelled, drunk on wine mixed with E&J Brandy. Crystal called her people for backup. They waited in the car. The women took their argument outside, and Patricia lost her balance and fell to the ground. Staring down, Crystal lifted her foot and brought it down on Patricia's face—again and again. Seeing this, one of Crystal's sisters ran up and hit Patricia with a hammer. "Bitch, try it again!" she yelled before pulling Crystal away. In pain, Patricia lay still on the sidewalk, in a fetal position. Crystal asked to be dropped off at St. Joseph's Hospital, where she spent the night.[2]

AFTER TRYING FOR seventy-three places, Vanetta and Crystal were approved for a $500-a-month two-bedroom apartment. Desperate tenants willing to overlook neglected repairs had found a desperate landlord willing to overlook evictions and convictions. The apartment's wood floors were sticky with grime, the front door didn't lock properly, and the bedrooms were so small they couldn't hold much more than a twin bed. In the kitchen, the sink was clogged, the floor tiles were chipped, and there was a wall of cabinets sealed shut with laminating paper. There were empty spaces where a stove and refrigerator once had been. There was, however, a tub. And the place was on Seventh and Maple, on the near South Side: you could see St. Stanislaus's twinned steeples from the kitchen window. Vanetta thought it was a dangerous block. She had known the drug dealer on the corner since childhood. "It's wretched, but I'm tired of looking," Vanetta said. "I don't want to take it . . . but it's the only option I got."

The new friends moved into the apartment with a few garbage

bags of clothes and toys between them. Crystal had left most of her things at Patricia's and considered them gone for good. The only piece of furniture in the place was an old upholstered rocking chair someone had left behind.

Vanetta and Crystal's plan was to stay for a year. But not long after moving in, Clara, a woman Crystal and Vanetta knew from the Lodge, came over and used up Crystal's cell-phone minutes. So Crystal put her through one of the apartment's windows. When the cops showed up, Crystal made herself a couple of sandwiches for the road. Vanetta used most of what she had saved at the shelter to pay for the shattered window—and told Crystal not to come back. It was the only way the landlord would allow Vanetta and her children to stay.

A few days later, Child Protective Services called Ebony's apartment, asking for Vanetta.[3] When Ebony called Vanetta to warn her, Vanetta suspected Crystal. "I'm gonna kill that bitch," she vented to Shortcake. "Do you know that bitch called social services on me!"

"You poured salt on her. Now she's gonna pour salt on you," Shortcake said.

"She pouring salt on my kids!" Vanetta cried.

The news about CPS had unnerved Vanetta. She didn't think they would allow her children to stay in an apartment with no stove or refrigerator. Vanetta was broke, but she went to a used-appliances corner store anyway. Spanish music played over a clutter of used dishwashers, dryers, and other appliances. The owner, Mr. Rodriguez, a pudgy Mexican man with thick hair, identified different units piled in his small store with a stick resembling a teacher's pointer.

"How much is your cheapest stove and cheapest refrigerator?" Vanetta asked.

"Baking? No baking?" Rodriguez asked with a thick accent.

Vanetta shook her head no. She would be fine with a nonworking oven.

Rodriguez poked his stick in the direction of a small gas stove.

"How much?" Vanetta asked.

"Ninety."

She shook her head no again. "Too high. How much?"

Rodriguez shrugged.

They went back and forth until Vanetta talked Rodriguez down to $80 including the hose piece, which he had wanted to sell separately. She found a refrigerator somewhere else and talked the guy down to $60. She borrowed the money from a friend, promising to pay it back the first of the month, and finished the day shopping at Aldi. At the checkout counter, she placed the ice-cream sandwiches and other junk food at the end of the conveyor belt in case she ran out of food stamps and needed to put something back.

After unloading the groceries, Vanetta slumped down exhausted in the rocking chair and lit a cigarette. If CPS came knocking, she was ready for them.

Then other thoughts drifted in. She was still undecided about who she wanted to care for her children if she was sent to prison for the robbery. Lately, she was leaning toward a woman from her children's day care. "I might go crazy, but I know they be taken care of," Vanetta told herself. Then there was Kendal's upcoming preschool graduation. Vanetta wanted to somehow find money to buy him a new pair of shoes for the big day. She wanted him to feel special, accomplished. In the inner city, much was made of early milestones. Later ones might never come.

THE MORNING OF her sentencing hearing, Vanetta roused her children, fed and dressed them, and began re-ironing her outfit on the living-room floor. Besides installing the stove and refrigerator, she hadn't been able to do much else in the apartment, and it felt empty, unlived-in. Kendal joined Vanetta in the living room, standing with his hands at his sides in the tawny glow of the morning. She had dressed him in a red-collared shirt and his new shoes. A few feet away, a picture of him at his preschool graduation, in a cap and gown, was displayed on the mantel.

"Momma," Kendal said, "kids aren't supposed to go to court. They're supposed to go to day care and school." He wasn't pouting. He was observing some strangeness in the world, a misalignment. He could have been saying, "Dogs aren't supposed to like cats," or "It's not supposed to snow in April."

Vanetta put down the iron and took a breath. "Kendal, will you come to court with me?" she asked, just as she had the night before.

Kendal saw that she needed him. "Momma, I *will* go to court with you," he said decisively.

"If they give Momma the punishment, what you supposed to do?"

"Stick together, take care of my sister and brother, and listen to my *titi*."

At the last minute, Vanetta had decided to ask her sister to care for her kids if she was sent away. She couldn't say why.

Vanetta arrived at court early, quietly shaking under a conservative black sweater and matching slacks. She had put on makeup and earrings and had pulled her hair tight around her head. She paced the hallway, trying to think of what she would say to the judge, periodically stopping to watch the ponderous gait of shackled black men in orange prison uniforms. Shortcake showed up in a knit cap and winter coat, along with Vanetta's twin brother and younger sister. Ebony stayed home and watched Tembi, Bo-Bo, and the rest of the kids. Later, the preacher's wife and another white woman from the All Bible Baptist Church, Vanetta's congregation, would join them in knit sweaters and thick glasses.

When it was time, Vanetta took a seat next to her public defender, a foot-tapping white man in a plain black suit. The courtroom didn't look like the kind you see on television, those open-air theaters with balconies, large ceiling fans, and people crowded into wooden pews. It was a small space, separated from the audience by a thick wall of glass. Ceiling speakers broadcast court proceedings to onlookers.

The prosecution went first, represented by a fit, pink-faced assistant district attorney with thinning hair and trimmed beard. Many things about Vanetta impressed him. She had not been arrested before and had "some employment history." "She apparently attended school into the eleventh grade. That is better education, as sad as that is, that's better education than many of the defendants that we see." He continued, "She has family support. That's good. . . . Unfortunately, that same level of emotional and family support was available at the time of this offense, and by itself wasn't sufficient. . . . I don't doubt that the decision was driven by desperation, but the fact that it was desperation does not minimize its impact on the victims." One of the victims didn't carry a purse anymore and didn't feel safe in her neighborhood, the prosecutor reported. "It is the state's view that people need to know when you use a gun to take things from other people, you go to prison."

Vanetta's public defender spoke next, offering a sprawling but impassioned case for leniency. Vanetta was remorseful, he said, and had confessed to the crime. She was younger and "less street smart" than her accomplices. Her friend had held the gun. It was a crime of mean circumstances. "I believe punishment can be accomplished in a community setting," the public defender concluded. "I don't believe that you have to send her away."

It was Vanetta's turn to speak next. She "took full responsibility" for her actions and apologized to the victims and the Court. "At the time of this situation, me and my kids were going through a difficult time in our lives and on the verge of being evicted and our lights being cut off. I was overwhelmed by the difficulties. But this doesn't excuse what I have done. . . . At this time I'm asking for leniency for me but, especially, for my children."

Then it was time for people to speak on Vanetta's behalf. The preacher's wife said, "I have observed in her a quiet calmness in the midst of trying circumstances." Shortcake offered four sentences. Vanetta's twin brother said that they "had just made twenty-one" and that his sister's children needed to wake up to their mother, not to their aunties and uncles.

Finally, it was the judge's turn. An older white man, he began to recap what he had just heard. "So this was a general discussion about the nature of this offense, basically, that it was an aberration . . . a crime of desperation. I look at that. But I'm also mindful of the fact that between then and now nothing has really changed. . . . I'm saying that the overall economic situation hasn't improved. Has it, Counsel?"

"No," the public defender answered. He had argued that Vanetta had been looking for work. He hadn't pointed out that Vanetta rose at five each morning but still had little time to find a job between searching for a new place to live, attending GED classes, and caring for her children—or that employers usually did not hire people who had recently confessed to committing a felony.

"No," the judge repeated. "And, quite honestly, I don't know that it got any better after that time, maybe a little worse, based upon what's occurred and the fact that she's kicked around and moved around."

What the judge was saying, in essence, was: We all agree that you were poor and scared when you did this violent, hurtful thing, and if you had been allowed to go on working five days a week at Old Country Buffet, refilling soup pots and mopping up frozen yogurt spills, none of us would be here right now. You might have been able to save enough to move to an apartment that was de-leaded and clean in a neighborhood without drug dealers and with safe schools. With time, you may have been able to get Bo-Bo the medical treatment he needs for his seizures, and maybe you could have even started taking night classes to become a nurse, like you always wanted. And, who knows, maybe you could have actually *become* a nurse, a real nurse with a uniform and everything. Then you could really give your kids a childhood that would look nothing like the one Shortcake gave you. If you did that, you would walk around this cold city with your head held high, and maybe you would eventually come to feel that you were worth something and deserving of a man who could support you other than by lending you his pistol for a stickup or at least one who didn't break down your door and beat you in front of your children. Maybe you would meet someone with a steady job and get married in a small church with Kendal standing proudly up front by the groom and Tembi as the poofy-dressed flower girl and Bo-Bo as the grinning, toddling ring bearer, just like you always dreamed it, and from that day on your groom would introduce you as "my *wife*." But that's not what happened. What happened was that your hours were cut, and your electricity was about to be shut off, and you and your children were about to be thrown out of your home, and you snatched someone's purse as your friend pointed a gun at her face. And if it was poverty that caused this crime, who's to say you won't do it again? Because you were poor then and you are poor now. We all see the underlying cause, we see it every day in this court, but the justice system is no charity, no jobs program, no Housing Authority. If we cannot pull the weed up from the roots, then at least we can cut it low at the stem."

The judge sighed, and a silent moment passed. The court stenographer steadied her hands above the keys and waited. Kendal, asleep on Shortcake's lap, breathed noiselessly. The judge ruled: "This is not . . . a probationary case. I am going to impose eighty-one months in the state prison system. It's going to break down to fifteen months of initial confinement and sixty-six months of extended supervision."

The bailiff approached Vanetta and told her to stand to be handcuffed.

"Oh, God," Shortcake let out. She shook Kendal awake and took him to the glass. "Wave goodbye, son."

Hands behind her back, Vanetta turned around, tears streaming down her cheeks. Kendal stared back stone-faced, strong, just like his momma had taught him.

AFTER GETTING INTO several conflicts with congregants, bishops, and eventually her minister, Crystal left Mt. Calvary and joined Restoration International Ministries, an inner-city church in a bland two-story office building on Forty-First and Burleigh.

One Sunday, Crystal sat in the third pew from the front and began clapping with the music. She wore a black shirt and green pants, unbuttoned and unzipped halfway to fit. The pastor, a black woman with hair falling in arching waves down to her shoulders, wore a white robe with gold accents. She paced with a queen's authority, stopping as the spirit led her. "God says He is the truth and the light," she said. The young man at the piano fluttered his hands, and the even younger fellow behind the drums began teasing a cymbal. "The truth! And the—*light*! You *hearing* me?"

"Amen," Crystal said. After being kicked out of her apartment with Vanetta, Crystal was admitted to a homeless shelter. Then through a weary, looping rhythm—make a friend, use a friend, lose a friend—Crystal found, for short bursts, dry and warm places to sleep. When those bridges burned, she dropped back into street homelessness, returning to St. Joseph's or the Amtrak station. Sometimes she would walk the streets all night and sleep on the bus once morning broke. But through it all, she almost never missed church.

"*Sha la la la YABA SHO TA tama ma ma,*" the pastor prayed into a microphone. The language of tongues was spoken in a cadence the shape of a heartbeat: a small entrance, followed by a spike, then a quivering trailing off. "Are you in the press? Are you squeezing yourself up into the crowd to see Jesus? Whoa!" She stumbled back as if bumped by an invisible force.

"All right, pastor!" Crystal hollered. Crystal had always believed that SSI was a more secure income source than a paycheck. You couldn't get fired from SSI; your hours couldn't get cut. "SSI always come," she said. Until one day it didn't. She had been approved for SSI as a minor, but her adult reevaluation found her ineligible. Now Crystal's only source of income came from food stamps.[4] She tried donating plasma but her veins were too small. She asked her spiritual, foster, and even biological mothers for money, but what they could give her didn't go very far. She didn't ask anything from her church because "it always led to conflict." Because she didn't know what else to do, Crystal went "on the stroll" and began selling sex. She had never been a morning person but soon learned that it was the best time to turn tricks, catching men on their way to work.

"Is Momma okay?" the pastor asked. She was looking at an older woman being held up by two people.

"No."

"Then we gonna stop everything and *pray* for her." The pastor knelt down in front of the woman. A dozen or so churchgoers surrounded her, some standing on chairs, some with their hands on the old woman's head. "Reach out your hands this way and pray!" the pastor commanded, and her congregation obeyed, even the children. "Oh, Jesus!" the pastor yelled into the microphone. "Oh, by the blood, oh you death spirit, you stroke spirit, come out!"

Crystal was bouncing and moving her hands from shoulders to hips, chanting, "By your stripes, Lord, by your stripes."

"By the blood," prayed the pastor. "The blood! *ShabbabmaSHOT-tala!* I bind you. Come back, Momma. Come back!"

The music simmered low, waiting. The clutch of people surrounding the older woman parted, revealing her limp and blood-drained face. She looked to be asleep or dead. Then the huddle closed in again. After a few minutes, the people encircling the woman grew louder and stepped outward to show the pastor kissing the woman about her face and hands. People began clapping as the woman rose to her feet.

"Praise God!" the pastor said. She let out a triumphant scream into the microphone and collapsed to her knees, praying. The piano and drums kicked up, and the church exploded. People began running up and down the aisle, shouting and singing. Someone found a tambourine and started pounding it. The drummer crashed the cymbals, and the pianist lingered on the high notes. A woman yelled and sprinted in place, sweat streaming down her face. "We ain't trying to have no funeral up in here!" the pastor boasted.

And there was Crystal, hands raised, fingers spread, beaming and dancing. "God got me," she cried. "God got me!"

23.

THE SERENITY CLUB

S cott had been eight days sober when he went to the Serenity Club, a smoke-filled, wood-paneled AA bar that served stale coffee and root-beer floats. "They're addictive," one regular with a rap sheet said about the floats. "But I don't do robberies for them." When it was time for the speakers, a light-skinned Puerto Rican woman in a black bandanna and vinyl jacket took the podium. This was Anna Aldea, an acid-dropping, coke-snorting, cowhide-tough biker lady turned high priestess of AA. A few months shy of her ten-year chip, Anna had helped dozens of addicts through the program. During her speech, she pointed to her newest project.

"I love you, Scott," she said. "Keep coming back. It works—"

"*If you work it,*" the room finished.

A week prior, Scott had woken up from his three-day bender, broke and hungover. To still his nerves, he dressed and left his apartment. It was early Saturday morning, and Scott walked as the city slept. He made it all the way to Pito's house and got him out of bed. Two years sober himself, Pito knew what to do with a detoxing junkie who wanted to get clean: plenty of water, coffee, vitamins, cigarettes, food, and, and, above all, constant monitoring. Pito stayed with Scott all day and that evening took him to meet his brother, David (fourteen years sober), and his wife, Anna. Anna lit a fire in their backyard pit and sat up with Scott until the bars closed at two a.m. It was a nauseating, painful, stretched-out day—Scott's first drug-free in years.

Day five was miserable in a different way. Scott passed it sobbing at Pito's house. "I can feel my body getting better," he said, "but when you have years and years and years of not feeling anything from drinking and dope, then it kind of hits you."

AA had its own binge for people starting to get sober: ninety meetings in ninety days. The idea was to surround the baby, their slang for newcomer, with a support structure that would replace his junkie network. And to never leave him alone. So Scott began showing up at Pito's before the liquor stores opened at eight a.m. and ending his days around Anna's fire pit after last call.

Scott was almost three weeks sober when his landlord told him to go. D.P.'s newly acquired pit bull had got out and somehow snuck into the downstairs neighbors' apartment. The neighbors called the police, who called the landlord, who, wanting to keep his long-term tenants, gave Scott and D.P. the boot. By that time, Scott was basically living at David and Anna's. They told him he might as well sleep there too.

David and Anna's working-class home was one of those places that seemed to belong to everybody. People would walk through the door without knocking and open the refrigerator without asking. "This is the Aldea Recovery House," Anna would say. "If somebody's not here, somebody's calling." She kept large bowls of rice and beans on hand and never locked the door.

Scott began sleeping on the Aldeas' couch and picking up their children from school. Soon, he began working with David, a freelance mason and, in lean weeks, a metal scrapper. Scott liked the work, especially the urban adventure of hunting for aluminum or steel scraps, even if it did involve the occasional Dumpster dive. A barrel-chested Puerto Rican man with pinched eyes and a ready grin, sometimes

David paid Scott and sometimes he didn't. Scott didn't complain. How could he, after what David and Anna had done for him?

AT FIRST, SCOTT liked cleaning the Serenity Club. The pay was piddly—$7.15 an hour, which would give him around $100 a week—but because he worked alone, from ten p.m. to one a.m. most nights, it gave him time to think. He thought about finding someone, although he didn't know where to start if not in a gay bar. Craigslist? He thought about his sister's wedding. Maybe he could make it home for that. He prayed, *"Please don't let me use tomorrow."*

But most of all, he would dream about returning to nursing. He thought that would be a "great way to stay sober because you start thinking about other people and not your poor, pathetic shit." But the road ahead felt daunting. The nursing board didn't just take Scott's license away. Understandably, it made it extremely difficult for him to earn it back. He would have to submit to "the testing of urine specimens at a frequency of not less than 56 times per year," which would cost thousands of dollars. He'd have to stay clean for five years and attend biweekly AA meetings.[1] Scott recognized his weaknesses. He didn't know if he would have tried harder to get clean years ago if the nursing board had not put license reinstatement so far out of reach. But giving up did come easier when things seemed impossible.

The "impaired professionals" gathering had left him discouraged too. One nurse said it had taken her over a year to find a job after being sober for about two years and passing all the requirements. And she had a master's degree.

There were stations between having a revoked nursing license and having one with full privileges. But to get a nursing job with a restricted license—one that didn't allow you to handle narcotics, say—was rare. Scott knew people. Over the years, he had stayed in touch with several nursing pals, and some had moved into positions of influence. He even had an aunt who was the dean of nursing at a large state university nearby. But staying in touch with these people had meant hiding his addiction and poverty, so approaching them for help was complicated. The last time Scott spoke with a friend who was the director of a local nursing home, he said he was doing fine. "So now I'd have to go back and say, 'Oh no, I really wasn't doing well. I was still a junkie. I totally lied to you.' . . . I guess that's where a lot of my reservations would come in." Scott didn't feel he could call in any favors.[2]

After four months of cleaning the club with only one night off in total, Scott began to grow weary. He was sober and bored. He would empty the ashtrays, scrub the toilets, and, at the end of the night, grade his performance: A–, C+. Then twenty-one hours later, he would do it all again. At least when he was a junkie, his life had purpose: get dope. Now he felt as though he were pacing in a small, dull loop. Anna had asked Scott to pay $200 a month to sleep on the couch and to put his food stamps toward groceries, which made it difficult for him to save much.

It was more than just his work at the club. As the initial high of sobriety wore off, Scott began to sour on AA in general. This post-honeymoon sensation was so common that AA had a phrase for it: "falling off your pink cloud."

"Ambivalence has turned into animosity," Scott said. It embarrassed him, spending nights in folding-chair semicircles with washed-up drunks and cokeheads, drinking Folgers out of styrofoam cups and swapping horror stories. Scott grew to hate the rituals, the stranger's hand on his shoulder, the hoary sayings—"But by the Grace of God," "Let go and let God"—not to mention the Serenity Club crowd's belief that fighting addiction with a prescription—methadone, say—was cheating. Scott was considering going to the county clinic to get something to help with the cravings and depression. But he couldn't tell Anna or David. Scott had puked and shivered and wept to push the poison out of his system only to look around and see that he was still broke and homeless, logging stupid hours at AA and dipping a mop into a bucket at midnight. "Fucking addicts and drunks," he would yell into an empty room whose folding chairs had not been put back. "This makes me crazy!"

AT 7:37 A.M., Scott signed into the Milwaukee County Behavioral Services Division Access Clinic. The clinic served residents with no insurance or only GAMP, Milwaukee County's public insurance. A sign on the wall announced: YOUR FIRST APPOINTMENT MAY LAST THREE TO FIVE HOURS. If you didn't have the money, you would pay with your time. Nurses and social workers bustled past patients strolling the hallways, doing nothing while they waited. Scott wouldn't mind working at the clinic, being one of the fast-walkers. But on that day, he was there for drugs. To him, what the AA converts didn't understand, because none of them were heroin users, was that his body was physically in need of something that would give him a boost and kick-start his motivation. His fingers were crossed for Suboxone, which was used to treat opiate addiction. After almost three hours, Scott's name was called. He stood up, relieved to be seen.

The psychiatrist was a skinny Asian man with a flattop and a voice just above a whisper. He led Scott into a drab, rectangular room that resembled an oversized closet. Scott sat on a couch and the psychiatrist bent over an old desk, reading Scott's file. The desk was pushed against the wall so that when Scott looked up from the couch, he saw the psychiatrist in profile.

"How long have you been depressed?" the psychiatrist asked, staring at the file.

"A long time," Scott answered.

"So, what kind of symptoms are you having?"

"I just really don't have any energy. . . . I'm thinking about looking into Suboxone. I can't tell if I'm in post-withdrawal."

"How long have you had trouble with the drugs?"

"I'd say about, about seven years."

"And how long have you been clean?"

"Four months."

After Scott filled him in about his drug use, the psychiatrist paused before the next question. "Um," he continued, "it says here that you were sexually abused when you were younger."

"Correct." Scott sniffed.

"How old were you?"

"Young. From four to"—Scott thought for a moment—"ten."

"Who was the perpetrator?"

Scott told him.

"So how did it end? Was someone told?"

"No. I never told anybody about it."

"Have you ever got any treatment for that?"

"No."

"You have any interest in that?"

"No."[3]

Scott walked out of the clinic with two bottles of antidepressants. He was to take 100 mgs of Zoloft twice a day and 50 mgs of amitriptyline at bedtime.[4] When Scott had asked, "Do you suggest anything to help with the cravings?" the doctor had mentioned treatment programs instead of Suboxone. Scott had been "a little bummed" at that response. But two out of three wasn't bad. It was cold outside, −1° without the windchill. Under Scott's boots, the snow squeaked.

THREE MONTHS LATER, while rooting around for loose change, David and Anna Aldea's twelve-year-old daughter found a syringe in Scott's swimming trunks. Oscar, the Aldeas' eldest son, who had recently moved back home, floated the possibility of it being an old needle, which was entirely plausible. When Scott had first moved in, he would periodically find paraphernalia in the pocket of a sweatshirt or pair of jeans he hadn't worn in a while. He even found a crack pipe once, looking at it and remembering, the way you do when finding a faded ticket stub in the laundry. But David and Anna weren't buying it. That night, after Scott had finished cleaning the Serenity Club, he discovered his things on the Aldeas' porch with a note. He tried the door. Locked. Theirs had been his home for seven months.

Scott didn't plead his case. He shunned confrontation, and David and Anna wouldn't have believed him anyway. "It's much easier for them to think that it was mine than his," Scott reflected. Besides, this was no time for Oscar to detox, having just become a father. The unselfish thing to do, in Scott's mind, was to allow Oscar to keep using so that he could be there for his girlfriend and baby daughter.

Scott knew the needle was Oscar's because Scott had shot up with him. Scott wouldn't use the term "relapse." He would say, "It just made me normal."

Several things had happened all at once. First, Scott learned that all those AA meetings he had sat through and all those group therapy sessions, which he hated even more, didn't count toward his nursing license. The nursing board had its own procedure, and Scott hadn't followed it. The board also had its own lab for urine screening, and since Scott hadn't used it, all those clean drops he'd been racking up didn't count either. "I went and pissed in the cup, and I did that for weeks and weeks and weeks. And finally, I contacted the board to make sure that it was all okay. And they were like, 'No.'"

Just days after hearing this defeat, Scott ran into Heroin Susie and Billy at a gas station. They offered, and he accepted, a quiet act of rebellion. That might have been an isolated incident, a small back-slip on his steep climb, but then Oscar moved in with a full-blown habit. The two began getting high on the weekends together. Scott would stop using by Monday so that he could piss clean on Friday. He was still going to counseling and AA meetings. But after a few months, he dropped the routine and started getting high whenever he could.

At two a.m., standing on the porch of the Aldea Recovery House with a sack of clothes and his memory box, Scott took the natural next step and called Susie and Billy. He spent that night in their trailer, right back where he started.

A FEW DAYS later, as Susie baked an apple pie, Scott called his mom, Joan. He had decided to give methadone a try and needed two things: heroin in his system, which he had, and $150, which he didn't. A month earlier, Scott had returned to his hometown for a two-day visit. He stayed at his mother's small but dignified home, visited his grandmother in the nursing home, played video games with his teenage nieces, and watched his sister model her new wedding dress. It had been two years since Scott had seen his mother. "I would drive up to see you if I could drive in the city," Joan apologized without apologizing. The visit had been pleasant. Scott was relaxed and calm, not like his last visit, when he seemed to Joan as nervous as a caged rabbit. "His legs would be shaking a mile a minute," she remembered. Joan had organized a special lunch and a big dinner so that all the relatives could see Scott. He'd traveled back to Milwaukee feeling loved, and that memory helped him pick up the phone.

"It's a methadone clinic," Scott was saying. "Do you know what that is? . . . I'll go to them every day to get the medication. And that'll help me with the opiate addiction and depression. . . . I've kind of tried to do all this and beat this without; I didn't want you guys really to know the whole, you know. But it's not working that way." Scott drew a breath. "Mom, does this make sense to you?"

All Joan knew was that her son, who almost never asked for anything, was asking for help. She came up with the $150.

The next morning, Scott sat in the Tenth Street Methadone Clinic, waiting his turn. The clinic had four stations. Reception took your money, and Collections took your piss. The nurses greeted regulars by their nicknames or numbers. "Hey, Deano!" "Your lucky day, 3322." The third station was the bathroom, equipped with a camera to make sure you weren't swapping urine. At the last station, the methadone dispensers sat behind a thick door on which someone had clipped an article from *The Onion* with the headline EVERYTHING TAKING TOO

LONG, accompanied by a photograph of a man staring impatiently at a microwave. Once buzzed in, patients stepped through the door and punched their number into a dispenser, which would squirt the bitter red liquid into a small plastic cup.

Scott thought the most diverse place in all of Milwaukee had to be the methadone clinic at seven a.m. Through its doors had walked a twenty-something white woman in full makeup carrying a designer purse, a grunting Mexican man leaning on a walker, a white woman holding a newborn, a tall black man with earrings whom Scott enjoyed looking at, a fat painter, a burly construction worker, a white woman in pressed slacks and a pink blouse, and a man in an accountant's suit. When a bent-over Chinese woman who looked to be in her eighties shuffled into the clinic, a Puerto Rican woman with a cane walked over and hugged her.

"You new?" someone asked.

Scott turned around to find a young white woman who looked like she belonged on the East High School track team. She was maybe eighteen with a ponytail, freckles, orthodontic-straightened teeth.

Scott nodded yes.

"Well, my advice"—the girl scooted closer—"is don't get on this stuff. I mean, they say they want to get you in to get you off, but it's all a lie. They just want your money. I've been on this for who knows how long, and I'm still taking a hundred milligrams."

Scott raised his eyebrows, recalling that 100 milligrams was the dose that had sent him to the hospital the last time he had tried methadone. As he remembered it, he had mixed the dose with Xanax and succumbed to the cocktail soon after leaving the clinic, stumbling into oncoming traffic. The responding officer injected him with Narcan, sending him into a convulsive withdrawal that landed him in the ICU.

"How much do you pay?" Scott asked.

"Three hundred and seventy," she answered, referencing her monthly bill.

He nodded and wondered how he would make the next installment.

When it was Scott's turn, he swallowed the red stuff, swished a little water in the cup, and downed the rinse. Those last drops could make a difference.

Before he left, Scott met with a methadone counselor, a black man around Scott's age.

"How many times in the last thirty days have you used heroin?" the counselor asked.

"Thirty." Scott went on to tell the counselor about his mother lending him the $150. "I guess it's my fault for underestimating her," he said. "Maybe I just cut her out of everything."

"You're as sick as your secrets," the counselor said.

Because he couldn't afford both methadone and rent on his Serenity Club check, Scott went homeless. He checked into an eighty-six-bed shelter called the Guest House. Every morning, he bused to the methadone clinic, and every evening he slept on a bunk bed in a large room with other homeless men. Methadone made him sweat and gain weight, and it smothered his libido. But it worked.[5]

Most people who began methadone treatment dropped out within a year.[6] Scott stuck with it. Over time, he became a resident manager at the Guest House and started helping people again. Four days a week, Scott worked in one of the Guest House's satellite shelters, an unmarked three-story home with bay windows, tucked in a quiet South Side neighborhood. He scrubbed bathrooms with bleach and guided old-timers to the backyard picnic table, where they sat and tapped their cigarette ash into a repurposed Folgers coffee can.

A year and almost $4,700 later, the county agreed to help Scott pay for his methadone, lowering his monthly bill to $35. Then, through a permanent housing program offered by the Guest House, Scott was able to move into his own place, paying one-third of his income to rent. He chose the Majestic Loft Apartments, on Wisconsin Avenue, right next to the Grand Avenue mall. He had always wanted to live downtown and had been a regular at the mall after first arriving in Milwaukee; back then, to an Iowa farm kid at least, the mall was a vibrant social scene. The fourteen-story Majestic was built in 1908, originally for offices and a vaudeville theater. After it was converted into residential apartments, developers installed a fitness center, an indoor basketball court, a small private movie theater, and a putting green with artificial turf.

Scott's apartment was on the tenth floor. It had clean, wheat-colored carpet, unblemished white walls, mini blinds over person-length windows, a generous bathroom, and a working stove and refrigerator. The Guest House furnished the apartment with a dark brown love seat and matching couch, a few lamps Scott preserved by leaving the plastic wrapping on the shades, and a full-size bed that Scott hardly used—falling asleep on the couch had become a habit. There was even a stacked washer and dryer. It felt too good to be true. At first, Scott half-believed that the Guest House would call and say they had made a mistake. The apartment rented for $775 a month; Scott only paid $141.

It took a good month before Scott was able to accept the apartment as his own. Once he did, he acquired a bathroom rug, a navy-blue coverlet, hand soap, scented candles, throw pillows, mouthwash, dishes, and a welcome mat on which to place his shoes. The apartment made Scott feel affirmed, deserving of something better. It motivated him. One day, Scott used a magnet from the Society of St. Vincent de Paul to stick a note on his refrigerator. It read:

> **5 YEAR PLAN**
> Back to nursing
> Make a lot more money
> Live as cheaply as possible
> Start a savings account

Two years and three months after losing his license, Scott was finally able to start scrimping for the lab tests he would need to become a nurse again. He even started collecting loose change for this purpose, keeping the coins in a kitchen jar.

In the trailer park, Scott had felt stuck. "I just didn't know how to fix anything," he remembered. "It felt like the end of the earth down there, like none of the rest of the city existed." During that time, Scott often thought about killing himself. He'd have done it with a monster hit of heroin; but he never could find enough money. Scott's new place was such a stark contrast to his trailer and everything it represented that he began to think back on his time in the park as "one big camping trip," removed from civilization. Sometimes, when he remembered those days and all he had lost, he would leave his apartment and wind his way through the Majestic's narrow, dimly lit hallways and come to a door. He'd open it and emerge in the middle of the Grand Avenue mall, as if stepping through a secret passageway. Walking the mall's floors, Scott would take in the lights, music, food smells, and people and remember how he used to feel, years ago, when the city was still full of wonder and promise.

24.

CAN'T WIN FOR LOSING

When Arleen dialed the number, she gave Jori her "here we go" look. A landlord, Number 90, had left her a voice mail, saying to give him a call. The message was from the landlord's son, actually, who had been the one to show Arleen the unit. He was in his early twenties with a backwards cap and a braided ponytail. "Call me Pana," he had said. Arleen remembered living in his father's building in 2003, in a two-bedroom unit that back then rented for $535. Now that same unit went for $625. So when Arleen applied this time, it was for a $525 one-bedroom unit. What a difference six years could make.

The phone rang, and Arleen thought about what she had told Pana. She had lied about her income, saying she received $250 a month in child support, but had been straight about her evictions. Mainly, she had begged him. She told him she'd take the unit before looking at it. She didn't much consider the neighborhood or the condition of the place. "Whatever I get is whatever I get," she figured. She had said, "I'm in a shelter. *Please.*"

Pana answered. "Yeah, so, we checked you out. Everything was what you said it was. So, we gonna work with you."

Arleen jumped up and let out a muffled "Yes!"

"But you know, there is no room for error here."

"I know."

"You're on a fixed income. So you need to pay your rent and not get into trouble."

Arleen thanked Pana. Getting off the phone, she thanked Jesus. She smiled. When she smiled she looked like a different person. The press had loosened its grip. From landlords, she had heard eighty-nine nos but one yes.

Jori accepted his mother's high five. He and his brother would have to switch schools. Jori didn't care. He switched schools all the time. Between seventh and eighth grades, he had attended five different schools—when he went at all. At the domestic-violence shelter alone, Jori had racked up seventeen consecutive absences. Arleen saw school as a higher-order need, something to worry about after she found a house. Plus, Jori was a big help. He would bound down the street and memorize numbers off rent signs or watch Jafaris when Arleen left with her HOUSE notepad. He was good for a laugh too. When things looked bleak, he would try to make his momma smile by freestyling (badly) as the city rolled past their bus window.

> *Aye, aye, aye*
> *Looking for me a house to move in.*
> *That was my old school.*
> *That's my old block.*
> *That's my old gas station.*
> *We looking for a house.*

If Jori worried about finding a home, he never showed it.

Jafaris cried when they left the shelter, holding on to the remote-control car and stuffed Elmo a social worker had given him as parting gifts. "I can't look," he said as the car pulled away. Arleen rubbed her boy's head and told him he should be happy leaving the shelter.

Jafaris didn't understand why. It was quiet and warm, and there were toys there.

Their new apartment building was at the busy intersection of Teutonia and Silver Spring, in a more industrial part of the North Side. Arleen climbed the steps to the third-floor apartment while Jori and Jafaris took a giggling ride in the creaking elevator. Inside, the walls were freshly painted, and the gray carpet was thick and clean. There was an air-conditioning unit and fixtures on every light. There was a small kitchen with light wood cupboards, each one of which had a handle. The hot water worked. Arleen took her time inspecting the place but couldn't find anything wrong. She opened a window and looked out over the cars driving by and Auer Steel & Heating's distribution center across the street. She felt "good but tired."

Once all the trash bags of clothes and boxes of canned food were moved in, Arleen sat on the floor. She found a soft bag and leaned back on it. She felt at peace, at home. It had been two months since her eviction hearing with Sherrena. Jori sat down beside Arleen and pitched his head into her shoulder. Jafaris followed, lying on Arleen's legs and resting his head on her belly. They stayed like that for a long time.

AFTER A FEW quiet days, Arleen learned that Terrance—everyone just called him "T"—was dead. T was one of the only people Arleen still kept in touch with on Larry's side of the family. His cousin P.A., whom Arleen also loved, had shot him. During an argument, T had hit P.A. over the head with an ax handle, and P.A. went to get a gun. Before he returned, he called T's mother, saying that he was going to kill her son. Then he did.

T's death interrupted Arleen's life in the usual way. She wept for him and reminisced with old friends and arranged for Jafaris to stay over at his old foster mother's home during the funeral. He was too young to go, Arleen thought. Some people were talking about going to Ponderosa Steakhouse after the funeral. Those who couldn't afford it donated plasma so they could have a place at the table.

When Arleen and Jori visited T's street memorial near Fond Du Lac Avenue, on the Northwest Side, she straightened the flowers and stuffed animals. It was a handsome memorial, adorned with a large cream ribbon, poems, silk roses, and several bouquets of white and yellow daisies, carnations, and alstroemeria. Arleen walked to T's house and stood on the steps, walked back to the memorial, then walked to the steps again.

"Time is going fast, ain't it?" Jori said. "I bet when we get down to the funeral, time will be going slow."

On the morning of the funeral, Arleen put on dark jeans, a Rocawear T-shirt, and a blue hoodie. As she and Jori descended the stairs on their way out, they met Pana on his way up.

"I need to talk with you," he said. "About two nights ago."

Arleen's mind raced. That was when she had called 911 because Jafaris was having an asthma attack.

"This is a nuisance building," Pana said. "We can't have police coming up in here."

"Just the fire department and ambulance came," Arleen said. "Police don't come for an asthma attack."

Still, that wasn't the only issue. A neighbor had complained that one of Arleen's friends had knocked on his door and asked for weed. (Trisha. She was babysitting the boys at the time.) And Jafaris had been caught dropping something out their third-story window. "If things don't get better, we are going to ask you to go."

Outside, on her way to New Pitts Mortuary, Arleen shook her head. "If it ain't one thing it's another," she said. Besides trying to stay in Pana's good graces, Arleen was having a problem with her food stamps. She had submitted the necessary change-of-address form, but there was some holdup. Then there was the problem of getting everything out of storage. She needed to find a way to move her things fast or, come the first of the month, she would fall behind on payments—either that or fall behind in rent. And now T was gone and, in a way, so was P.A. Poverty could pile on; living it often meant steering through

gnarled thickets of interconnected misfortunes and trying not to go
crazy. There were moments of calm, but life on balance was facing one
crisis after another.[1] At least Arleen had a home, a floor of her own to
sleep on.

Arleen hesitated in front of the door at Pitts. Built in the 1930s,
the funeral home on West Capitol Drive was a North Side institution.
Fashioned in the French Revival style, the Lannon stone building was
adorned with an octagonal stair tower; thin, elegant windows; a deep-
maroon entrance canopy stretching across the sidewalk; and steep roof
lines, with a towering chimney. Jori drew up next to his mother, and
they walked in together. The sanctuary was packed. Teenagers and
children huddled together wearing personalized shirts with T's face or
the face of someone else who had been cut down young. Grandmothers and grandfathers were there in cream and brown suits with matching felt hats. Big C, T's brother, was up front in a crisp blue T-shirt
with matching bandanna and sunglasses. Uncle Link showed up with
a half-finished cigarette behind his ear. A towering man walked down
the aisle slowly as his wife leaned her face on his back and wept. Arleen
took a seat at the rear, reflecting her status in the family.

T looked good, dressed in a long-sleeved black T-shirt and a new
Oakland Raiders cap. He had almost made forty. The preacher looked
down on him. "It seems like every time I come over here, I see someone who looks like me, lying in a casket, gone too young," he said,
shaking his head above a fat Windsor knot. Then he boomed, raspy
and impassioned, "What has happened to the love amongst us? What
has happened to the concern? . . . Can't nobody help us but *us*!"

"*Go on!*"

"*Tha's right.*"

"*That was my baby!*"

After it was over, Arleen joined Uncle Link and a few others outside. Someone handed her a can of Olde English malt liquor, and she
poured it out for T, making pretty amber circles in the snow. At the
repast, the family ate fried chicken on bread, greens, and mac and

cheese in the basement of the Wisconsin African American Women's Center, on Thirtieth and Vliet. Through it all, Arleen was embraced and kissed and welcomed. She felt held by her people. They weren't much help if you needed a place to stay or money to keep the heat on, but they knew how to throw a funeral.

THE NEXT DAY, no one was calling, and Arleen got back to making her apartment a home. She enrolled the boys in new schools. She got her stuff out of storage and hung pictures on the wall. A neighbor gave her a couch. Arleen's old apartment on Thirteenth Street was usually messy because cleaning didn't do it much good, what with its cracked windows, ravaged carpet, and broken bathroom. But Pana's father kept a nice place. It could look respectable if Arleen kept it nice. She did. Over the sink, she wrote a little note to Jori: "*If you don't clean up after yourself, we are going to have problems.*" On the counter she set out a candle for St. Jude, patron saint of difficult cases. When people saw Arleen's apartment, they would say, "Your house so *pretty*." Some even asked if they could move in. Arleen would feel proud and say no.

Jori tried to adjust to his new school. He was technically in eighth grade but so far behind that he might as well have been in seventh. It was frustrating. And on top of that, T's death had unsettled him. It had come out that when P.A. called T's mother, he had called from Larry's phone. The police questioned Larry but released him. It still twisted Jori up inside. Why was his daddy with P.A. that night? Exactly two weeks after the funeral, a teacher snapped at Jori and he snapped back. He kicked the teacher in the shin and ran home. The police followed him there, the teacher having called them.

When Pana heard about it, he made Arleen a deal. If she left by Sunday, he'd return her rent and security deposit; if she didn't, he would keep her money and evict her. Children didn't shield families from eviction; they exposed them to it.[2]

Arleen took the deal, and Pana was nice enough to help her move. She pulled her dishes out of the clean cupboards and took her decorations off the walls. When Arleen had finished stuffing every-thing into trash bags and recycled boxes, Pana loaded his truck and drove Arleen's things right back to storage.

Arleen had lost the pretty house and felt miserable about it.[3] "Why it's like I got a curse on me?" she wondered. "I can't win for losing. No matter how hard I try."

ARLEEN CALLED TRISHA and told her how angry the landlord was when he found out she had been going door-to-door asking for a joint. It really was the police visit that did her in, but years of hardship had taught Arleen how to ask for help, and one particularly effective method involved addressing a person's guilt, framing things so that someone looked like a real bastard if he or she turned you down.[4] "The least you can do is to help me if you're the one that got *me put out*."

Trisha told Arleen to come on over.

There was a new street memorial on Thirteenth Street. Jafaris no-ticed it. "Someone got shot there," he said in his six-year-old voice. When they arrived at the old address, the boys ran up to Trisha's apartment to see Little. But Little was dead. A car had ground him into the pavement. When Trisha told Jori, he tried to keep himself from crying. He paced around Trisha's apartment and sleeve-attacked the snot sliding from his nose. He found a foam mannequin's head. There was always random stuff like that lying around Trisha's place. Jori knelt over the head and turned it faceup. He hit the face with a closed fist. He kept hitting it. Soon he was grunting, and his punches flew faster and harder and louder until Arleen and Trisha screamed at him to stop.

Trisha didn't hide the fact that she had begun turning tricks. She couldn't even if she wanted to. Men would just show up, and Trisha would take them into her bedroom, telling Arleen, "Look, I'm about to get us some cigs." Trisha would emerge later with eight or ten dol-lars. Once, Jori walked in to find a man in bed with Trisha, his pants on the floor next to them and her lipstick smeared. In crowded houses, there were no separate spaces, and children quickly learned the ways of adults.

Trisha kept at it even after her new boyfriend moved in. Arleen sensed that he encouraged her to. She also figured it was the boyfriend who told Trisha to raise Arleen's monthly rent to $150, from $60. The man went by a string of nicknames; Trisha called him Sunny. He was a thirty-year-old man who had just served five years for selling drugs. Skinny, with a smooth walk, he bragged about having nine children by five different women and joked about taking a spatula to Trisha. When Trisha got money from johns or her payee, Sunny would take it. If Trisha called after Sunny on the street, he would ignore her and later hiss, "Don't call me 'babe' in public." Trisha would ball up under the covers with her clothes on or sit on a windowsill and light a cigarette, its smoke coming alive in the breeze like a raging spirit that had only seconds to live.

Sunny's parents and one of his sisters moved in soon after Arleen did. Trisha's small one-bedroom apartment, which was in bad shape to begin with, began to buckle under the weight of eight people. The toilet broke and the kitchen sink started leaking. The leak got so bad that the floor filled with water that would ripple when Jori stepped in it. He spread old clothes on the ground to sop it up.

"It looks like slums," Arleen said. "Kitchen all nasty, floor all nasty. Bathroom." She thought about what to do next. "What's beyond this? What's to come? It can't get no worser."

Then a Child Protective Services caseworker showed up asking for "Ms. Belle." It was not Arleen's usual caseworker but one she'd never met before. She knew Arleen was living there—Sherrena didn't even know that—and she knew about the toilet and the sink. The caseworker opened the refrigerator and grimaced. Arleen pointed out that it was the end of the month. She had gone shopping, but there were eight mouths to feed.[5]

The CPS worker said she'd be back. Arleen became nauseous with anxiety and secretly suspected Trisha had reported her. She needed to escape, somehow. So she called J.P. Her dependable cousin picked her up and rolled her a blunt. It helped. So he rolled another. "J.P. always tries to make me forget about all my stress," Arleen said the next day.

FINALLY, SPRING HAD come to the city. The snow had melted, leaving behind wet streets edged in soggy garbage. On the same day, the whole ghetto realized there was no longer a need to brace and tighten when stepping outside. People overreacted without regret. Boys went shirtless, and girls put lotion and sun on their legs long before it was actually hot. Chairs and laughter returned to porches. Children found their jump ropes.

Arleen and her boys had spent the past several days alone in Trisha's apartment. She relished the peace and quiet. Trisha and Sunny and Sunny's people had disappeared. Arleen didn't give it any thought, figuring they were visiting kin or friends. But on May 1, movers stormed Trisha's apartment. They came with gloved hands, ready to work, but ended up looking at each other bewildered, trying to figure out what they should pack and what they should trash. Belinda, Trisha's payee, had contracted the men. She would later come check on their progress, pulling up in a new Ford Expedition XLT with temporary license plates from the dealership. Chris had been released and came by the apartment looking for Trisha. Belinda didn't think her client was safe on Thirteenth Street anymore.

Arleen stared out the front window. "This is too much for me," she mumbled. She had stayed with Trisha for a month and a half.

Jafaris came home from school with braids on one side of his head. He watched the movers lugging out mattresses and dressers and shoving handfuls of clothes into black trash bags. To this scene, he had no reaction. He did not cry or ask a question or run to check on a special possession. He simply turned around and went outside.

THEY STAYED A while with Arleen's sister, who wanted $200 a month even though Arleen and the boys didn't have their own room. During that time Arleen lost everything she had in storage: her glass dining table, the armoire and bedroom dresser she had acquired at Thirteenth Street, her air-conditioning units. She had given Boosie the money to pay it, but he lost or stole it. Then Arleen's welfare case was closed because she missed three appointments; the letters had once again been mailed to an address she was evicted from. "It won't stop for nothing," she said. Arleen eventually found another run-down apartment on Thirty-Fourth and Clarke, by the Master Lock factory. "Maybe this will be the end of it," she told herself. Arleen found enough stability to start looking for jobs. But not long after an interview at Arby's, she and her boys were robbed. Two men ran into her apartment and stuck a pistol in Jori's face. Arleen's caseworker told her the place was no longer safe, causing Arleen to flee once again to a shelter. Rents continued to rise. Arleen's next apartment took $600 of her $628 monthly check. It was only a matter of time before her lights were shut off. When that finally happened, Jori went to live with Larry, and Child Protective Services placed Jafaris with Arleen's sister.

Arleen began to unravel. "Just my soul is messed up," she said. "Sometimes I find my body trembling or shaking. I'm tired, but I can't sleep. I'm fitting to have a nervous breakdown. My body is trying to shut down."

Arleen stood back up. She borrowed money from her aunt Merva to get her lights back on, and her boys came back. She took another apartment on Tamarack Street, near Tabernacle Community Baptist Church. This apartment had no stove or refrigerator, but they boiled hot dogs in a crockpot or went to St. Ben's to eat beef stroganoff with the winos.

Sometimes Arleen would head out to a food pantry and Jafaris would ask, "Will you get me some cakes, Momma?"

Arleen would smile and say, "You know I'll try if they have them."

Jori had been thinking about his future. He wanted to become a carpenter so he could build Arleen a house. "People be not thinking that I can do this. But you watch," he said.

Arleen smiled at Jori. "I wish my life were different," she said. "I wish that when I be an old lady, I can sit back and look at my kids. And they be grown. And they, you know, become something. Something more than me. And we'll all be together, and be laughing. We be remembering stuff like this and be laughing at it."

Epilogue

HOME AND HOPE

The home is the center of life. It is a refuge from the grind of work, the pressure of school, and the menace of the streets. We say that at home, we can "be ourselves." Everywhere else, we are someone else. At home, we remove our masks.

The home is the wellspring of personhood. It is where our identity takes root and blossoms, where as children, we imagine, play, and question, and as adolescents, we retreat and try. As we grow older, we hope to settle into a place to raise a family or pursue work. When we try to understand ourselves, we often begin by considering the kind of home in which we were raised.

In languages spoken all over the world, the word for "home" encompasses not just shelter but warmth, safety, family—the womb. The ancient Egyptian hieroglyph for "home" was often used in place of "mother." The Chinese word *jiā* can mean both family and home. "Shelter" comes from two Old English words: *scield* (shield) and *truma* (troop), together forming the image of a family gathering itself within a protective shell.[1] The home remains the primary basis of life. It is where meals are shared, quiet habits formed, dreams confessed, traditions created.

Civic life too begins at home, allowing us to plant roots and take ownership over our community, participate in local politics, and reach out to neighbors in a spirit of solidarity and generosity. "It is difficult to force a man out of himself and get him to take an interest in the affairs of the whole state," Alexis de Tocqueville once observed. "But if it is a question of taking a road past his property, he sees at once that this small public matter has a bearing on his greatest private interests."[2] It is only after we begin to see a street as *our* street, a public park as *our* park, a school as *our* school, that we can become engaged citizens, dedicating our time and resources for worthwhile causes: joining the Neighborhood Watch, volunteering to beautify a playground, or running for school board.

Working on behalf of the common good is the engine of democracy, vital to our communities, cities, states—and, ultimately, the nation. It is "an outflow of the idealism and moralism of the American people," wrote Gunnar Myrdal.[3] Some have called this impulse "love of country" or "patriotism" or the "American spirit." But whatever its name, its foundation is the home. What else is a nation but a patchwork of cities and towns; cities and towns a patchwork of neighborhoods; and neighborhoods a patchwork of homes?

America is supposed to be a place where you can better yourself, your family, and your community. But this is only possible if you have a stable home. When Scott was provided with an affordable apartment through the Guest House's permanent housing program, he was able to stay off heroin, find meaningful work as a resident manager for homeless people, and begin striving for independence. He remains stably housed and sober. And then there are the Hinkstons. After Malik Jr. was born, Patrice and Doreen finally did move to Brownsville, Tennessee, a town of about 10,000. They found a nice three-bedroom place. Out of the rat hole, Patrice earned her GED, impressing her teacher so much that she was named Adult Learner of the Year. Patrice went on to enroll in a local community college, where she took online classes in computers and criminal justice, hoping to one day become a parole officer. She liked to half joke, "I got a lot of friends who are criminal who are going to need my help!"

The persistence and brutality of American poverty can be disheartening, leaving us cynical about solutions. But as Scott and Patrice will tell you, a good home can serve as the sturdiest of footholds. When people have a place to live, they become better parents, workers, and citizens.

If Arleen and Vanetta didn't have to dedicate 70 or 80 percent of their income to rent, they could keep their kids fed and clothed and off the streets. They could settle down in one neighborhood and enroll their children in one school, providing them the opportunity to form long-lasting relationships with friends, role models, and teachers. They could start a savings account or buy their children toys and books, perhaps even a home computer. The time and emotional energy they spent making rent, delaying eviction, or finding another place to live when homeless could instead be spent on things that enriched their lives: community college classes, exercise, finding a good job, maybe a good man too.

But our current state of affairs "reduces to poverty people born for better things."[4] For almost a century, there has been broad consensus in America that families should spend no more than 30 percent of their income on housing.[5] Until recently, most renting families met this goal. But times have changed—in Milwaukee and across America. Every year in this country, people are evicted from their homes not by the tens of thousands or even the hundreds of thousands but by the millions.[6]

UNTIL RECENTLY, WE simply didn't know how immense this problem was, or how serious the consequences, unless we had suffered them ourselves. For years, social scientists, journalists, and policymakers all but ignored eviction, making it one of the least studied processes affecting the lives of poor families. But new data and methods have allowed us to measure the prevalence of eviction and document its effects. We have learned that eviction is commonplace in poor neighborhoods and that it exacts a heavy toll on families, communities, and children.

Residential stability begets a kind of psychological stability, which allows people to invest in their home and social relationships. It begets school stability, which increases the chances that children will excel and graduate. And it begets community stability, which encourages neighbors to form strong bonds and take care of their block.[7] But poor families enjoy little of that because they are evicted at such high rates. That low-income families move often is well known. *Why* they do is a question that has puzzled researchers and policymakers because they have overlooked the frequency of eviction in disadvantaged neighborhoods.[8] Between 2009 and 2011, roughly a quarter of all moves undertaken by Milwaukee's poorest renters were involuntary. Once you account for those dislocations (eviction, landlord foreclosure), low-income households move at a similar rate as everyone else.[9] If you study eviction court records in other cities, you arrive at similarly startling numbers. Jackson County, Missouri, which includes half of Kansas City, saw 19 formal evictions a day between 2009 and 2013. New York City courts saw almost 80 nonpayment evictions a day in 2012. That same year, 1 in 9 occupied rental households in Cleveland, and 1 in 14 in Chicago, were summoned to eviction court.[10] Instability is not inherent to poverty. Poor families move so much because they are forced to.

Along with instability, eviction also causes loss. Families lose not only their home, school, and neighborhood but also their possessions: furniture, clothes, books. It takes a good amount of money and time to establish a home. Eviction can erase all that. Arleen lost everything. Larraine and Scott too. Eviction can cause workers to lose their jobs. The likelihood of being laid off is roughly 15 percent higher for workers who have experienced an eviction. If housing instability leads to employment instability, it is because the stress and consuming nature of being forced from your home wreak havoc on people's work performance.[11] Often, evicted families also lose the opportunity to benefit from public housing because Housing Authorities count evictions and unpaid debt as strikes when reviewing applications. And so people who have the greatest need for housing assistance—the rent-burdened and evicted—are systematically denied it.[12]

This—the loss of your possessions, job, home, and access to government aid—helps explain why eviction has such a pronounced effect on what social scientists call "material hardship," a measure of the texture of scarcity. Material hardship assesses, say, whether families experience hunger or sickness because food or medical care is financially out of reach or go without heat, electricity, or a phone because they can't afford those things. The year after eviction, families experience 20 percent higher levels of material hardship than similar families who were not evicted. They go without food. They endure illness and cold. Evicted families continue to have higher levels of material hardship at least two years after the event.[13]

These families are often compelled to accept substandard housing conditions. In Milwaukee, renters whose previous move was involuntary were 25 percent more likely to experience long-term housing problems than similar renters who moved under less trying circumstances.[14]

And families forced from their homes are pushed into undesirable parts of the city, moving from poor neighborhoods into even poorer ones; from crime-filled areas into still more dangerous ones. Arleen's favorite place was nested in a working-class black neighborhood. After the city condemned it and forced her out, she moved into an apartment complex teeming with drug dealers. Even after controlling for a host of important factors, families who experience a forced move relocate to worse neighborhoods than those who move under less demanding circumstances.[15] Concentrated poverty and violence inflict their own wounds, since neighborhoods determine so much about your life, from the kinds of job opportunities you have to the kinds of schools your children attend.[16]

Then there is the toll eviction takes on a person's spirit. The violence of displacement can drive people to depression and, in extreme cases, even suicide. One in two recently evicted mothers reports multiple symptoms of clinical depression, double the rate of similar mothers who were not forced from their homes. Even after years pass, evicted mothers are less happy, energetic, and optimistic than their peers.[17] When several patients committed suicide in the days leading up to their eviction, a group of psychiatrists published a letter in *Psychiatric Services*, identifying eviction as a "significant precursor of suicide." The letter emphasized that none of the patients were facing homelessness, leading the psychiatrists to attribute the suicides to eviction itself. "Eviction must be considered a traumatic rejection," they wrote, "a denial of one's most basic human needs, and an exquisitely shameful experience." Suicides attributed to evictions and foreclosures doubled between 2005 and 2010, years when housing costs soared.[18]

Eviction even affects the communities that displaced families leave behind. Neighbors who cooperate with and trust one another can make their streets safer and more prosperous. But that takes time. Efforts to establish local cohesion and community investment are thwarted in neighborhoods with high turnover rates. In this way, eviction can unravel the fabric of a community, helping to ensure that neighbors remain strangers and that their collective capacity to combat crime and promote civic engagement remains untapped.[19] Milwaukee neighborhoods with high eviction rates have higher violent crime rates the following year, even after controlling for past crime rates and other relevant factors.[20]

Losing your home and possessions and often your job; being stamped with an eviction record and denied government housing assistance; relocating to degrading housing in poor and dangerous neighborhoods; and suffering from increased material hardship, homelessness, depression, and illness—this is eviction's fallout. Eviction does not simply drop poor families into a dark valley, a trying yet relatively brief detour on life's journey. It fundamentally redirects their way, casting them onto a different, and much more difficult, path. Eviction is a cause, not just a condition, of poverty.

Eviction affects the old and the young, the sick and able-bodied. But for poor women of color and their children, it has become ordinary. Walk into just about any urban housing court in America, and you can see them waiting on hard benches for their cases to be called. Among Milwaukee renters, over 1 in 5 black women report having been evicted in their adult life, compared with 1 in 12 Hispanic women and 1 in 15 white women.[21]

Most evicted households in Milwaukee have children living in them, and across the country, many evicted children end up homeless. The substandard housing and unsafe neighborhoods to which many evicted families must relocate can degrade a child's health, ability to learn, and sense of self-worth.[22] And if eviction has lasting effects on mothers' depression, sapping their energy and happiness, then children will feel that chill too. Parents like Arleen and Vanetta wanted to provide their children with stability, but eviction ruined that, pulling kids in and out of school and batting them from one neighborhood to the next. When these mothers finally did find another place to live, they once again began giving landlords most of their income, leaving little for the kids. Families who spend more on housing spend less on their children.[23] Poor families are living above their means, in apartments they cannot afford. The thing is, those apartments are already at the bottom of the market.[24] Our cities have become unaffordable to our poorest families, and this problem is leaving a deep and jagged scar on the next generation.

ALL THIS SUFFERING is shameful and unnecessary. Because it is unnecessary, there is hope. These problems are neither intractable nor eternal. A different kind of society is possible, and powerful solutions are within our collective reach.

But those solutions depend on how we answer a single question: do we believe that the right to a decent home is part of what it means to be an American?

The United States was founded on the noble idea that people have "certain unalienable Rights, that among these are Life, Liberty and the pursuit of Happiness." Each of these three unalienable rights—so essential to the American character that the founders saw them as God-given—requires a stable home.

Life and home are so intertwined that it is almost impossible to think about one without the other. The home offers privacy and personal security. It protects and nurtures. The ideal of liberty has always incorporated not only religious and civil freedoms but also the right to flourish: to make a living however one chooses, to learn and develop new skills. A stable home allows us to strive for self-reliance and personal expression, to seek gainful employment and enjoy individual freedoms.

And happiness? It was there in the smile that flashed across Jori's face when Arleen was able to buy him a new pair of sneakers, in the church hymn Larraine hummed when she was able to cook a nice meal, in the laughter that burst out of the Hinkstons' house after a good prank. The pursuit of happiness undeniably includes the pursuit of material well-being: minimally, being able to secure basic necessities. It can be overwhelming to consider how much happiness has been lost, how many capabilities snuffed out, by the swell of poverty in this land and our collective decision not to provide all our citizens with a stable and decent place to live.

We have affirmed provision in old age, twelve years of education, and basic nutrition to be the right of every citizen because we have recognized that human dignity depends on the fulfillment of these fundamental human needs. And it is hard to argue that housing is not a fundamental human need. Decent, affordable housing should be a basic right for everybody in this country. The reason is simple: without stable shelter, everything else falls apart.

HOW CAN WE deliver on this obligation? The good news is that much has already been accomplished. America has made impressive strides over the years when it comes to housing. In generations past, the poor crowded into wretched slums, with many apartments lacking toilets, hot water, heat, or windows.[25] Death and disease were rampant. Over the generations, the quality of housing improved dramatically. And to address the problem of affordability, bold and effective programs were developed. In the middle part of the twentieth century, housing was at the forefront of the progressive agenda. High-rise housing projects were erected to replace slums, sometimes in a single, massive sweep. "Cutting the ribbon for a new public housing project was an occasion to celebrate," the late housing economist Louis Winnick remembered. "Big-city mayors and aldermen trolled for votes by pledging a towering public housing project for the ward." When public housing residents saw their apartments—all airy and new, nested in complexes surrounded by expansive grassy fields and playgrounds—they were thrilled. "It is a very beautiful place," one said, "like a big hotel resort."[26]

But soon the great towers erected to replace slums became slums themselves. After politicians choked off funding, public housing fell into a miserable state of disrepair. Broken windows, plumbing, and elevators stayed that way; outside, sewer openings were left uncovered and trash piled up. Families who could move did, leaving behind the city's poorest residents. Soon, public housing complexes descended into chaos and violence. It got to the point where the police refused to go to St. Louis's Pruitt-Igoe Towers, which would be demolished in front of a televised audience only eighteen years after the first residents moved in. Across the United States, the wrecking ball and dynamite stick visited other infamous housing projects, such as Chicago's Robert Taylor Homes and Atlanta's McDaniel-Glenn Homes—joyless towers casting shadows over segregated and desolate areas of their cities. Given what the projects had become, blowing them up was not only the cheaper option; it was the most humane one, like bulldozing a house in which some unspeakable thing had once transpired.[27]

Out of this rubble, the voucher program sprung to life. Whatever else vouchers were, they were not Pruitt-Igoe or Robert Taylor or all the other public housing complexes that had come to be synonymous with urban violence, bitter poverty, and policy failure. Today, the federally funded Housing Choice Voucher Program helps families secure decent housing units in the private rental market. Serving over 2.1 million households, this program has become the largest housing subsidy program for low-income families in the United States. An additional 1.2 million families live in public housing.[28] Cities such as Philadelphia, Seattle, and Oakland have reimagined public housing, often as low-rise, attractive buildings dispersed over several neighborhoods. By and large, both public housing residents and voucher holders pay only 30 percent of their income on rent, with government funds covering the remaining costs.[29]

Public initiatives that provide low-income families with decent housing they can afford are among the most meaningful and effective anti-poverty programs in America. Not every public housing resident or voucher holder is poor—many are elderly or disabled; others have modest incomes—but every year rental assistance programs lift roughly 2.8 million people out of poverty. These programs reduce homelessness and allow families to devote more resources to health care, transportation—and food.[30] When families finally receive housing vouchers after years on the waiting list, the first place many take their freed-up income is to the grocery store. They stock the refrigerator and cupboards. Their children become stronger, less anemic, better nourished.[31]

But the majority of poor families aren't so lucky, and their children—children like Jori, Kendal, and Ruby—are not getting enough food because the rent eats first. In 2013, 1 percent of poor renters lived in rent-controlled units; 15 percent lived in public housing; and 17 percent received a government subsidy, mainly in the form of a rent-reducing voucher. The remaining 67 percent—2 of every 3 poor renting families—received no federal assistance.[32] This drastic shortfall in government support, coupled with rising rent and utility costs alongside stagnant incomes, is the reason why most poor renting families today spend most of their income on housing.[33]

Imagine if we didn't provide unemployment insurance or Social Security to most families who needed these benefits. Imagine if the vast majority of families who applied for food stamps were turned away hungry. And yet this is exactly how we treat most poor families seeking shelter.

A PROBLEM AS big as the affordable-housing crisis calls for a big solution. It should be at the top of America's domestic-policy agenda—because it is driving poor families to financial ruin and even starting to engulf families with moderate incomes. Today, over 1 in 5 of *all* renting families in the country spends half of its income on housing.[34] America can and should work to make its cities livable again.

Meaningful change comes in various shapes and sizes. Some solutions are slow-going and costly, especially those involving fundamental reform. Other solutions, smaller ones, are more immediately feasible. Consider the courts.

Legal aid to the poor has been steadily diminishing since the Reagan years and was decimated during the Great Recession. The result is that in many housing courts around the country, 90 percent of landlords are represented by attorneys, and 90 percent of tenants are not.[35] Low-income families on the edge of eviction have no right to counsel. But when tenants have lawyers, their chances of keeping their homes increase dramatically.[36] Establishing publicly funded legal services for low-income families in housing court would be a cost-effective measure that would prevent homelessness, decrease evictions, and give poor families a fair shake.

In the 1963 landmark case *Gideon v. Wainwright*, the Supreme Court unanimously established the right to counsel for indigent defendants in criminal cases on the grounds that a fair trial was impossible without a lawyer. Eighteen years later, the court heard the case of Abby Gail Lassiter, a poor black North Carolinian, who appeared without counsel at a civil trial that resulted in her parental rights being terminated. This time, a divided court ruled that defendants had a right to counsel only when they risked losing their physical liberty. Incarceration is a misery, but the outcomes of civil cases also can be devastating. Just ask Ms. Lassiter.

Good lawyers would raise defenses tenants often don't, because they either are unaware of them or, like Arleen, are too nervous and intimidated to mount a strong argument. They would curb frivolous evictions and unchecked abuses and help prevent tenants from signing bad stipulations. If it weren't so easy to evict someone, tenants like Doreen and Patrice could report dangerous or illegal conditions without fearing retaliation. If tenants had lawyers, they wouldn't need to go to court. They could go to work or stay home with their children while their attorney made their case. And their case would actually be made.

Courts have shown little interest in addressing the fact that the majority of tenants facing eviction never show up. If anything, they have come to depend on this because each day brings a pile of eviction cases, and the goal of every person working in housing court, no matter where their sympathies lie, is just to get through the pile because the next day another pile will be there waiting. The principle of due process has been replaced by mere process: pushing cases through. Tenant lawyers would change that. This would cost money, not only in attorney salaries, but also in the hiring of more commissioners, judges, and clerks to handle the business of justice. Every housing court would need to be adequately funded so that it could function like a court, instead of an eviction assembly line: *stamp, stamp, stamp.*

It would be a worthwhile investment in our cities and children. Directing aid upstream in the form of a few hours of legal services could lower costs downstream. For example, a program that ran from 2005 to 2008 in the South Bronx provided more than 1,300 families with legal assistance and prevented eviction in 86 percent of cases. It cost around $450,000, but saved New York City more than $700,000 in estimated shelter costs alone.[37] The consequences of eviction are many—and so are its burdens on the public purse.[38]

The right to counsel in civil matters has been established around the world: not just in France and Sweden but also in Azerbaijan, India, Zambia, and many other countries we like to think of as less progressive than our own.[39] If America extended the right to counsel in housing court, it would be a major step on the path to a more fair and equitable society. But it would not address the underlying source of America's eviction epidemic: the rapidly shrinking supply of affordable housing.

IF WE ACKNOWLEDGE that housing is a basic right of all Americans, then we must think differently about another right: the right to make as much money as possible by providing families with housing—and especially to profit excessively from the less fortunate. Since the founding of this country, a long line of American visionaries have called for a more balanced relationship, one that protects people from the profit motive, "not to destroy individualism," in Franklin D. Roosevelt's words, "but to protect it."[40] Child labor laws, the minimum wage, workplace safety regulations, and other protections we now take for granted came about when we chose to place the well-being of people above money.

There are losers and winners. There are losers because there are winners. "Every condition exists," Martin Luther King Jr. once wrote, "simply because someone profits by its existence. This economic exploitation is crystallized in the slum."[41]

Exploitation. Now, there's a word that has been scrubbed out of the poverty debate.[42] It is a word that speaks to the fact that poverty is not just a product of low incomes. It is also a product of extractive markets. Boosting poor people's incomes by increasing the minimum wage or public benefits, say, is absolutely crucial. But not all of those extra dollars will stay in the pockets of the poor. Wage hikes are tempered if rents rise along with them, just as food stamps are worth less if groceries in the inner city cost more—and they do, as much as 40 percent more, by one estimate.[43] Poverty is two-faced—a matter of income and expenses, input and output—and in a world of exploitation, it will not be effectively ameliorated if we ignore this plain fact.

History testifies to this point. When the American labor movement rose up in the 1830s to demand higher wages, landed capital did not lock arms with industrial capital. Instead landlords rooted for the workers because higher wages would allow them to collect higher rents. History repeated itself 100 years later, when wage gains that workers had made through labor strikes were quickly absorbed by rising rents. In the interwar years, the industrial job market expanded, but the housing market, especially for blacks, did not, allowing landlords to recoup workers' income gains. Today, if evictions are lowest each February, it is because many members of the city's working poor dedicate some or all of their Earned Income Tax Credit to pay back rent. In many cases, this annual benefit is as much a boost to landlords as to low-income working families.[44] In fixating almost exclusively on what poor people and their communities *lack*—good jobs, a strong safety net, role models—we have neglected the critical ways that exploitation contributes to the persistence of poverty. We have overlooked a fact that landlords never have: there is a lot of money to be made off the poor.[45] The 'hood *is* good.

Exploitation thrives when it comes to the essentials, like housing and food. Most of the 12 million Americans who take out high-interest payday loans do so not to buy luxury items or cover unexpected expenses but to pay the rent or gas bill, buy food, or meet other regular expenses. Payday loans are but one of many financial techniques—from overdraft fees to student loans for for-profit colleges—specifically designed to pull money from the pockets of the poor.[46] If the poor pay more for their housing, food, durable goods, and credit, and if they get smaller returns on their educations and mortgages (if they get returns at all), then their incomes are even smaller than they appear. This is fundamentally unfair.

Those who profit from the current situation—and those indifferent to it—will say that the housing market should be left alone to regulate itself. They don't really mean that. Exploitation within the housing market relies on government support. It is the government that legitimizes and defends landlords' right to charge as much as they want; that subsidizes the construction of high-end apartments, bidding up rents and leaving the poor with even fewer options; that pays landlords when a family cannot, through onetime or ongoing housing assistance; that forcibly removes a family at landlords' request by dispatching armed law enforcement officers; and that records and publicizes evictions, as a service to landlords and debt collection agencies. Just as the police and the prison have worked to triage the ill effects of rising joblessness in the inner city (like social unrest or the growth of the underground economy), civil courts, sheriff deputies, and homeless shelters manage the fallout of rising housing costs among the urban poor and the privatization of the low-income housing market.[47]

Landlords like to describe themselves as a special breed. But they are neither alone in making a living off the poor nor are they so different from the rest of us. Large-scale historical and structural changes have given urban landlords the opportunity to make good money, sometimes spectacular money, by providing housing to struggling families at a cost the law has deemed fair and just. If given the same opportunity, would any of us price an apartment at half of what it could fetch or simply forgive and forget losing thousands of dollars when the rent checks didn't arrive? Emphasizing the importance of exploitation does not mean haranguing landlords as greedy or heartless. It means uncovering the ironies and inefficiencies that arise when policymakers try to help poor families without addressing the root causes of their poverty. It means trying to understand landlords' and tenants' acceptance of extreme inequality—and our own.

Regardless of how landlords came to own property—sweat, intelligence, or ingenuity for some; inheritance, luck, or fraud for others—rising rents mean more money for landlords and less for tenants. Their fates are bound and their interests opposed. If the profits of urban landlords were modest, that would be one thing. But often they are not. The annual income of the landlord of perhaps the worst trailer park in the fourth-poorest city in America is 30 times that of his tenants working full-time for minimum wage and 55 times the annual income of his tenants receiving welfare or SSI. There are two freedoms at odds with each other: the freedom to profit from rents and the freedom to live in a safe and affordable home.[48]

THERE IS A way we can rebalance these two freedoms: by significantly expanding our housing voucher program so that *all* low-income families could benefit from it. What we need most is a housing program for the unlucky majority—the millions of poor families struggling unassisted in the private market—that promotes the values most of us support: security, fairness, and equal opportunity. A universal housing voucher program would carve a middle path between the landlord's desire to make a living and the tenant's desire, simply, to live.

The idea is simple. Every family below a certain income level would be eligible for a housing voucher. They could use that voucher to live anywhere they wanted, just as families can use food stamps to buy groceries virtually anywhere, as long as their housing was neither too expensive, big, and luxurious nor too shabby and run-down. Their home would need to be decent, modest, and fairly priced. Program administrators could develop fine-grained analyses, borrowing from algorithms and other tools commonly used in the private market, to prevent landlords from charging too much and families from selecting more housing than they need. The family would dedicate 30 percent of their income to housing costs, with the voucher paying the rest.

A universal voucher program would change the face of poverty in this country. Evictions would plummet and become rare occurrences. Homelessness would almost disappear. Families would immediately feel the income gains and be able to buy enough food, invest in themselves and their children through schooling or job training, and start modest savings. They would find stability and have a sense of ownership over their home and community.

Universal housing programs have been successfully implemented all over the developed world. In countries that have such programs, every single family with an income below a certain level who meets basic program requirements has a right to housing assistance. Great Britain's Housing Benefit is available to so many households that a journalist recently reporting on the program asked, "Perhaps it is easier to say who does not get it?" "Indeed," came the answer. This benefit, transferred directly to landlords in most cases, ensures that paying rent does not plunge a family into poverty. The Netherlands' Housing Allowance operates in a similar way and helps provide good homes to nearly one-third of all its tenants. It has been remarkably successful at housing the country's poorest citizens.[49]

There is a reason why these countries have come to rely on vouchers. Although vouchers are not everywhere the most efficient option—particularly in expensive cities—they are the best way to deliver a national program. In theory, you could solve the problem by expanding public housing, tax credits, homeownership initiatives, or developer incentives. But each of these options quickly confronts the problem of scale. Vouchers are far more cost-effective than new construction, whether in the form of public housing or subsidized private development. We can't build our way out. Given mounting regulatory and construction costs, offering each low-income family the opportunity to live in public housing would be prohibitively expensive. Even if it weren't, building that much public housing risks repeating the failures of the past, by drawing the nation's poorest citizens under the same roof and contributing to racial segregation and concentrated poverty.[50]

Would a universal housing program be a disincentive to work? It is a fair and important question. One study has shown that housing assistance leads to a modest reduction in work hours and earnings, but others have found no effect.[51] In truth, the status quo is much more of a threat to self-sufficiency than any housing program could be. Families crushed by the high cost of housing cannot afford vocational training or extra schooling that would allow them to acquire new skills; and many cannot stay in one place long enough to hold down the same job. Affordable housing is a human-capital investment, just like job programs or education, one that would strengthen and steady the American workforce. By and large, the poor do not want some small life. They don't want to game the system or eke out an existence; they want to thrive and contribute: to become nurses (that was Vanetta's dream) or run their own charities (that was Arleen's). A stable home would extend to them the opportunity to realize those dreams.

Landlords in most states are not obligated to accept families with housing vouchers, and many don't because they shun extra building-code mandates or the administrative hassle. A universal voucher program would take their concerns seriously. Some building codes are critical to maintaining safe and decent housing; others are far less so. Enforcing a strict building code in apartments where voucher holders live can be an unnecessary burden on landlords and drive up costs.[52] But even if code enforcement and program administration were made much more reasonable and landlord-friendly, some property owners—particularly those operating in prosperous areas—would still turn away voucher holders. They simply don't want to house "those people." If we continue to permit this kind of discrimination, we consign voucher holders to certain landlords who own property in certain neighborhoods. Doing so denies low-income families the opportunity to move into economically healthy and safe neighborhoods and hobbles our ability to promote integration through social policy. Accordingly, a universal voucher program would not only strive to make participation attractive to landlords, it would also mandate participation. Just as we have outlawed discrimination on the basis of race or religion, discrimination against voucher holders would be illegal under a universal voucher program.

A well-designed program would ensure a reasonable rent that rose at the rate of inflation and include flexible provisions allowing land-lords to receive a modest rate of return. It would also provide them with steadier rental income, less turnover, and fewer evictions. If we are going to house most low-income families in the private rental market, then that market must remain profitable. "The business of housing the poor," Jacob Riis wrote 125 years ago, "if it is to amount to anything, must be a business, as it was business with our fathers to put them where they are. As charity, pastime, or fad, it will miserably fail, always and everywhere."[53] And yet, housing is too fundamental a human need, too central to children's health and development, too important to expanding economic opportunities and stabilizing communities to be treated as simply a business, a crude investment vehicle, something that just "cashes out."

Making a universal housing program as efficient as possible would require regulating costs. Expanding housing vouchers without stabilizing rent would be asking taxpayers to subsidize landlords' profits.[54] Today, landlords overcharge voucher holders simply because they can. In distressed neighborhoods, where voucher holders tend to live, market rent is lower than what landlords are allowed to charge voucher holders, according to metropolitan-wide rent ceilings set by program administrators. So the Housing Choice Voucher Program likely costs not millions but billions of dollars more than it should, resulting in the unnecessary denial of help to hundreds of thousands of families. In fact, economists have argued that the current housing voucher program could be expanded to serve all poor families in America *without additional spending* if we prevented overcharging and made the program more efficient.[55]

Even if we did nothing to make the voucher program more cost-effective, we still could afford to offer this crucial benefit to all low-income families in America. In 2013, the Bipartisan Policy Center estimated that expanding housing vouchers to all renting families below the 30th percentile in median income for their area would require an additional $22.5 billion, increasing total spending on housing assistance to around $60 billion. The figure is likely much less, as the estimate does not account for potential savings the expanded program would bring in the form of preventing homelessness, reducing health-care costs, and curbing other costly consequences of the affordable-housing crisis.[56] It is not a small figure, but it is well within our capacity.

We have the money. We've just made choices about how to spend it. Over the years, lawmakers on both sides of the aisle have restricted housing aid to the poor but expanded it to the affluent in the form of tax benefits for homeowners.[57] Today, housing-related tax expenditures far outpace those for housing assistance. In 2008, the year Arleen was evicted from Thirteenth Street, federal expenditures for direct housing assistance totaled less than $40.2 billion, but homeowner tax benefits exceeded $171 billion. That number, $171 billion, was equivalent to the 2008 budgets for the Department of Education, the Department of Veterans Affairs, the Department of Homeland Security, the Department of Justice, and the Department of Agriculture combined.[58] Each year, we spend three times what a universal housing voucher program is estimated to cost (in *total*) on homeowner benefits, like the mortgage-interest deduction and the capital-gains exclusion.

Most federal housing subsidies benefit families with six-figure incomes.[59] If we are going to spend the bulk of our public dollars on the affluent—at least when it comes to housing—we should own up to that decision and stop repeating the politicians' canard about one of the richest countries on the planet being unable to afford doing more. If poverty persists in America, it is not for lack of resources.

A UNIVERSAL VOUCHER program is but one potential policy recommendation. Let others come. Establishing the basic right to housing in America could be realized in any number of ways—and probably should be. What works best in New York might fail in Los Angeles. The solution to housing problems in booming Houston or Atlanta or Seattle is not what is most needed in the deserted metropolises of the Rust Belt or Florida's impoverished suburbs or small towns dotting the landscape. One city must build; another must destroy. If our cities and towns are rich in diversity—with unique textures and styles, gifts and problems—so too must be our solutions.

Whatever our way out of this mess, one thing is certain. This degree of inequality, this withdrawal of opportunity, this cold denial of basic needs, this endorsement of pointless suffering—by no American value is this situation justified. No moral code or ethical principle, no piece of scripture or holy teaching, can be summoned to defend what we have allowed our country to become.

ABOUT THIS PROJECT

When I was growing up, my father was a preacher, and my industrious mother worked everywhere. Money was always tight. Sometimes the gas got shut off, and Mom cooked dinner on top of our wood-burning stove. She knew how to make do, having grown up across from a junkyard in Columbus, Georgia, and, later, in San Francisco's infamous Ford Hotel. She had done better for herself and expected us kids to do the same, to go off to college even if she and my father weren't able to help pay for it. My father drilled this point home in his own way. Whenever we drove past a line of bent-over people, sweating in the sun for some lousy job, my father would turn to us and ask, "Do you want to do that for the rest of your life?"

"No."

"Then go to college."

Thanks to some loans and scholarships, I was able to attend Arizona State University, a four-hour drive from my hometown of Winslow. I thought I might want to be a lawyer, so I enrolled in courses on communication, history, and justice. In those classes, I began learning things that did not square with the image of America passed down to me from my parents, Sunday-school teachers, and Boy Scout troop leaders. Was the depth and expanse of poverty in this country truly unmatched in the developed world? Was the American Dream widely attainable or reserved for a privileged few? When I wasn't working or studying, I was thumbing through books in the library, seeking answers about the character of my country.

It was around that time that the bank took my childhood home. A friend and I made the four-hour drive and helped my parents move. I remember being deeply sad and embarrassed. I didn't know how to make sense of it, but maybe something worked its way inside because, once back on campus, I found myself spending weekends helping my girlfriend build houses with Habitat for Humanity. Then I began hanging out with homeless people around Tempe's Mill Avenue several nights a week. The people I met living on the street were young and old, funny, genuine, and troubled. When I graduated, I felt a need to understand poverty in America, which I saw as the wellspring of so many miseries. I figured sociology would be the best place to do that. So I enrolled in a PhD program at the University of Wisconsin at Madison, a town that grizzled Milwaukeeans refer to as "thirty square miles surrounded by reality."

When I began studying poverty as a graduate student, I learned that most accounts explained inequality in one of two ways. The first referenced "structural forces" seemingly beyond our control: historical legacies of discrimination, say, or massive transformations of the economy. The second emphasized individual deficiencies, from "cultural" practices, like starting a family outside of wedlock, to "human capital" shortfalls, like low levels of education. Liberals preferred the first explanation and conservatives the second. To me, both seemed off. Each treated low-income families as if they lived in quarantine. With books about single mothers, gang members, or the homeless, social scientists and journalists were writing about poor people as if they were cut off from the rest of society. The poor were said to be "invisible" or part of "the other America." The ghetto was treated like "a city within a city." The poor were being left out of the inequality debate, as if we believed the livelihoods of the rich and the middle class were intertwined but those of the poor and everyone else were not. Where were the rich people who wielded enormous influence over the lives of low-income families and their communities—who were rich precisely because they did so? Why, I wondered, have we documented how the poor make ends meet without asking why their bills are so high or where their money is flowing?

I wanted to try to write a book about poverty that didn't focus exclusively on poor people or poor places. Poverty was a relationship, I thought, involving poor and rich people alike. To understand poverty, I needed to understand that relationship. This sent me searching for a process that bound poor and rich people together in mutual dependence and struggle. Eviction was such a process.[1]

I MOVED INTO Tobin's trailer park in May 2008, after reading in the newspaper that its residents could face mass eviction. That didn't happen. (Tobin eventually did sell the trailer park, and Lenny and Office Susie moved elsewhere.) But I stayed anyway because the park proved a fine place to meet people getting the pink papers. It also allowed me to spend time with Tobin and Lenny.

My trailer was considered to be one of the nicest in the park. It was clean with wood paneling and thick, rust-orange carpet. But for most of the four months I lived in it, I did not have hot water because, despite multiple requests, Tobin and Lenny neglected to fix the chimney to my water heater. They just didn't get around to it, even though I told them I was a writer working on a book about them and their trailer park. If used, the water heater would have emitted carbon monoxide straight into the trailer. Office Susie tried to fix it once. She jammed a wooden board underneath and, with two inches still separating the water heater from the chimney, pronounced it safe.

To me, ethnography is what you do when you try to understand

people by allowing their lives to mold your own as fully and genuinely
as possible. You do this by building rapport with the people you want
to know better and following them over a long stretch of time, observing and experiencing what they do, working and playing alongside
them, and recording as much action and interaction as you can until
you begin to move like they move, talk like they talk, think like they
think, and feel something like they feel. In this line of work, living
"in the field" helps quite a lot. It's the only way to have an immersive
experience; and practically speaking, you never know when important things are going to happen. Renting a trailer allowed me to meet
dozens of people, pick up on rumors, absorb tenants' concerns and
perspectives, and observe everyday life all hours of the day.

I began my fieldwork in the trailer park hanging out in the office,
where some of my neighbors spent most of their days. I was in the office the evening Larraine walked in, shaking and gripping a warning
from the sheriff's eviction squad. I watched her pay Tobin what she
could before dragging herself back to her trailer. I followed her there.
Larraine opened the door, wiping away tears with the bottom of her
shirt. That's how we met. After word spread that I was interested in
talking to people going through an eviction, Pam got ahold of my
phone number and called me up. A few days after we met, I began
trailing her and her family as they looked for a new place to live. Pam
told Scott about my project, and he told me to stop by his trailer.
When I did one morning, Scott stepped outside and said, "Let's walk."
Then he said, "Well, let's just get this out in the open. I was a nurse
for . . . years. But then I got addicted to painkillers and lost everything. My job, my car, my house."

No one really knows why some people unfurl like this in front of
a stranger with a notepad and pen, why they open the door and let
you in. With tenants on the verge of homelessness, there were material
benefits, like access to a car and phone, and psychological ones, too.
Several called me their "shrink." But there is another truth too, which
is that some people at the bottom don't think they have anything left

to lose. One evening at the Aldea Recovery House, where Scott had been living sober for a few months, Scott nodded to me scribbling away in my notepad and asked AA diehard Anna Aldea, "Does it make you nervous, having Matt here?"

"Fuck no," Anna said. "My life is an open book."

Said Scott, "I am the same way. You know, I've got no pride or anything left."

WHEN FALL ARRIVED, having seen Scott, Larraine, and Pam and Ned evicted from the trailer park, I began looking for a new place to live on the North Side. One day, I mentioned this to Officer Woo, one of the security guards Tobin had been forced to hire to appease Alderman Witkowski. Woo's real name was Kimball, but he told everyone to call him by his childhood nickname. A gregarious black man who tried to make friends with everyone in the park, he wore size 6 XL T-shirts and a security badge he had picked up at an army surplus shop.

"You talkin' about moving out by Silver Spring?" Woo asked, thinking about an area where Milwaukee's black inner city gave way to the northern suburbs of Glendale and Brown Deer.

"I'm thinking like city center," I clarified.

"You want to be by Marquette?" Woo asked again, referencing the Jesuit university located downtown.

"Not by Marquette. I'm looking for an inner-city neighborhood."

Woo squinted at me, assuming he had misunderstood. It took a few more conversations for Woo to realize that I wanted to live on the North Side, in a neighborhood like his, where the street signs were green, not blue like in the suburb of Wauwatosa. Once he did, Woo invited me to live with him in a rooming house on First and Locust. The rent was $400, utilities included. I accepted and paid the landlords: Sherrena and Quentin.

The rooming house was on the second floor of a duplex, white with green trim. Woo and I shared a living room, bathroom, and kitchen, whose cupboards could be padlocked to keep your roommates from eating your food. My room came with a window, draped with a heavy blanket, and a full-size bed, under which I found an empty can of Classic Ice, Narcotics Anonymous pamphlets, toenail clippers, and a typewriter in a hard plastic case. Behind the rooming house was an alley, tagged in rushed Gangster Disciples graffiti, and a small weedy backyard with a cherry tree that, come May, unveiled soft blossoms that looked like a spray of confetti. I lived in the rooming house until June 2009.

Woo had told Sherrena that I was "working on a book about landlords and tenants." Sherrena agreed to an interview, at the end of which I made my pitch.

"Sherrena, I would love to be kind of like your apprentice," I said, explaining that my goal was to "walk in [her] shoes as closely as possible."

Sherrena was all-in. "I'm committed to this," she said. "You have your person." She was in love with her work and proud of it too. She wanted people to know "what landlords had to go through," to share her world with a wider public that rarely stopped to consider it.

I began shadowing Sherrena and Quentin as they bought property, screened tenants, unclogged sewer pipes, and delivered eviction notices, just as I had done with Tobin and Lenny. I met Arleen, Lamar, and the Hinkston clan through Sherrena. Later, I met Crystal through Arleen, and Vanetta through Crystal. Doreen was lonely and happy to have someone to sit and talk with. Lamar warmed to me after I helped him paint Patrice's old unit; I later sealed the deal by being decent at spades, which I used to play regularly during my days working as a firefighter in college.

Arleen was a much tougher case. At first, she kept me at a distance and would remain silent when I explained my project to her. When I tried to fill the silence, she would cut me off, saying, "You don't need to keep talking." Her biggest worry was that I worked for Child Protective Services. "I feel uncomfortable talking with you," Arleen told me during one of our early conversations, "not because of how you are, but just because of all this stuff that's happened to me. I've been in the [child welfare] system so long that I just don't trust people anymore." I responded by saying that I understood, giving her some of my published work—which I had learned to keep in my car for moments like this—and, later, taking it very slowly, limiting myself to only a handful of questions per meeting.

Other people thought I was a police officer or, in the trailer park, a spy for the alderman. Still others thought I was a drug addict or a john. (For a time, Woo and I lived with sex workers in the rooming house.) Sherrena introduced me as her assistant. To Tobin, I was nobody.

Some tenants suspected I was in cahoots with their landlord, whom they referred to as "your friend." On several occasions, they tried to get me to admit to their landlord's wrongdoing, like the time Lamar pressured me to admit Sherrena was "a slumlord." When I refused, Lamar accused me of being her snoop. Some landlords refused to discuss the details of a tenant's case or, in the opposite direction, asked me to weigh in on a specific case. My policy was to intervene as little as possible (although, as I describe below, I abandoned that policy on two occasions), but landlords often forced my hand. To my knowledge, the only time I had any real effect on a case was the time Sherrena asked me repeatedly if she should call the sheriff on Arleen. I finally said no, and she didn't. Sherrena later told me, "Had you not been involved, honestly, truly, I would have done the writ and been waiting on the sheriff. . . . If you didn't intervene, she would have been dead meat." So instead of Eagle Moving taking her things, Arleen got to store them in Public Storage until they were trashed for missed payments.

After a while, both tenants and landlords began to accept me and get on with their lives. They had more important things to worry about. I sat beside tenants at eviction court, helped them move, followed them into shelters and abandoned houses, watched their children, fought with them, and slept at their houses. I attended church with them, as well as counseling sessions, AA meetings, funerals, and births. I followed one family to Texas. I visited Iowa with Scott. As I spent more time with people, something like trust emerged, even if it remained a fragile, heavily qualified trust.[2] Years after meeting, Arleen would still ask me, during a quiet moment, if I worked for Child Protective Services.

IF MOVING TO the North Side initially confused Woo, it deeply disturbed my neighbors in the trailer park. When I told Larraine, she nearly cried, "No, Matt. You don't know how dangerous it is." Beaker chimed in: "They don't cotton to white folks over there."

But the truth is that white people are afforded special privileges in the ghetto. For one, my interactions with the police were nonintrusive and quick, even after a pair of separate shootings happened outside my front door. Once, I watched a police officer pull his patrol car up to Ger-Ger, Arleen's eldest son, and say, "Man, you're fucked up!" (Ger-Ger had a learning disability that caused him to move and talk slowly.) When I came out of the apartment for a closer look, the officer looked at me and drove away. He might have acted differently had I not been a white man with a notepad.

There were other moments like this. Take Crystal and Vanetta's exchange with the discriminating landlord on Fifteenth Street. When that went down, I was outside in the car, watching Vanetta's kids. The women told me about it when they returned, immediately afterward. I copied down the landlord's number from the rent sign and called him up the next day. Meeting him in the same unit Vanetta and Crystal had been shown, I told him I took home about $1,400 a month (Vanetta and Crystal's combined income), that I had three kids (like Vanetta), and that I'd really like a unit with a bathtub. The landlord told me that he had another unit available. He even drove me to it in his Saab. I reported him to the Fair Housing Council. They took down my report and never called me back.

Inner-city residents took care to protect me and make sure I wasn't taken advantage of, as when Lamar would snap at his boys—"Cut that shit out!"—when they asked me for a dollar. One day at the rooming house, C.C., one of my downstairs neighbors, asked to borrow a few dollars so she could buy trash bags. I obliged and went back to writing. But Keisha, Woo's young niece who was living with us at the time, kept an eye on C.C. as she left and claimed to see her call her dope man. Oblivious to this, I soon headed out for the store. When Woo got home, Keisha told him about the exchange, and he called me, angry. "Matt, you don't ever give her nothing!" he said. "They think because you not like us, because you not from around here, that they can just come at you like that. . . . I'm about to go down there and tell them to give you your fucking money back."

"Well, Woo, look—"

"Uh-uh, Matt."

Woo hung up. I don't know exactly what he said to C.C., but when I got home, she met me outside, wearing a wig, cut-off shorts, a revealing halter top, and strappy heels. C.C. handed me the money. I didn't ask how she got it.

It felt terrible. "You're too protective of me," I told Woo when I got upstairs.

He was leaning over the kitchen sink, washing dishes shirtless. "You suburbs. We 'hood," he began, using his low, father-to-son voice he reserved for moments like this. "And you came down here, took a chance living in the 'hood with me. And that was a real honor for me, and I feel responsible for you here. I ain't let nothing happen to you."

A white person living in and writing about the inner city is not uniquely exposed to threats but uniquely shielded from them. And inner-city residents sometimes stiffened in my presence. People often started cleaning up and apologizing after meeting me for the first time. In my late twenties, I was called "sir" countless more times than I was told by some young tough to get a "G pass"—a "gangster pass," essentially to account for my white self. These are nontrivial issues for someone trying to record life as it is actually lived. The only thing to do is to spend as much time on the ground as you can, transforming yourself from novelty to perpetual foreigner. People generally relax and go about their business with enough time, even if their guard can fly up again in certain circumstances.

It takes time too, to be taught how to notice things by people like Keisha, who have learned when to listen and what to look for. The people I met in Milwaukee trained my vision by modeling how to see and showing me how to make sense of what I saw. Still, I know I missed a lot, especially in the beginning, not only because I was an outsider but also because I was constantly overanalyzing things. A buzzing inner monologue would often draw me inward, hindering my ability to remain alert to the heat of life at play right in front of me. It's safer that way. Our ideas allow us to tame social life, to order it according to typologies and theories. As Susan Sontag has warned, this comfort can "deplete the world" and get in the way of seeing.[3]

RESEARCHING THIS BOOK involved spending long stretches of time with women, often in their homes, which raised suspicions. In two incidents, men accused me of sleeping with their girlfriends. The first occurred during a drunken argument between Ned and Pam, when Ned snapped: "You're the one talking to Matt, like he's a fucking psychologist. . . . Why don't you go fuck him." After Ned stormed off, Pam said to me, "He thinks we're fucking. How pathetic is that?" The fight died down, and Ned backed off from the accusation. But several weeks after that happened, I kept my distance from Pam and tried spending as much time with Ned as I could. On another occasion, I stopped by to see Vanetta the month before she was sentenced to prison and found her with Earl, an older man she had met at the Lodge. Earl had taken a strong romantic interest in Vanetta, an interest she entertained, and he was not happy to see me. Said Earl, "You see, this is my woman. And I should know what my woman is doing." I took my time explaining my job to Earl and showed him my previous work. I thought he was capable of hurting Vanetta—his rap sheet contained domestic-abuse charges—or at least of leaving her and taking his VA check with him. Earl eventually apologized to me, but the exchange was deeply unsettling. When I left, I asked Vanetta's sister, Ebony, to check on Vanetta, which she did. And the next morning, I called to make sure everything was okay. "He don't scare me, though," Vanetta told me. He should have. After Vanetta got out of prison and broke it off with Earl, someone shot up Ebony's apartment, where Vanetta and her children were staying. Everyone suspected Earl.

I've always felt that my first duty as an ethnographer was to make sure my work did not harm those who invited me into their lives. But this can be a complicated and delicate matter because it is not always obvious at first what does harm.[4] Especially in poor neighborhoods, nothing is free. People get compensated for favors one way or another. Ned and Earl figured that if I was giving their girlfriends rides as they looked for housing and went about their business, I must be getting something in return. I was, of course: stories. That was the strange thing. Their accusations were perfectly valid, and I took them seriously.

Gender influenced how people behaved and talked in my presence in other ways too. After prison, Vanetta found a job running tables at a George Webb restaurant and met a new man, Ben, who aspired to be a truck driver. One night in their apartment, Ben left abruptly. "Are you guys okay?" I asked.

"Not really." Vanetta sighed. "He thinks I act too much like a man."

"What's that mean?" I asked.

"It's like I know too much. . . . He's always like, 'You acting like a man. Like, you always have to have an answer to everything.'"

"You ever pretend not to know stuff?"

"Sometimes."

Right then I wondered how often Vanetta had played dumb with me, how often she had faked ignorance to appear more ladylike.

Everything about you—your race and gender, where and how you were raised, your temperament and disposition—can influence whom you meet, what is confided to you, what you are shown, and how you interpret what you see. My identity opened some doors and closed others. In the end, we can only do the best we can with who we are, paying close attention to the ways pieces of ourselves matter to the work while never losing sight of the most important questions.[5]

WHILE LIVING IN Milwaukee, I was a full-time fieldworker. Most days, I carried a digital recorder and just let it run. This allowed me to capture people's words verbatim. I also carried a small notepad and wrote down observations and conversations, usually as they were happening. I never hid the fact that I was a writer trying to record as much as I could. In the evenings and early mornings, I would spend hours typing up the jottings from my notebooks and writing about the day's events. I took thousands of photographs. I conducted more than one hundred interviews with people not featured in this book, including thirty landlords. I spoke with and observed court officers, social workers, building inspectors, property managers, and other people who lived in the trailer park or inner city.

When I left the field, I began a long process of transcribing the recorded material. Some people helped me with this, but I did a significant amount myself. After everything was down on paper, my notes spanned over five thousand single-spaced pages. I began poring over the words, calling up the photographs, and listening to recordings on my way to work or when rocking my newborn to sleep. I read and reread everything several times before I felt ready to begin writing.[6] I wanted to be as close to the material as possible, to experience a kind of second immersion in the words and scenes. And I missed everyone. Moving from the North Side of Milwaukee to Cambridge, Massachusetts—a rich, rarefied community—was profoundly disorienting. At first, all I wanted was to be back in the trailer park or the inner city. I returned as often as I could.

Writing this book, I have prioritized firsthand observation. When something important happened that I didn't see, I spoke to multiple people about the event whenever possible and checked details by drawing on other sources, such as news reports, medical or court records, and mortgage files. I have indicated in the notes all events sourced from secondhand accounts. I said that someone "thought" or "believed" something only when they said as much to me. When writing about things that happened in people's past, I said someone "remembered" or "recalled" it a certain way. To interrogate those details, I would ask the same person the same questions multiple times over several years. This proved to be incredibly useful, as some things people told me at the beginning turned out to be inaccurate. Sometimes, the truth comes out slow.

As much as possible, I vetted the material in this book by reaching out to third parties. Often, this meant confirming the possibility of something happening, if not the thing itself. For example, I was able to verify with the Wisconsin Department of Children and Families that the welfare sanctions Arleen experienced were not uncommon. I had overheard Arleen explain the sanctions to Sherrena and had accompanied Arleen as she met with a caseworker to sort out the details; but because this was something I could corroborate with a few emails and phone calls, I did. After all, eyewitnessing is a fraught and imperfect thing, as any defense attorney will tell you. Things hide in plain sight and misdirection is everywhere. I dropped stories that could not be verified through this method. Once, Natasha Hinkston told me that she stopped going to high school after there was a shooting in her cafeteria. After confirming this story with Doreen, I found myself drawn to it, eager to include it somewhere, which is an impulse I've learned to mistrust. So I spoke with three separate Milwaukee Public School administrators, none of whom could confirm that a shooting occurred around the time Natasha said it did. Perhaps something did happen and the administrators were wrong; perhaps the gist (if not the details) of Natasha's story was true; perhaps not. Whatever the case, I excluded this account and two others that could not be corroborated in this manner. Once the book was fully drafted, I hired an independent fact-checker.[7] I also traveled to Milwaukee and Brownsville, Tennessee, to tie up loose ends.[8]

I am frequently asked how I "handled" this research, by which people mean: How did seeing this level of poverty and suffering affect you, personally? I don't think people realize how raw and intimate a question this is. So I've developed several dishonest responses, which I drop like those smoke bombs magicians use when they want to glide offstage, unseen. The honest answer is that the work was heartbreaking and left me depressed for years. You do learn how to cope from those who are coping. After several people told me, "Stop looking at me like that," I learned to suppress my shock at traumatic things. I learned to tell a real crisis from mere poverty. I learned that behavior that looks lazy or withdrawn to someone perched far above the poverty line can actually be a pacing technique. People like Crystal or Larraine cannot afford to give all their energy to today's emergency only to have none left over for tomorrow's. I saw in the trailer park and inner city resilience and spunk and brilliance. I heard a lot of laughter. But I also saw a lot of pain. Toward the end of my fieldwork, I wrote in my journal, "I feel dirty, collecting these stories and hardships like so many trophies." The guilt I felt during my fieldwork only intensified after I left. I felt like a phony and like a traitor, ready to confess to some unnamed accusation. I couldn't help but translate a bottle of wine placed in front of me at a university function or my monthly day-care bill into rent payments or bail money back in Milwaukee. It leaves an impression, this kind of work. Now imagine it's your life.

As I spent more time with tenants and landlords, I found myself needing answers to basic questions that were beyond the reach of my fieldwork. How prominent is eviction? What are its consequences? Who gets evicted? If poor families are spending so much on housing, what are they going without? So I went looking for studies that answered these questions. Urban poverty, community, slums—these topics had been foundational to American sociology from the beginning. Surely someone had looked into it.

But I found no study—and no readily available data—that adequately addressed my questions. This was strange, especially given what I was seeing every day in Milwaukee. I wondered how we in the research community could have overlooked something so fundamental to poverty in America: the dynamics of the private housing market. The answer, I would later come to realize, was in the way we had been studying housing. By and large, poverty researchers had focused narrowly on public housing or other housing policies; either that, or they had overlooked housing because they were more interested in the character of urban neighborhoods—their levels of residential segregation or resistance to gentrification, for example.[9] And yet here was the private rental market, where the vast majority of poor people lived, playing such an imposing and vital role in the lives of the families I knew in Milwaukee, consuming most of their income; aggravating their poverty and deprivation; resulting in their eviction, insecurity, and homelessness; dictating where they lived and whom they lived with; and powerfully influencing the character and stability of their neighborhoods. And we hardly knew a thing about it.

I tried to ignore this problem, wanting to spend all my time with landlords and tenants on the ground. But when my questions didn't go away, I set out to gather the data myself. I began by designing a survey of tenants in Milwaukee's private housing sector. The survey began small, but with the support of the MacArthur Foundation it grew into something more. I called it the Milwaukee Area Renters Study, MARS for short. From 2009 to 2011, roughly 1,100 tenants were interviewed in their homes by professional interviewers trained and supervised by the University of Wisconsin Survey Center, which reported to me. To facilitate estimates generalizable to Milwaukee's entire rental population, households from across the city were interviewed. Clipboards and portable Lenovo ThinkPad computers in hand, interviewers ventured into some of the city's worst neighborhoods. One was bitten by a dog and, later, mugged.

Thanks to the heroic efforts of the Survey Center, MARS had an extraordinarily high response rate for a survey of such a highly mobile and poor population (84 percent). What I was learning during my fieldwork deeply informed MARS's 250 questions: not only what I asked but how I asked it. For example, when I was living in the trailer park, I learned that asking why someone moved was no simple task. Tenants often provided an explanation for a move that maximized their own volition. And asking about involuntary mobility, for its part, came with its own set of complications, as tenants tended to have strict conceptions of eviction. Take Rose and Tim, my neighbors in the trailer park. Rose and Tim were forced to leave their trailer after Tim sustained a back injury at work. They did not go to court but undeniably were evicted. (Their names appear in the eviction records.) Nevertheless, they didn't see things this way. "When you say 'eviction,'" Rose explained, "I think of the sheriffs coming and throwing you out and changing your locks, and Eagle Movers tosses your stuff on the curb. That's an eviction. We were *not* evicted." If Rose and Tim had been asked during a survey, "Have you ever been evicted?," they would have answered no. Accordingly, surveys that have posed this question vastly underestimate the prevalence of involuntary removal from housing. I learned to ask the question differently, in light of tenants' understanding of the matter, and designed the survey accordingly.

MARS collected new data on housing, residential mobility, eviction, and urban poverty. These data provide the only comprehensive estimate of the frequency of involuntary displacement from housing among urban renters. When I ran the numbers, I was shocked to discover that 1 in 8 Milwaukee renters experienced at least one forced move—formal or informal eviction, landlord foreclosure, or building condemnation—in the two years prior to being surveyed.

The survey also showed that nearly half of those forced moves (48 percent) were informal evictions: off-the-books displacements not processed through the court, as when a landlord pays you to leave or hires a couple of heavies to throw you out. Formal eviction was less common, constituting 24 percent of forced moves. An additional

23 percent of forced moves were due to landlord foreclosure, with building condemnations accounting for the remaining 5 percent.[10]

In other words, for every eviction executed through the judicial system, there are two others executed beyond the purview of the court, without any form of due process. This means that estimates that do not account for informal evictions downplay the crisis in our cities. If public attention and resources are a product of how widespread policymakers think a problem is, then studies that produce artificially low eviction rates are not just wrong; they're harmful.

Some of the most important findings to come out of the Milwaukee Area Renters Study have to do with eviction's fallout. The data linked eviction to heightened residential instability, substandard housing, declines in neighborhood quality, and even job loss. These findings led me to analyze the consequences of eviction in a national-representative data set (the Fragile Families and Child Wellbeing Study), which showed that evicted mothers suffer from increased material hardship as well as poor physical and mental health.

The prevalence of informal eviction notwithstanding, you can still learn something from eviction court records. They provide an accurate measure of the frequency and location of formal evictions in the city. So I extracted records for all eviction cases that took place in Milwaukee between 2003 and 2013, hundreds of thousands of them. According to these official records, each year almost half of all formal, court-ordered evictions in Milwaukee take place in predominantly black neighborhoods. Within those neighborhoods women are more than twice as likely to be evicted as men.[11]

Last, I designed another survey that would help me understand why certain people escaped eviction while others did not. The Milwaukee Eviction Court Study was an in-person survey of 250 tenants appearing in eviction court over a six-week period in January and February 2011 (66 percent response rate). These interviews, conducted immediately after tenants' court hearings, provided a snapshot into Milwaukee's evicted population. The data show that the median age of a tenant in Milwaukee's eviction court was thirty-three. The youngest was nineteen; the oldest, sixty-nine. The median monthly household income of tenants in eviction court was $935, and the median amount of back rent owed was about that much. The eviction court survey also showed that much more than rental debt separates the evicted from the almost evicted. When I analyzed these data, I found that even after accounting for how much the tenant owed the landlord—and other factors like household income and race—the presence of children in the household almost tripled a tenant's odds of receiving an eviction judgment. The effect of living with children on receiving an eviction judgment was equivalent to falling four months behind in rent.[12]

The multiple methods and different data sources used in this book informed one another in important ways. I began this project with a set of questions to pursue, but lines of inquiry flexed and waned as my fieldwork progressed. Some would not have sprung to mind had I never set foot in the field. But it was only after analyzing court records and survey data that I was able to see the bigger picture, grasping the magnitude of eviction in poor neighborhoods, identifying disparities, and cataloguing consequences of displacement. My quantitative endeavors also allowed me to assess how representative my observations were. Whenever possible, I subjected my ground-level observations to a kind of statistical check, which determined whether what I was seeing on the ground was also detectable within a larger population. When an idea was clarified or refined by aggregate comparisons, I would return to my field notes to identify the mechanisms behind the numbers. Working in concert with one another, each method enriched the others. And each kept the others honest.

In addition to the larger endeavors—conducting original surveys and analyzing big data from court records—I also sought out a wide variety of evidence to bolster the validity of my observations and deepen my understanding of the issues. I analyzed two years' worth of nuisance property citations from the Milwaukee Police Department;

obtained records of more than a million 911 calls in Milwaukee; and collected rent rolls, legal transcripts, public property records, school files, and psychological evaluations.

Together, these combined data sources provide a new portrait of the powerful ways the private housing sector is shaping the lives of poor American families and their communities. They have shown that problems endemic to poverty—residential instability, severe deprivation, concentrated neighborhood disadvantage, health disparities, even joblessness—stem from the lack of affordable housing in our cities. I have made all survey data publicly available through the Harvard Dataverse Network.[13]

THIS BOOK IS based in Milwaukee. Wisconsin's largest city is not every city, but it is considerably less unique than the small clutch of iconic but exceptional places that have come to represent the American urban experience. Every city creates its own ecosystem, but in some cities this is much more pronounced. Milwaukee is a fairly typical midsize metropolitan area with a fairly typical socioeconomic profile and housing market and fairly typical renter protections.[14] It is far better suited to represent the experiences of city dwellers living in Indianapolis, Minneapolis, Baltimore, St. Louis, Cincinnati, Gary, Raleigh, Utica, and other cities left out of the national conversation because they are not America's biggest successes (San Francisco, New York City) or biggest failures (Detroit, Newark).

That said, it is ultimately up to future researchers to determine whether what I found in Milwaukee is true in other places. A thousand questions remain unanswered. We need a robust sociology of housing that reaches beyond a narrow focus on policy and public housing. We need a new sociology of displacement that documents the prevalence, causes, and consequences of eviction. And perhaps most important, we need a committed sociology of inequality that includes a serious study of exploitation and extractive markets.

Still, I wonder sometimes what we are asking when we ask if

findings apply elsewhere. Is it that we really believe that something could happen in Pittsburgh but never in Albuquerque, in Memphis but never in Dubuque? The weight of the evidence is in the other direction, especially when it comes to problems as big and as widespread as urban poverty and unaffordable housing. This study took place in the heart of a major American city, not in an isolated Polish village or a brambly Montana town or on the moon.[15] The number of evictions in Milwaukee is equivalent to the number in other cities, and the people summoned to housing court in Milwaukee look a lot like those summoned in Charleston and Brooklyn. Maybe what we are really asking when we ask if a study is "generalizable" is: Can it really be this bad everywhere? Or maybe we're asking: Do I really have to pay attention to this problem?

ETHNOGRAPHY RECENTLY HAS come to be written almost exclusively in the first person. It is a straightforward way of writing and an effective one. If ethnographers want people to take what they say seriously, the cultural anthropologist Clifford Geertz once observed, they have to convince readers that they have "been there." "And that," Geertz said, "persuading us that this offstage miracle has occurred, is where the writing comes in."[16] The first person has become the chosen mule for this task. *I was there. I saw it happen. And because I saw it happen, you can believe it happened.* Ethnographers shrink themselves in the field but enlarge themselves on the page because first-person accounts convey experience—and experience, authority.

But first-person narration is not the only technique available to us.[17] In fact, it may be the least well-suited vehicle for capturing the essence of a social world because the "I" filters all. With first-person narration, the subjects and the author are each always held in view, resulting in every observation being trailed by a reaction to the observer. No matter how much care the author takes, the first-person ethnography becomes just as much about the fieldworker as about anything she or he saw. I have sat through countless conversations about a work of ethnography or reportage that have nothing to do with the book's sub-ject matter and everything to do with its author's decisions or mistakes or "ethical character." And after almost every academic talk I have given on the material in this book, I have been asked questions like: "How did you feel when you saw that?" "How did you gain this sort of access?" These are fine questions, but there is bigger game afoot. There is an enormous amount of pain and poverty in this rich land. At a time of rampant inequality and widespread hardship, when hunger and homelessness are found throughout America, I am interested in a different, more urgent conversation. "I" don't matter. I hope that when you talk about this book, you talk first about Sherrena and Tobin, Arleen and Jori, Larraine and Scott and Pam, Crystal and Vanetta— and the fact that somewhere in your city, a family has just been evicted from their home, their things piled high on the sidewalk.

There are costs to abandoning the first person. In the context of this study, it meant disguising when I intervened in nontrivial ways. There are two such instances in this book. When a "friend" rented Arleen a U-Haul truck to move from Thirteenth Street and when Vanetta borrowed money from a "friend" to buy a stove and refrigera-tor in anticipation of a visit from Child Protective Services, that was me. It is also important to recognize that none of the tenants in this book had a car. I did, and I sometimes drove people around when they were looking for housing. When I didn't, people relied on Milwaukee's irregular bus system or set off on foot. It would have taken families much longer to find subsequent housing if they hadn't had access to my car (or phone).

I didn't pay people for interviews or for their time. People asked me for money because they asked everyone for money. I stopped carry-ing a wallet and learned how to say no like everyone around me did. If I had a few dollars on me, I'd sometimes give it. But as a rule I didn't give out large sums.

In Milwaukee, people bought me food, and I bought them food. People bought me gifts, and I bought them gifts. The Hinkstons once

sent me into their basement to see if I couldn't bang the furnace back
to life. When I emerged unsuccessful, I found a birthday cake waiting for me. Once, Arleen bought me a tin of cookies and one of those
cards that play a silly song. We kept it in my car and would open it
when we needed a laugh. Scott still sends my eldest son a birthday
card with a ten-dollar bill tucked inside, just like he did when he was
homeless.

The harder feat for any fieldworker is not getting in; it's leaving.
And the more difficult ethical dilemma is not how to respond when
asked to help but how to respond when you are given so much. I have
been blessed by countless acts of generosity from the people I met in
Milwaukee. Each one reminds me how gracefully they refuse to be reduced to their hardships. Poverty has not prevailed against their deep
humanity.

ACKNOWLEDGMENTS

To the people I met in Milwaukee: thank you for everything. You invited me into your homes and work, taught me so much more than I could report here, and were patient, courageous, generous, and honest.

My editor, Amanda Cook, read this book several times and provided thirty single-spaced pages of comments on earlier drafts. Thank you, Amanda, for your brilliant reads, broad vision, flat-out hard work, and most of all, for getting it. I'd also like to thank the rest of the team at Crown, including Penny Simon, for being hands down the best publicist a guy could ask for, Molly Stern, for her commitment to serious nonfiction, and Emma Berry, for her careful eye.

Jill Kneerim, my deep-thinking and resolute agent, worked closely with me to develop a proposal, a rigorous and clarifying ordeal. I owe Jill, and everyone at Kneerim and Williams, a huge debt of gratitude.

I began this project while studying sociology at the University of Wisconsin at Madison. Mustafa Emirbayer, my dissertation advisor and total sociologist, spent untold hours reviewing my work and pushing me hard. Thank you, Mustafa, for teaching me so much about the craft. Robert Hauser supported this work in many ways, including by funding my final semester at Wisconsin. Ruth López Turley and Felix Elwert coached me in statistics and much more. Timothy Smeeding connected my ideas and findings to public policies. Chad Goldberg, Myra Marx Ferree, Douglas Maynard, and Pamela Oliver offered their time and guidance.

The University of Wisconsin Survey Center helped me design and implement the Milwaukee Area Renters Study and the Milwaukee Eviction Court Study. I thank everyone at the Survey Center, especially Kerryann DiLoreto, Charlie Palit, Jessica Price, and John Stevenson, who went above and beyond the call of duty (and my budget).

While writing this book, I have benefited enormously from my colleagues and students at Harvard. I would like to thank Bruce Western, for reading this manuscript in full and fundamentally shaping how I think about poverty and justice in America; Robert Sampson, for deepening my perspective on cities, crime, and the purpose of social science; William Julius Wilson, for setting the agenda and encouraging me every step of the way; Kathryn Edin, for trusted advice and contagious optimism; Christopher Jencks, for accepting zero easy answers; Devah Pager, for clarity of mind and generosity of spirit; Christopher Winship, for stimulating conversations about theory, methods, and making a difference; and Michèle Lamont, for stretching my understanding of inequality beyond these shores. I have also relied on insights from William Apgar, Mary Jo Bane, Jason Beckfield, Lawrence Bobo, Alexandra Killewald, Jane Mansbridge, Orlando Patterson, James Quane, Mario Small, and Mary Waters. Deborah De Laurell helped in countless ways, including by offering comments on the manuscript. Nancy Branco and Dotty Lukas aptly handled grant management. And a special thanks to a Brisbane taxi driver.

I have worked with a number of incredible research assistants and collaborators on this project. I thank Weihua An, Monica Bell, Thomas Ferriss, Carl Gershenson, Rachel Tolbert Kimbro, Barbara Kiviat, Jonathan Mijs, Kristin Perkins, Tracey Shollenberger, Adam Travis, Nicol Valdez, Nate Wilmers, and Richelle Winkler. Jasmin Sandelson gave smart comments on the full manuscript.

The Harvard Society of Fellows provided a warm and energetic intellectual environment, not to mention time to think and write. At the Society, I am especially indebted to Daniel Aaron, Lawrence David, Walter Gilbert, Joanna Guldi, Noah Feldman, Sarah Johnson, Kate Manne, Elaine Scarry, Amartya Sen, Maura Smyth, Rachel Stern, William Todd, Glen Weyl, Winnie Wong, and Nur Yalman. Kelly Katz and Diana Morse: thank you for your hospitality and for allowing me to finish this book in Green House.

At Harvard Law School, Esme Caramello and the late (and heroic) David Grossman taught me about the promise and pitfalls of poverty law. Anne Harrington, John Durant, and everyone at Pforzheimer House provided my family and me with community.

This project was supported in a major way by the John D. and Catherine T. MacArthur Foundation, through its "How Housing Matters" initiative, as well as by the Ford Foundation, the American Philosophical Society, the National Science Foundation, the US Department of Housing and Urban Development, the Horowitz Foundation for Social Policy, the Institute for Research on Poverty, the William F. Milton Fund, the Joint Center for Housing Studies, Harvard University's Faculty of Arts and Sciences, and the Malcolm Wiener Center for Social Policy at the John F. Kennedy School of Government.

Barry Widera at Court Data Technologies helped me collect hundreds of thousands of eviction records. Jeffrey Blossom at Harvard's Center for Geographic Analysis geo-coded huge data sets, merging them with population estimates. Chrissy Greer and Liza Karakashian accurately transcribed challenging ethnographic material. In Wisconsin, I also thank Tim Ballering, David Brittain, April Hartman, Michael Kienitz, Maudwella Kirkendoll, and Bradley Werginz for lending me their expertise.

Gillian Brassil, my obsessive and tireless fact-checker, made this book better. Michael Carliner answered several questions about housing data and policy. Marion Fourcade hosted me at Sciences Po for a week, where I began to outline this book on large sheets of paper. For their intellectual guidance and support, I also thank Elijah Anderson, Javier Auyero, Jacob Avery, Vicki Been, Rogers Brubaker, Megan Comfort, Kyle Crowder, John Diedrich, Mitchell Duneier, Ingrid Gould Ellen, Russell Engler, Joseph "Piko" Ewoodzie Jr., Daniel Fetter, Gary Alan Fine, Herbert Gans, Phillip Goff, Mark Granovetter, Suzi Hall, Peter Hart-Brinson, Chester Hartman, Christopher Herbert, Neil Fligstein, Colin Jerolmack, Nikki Jones, Jack Katz, Shamus Khan, Eric Klinenberg, Issa Kohler-Hausmann, John Levi Martin, Kate McCoy, Alexandra Murphy, Tim Nelson, Amanda Pallais, Andrew Papachristos, Mary Pattillo, Victor Rios, Eva Rosen, Megan Sandel, Barbara Sard, Hilary Silver, Adam Slez, Diane Vaughan, Loïc Wacquant, Christopher Wildeman, Eva Williams, and Robb Willer.

I thank the reviewers of this book as well as dozens of anonymous readers of related academic papers. I am grateful for having presented parts of this project at the following institutions, where I received helpful feedback: the Association for Public Policy Analysis and Management, American Sociological Association, Australian National University, Brandeis University, British Sociological Association, Brown University, Center for Housing Policy, Columbia University, Duke University, Harvard University, Harvard Business School, Harvard Law School, Harvard School of Public Health, the Housing Justice Network, King's College London, London School of Economics, National Low Income Housing Coalition Legislative Forum, Marquette University, Max Planck–Sciences Po Center, Massachusetts Institute of Technology, New York Law School, New York University Law School, Northwestern University, Population Association of America, Purdue University, Rice University, Stanford University, the State University of New York at Buffalo, Université de Paris, University of Aarhus, University of Amsterdam, University of California at Berkeley and the Boalt Law School, University of California at Los Angeles, University of Chicago, University of Georgia, University of Michigan, University of Pennsylvania, University of Queensland, University of

Texas at Austin, University of Washington, University of Wisconsin at Madison, University of York, Urban Affairs Association, West Coast Poverty Center, Yale University, and the Yale Law School.

This book is dedicated to my sister, Michelle, who continues to inspire me with her pure curiosity and heart for the poor. Thank you, Shavon, Nick, and Maegan Desmond, for your unceasing support and love. And thank you, Sterling and Walter, my lights, my joy.

Tessa—what can I say? Thank you for anchoring me and empowering this work. You have been there in every moment, and I am overwhelmed with gratitude for your wisdom, sacrifice, and love. *"Thy firmness makes my circle just / And makes me end where I begun."**

---

*John Donne, "A Valediction: Forbidding Mourning."

NOTES

PROLOGUE: COLD CITY

1. Frances Fox Piven and Richard Cloward, *Poor People's Movements: Why They Succeed, How They Fail* (New York: Vintage, 1979), 53–55; St. Clair Drake and Horace Cayton, *Black Metropolis: A Study of Negro Life in a Northern City* (New York: Harcourt, Brace, and World, 1945), 85–86; Beryl Satter, *Family Properties: How the Struggle over Race and Real Estate Transformed Chicago and Urban America* (New York: Metropolitan Books, 2009). Although nationally representative historical data on eviction do not exist, these historical accounts of the first half of the twentieth century depict evictions as rare and shocking events. Some local studies from the second half of the twentieth century, however, document nontrivial rates of involuntary displacement in American cities. See Peter Rossi, *Why Families Move*, 2nd ed. (Beverly Hills: Sage, 1980 [1955]); H. Lawrence Ross, "Reasons for Moves to and from a Central City Area," *Social Forces* 40 (1962): 261–63.

2. Rudy Kleysteuber, "Tenant Screening Thirty Years Later: A Statutory Proposal to Protect Public Records," *Yale Law Journal* 116 (2006): 1344–88.

3. These estimates draw on the American Housing Survey (AHS), 1991–2013. They are conservative, since they exclude renter households reporting no cash income as well as those reporting zero or negative income. The AHS records renting households that reported housing costs in excess of 100 percent of family income. For some households, this scenario reflects response error. For others, including those living off savings and those whose rent and utility bill actually is larger than their income, it does not. Analyses that have examined renter households reporting a housing cost burden in excess of 100 percent of their family income have found that only a minority of these households report receiving some assistance with rent (11 percent) or utilities (5 percent)—assistance which may be ongoing or take place on a single occasion. If you include households reporting a housing cost burden in excess of 100 percent of family income, you find that in 2013, 70 percent of poor renting families were

dedicating half of their income to housing costs, and 53 percent were dedicating 70 percent or more of their income. If you exclude these households, you find that 51 percent of poor renting families were dedicating at least half of their income to housing costs, and almost one-quarter were dedicating over 70 percent of their income to it. The right number rests somewhere in the middle of these two point estimates, meaning that in 2013 between 50 and 70 percent of poor renting families spent half of their income on housing and between 25 and 50 percent spent at least 70 percent on it.

The number of renter households dedicating less than 30 percent of family income to housing costs fell from 1.3 million in 1991 to 1.07 million in 2013, even as the total renter households grew by almost 6.3 million during that time. During those same years, the number of renter households dedicating 70 percent or more of their income to housing costs grew from 2.4 million to 4.7 million (if you include households reporting housing cost burden in excess of 100 percent of family income) or from 901,000 to 1.3 million (if you exclude those households).

Housing costs include contract rent, utilities, property insurance, and mobile-home park fees. Here, income refers to the sum of all wages, salaries, benefits, and some in-kind aid (food stamps) for the householder, relatives living under the same roof, and a "primary individual" living in the same household but unrelated to the householder. When calculating housing burden, the AHS chose to use this income measure, called *family* income, over *household* income to "approximate whose income may be available for housing and other shared living expenses." (The AHS poverty status definitions, however, are based on household income.) See Frederick Eggers and Fouad Moumen, *Investigating Very High Rent Burdens Among Renters in the American Housing Survey* (Washington, DC: US Department of Housing and Urban Development, 2010); Barry Steffen, *Worst Case Housing Needs 2011: Report to Congress* (Washington, DC: US Department of Housing and Urban Development, 2013).

4. Milwaukee County Eviction Records, 2003–2007, and GeoLytics Population Estimates, 2003–2007; Milwaukee Area Renters Study, 2009–2011. For a detailed explanation of the methodology, see Matthew Desmond, "Eviction and the Reproduction of Urban Poverty," *American Journal of Sociology* 118 (2012): 88–133; Matthew Desmond and Tracey Shollenberger, "Forced Displacement from Rental Housing: Prevalence and Neighborhood Consequences," *Demography*, forthcoming. Throughout this book, I use custom design weights to facilitate estimates generalizable to Milwaukee's rental population. All descriptive statistics that draw on the Milwaukee Area Renters Study are weighted.

The American Housing Survey (AHS) collects data on the reasons renters relocated with the question, "What are the reasons you moved from your last residence?" and reports this information with respect to the most recent move of renters who moved within the previous year. According to the 2009 AHS (Table 4-11), among renters nationwide who had moved in the past year, between 2.1 and 5.5 percent were forced from their previous unit on account of private displacement (e.g., owner moved into unit, converted to condominium), government displacement (e.g., unit was found unfit for occupancy), or eviction. (The 2.1 percent estimate is based on renters' reported "main reason for moving," which is too limiting because those who were involuntarily displaced but listed another factor as their "main" reason for moving [e.g., poor housing conditions] would be excluded from this figure. The 5.5 percent estimate is based on all reasons given for moving, which may double-count some renters who report multiple kinds of forced moves. The most appropriate measure, therefore, is somewhere between the two point estimates.) According to the Milwaukee Area Renters Study (2009–2011), 10.8 percent of the most recent moves of renters who had moved within the previous year were forced. My estimate is larger—and more accurate—because MARS captured informal evictions. When informal evictions were excluded, my estimate drops to 3 percent, which aligns with the AHS estimate. The AHS, along with most material-hardship studies, *significantly underestimates* the prevalence of involuntary removal among renters by relying on open-ended questions that do not adequately capture informal evictions that many renters do not consider to be "evictions."

5. The national estimates about the proportion of poor renting families being unable to pay all of their rent and believing they soon would be evicted come from the American Housing Survey, 2013, Table S-08-RO, which also reported that over 2.8 million renting households in the US believed it was "very likely" or "somewhat likely" that they would be evicted within the next two months. Chester Hartman and David Robinson ("Evictions: The Hidden Housing Problem," *Housing Policy Debate* 14 [2003]: 461–501, 461) estimate that the number of Americans evicted every year "is likely in the many millions." See also Kathryn Edin and Laura Lein, *Making Ends Meet: How Single Mothers Survive Welfare and Low-Wage Work* (New York: Russell Sage Foundation, 1997), 53.

 With respect to statewide eviction estimates: The Neighborhood Law Clinic at the University of Wisconsin Law School has begun to record state-level eviction filings. (Eviction *filings* [being called to eviction court] are different from eviction *judgments* [being ordered to move out by court order]. In all cities, there are more filings than judgments. My estimate of Milwaukee's formal, court-ordered eviction rate is based on judgments, which is a much harder metric to obtain and validate in other cities.) In 2012, the numbers broke down like this: Alabama, 22,824 evictions filed in court (pop. 4.8 million); Minnesota, 22,165 evictions filed in court (pop. 5.4 million); Oregon, 23,452 evictions filed in court (pop. 3.9 million); Washington, 18,060 evictions filed in court (pop. 6.9 million); Wisconsin, 28,533 evictions filed in court (pop. 5.7 million). See the epilogue for eviction estimates in cities other than Milwaukee. On measuring involuntary displacement, see Desmond and Shollenberger, "Forced Displacement from Rental Housing"; Hartman and Robinson, "Evictions: The Hidden Housing Problem."

1. THE BUSINESS OF OWNING THE CITY

1. The median annual household income among Milwaukee renters is $30,398, almost $5,500 lower than that of the city's overall population. See Nicolas Retsinas and Eric Belsky, *Revisiting Rental Housing* (Washington, DC: Brookings Institution Press and the Harvard University Joint Center for Housing Studies, 2008).

2. Where you bought in the city depended on who you were, especially when it came to race. Milwaukee landlords were more likely than not to share their tenants' racial or ethnic identity. Most white tenants in the city (87 percent) rented from white landlords; and most black tenants (51 percent) rented from black landlords. Overall, the majority of tenants in Milwaukee (63 percent) rented from a white landlord. But almost 1 in 5 rented from a black landlord, while almost 1 in 9 rented from a Hispanic landlord.

   Among Hispanic renters, roughly half rented from Hispanic landlords and half from white landlords, and 41 percent of Hispanic renters in Milwaukee believed their landlord was born outside the United States. Landlording had long been a way for immigrants to break into the American middle class. In the early twentieth century, Polish immigrants in Milwaukee took to jacking up their houses, building basement apartments, and renting them out. As the South Side of Milwaukee transitioned from Polish to Hispanic, immigrants from Mexico and Puerto Rico became the ones renting out those "Polish Flats." See John Gurda, *The Making of Milwaukee*, 3rd ed. (Milwaukee: Milwaukee County Historical Society, 2008 [1999]), 173.

   Unlike in past decades, when the typical inner-city landlord was white, the deeper you went into the inner city, the more likely it became that your landlord was black: in neighborhoods where at least two-thirds of the residents were African American, 3 in 4 renters had a black landlord. On white landlords in black neighborhoods in past eras, see St. Clair Drake and Horace Cayton, *Black Metropolis: A Study of Negro Life in a Northern City* (New York: Harcourt, Brace, and World, 1945), 718.

   Most tenants in Milwaukee rented from a man. (Eighty-two percent of Milwaukee tenants reported renting from a single individual, as opposed to a couple, and 62 percent of those lone-wolf landlords were men.) Sherrena was bucking that trend. But when she stepped out of the car in front of Lamar's house, as a black landlord meeting her black tenants, she was more norm than exception. Milwaukee Area Renters Study, 2009–2011.

3. I did not personally witness this event. The scene was reconstructed through interviews with Sherrena, Quentin, and Community Advocates social workers.

4. Of those, about 1 in 7 had their utilities shut off. A family renting crumbling housing on a dangerous street paid less rent than an affluent one living in a swanky downtown loft—but their utility costs often were equivalent. In some cases, renters living at the bottom of the market paid more for utilities than those living at the top because they could not afford new construction with

thick insulation, double-paned windows, or Energy Star appliances. Nation-wide, renting families responsible for utilities with incomes less than $15,000 spend an average of $116 a month on utilities; those with incomes in excess of $75,000 spend $151 a month. Bureau of Labor Statistics, *Consumer Price Index*, 2000–2013; American Housing Survey, 2013, Table S-08-R0; Michael Carliner, *Reducing Energy Costs in Rental Housing: The Need and the Potential* (Cambridge: Joint Center for Housing Studies of Harvard University, 2013).

5. We Energies, whose service area extends beyond Milwaukee to other parts of Wisconsin and Michigan's Upper Peninsula, processes roughly 4,000 cases of theft every year. (Personal communication, Brian Manthey, We Energies, July 22, 2014.) See Peter Kelly, "Electricity Theft: A Bigger Issue Than You Think," *Forbes*, April 23, 2013; "Using Analytics to Crack Down on Electricity Theft," *CIO Journal*, from the *Wall Street Journal*, December 2, 2013.

6. The moratorium applies to both gas and electric heating sources. The disconnection estimates come from a personal communication with Brian Manthey, We Energies, July 24, 2014. On monthly eviction trends, see Matthew Desmond, "Eviction and the Reproduction of Urban Poverty," *American Journal of Sociology* 118 (2012): 88–133, Figure A2.

2. MAKING RENT

1. John Gurda, *The Making of Milwaukee*, 3rd ed. (Milwaukee: Milwaukee County Historical Society, 2008 [1999]), 421–22; see also 416–18; Sammis White et al., *The Changing Milwaukee Industrial Structure, 1979–1988* (Milwaukee: University of Wisconsin–Milwaukee Urban Research Center, 1988).

2. William Julius Wilson, *The Truly Disadvantaged: The Inner City, the Underclass, and Public Policy*, 2nd ed. (Chicago: University of Chicago Press, 2012 [1987]); Marc Levine, *The Crisis Continues: Black Male Joblessness in Milwaukee* (Milwaukee: University of Wisconsin–Milwaukee, Center for Economic Development, 2008).

3. Jason DeParle, *American Dream: Three Women, Ten Kids, and the Nation's Drive to End Welfare* (New York: Penguin, 2004), 16, 164–68.

4. State of Wisconsin, Department of Children and Families, *Rights and Responsibilities: A Help Guide*, 2014, 6.

5. I did not personally witness Lamar's interaction with his caseworker. This quotation is from Lamar's account of the conversation. And I did not personally witness the painting scene. It was reconstructed through conversations with Lamar, his sons, and the neighborhood boys.

6. Landlording is one of the last vestiges of family capitalism in America. Rental properties get handed down from fathers to sons, and it is not unusual to meet a second- or even a fourth-generation landlord. See Daniel Bell, *The End of Ideology: On the Exhaustion of Political Ideas in the Fifties* (New York: Collier Books, 1961), chapter 2.

7. A 1960s study found that 8 in 10 rental properties in Newark, New Jersey, were owned by people for whom rent contributed less than three-quarters of

their income. George Sternlieb, *The Tenement Landlord* (New Brunswick, NJ: Rutgers University Press, 1969).

8. This happened during a time when the entire American labor force grew by only 50 percent. David Thacher, "The Rise of Criminal Background Screening in Rental Housing," *Law and Social Inquiry* 33 (2008): 5–30.

9. Author's calculations based on the Library of Congress call number HD1394 (rental property, real estate management). This idea is indebted to Thacher, "Rise of Criminal Background Screening in Rental Housing."

10. In 2009, the going rate for a two-bedroom apartment in inner-city Milwaukee was $550, utilities not included. The going rate for a room in a rooming house in the same neighborhood was $400 per room, utilities included. The profit margins of rooming houses often were better. Milwaukee Area Renters Study, 2009–2011.

3. HOT WATER

1. In previous academic publications, I represented the trailer park under a pseudonym. I have used its real name here.

2. Patrick Jones, *The Selma of the North: Civil Rights Insurgency in Milwaukee* (Cambridge: Harvard University Press, 2009), 1, 158, 176–77, 185; "Upside Down in Milwaukee," *New York Times*, September 13, 1967.

3. On the history of Hispanics in Milwaukee, see John Gurda, *The Making of Milwaukee*, 3rd ed. (Milwaukee: Milwaukee County Historical Society, 2008 [1999]), 260. On segregation, see John Logan and Brian Stults, *The Persistence of Segregation in the Metropolis: New Findings from the 2010 Census* (Washington, DC: US Census, 2011); Harrison Jacobs, Andy Kiersz, and Gus Lubin, "The 25 Most Segregated Cities in America," *Business Insider*, November 22, 2013.

4. This figure is based on the trailer park's rent rolls from April to July 2008. (Lenny Lawson allowed me to copy them.) Because these arrears estimates are based on summer month totals, when nonpayment and evictions are highest, they are inflated.

5. I did not personally witness this exchange but reconstructed the details by talking with Jerry, Lenny, and other trailer park residents. The quotation is verbatim in Jerry's recollection.

6. Later, Tobin would look for a way to evict Phyllis, who paid her rent every month. Lenny suggested giving her an eviction notice for having a dog. Tobin's lease, with its faded and crowded type pushing forward in all caps over three pages, clearly stipulated: NO DOGS OR FARM ANIMALS ARE ALLOWED. But many residents had pets because Tobin and Lenny told them they could. "I'm kind of looking the other way," Tobin would say. Lenny was suggesting they deny what was said aloud and point to what they had in writing. The lease also outlawed the consumption of alcohol on trailer park grounds.

4. A BEAUTIFUL COLLECTION

1. Throughout American history, city politicians have attempted to place checks on landlords' power and improve tenants' lives by laying down rules—from slum clearance to building code enforcement—as if the underlying problem were not America's abundance of poverty and lack of affordable housing but disorder and inefficiency. This often brings unanticipated consequences that increase tenants' hardship. Marc Bloch, *Feudal Society*, vol. 1, *The Growth of Ties of Dependence* (Chicago: University of Chicago Press, 1961), 147; Beryl Satter, *Family Properties: How the Struggle over Race and Real Estate Transformed Chicago and Urban America* (New York: Metropolitan Books, 2009), 135–45.

2. One's sovereignty over the land is expressed most powerfully in the act of banishment. Perhaps the first eviction recorded in human history was Adam and Eve's. See Lewis Mumford, *The City in History: Its Origins, Its Transformations, and Its Prospects* (New York: MJF Books, 1961), 107–10. On the link between sovereignty and expulsion, see Hannah Arendt, *The Origins of Totalitarianism* (Orlando: Harcourt, 1968).

3. The distinctly American desire to own a home is just as pronounced among the poor as it is among the middle class. Since the pioneer days, freedom and citizenship and landholding have advanced in lockstep in the American mind. To be American was to be a homeowner. As for tenancy: it was "unfavorable to freedom," Thomas Hart told Congress in 1820. "It lays the foundation for separate orders in society, annihilates the love of country, and weakens the spirit of independence." Cited in Lawrence Vale, *From the Puritans to the Projects: Public Housing and Public Neighbors* (Cambridge: Harvard University Press, 2000), 96.

4. The nationwide vacancy rate for units renting at $300–$349, for example, fell from almost 16 percent in 2004 to below 6 percent in 2011. Author's calculations based on the Current Population Survey, 2004–2013.

5. Trailer park vacancy rates are based on Lenny's rent rolls (April to July 2008).

6. This event happened before my fieldwork, and I did not witness it. The quotation is based on Pam's recollection.

5. THIRTEENTH STREET

1. In 1997, Milwaukee's federal Fair Market Rent (FMR)—rent and utility costs that reflect the 40th percentile of the city's rental distribution—was $466 for a one-bedroom apartment. If Arleen had rented that apartment, she would have had $162 left over each month. Ten years later, when the FMR for that same apartment was $608 and her welfare check was still $628, she would have to find a way to make $20 stretch over the entire month. FMR and welfare stipend data come from the US Department of Housing and Urban Development; Wisconsin Department of Children and Families; and State of Wisconsin Equal Rights Division. On the virtual impossibility of surviving on welfare

alone, see Kathryn Edin and Laura Lein, *Making Ends Meet: How Single Mothers Survive Welfare and Low-Wage Work* (New York: Russell Sage Foundation, 1997).

2. In 2013 there were roughly 3,900 Milwaukee families in public housing and roughly 5,800 who received housing vouchers. There were roughly 105,000 renter households in the city. See Georgia Pabst, "Waiting Lists Soar for Public Housing, Rent Assistance," *Milwaukee Journal Sentinel*, August 10, 2013.

3. Adrianne Todman, "Public Housing Did Not Fail and the Role It Must Play in Interrupting Poverty," Harvard University, Inequality and Social Policy Seminar, March 24, 2014.

4. To make matters worse for the very poor, the shortfall of federal housing assistance has coincided with the emergence of an employment-based safety net, which directs aid to working families through programs like the Earned Income Tax Credit or public housing reserved for parents with low-wage jobs. The result is that families just above and below the poverty line receive significantly more help today than they did twenty years ago, but those far below the poverty line receive significantly less. For families living in deep poverty, both income and housing assistance have been scaled back. On spending patterns, see Janet Currie, *The Invisible Safety Net: Protecting the Nation's Poor Children and Families* (Princeton: Princeton University Press, 2008); Robert Moffitt, "The Deserving Poor, the Family, and the US Welfare System," *Demography* 52 (2015): 729–49. On the gap between housing assistance and need, see Danilo Pelletiere, Michelle Canizio, Morgan Hargrave, and Sheila Crowley, *Housing Assistance for Low Income Households: States Do Not Fill the Gap* (Washington, DC: National Low Income Housing Coalition, 2008); Douglas Rice and Barbara Sar, *Decade of Neglect Has Weakened Federal Low-Income Programs: New Resources Required to Meet Growing Needs* (Washington, DC: Center on Budget and Policy Priorities, 2009).

5. I did not personally witness this event. The scene was reconstructed through interviews with Arleen and Trisha.

6. The Milwaukee Housing Authority's general-occupancy list for merely poor families seeking assistance was closed and backlogged, but its lists for elderly low-income adults as well as those with disabilities were kept continuously open. The Housing Authority may deny even these applicants for any number of reasons, however, including if they have a criminal record, a drug problem, or a history of missing rent payments. Housing Authority of the City of Milwaukee, *Admissions and Continued Occupancy Policy (ACOP)*, October 2013, Section 7.4: "Grounds for Denial."

7. As state services for the needy have been scaled back, social service agencies, like Belinda's, have sprung up in poor neighborhoods across the nation to fill the void. Some are nonprofits; others are business ventures. Lester Salamon, "The Rise of the Nonprofit Sector," *Foreign Affairs* 73 (1994): 111–24, 109; John McKnight, *The Careless Society: Community and Its Counterfeits* (New York: Basic Books, 1995); Jennifer Wolch, *The Shadow State: Government*

and Voluntary Sector in Transition (New York: The Foundation Center, 1990). Urban ethnographies published during the 1960s and 1970s are striking in their lack of references to social service agencies. After reading these accounts, one cannot but arrive at the conclusion that social workers were not a major force in the lives of the urban poor fifty years ago. Carol Stack's *All Our Kin: Strategies for Survival in a Black Community* (New York: Basic Books, 1974) mentions but a single social worker and says almost nothing about child welfare services or similar agencies. And there are no job centers or employment counselors milling around *Tally's Corner*, which Liebow published in 1967, a book (mainly) about unemployed black men. See Elliot Liebow, *Tally's Corner: A Study of Negro Streetcorner Men* (Boston: Little, Brown and Company, 1967).

8. When lawmakers reformed welfare, they required states to develop sanctions for TANF recipients, procedures that involved suspending all or some of their benefit if recipients were found to be noncompliant. When W-2 began in Wisconsin, nearly two-thirds of those who entered the program were sanctioned at some point during the first four years. Chi-Fang Wu, Maria Cancian, Daniel Meyer, and Geoffrey Wallace, "How Do Welfare Sanctions Work?," *Social Work Research* 30 (2006): 33–50; Matthew Fellowes and Gretchen Rowe, "Politics and the New American Welfare States," *American Journal of Political Science* 48 (2004): 362–73; Richard Fording, Joe Soss, and Sanford Schram, "Race and the Local Politics of Punishment in the New World of Welfare," *American Journal of Sociology* 116 (2011): 1610–57.

6. RAT HOLE

1. For the full models and methodology, see Matthew Desmond, Carl Gershenson, and Barbara Kiviat, "Forced Relocation and Residential Instability Among Urban Renters," *Social Service Review* 89 (2015): 227–62. Tenants represented in the Milwaukee Area Renters Study were classified as having experienced long-term housing problems if they suffered any of the following issues the year prior to being interviewed: (a) a broken stove or other appliance, (b) a broken window, (c) a broken exterior door or lock, (d) mice, rats, or other pests, or (e) exposed wires or other electrical problems *for at least three days* as well as (f) no heat, (g) no running water, or (h) stopped-up plumbing *for at least 24 hours*. To estimate the effect of a forced move on housing quality, we used doubly robust regression models that employed coarsened exact matching. Vouchered tenants were included in these analyses.

2. While involuntary displacement by definition causes residential instability, the impact of a forced move on residential instability can last beyond the relocation immediately following eviction. Housing dissatisfaction is the key mechanism linking eviction's direct (involuntary) move and its subsequent indirect (voluntary) one, as forced movers relocating under duress often accept subpar housing but then seek to move to better conditions. An analysis of the Milwaukee Area Renters Study that employed doubly robust regression on a data

set processed by coarsened exact matching found that renters who experienced a forced move were 24 percentage points more likely to undertake an unforced move soon thereafter, compared to those who did not experience involuntary displacement. Additionally, 53 percent of renters who experienced a forced move followed by an unforced move attributed their latest move to a desire to move to a better housing unit or neighborhood, while only 34 percent of renters with two consecutive unforced moves did so. In other words, unforced movers whose previous move was involuntary were far more likely to cite housing or neighborhood problems as the reason for moving than were unforced movers whose previous move was also unforced. Not only do poor renters disproportionately experience involuntary displacement, but involuntary displacement itself brings about subsequent residential mobility. See Desmond et al., "Forced Relocation and Residential Instability Among Urban Renters."

3. Jane Jacobs, *The Death and Life of Great American Cities* (New York: Random House, 1961), 31–32; Robert Sampson, *Great American City: Chicago and the Enduring Neighborhood Effect* (Chicago: University of Chicago Press, 2012), especially 127, 146–47, 151, 177, 231–32. For an ethnographic take on the uses of public space, see Mitchell Duneier, *Sidewalk* (New York: Farrar, Straus and Giroux, 1999).

4. Jacobs, *Death and Life of Great American Cities*, 271, emphasis mine.

5. This strategy, if it was that, backfired when tenants didn't report housing problems that bit into Sherrena and Quentin's bottom line, like a running toilet.

6. Landlords were required to disclose code violations before entering into a rental agreement with prospective tenants. City of Milwaukee, *Landlord Training Program: Keeping Illegal and Destructive Activity Out of Rental Property*, 7th ed. (Milwaukee: City of Milwaukee, Department of Neighborhood Services, 2006), 12; Wisconsin Administrative Code, ATCP134.04, "Disclosure Requirements."

7. Housing problems motivate a significant number of moves among Milwaukee renters. Consider "responsive moves," which are neither forced displacements (e.g., eviction, building condemnation) nor completely voluntary relocations (to gain residential advantage) but something in between. Data from the Milwaukee Area Renters Study reveal that the most common type of responsive move among Milwaukee renters between 2009 and 2011 was that initiated by a housing problem. These moves accounted for 23 percent of responsive moves and 7 percent of all moves undertaken by renters in the two years prior to being surveyed. These moves were not motivated by a positive impulse (moving to a bigger apartment) but by a negative one (the need to leave units after housing conditions deteriorated). See Desmond et al., "Forced Relocation and Residential Instability Among Urban Renters."

8. As thousands of underwater homeowners learned when the housing bubble popped, defaulting can be far more rational than throwing money into a black hole. Timothy Riddiough and Steve Wyatt, "Strategic Default, Workout, and Commercial Mortgage Valuation," *Journal of Real Estate Finance and Economics*

9 (1994): 5–22; Lindsay Owens, "Intrinsically Advantaged? Middle-Class (Dis)advantage in the Case of Home Mortgage Modification," *Social Forces* 93 (2015): 1185–209.

9. Milwaukee Area Renters Study, 2009–2011. Between 2009 and 2011, the median rent for a one-bedroom apartment was $550; for a three-bedroom it was $775.

The professionalization of the rental market, combined with the spread of information technology, may have contributed to compressing rents within cities through either competition or price coordination. Large-scale property managers often rely on products with names like Rainmaker LRO, RentPush, and RENTmaximizer—complex algorithms that draw on hundreds of current and historical market indicators to adjust lease prices daily, even hourly. The RENTmaximizer, used in over 8 million residential units worldwide, offers property owners "higher revenue by quicker adjustments to market conditions" (www.yardi.com). For do-it-yourself types, how-to real estate books advised landlords to conduct monthly market surveys. "You call nearby complexes and check out what their rental rates are to make sure you are not too high and not too low," writes Bryan Chavis in *Buy It, Rent It, Profit! Make Money as a Landlord in Any Real Estate Market* (New York: Touchstone, 2009), 51. Picking up the phone was an extra measure, since several websites stood ready to report whether an apartment was above or below rent in the surrounding area (www.rentometer.com).

10. Milwaukee Area Renters Study, 2009–2011; merged with neighborhood-level data from the American Community Survey (2006–2010) and Milwaukee Police Department crime records (2009–2011). Consider one other statistic: the median rent for a two-bedroom apartment was $575 in Milwaukee's most dangerous neighborhoods (those at or above the 75th percentile in violent crime rate) and $600 in its least dangerous (those at or below the 25th percentile in violent crime rate).

11. Jacob Riis, *How the Other Half Lives: Studies Among the Tenements of New York* (New York: Penguin Books, 1997 [1890]), 11; Allan Spear, *Black Chicago: The Making of a Negro Ghetto, 1890–1920* (Chicago: University of Chicago Press, 1967), 24–26; Joe William Trotter Jr., *Black Milwaukee: The Making of an Industrial Proletariat, 1915–45,* 2nd ed. (Urbana: University of Illinois Press, 2007), 179; Thomas Sugrue, *The Origins of the Urban Crisis: Race and Inequality in Postwar Detroit* (Princeton: Princeton University Press, 2005), 54; Marcus Anthony Hunter, *Black Citymakers: How the Philadelphia Negro Changed Urban America* (New York: Oxford University Press, 2013), 80.

12. According to the Community Advocates rent abatement guidelines at the time of this fieldwork, a tenant could withhold 5 percent for no door or if the apartment was infested with roaches; 10 percent for a broken toilet; and 25 percent for no heat.

13. Landlords with vacant units could lower their rent, but some would prefer the vacancy. Sherrena once showed a prospective tenant, a truck driver, a

ground-floor unit in a four-family complex. It had sat empty for two months. The man looked at the patches of carpet a dog had mangled, fingered the unhinged cupboards, squeaked his shoe on the grimy kitchen floor. "This just isn't the kind of living I'm used to," he said. "How about $380?"

"No way," Sherrena responded, offended.

Collecting $380 would have been better than collecting nothing for that particular unit—but not if it meant that rent for everyone else in the building would drop. The three other units in the complex were occupied with tenants paying $600 a month. If Sherrena took the truck driver's deal, the other tenants would learn about it and likely demand a similar rate. If she allowed it, her take-home would be less than it was renting three units at $600. If she refused, some tenants might leave, causing more vacancies. Sherrena showed the truck driver out and locked the door behind him.

14. Forty-four percent, to be exact. Serious and lasting housing problems are defined above (chapter 6, note 1). Milwaukee Area Renters Study, 2009–2011.

15. Comparing two-bedroom units in the Milwaukee Area Renters Study, 2009–2011. In the 1970s and 1980s, rents increased primarily because housing quality did; see Christopher Jencks, *The Homeless* (Cambridge: Harvard University Press, 1994), 84–89. But since then, housing quality across America had remained virtually unchanged—if anything, the 2000s saw small declines in quality nationwide—while rents shot up. According to the American Housing Survey, there were approximately 909,000 renter-occupied units with severe physical problems in 1993. That number increased to 1.2 million by 2011. The proportion of all rental households with severe physical problems has remained flat over the last two decades (at roughly 3 percent). The same is true for other measures of housing quality. For example, in 1993, 9 percent of renters reported being "uncomfortably cold for 24 hours or more" because the heating broke. In 2011, 10 percent did. During the 2000s, rental housing across America did not undergo drastic improvements that kept pace with rent increases.

16. When those properties stopped cashing out, because they amassed too many fines or required costly repairs, Sherrena would "let 'em go back to the city." This meant she would simply stop paying taxes on those properties until the city eventually took control of them through tax foreclosures. Sherrena shielded herself from any personal liability by registering each of her properties under a different Limited Liability Company (LLC). In the eyes of the law, it was the company, not Sherrena, that defaulted. Milwaukee saw between 1,100 and 1,200 properties go into tax foreclosure every year. When the city inherited these used-up and discarded houses, it sold or demolished them, further shrinking the affordable housing stock. For Sherrena, losing property this way was not a mistake or the result of a financial setback. It was a basic part of her business model. "When I get tired of a property," she said, "I just let it go. Why would you keep throwing good money at the bad?"

Sherrena created LLCs online, through the Wisconsin Department of Financial Institutions (DFI). The DFI records a registered agent for each LLC but not owner names or Wisconsin tax information (www.wdfi.org). The estimates for the number of tax foreclosures in Milwaukee come from Kevin Sullivan, Assistant City Attorney (personal communication, August 13, 2015).

Policymakers and researchers focused on poor people's housing, most of whom have never set foot in an apartment like Doreen's, often point out that America has made impressive strides toward improving housing quality for its poor. "The affordability of housing is today of far greater concern than physical condition or crowding," Alex Schwartz writes, echoing the prevailing view (Alex Schwartz, *Housing Policy in the United States*, 2nd ed. [New York: Routledge, 2010], 26). This view is not wrong, but it gives the impression that the two problems are independent of each other; that since cities have razed tenements and criminalized lead paint, it is now time to confront the lack of affordable housing. But the two problems—poor housing conditions and high costs—are interlocked. At the bottom of the housing market, each permits the other.

17. Kenneth Clark, *Dark Ghetto: Dilemmas of Social Power* (New York: Harper and Row, 1965), 72; Carol Stack, *All Our Kin: Strategies for Survival in a Black Community* (New York: Basic Books, 1974), 46–47; Kathryn Edin and Timothy Nelson, *Doing the Best I Can: Fatherhood in the Inner City* (Berkeley: University of California Press, 2013), chapter 2.

18. The sociologist Linda Burton refers to the process of young people being prematurely exposed to the world of adults as "childhood adultification." See Linda Burton, "Childhood Adultification in Economically Disadvantaged Families: A Conceptual Model," *Family Relations* 56 (2007): 329–45.

19. I didn't witness this, but I did see the broken table and discussed the matter with Doreen, Patrice, Natasha, and Patrice's children. This is how Patrice's ten-year-old son, Mikey, interpreted that event: "You know, some people just be stressed. Everybody gets stressed, gets mad sometimes. And they was stressed and just had to let it out." He said it made him feel "embarrassed because of how it makes our family look, as a unit."

7. THE SICK

1. Since the early 1990s, opioid prescriptions have tripled in the United States, as have overdoses. Centers for Disease Control, *Policy Impact: Prescription Pain Killer Overdoses* (Washington, DC: Centers for Disease Control, 2011); National Institutes of Health, *Analysis of Opioid Prescription Practices Finds Areas of Concern* (Washington, DC: NIH News, US Department of Health and Human Services, 2011).

2. Stacey Mayes and Marcus Ferrone, "Transdermal System for the Management of Acute Postoperative Pain," *Annals of Pharmacotherapy* 40 (2006): 2178–86.

3. This quotation and other events of Scott's drug use during his time as a nurse come from the record of Scott's disciplinary proceedings in front of the Wisconsin Board of Nursing. I corroborated the details with Scott.

4. See Wisconsin Statutes 19.31–19.39 and 59.20(3).

5. City of Milwaukee, *Landlord Training Program: Keeping Illegal and Destructive Activity Out of Rental Property*, 7th ed. (Milwaukee: City of Milwaukee, Department of Neighborhood Services, 2006).

6. RentGrow has since become Yardi Resident Screening, which offers "terrorist, drug trafficker, sex offender, and Social Security fraud screening" (www .yardi.com). In the United States there are approximately 650 tenant-screening companies. Although these reports are often riddled with errors, landlords increasingly have come to rely on them. See Rudy Kleysteuber, "Tenant Screening Thirty Years Later: A Statutory Proposal to Protect Public Records," *Yale Law Journal* 116 (2006): 1344–88; Matthew Callanan, "Protecting the Unconvicted: Limiting Iowa's Rights to Public Access in Search of Greater Protection for Criminal Defendants Whose Charges Do Not End in Convictions," *Iowa Law Review* 98 (2013): 1275–308.

7. "These tenants, a lot of them it's like pigs in a dollhouse," Wilbur Bush told me. An older African American man with a flattop, leather jacket, and gold crucifix, Bush had been a landlord since the 1960s. Bush personally inspected applicants' current apartments, making sure to open the refrigerator. (I accompanied him on apartment screening visits and sat in his office as he interviewed tenants.) "So what you're doing here, if you can relate," he continued, "you're trying to get the best of the worst. . . . Because I've been in places where it's an upward climb to zero."

8. Some screening techniques were not mentioned that Saturday morning. One landlord, whose father was also a landlord, told me he uses the following strategy: Upon receiving an application from a woman with children, he looks first not at her income or previous residence but at the emergency contacts. "If they list a mother *and* a father, I know I won't have any trouble with the lease." But if she lists just a mother, he then looks at the applicant's last name. If it differs from her mother's, he infers the applicant is divorced or remarried, a plus. If the surnames match, he considers the applicant a single mother by a single mother—and usually turns her down.

9. This is a very different way of understanding how certain people get sorted into certain neighborhoods, compared to conventional perspectives—one that pays attention to the people doing the sorting: *the landlords*. For the Chicago School, the city was a space of sentiments and its pattern of physical and social segregation primarily the result of tens of thousands of individual decisions based on where one best fits. "In the long run," wrote Robert Park, "every individual finds somewhere among the varied manifestations of city life the sort of environment in which he expands or feels at ease." See Robert Park, "The City: Suggestions for the Investigation of Human Behavior in the Urban Environment," in *The City*, eds. Robert Park, Ernest Burgess, and Roderick McKenzie (Chicago: University of Chicago Press, 1925), 41. The sentimental neighborhood, like the plant habitat on which the urban ecology perspective was based, becomes for all purposes sentient, drawing to it those who belong.

R. D. McKenzie would explain residential sorting as being steered by "a selective or magnetic force [emanating from various neighborhoods] attracting to itself appropriate population elements and repelling incongruous units, thus making for biological and cultural subdivisions of a city's population." R. D. McKenzie, "The Ecological Approach to the Study of the Human Community," in Park, Burgess, and McKenzie, eds., *The City*, 63–79, 78.

The most influential perspective on residential mobility—the residential attainment model—is deeply influenced by the Chicago School's vision of mobility and neighborhood sorting. But those working within this tradition substitute the Chicago School's emphasis on sentimentality and morality with one focused on instrumentality and economic advancement. The residential attainment model perceives mobility as a result of social climbing and views the city not as a patchwork of isolated moral worlds but as a geography of advantage and disadvantage. According to this perspective, when people move, they try to move up, parlaying economic capital for residential capital. See John Logan and Richard Alba, "Locational Returns to Human Capital: Minority Access to Suburban Community Resources," *Demography* 30 (1993): 243–68; Scott South and Kyle Crowder, "Escaping Distressed Neighborhoods: Individual, Community, and Metropolitan Influences," *American Journal of Sociology* 102 (1997): 1040–84.

What each perspective overlooks is the crucial fact that *urban neighborhoods are markets*, largely owned, in the case of the inner city, by those who do not live within their borders. Consequentially, market actors in general—and landlords, in particular—should be seen as central players in our theories of neighborhood selection and mobility. See John Logan and Harvey Molotch, *Urban Fortunes: The Political Economy of Place* (Berkeley: University of California Press, 1987), 33–34.

10. On neighborhood variation, see Robert Sampson, *Great American City: Chicago and the Enduring Neighborhood Effect* (Chicago: University of Chicago Press, 2012); Peter St. Jean, *Pockets of Crime: Broken Windows, Collective Efficacy, and the Criminal Point of View* (Chicago: University of Chicago Press, 2007).

11. See John Caskey, *Fringe Banking: Check-Cashing Outlets, Pawnshops, and the Poor* (New York: Russell Sage Foundation, 2013); Gary Rivlin, *Broke, USA: From Pawnshops to Poverty, Inc.* (New York: Harper, 2010).

8. CHRISTMAS IN ROOM 400

1. Matthew Desmond, "Eviction and the Reproduction of Urban Poverty," *American Journal of Sociology* 118 (2012): 88–133.

2. In 2013, Milwaukee County processed almost 64,000 civil cases, roughly double the number of its criminal cases. Nationwide, the incoming civil caseload in 2010 was 13.8 million, compared to 10.6 million criminal cases. Wisconsin Circuit Court, *Caseload Summary by Responsible Court Official, County Wide Report* (Madison, WI: Wisconsin Courts, 2014). Court Statistics Project,

National Civil and Criminal Caseloads and *Civil/Criminal Court Caseloads: Total Caseloads* (Williamsburg, VA: National Center for State Courts, 2010).

3. One Milwaukee landlord who owned roughly 100 units in low-income neighborhoods told me he gave approximately 30 percent of his tenants five-day eviction notices each month. A $50 late fee accompanied each notice. He estimated that 90 percent of those cases were settled via stipulation; the remaining 10 percent were evicted. This meant that he collected roughly $1,350 in late fees each month from tenants he did not evict. That amounted to over $16,000 a year in late fees alone.

4. Milwaukee Eviction Court Study, 2011. In addition to surveying tenants, interviewers took eviction court attendance every weekday (save one) between January 17 and February 26, 2011. During this six-week period, in 945 out of 1,328 cases, tenants did not appear in court, with most receiving an eviction judgment. Of those that did appear in court, slightly more than one-third signed stipulation agreements. Some would later be evicted; some would not. One-quarter had to return to court on another day, owing to paperwork errors or because their case was complicated enough to be sent to a judge. Twelve percent had their cases dismissed. The remaining 29 percent received eviction judgments.

   Documented default rates in other cities and states range from 35 percent to over 90 percent. See Randy Gerchick, "No Easy Way Out: Making the Summary Eviction Process a Fairer and More Efficient Alternative to Landlord Self-Help," *UCLA Law Review* 41 (1994): 759–837; Erik Larson, "Case Characteristics and Defendant Tenant Default in a Housing Court," *Journal of Empirical Legal Studies* 3 (2006): 121–44; David Caplovitz, *Consumers in Trouble: A Study of Debtors in Default* (New York: The Free Press, 1974).

5. With Jonathan Mijs, I combined all eviction court records between January 17 and February 26, 2011 (the Milwaukee Eviction Court Study period) with information about aspects of tenants' neighborhoods, procured after geocoding the addresses that appeared in the eviction records. Working with the Harvard Center for Geographic Analysis, I also calculated the distance (in drive miles and time) between tenants' addresses and the courthouse. Then I constructed a statistical model that attempted to explain the likelihood of a tenant appearing in court based on aspects of that tenant's case and her or his neighborhood. The model generated only null findings. How much a tenant owed a landlord, her commute time to the courthouse, her gender—none of these factors were significantly related to appearing in court. I also investigated whether several aspects of a tenant's neighborhood—e.g., its eviction, poverty, and crime rates—mattered when it came to explaining defaults. None did. None of the explanatory variables I tried were statistically associated with showing up to eviction court. The absence of a clear pattern in the data implies that defaults are more or less random. Other studies have arrived at similar conclusions, as have the housing specialists at Community Advocates. One told me: "As for going down to the courthouse . . . well, they have to eat; they've got to ride the

bus; got to find someone to watch their kids. Everything is pretty much driven by the moment." See Barbara Bezdek, "Silence in the Court: Participation and Subordination of Poor Tenants' Voices in Legal Process," *Hofstra Law Review* 20 (1992): 533–608; Larson, "Case Characteristics and Defendant Tenant Default in a Housing Court."

6. Milwaukee Eviction Court Study, 2011. For more information about the Milwaukee Eviction Court Study, see Desmond, "Eviction and the Reproduction of Urban Poverty"; Matthew Desmond et al., "Evicting Children," *Social Forces* 92 (2013): 303–27. According to the 2013 American Housing Survey (Table S-08-RO), 71 percent of poor renting families who reported receiving an eviction notice within the last three months did so because of missed rent payments.

7. Milwaukee Eviction Court Study, 2011. The 2013 American Housing Survey asked all renters where they would move in the event of an eviction (Table S-08-RO). Most reported, optimistically enough, that they would move to "a new home." But when you step from the hypothetical to the actual and ask tenants who have just received an eviction judgment where they are planning to go, most haven't a clue.

8. Milwaukee Eviction Court Study, 2011.

9. In Milwaukee's poorest black neighborhoods, 1 male renter in 33 was evicted through the court system each year, compared to 1 male renter in 134 and 1 female renter in 150 in the city's poorest white neighborhoods. By "poorest neighborhoods," I mean census block groups in which at least 40 percent of families lived below the poverty line. By "white/black neighborhoods," I mean block groups in which at least two-thirds of the residents were white/black. Because eviction records do not include sex identifiers, two methods were employed to impute sex. First, a pair of research assistants assigned a sex to each person—over 90,000 of them—based on first names. Second, with the help of Felix Elwert, I imputed gender by drawing on Social Security card applications for US births. Each method produced virtually identical point estimates. An annual household eviction rate was calculated by dividing the number of eviction cases in a year by the number of occupied rental units estimated for that year. Additionally, for each neighborhood (block group), I estimated the eviction rate for male and female renters by dividing the number of evictees of one sex by the number of adults of the same sex living in rental housing. All statistics were calculated for each block group for each year. The results were then pooled and annual averages calculated. For a fuller explanation of the methods used to arrive at these estimates, see Desmond, "Eviction and the Reproduction of Urban Poverty."

In an average year between 2003 and 2007, 276 court-ordered evictions took place in predominantly Hispanic neighborhoods, compared to 1,187 and 2,759 in white and black neighborhoods, respectively. Like women in black neighborhoods, women in Hispanic neighborhoods were evicted at higher rates. On average, in high-poverty Hispanic neighborhoods, 1 male renter in

86 and 1 female renter in 40 were evicted through the court system every year. Estimates that considered informal evictions and landlord foreclosures were even more alarming. Between 2009 and 2011, roughly 23 percent of Hispanic renters in Milwaukee were forcibly removed from their homes sometime in the previous two years, via formal or informal eviction, landlord foreclosure, or building condemnation. This extraordinarily high rate of forced mobility— almost twice that of black renters—was attributed to the fact that the foreclosure crisis hit Milwaukee's Hispanic *renters* particularly hard. When landlord foreclosures were excluded from the estimate of involuntary displacement prevalence, the percentage of renters who had experienced a forced move within two years fell from 13.2 percent to 10.2 percent. This exclusion caused the rates of involuntary mobility among white and black renters to fall from 9 to 7 percent and from 12 to 10 percent, respectively. But its biggest impact was seen in the rate of involuntary mobility among Hispanic renters, which fell from 23 percent to 14 percent after landlord foreclosures were dropped. Milwaukee County eviction court records, 2003–2007; Milwaukee Area Renters Study, 2009–2011.

10. In poor black communities, women were more likely to work in the formal economy than men, many of whom were marked by a criminal record and unemployed at high rates. Many landlords did not approve the rental applications of unemployed persons or those with criminal records. In the inner city, women were more likely to provide the necessary income documentation when securing a lease, either from an employment check or public assistance like welfare. In Milwaukee, half of working-age black men were out of work and half in their thirties had done prison time—twinned trends not unrelated. WUMN, *Project Milwaukee: Black Men in Prison*, Milwaukee Public Radio, July 16, 2014; Marc Levine, *The Crisis Continues: Black Male Joblessness in Milwaukee* (Milwaukee: University of Wisconsin–Milwaukee, Center for Economic Development, 2008). Audit studies have shown that Milwaukee employers are more likely to call back white job seekers with criminal records than black job seekers with clean backgrounds. Black job seekers with criminal records are doubly disadvantaged. Devah Pager, "The Mark of a Criminal Record," *American Journal of Sociology* 108 (2003): 937–75.

If court records usually listed only leaseholders, it could be the case that women from poor black neighborhoods actually weren't evicted at higher rates than men but were just more likely to collect eviction records than their male counterparts who lived in apartments off lease. Yet in black neighborhoods, a gender gap in formal evictions remained even after accounting for adults not listed on the lease. The Milwaukee Eviction Court Study (2011) accounted for all adults in the household, including those not listed on the Summons and Complaint. After doing so, black women continued to outnumber all other groups. They accounted for half of all adults living in households appearing in eviction court and 44 percent living in households that received eviction judgments. Black women were not only "marked" by eviction at higher rates; they were actually displaced at higher rates as well. A clerical tick did not explain away the high rate of eviction among black women.

Another consideration: in the inner city, women had a harder time making rent than male leaseholders. Although many black men were closed off from the workforce, those with jobs worked longer hours and got paid better wages than black women workers. In 2010, the median annual income for full-time workers in Milwaukee was $33,010 for black men and $29,454 for black women—a difference equivalent to five months of rent for the average Milwaukee apartment. Many women in the inner city also had more expenses. This was particularly true for single-mother households, which made up the majority of black households in Milwaukee. Single mothers often could not rely on regular support from their children's fathers, and because of their children, they had to seek out larger and more expensive housing options than noncustodial fathers, who could sleep on someone's couch or rent a room. Sherrena rented her inner-city rooming house rooms for $400 a month (utilities included), a good deal less than the two-bedroom units Arleen and other single mothers rented for $550 (utilities excluded). With Milwaukee's maximum occupancy limits in mind—widely interpreted as two heartbeats per bedroom—many landlords refused to rent single mothers smaller units. More heartbeats meant more bedrooms—and more rent. See City of Milwaukee Code of Ordinances, Chapter 200: Building and Zoning Code, Subchapter 8: "Occupancy and Use." See Desmond, "Eviction and the Reproduction of Urban Poverty."

11. Manny Fernandez, "Still Home for the Holidays, When Evictions Halt," *New York Times*, December 21, 2008.

12. The "second cause" deals with unpaid rent; the "third cause" deals with property damage. In court, both causes are processed at the same time, leading to the legal lingo "second and third causes."

13. Between 2006 and 2010, Milwaukee Small Claims Court each year processed roughly 12,000 eviction cases but only 200 garnishments. I have excluded from this estimate garnishments in 2009, which for some reason were exceptionally high at 537. On eviction and garnishment filings, see State of Wisconsin, *2010 Annual Report: Milwaukee County Circuit Court, First Judicial District*, 2. On garnishment and execution statutes, see *Wisconsin Statues* §814 and §815.

14. In Milwaukee's Landlord Training course, landlords were strongly encouraged to docket judgments. "The most important thing I'm going to ask you to do is to spend an extra five dollars and docket that judgment with the clerk of courts," instructor Karen Long advised. "You want to add it to the credit report so that everyone out there knows that they owe you money. . . . I'm asking you to do it for all of us who need to run credit reports on people. . . . And also a couple years from now you might get a call, saying, 'I'm George Jones. Remember me?' 'Nope.' 'Well, I was your tenant three years ago. You have a judgment against me for seven hundred and fifty bucks. I need to buy this car. Can I give you five hundred bucks and you call it even?'" Karen went on to advise landlords to tell tenants about docketing: "I'm going to put this on your

credit report, and nobody is going to lend you any money or lend you anything until you pay me. So it behooves you, you know, to not let any of this go on your record."

15. Rent Recovery Service will report tenants to major credit bureaus even if landlords do not have money judgments (www.rentrecoveryservice.com).

16. In Milwaukee and many cities across the United States, the law offers few protections for tenants in arrears. "It's the *'what'* not the *'why'* that matters," the landlord saying goes. In other words, the court typically does not care why tenants fell behind, only that they did. Arleen could have articulated her housing problems clearly; she could have brought pictures. Doing so probably wouldn't have made any difference. Once, upon learning that an elderly woman being evicted had lived without electricity for a month because her landlord was slow to repair the wiring, a court commissioner replied, "That isn't necessarily a fact we need to work out today." Another time, a housing court judge listened patiently as a tenant described sewage in her bathtub and rotting floorboards. Then he responded, "You've told me everything except that you are current on your rent."

17. Tenants may have the right argument but the wrong presentation: too rough or meandering, too angry or meek. It would be naïve to think these considerations are uninformed by class, gender, and racial dynamics between tenants, landlords, and court actors. In the Landlord Training course, property owners are told, "The person who gets the loudest, and the noisiest, and the feistiest loses. So bite your tongue and go through it." And even if landlords are new to eviction, many are educated members of the middle class, just like the court clerks, commissioners, and judges, who on account of their similar class position all speak the same language and speak it in the same way.

18. Almost every landlord and building manager in Milwaukee that I met would agree. They felt that the court system was brazenly "pro-tenant," that it resembled an "uneven playing field" tilted against property owners, or that commissioners liked to play *Let's Make a Deal* when they should just be issuing writs of restitution. Lenny Lawson was the sole exception. The court system "used to be for the tenants. It's not anymore," he told me.

9. ORDER SOME CARRYOUT

1. According to Maudwella Kirkendoll, chief operating officer at Community Advocates (personal communication, December 19, 2014), 946 households benefited from the Homelessness Prevention Program in 2013. That year, the annual budget for that program was $646,000—all state- and city-distributed HUD dollars.

2. The notice the Sheriff's Office sends to tenants states, "movers will not take food left in your refrigerator or freezer." Movers do not take food to bonded storage, but they do place it on the curb.

3. Jacob Riis, *How the Other Half Lives: Studies Among the Tenements of New York* (New York: Penguin Books, 1997 [1890]), 129. On the psychology of scarcity,

see Sendhil Mullainathan and Eldar Shafir, *Scarcity: Why Having So Little Means So Much* (New York: Times Books, 2013).

4. After the foreclosure crisis, several states passed laws requiring landlords to provide tenants in foreclosed properties with advance notice, and in May 2009 Congress passed the Protecting Tenants at Foreclosure Act, which requires landlords who acquire property through foreclosure to honor existing leases. But when riding along with Milwaukee's eviction squad in 2014, I met several tenants who simply did not know who their landlord was. The foreclosure crisis has caused urban rental property to be shuffled through many institutions, real estate companies, property-management firms, and private investors, leaving tenants bewildered. See Vicki Been and Allegra Glashausser, "Tenants: Innocent Victims of the Foreclosure Crisis," *Albany Government Law Review* 2 (2009): 1–28; Creola Johnson, "Renters Evicted En Masse: Collateral Damage Arising from the Subprime Foreclosure Crisis," *Florida Law Review* 62 (2010): 975–1008.

5. Sheriff John and several movers told me about the eviction scenes listed in this paragraph.

6. Results from the Milwaukee Area Renters Study revealed that while some low-income families suffer from "double disadvantage," living in distressed neighborhoods and being embedded in impoverished networks, others, to put it plainly, live in relatively bad neighborhoods but have good networks and still others live in relatively good neighborhoods but have bad networks. Matthew Desmond and Weihua An, "Neighborhood and Network Disadvantage Among Urban Renters," *Sociological Science* 2 (2015): 329–50. See also Kathryn Edin and Laura Lein, *Making Ends Meet: How Single Mothers Survive Welfare and Low-Wage Work* (New York: Russell Sage Foundation, 1997), 189; Xavier de Souza Briggs, "Brown Kids in White Suburbs: Housing Mobility and the Many Faces of Social Capital," *Housing Policy Debate* 9 (1998): 177–221; Matthew Desmond, "Disposable Ties and the Urban Poor," *American Journal of Sociology* 117 (2012): 1295–335; Carol Stack, *All Our Kin: Strategies for Survival in a Black Community* (New York: Basic Books, 1974), 77–78.

7. Jacob Rugh and Douglas Massey, "Racial Segregation and the American Foreclosure Crisis," *American Sociological Review* 75 (2010): 629–51; Signe-Mary McKernan et al., *Less Than Equal: Racial Disparities in Wealth Accumulation* (Washington, DC: Urban Institute, 2013); Thomas Shapiro, Tatjana Meschede, and Sam Osoro, *The Roots of the Widening Racial Wealth Gap: Explaining the Black-White Economic Divide* (Waltham, MA: Institute for Assets and Social Policy, 2013).

8. According to Lenny's rent rolls, the month Larraine fell behind, so did forty-seven other families in the trailer park. The least amount owed was $3.88; the largest debt was Britney's.

9. When I asked landlords what factors informed their decision to move forward with an eviction, they typically provided canned answers that had to do with only the financial side of things. But as I learned after spending a considerable

amount of time with landlords, the reality was much more messy and arbitrary.

10. Although unequal in status, male landlords and their male tenants, both having been socialized to the rhythms and postures of masculinity, could engage one another in ways they could each understand. Among landlords represented in Milwaukee's eviction records, men outnumber women almost 3 to 1. Milwaukee County eviction court records, 2003–2007.

11. I observed some men avoid their landlords after receiving an eviction notice, just as I witnessed some women confront their landlords after receiving one. But because of the powerful ways gender guides interaction, providing individuals with expectations about appropriate ways to behave, a woman who aggressively confronted a landlord commonly was branded rude or out of line. This may be why Bob Helfgott, a landlord of twenty years who owned dozens of properties in poor neighborhoods, believed lesbians to be difficult tenants. "The gay women," he said with a sigh. "That angry dyke thing, it drives me crazy. They're just terrible. Always complaining." See Cecilia Ridgeway, "Interaction and the Conservation of Gender Inequality: Considering Employment," *American Sociological Review* 62 (1997): 218–35.

12. Lewis Mumford, *The City in History: Its Origins, Its Transformations, and Its Prospects* (New York: MJF Books, 1961), 107, 110.

13. Tobin and Lenny had had enough. But it is important to recognize that Larraine had nearly avoided eviction, as she had in the past, by borrowing money from a family member. Petitioning acquaintances, friends, or family members for help sometimes worked. But this was less often the case for black women. If black women "ducked and dodged" more than their white counterparts, the reason was that their social networks tended to be far more resource-deprived. Because white women tended to be connected to more people in better positions to help, they were more likely to avoid eviction. See Colleen Heflin and Mary Pattillo, "Poverty in the Family: Race, Siblings, and Socioeconomic Heterogeneity," *Social Science Research* 35 (2006): 804–22; Matthew Desmond, "Eviction and the Reproduction of Urban Poverty," *American Journal of Sociology* 118 (2012): 88–133.

14. I did not personally witness this event. The scene was reconstructed through multiple interviews with Larraine, Dave Brittain, some members of the moving crew, and other trailer park residents.

15. Thanks to a new law (Wisconsin Act 76, Senate Bill 179), Wisconsin landlords now may dispose of evicted tenants' things in whatever manner they see fit. They now have the option of removing tenants' personal belongings themselves and are no longer required to store them. When the law was being debated, the Brittain brothers dipped into their personal savings to support constituents mobilizing against its passage. But they were up against big money. The Apartment Association of Southeastern Wisconsin, the Wisconsin Realtors, and the Wisconsin Apartment Association joined forces to support the bill they had helped craft. As one commenter put it: "This new law will benefit landlords

and 'good' tenants. 'Bad' tenants (i.e., those that don't pay rent on time . . .) will not like this new law." See Tristan Pettit, "ACT 76—Wisconsin's New Landlord-Tenant Law—Part 1: Background and Overview," *Tristan's Landlord-Tenant Law* (blog), November 21, 2013.

10. HYPES FOR HIRE

1. The declaration "I keep to myself" is commonly heard throughout poor communities. The practice of actually keeping to oneself is not commonly seen in those communities. Alexandra Murphy plumbs this tension in her paper "'I Stay to Myself': What People Say Versus What They Do in a Poor Black Neighborhood," working paper, University of Michigan, Department of Sociology.

2. Most work on the underground economy focuses on the drug trade or sex work. But for every kid slinging dope or every prostitute on the stroll, there must be dozens and dozens of formally unemployed men working for cash or reduced rent, preparing landlords' properties. On the blurry line separating the formal and informal economy in American cities, see Sudhir Venkatesh, *Off the Books: The Underground Economy of the Urban Poor* (Cambridge: Harvard University Press, 2006).

11. THE 'HOOD IS GOOD

1. Researchers and legal scholars typically speculate that rents respond to market pressures (a city's vacancy rate) or policy interventions (providing legal aid). But sometimes landlords raise rents when they intuit that tenants can pay more. If Ricky One Leg couldn't pay, Belinda could. As Sherrena would say: "Ricky's in for a rude awakening. His rent is going up. I don't care. He can move. . . . Because I'm sure Belinda's going to have some more . . . tenants. I'm taking his rent up fifty bucks."

2. Technically, gross rent may exceed the FMR payment standard if voucher holders are willing to pay the difference and if the unit passes rent reasonableness inspection.

3. Deborah Devine, *Housing Choice Voucher Location Patterns: Implications for Participant and Neighborhood Welfare* (Washington, DC: US Department of Housing and Urban Development, 2003); George Galster, "Consequences from the Redistribution of Urban Poverty During the 1990s: A Cautionary Tale," *Economic Development Quarterly* 19 (2005): 119–25.

4. Milwaukee Area Renters Study, 2009–2011; US Department of Housing and Urban Development, *Final FY 2008 Fair Market Rent Documentation System*.

5. Robert Collinson and Peter Ganong, "Incidence and Price Discrimination: Evidence from Housing Vouchers," working paper, Harvard University and the US Department of Housing and Urban Development, 2014; Eva Rosen, *The Rise of the Horizontal Ghetto: Poverty in a Post–Public Housing Era*, PhD diss. (Cambridge: Harvard University, 2014).

6. The Milwaukee Area Renters Study offered a unique opportunity to investigate

if voucher holders were being overcharged because the sample included assisted and unassisted renters. Working with Kristin Perkins, I merged addresses represented in the Milwaukee Area Renters Study data set with property records. Doing so provided detailed information on housing quality, including square footage, building age, assessed value per square foot, building type (duplex, single-family), amenities (fireplace, air-conditioning, garage), and housing problems. We also gathered several measures of neighborhood quality, including an area's poverty rate, racial composition, and median home value. Next, we controlled for neighborhood amenities like the distance to the nearest park, bus stop, and grocery store, as well as the average test scores for the school to which the address was zoned. A run of demographic variables about the renters was also included. Hedonic regression models estimated a significant relationship between holding a voucher and rent, with the voucher premium being an additional $49 to $70 a month, depending on model specification. Voucher holders also experienced more housing problems, which casts doubt on the idea that their higher rents reflect newer appliances or other perks not captured in the data. (For full models, see Matthew Desmond and Kristin Perkins, "Are Landlords Overcharging Voucher Holders?," working paper, Harvard University, June 2015.) In 2010, 5,455 households in Milwaukee subsidized their housing costs with a rent-reducing voucher. Taking the results of our primary model, which includes 27 control variables and finds a $55 monthly rent premium for voucher holders, we estimate that the Housing Choice Voucher Program costs an additional $3.6 million each year in Milwaukee alone ($55 × 12 months × 5,455 vouchers). According to the City of Milwaukee, the average per-unit cost for a voucher-assisted household was $511 per month in 2010, or $6,126 a year. Dividing $3.6 million by $6,126 comes to roughly 588 additional families who could have been provided assistance if voucher holders were not overcharged. Some real estate manuals now include sections documenting profits that can be made from renting to voucher holders. See, e.g., Carleton H. Sheets, *Real Estate: The World's Greatest Wealth Builder* (Chicago: Bonus Books, 1998), 121.

7. Charles Orlebeke, "The Evolution of Low-Income Housing Policy, 1949 to 1999," *Housing Policy Debate* 11 (2000): 489–520, 502.

8. When Congress was debating the Taft-Ellender-Wagner bill, which would eventually become the Housing Act of 1949, the president of the National Association of Real Estate Boards called public housing "the cutting edge of the Communist front." The association waged a fierce battle—it funded radio appeals, penned editorials, and rallied its members to call their congressman—and might have won if the construction industry and its union, eager to pour concrete, hadn't flexed their muscle. The act passed by five votes. If it had not, federal provisions for public housing would have disappeared. See Louis Winnick, "The Triumph of Housing Allowance Programs: How a Fundamental Policy Conflict Was Resolved," *Cityscape* 1 (1995): 95–118, 101; Lawrence Vale, *From the Puritans to the Projects: Public Housing and Public Neighbors* (Cambridge: Harvard University Press, 2000), 238–41.

When real estate developers in the mid-twentieth century backed public housing efforts to release coveted urban land for private enterprise, they were more the exception than the rule. Plus, those developers did not support public housing per se; they viewed it as a necessary vehicle through which to execute slum clearance and land grabs. Arnold Hirsch, *Making the Second Ghetto: Race and Housing in Chicago, 1940–1960* (New York: Cambridge University Press, 1983), 104–34.

9. See Philip Tegeler, Michael Hanley, and Judith Liben, "Transforming Section 8: Using Federal Housing Subsidies to Promote Individual Housing Choice and Desegregation," *Harvard Civil Rights–Civil Liberties Law Review* 30 (1995): 451–86; Housing and Community Development Act of 1974, Pub. L. No. 93–383, § 101(a)(1), (c)(6), 88 Stat. 633, 633–34.

10. On foreclosures of rental property, see Gabe Treves, *California Renters in the Foreclosure Crisis, Third Annual Report* (San Francisco: Tenants Together, 2011); Vicki Been and Allegra Glashausser, "Tenants: Innocent Victims of the Foreclosure Crisis," *Albany Government Law Review* 2 (2009); Matthew Desmond, "Housing Crisis in the Inner City," *Chicago Tribune*, April 18, 2010; and Craig Karmin, Robbie Whelan, and Jeannette Neumann, "Rental Market's Big Buyers," *Wall Street Journal*, October 3, 2012. Real estate investment manuals promoted investing in foreclosed and damaged properties long before the crash. "Distressed properties can literally make you rich," one advised in 1998. "Banks don't like foreclosures. But real estate investors do, because foreclosures can be quick bargain buys." Sheets, *Real Estate*, 231, 234.

11. Dwight Jaffee, Anthony Lynch, Matthew Richardson, and Stijn Van Nieuwerburgh, "Mortgage Organization and Securitization in the Financial Crisis," in *Restoring Financial Stability: How to Repair a Failed System*, eds. Viral Acharya and Matthew Richardson (Hoboken: John Wiley & Sons, 2009), 61–82.

12. Kenneth Harney, "Even with Great Credit and Big Down Payment, Home Loans Will Cost More in 2011," *Washington Post*, January 8, 2011.

13. By one estimate, foreclosure discounts are on average 27 percent of the value of the property. John Campbell, Stefano Giglio, and Parag Pathak, "Forced Sales and House Prices," *American Economic Review* 101 (2011): 2108–121.

14. I wasn't there when the door fell on Ruby and then Doreen. Later, I did see the door off its hinges and Doreen's swollen foot and confirmed this story with several Hinkstons.

12. DISPOSABLE TIES

1. This was done so that the apartment would not sit vacant for any amount of time.

2. I did not personally witness this event but reconstructed the scene after speaking with Arleen, Crystal, and Sherrena.

3. A recent study estimated that between one-third and a half of youths aging out of foster care experience homelessness by the time they turn twenty-six. Amy Dworsky, Laura Napolitano, and Mark Courtney, "Homelessness During the

Transition from Foster Care to Adulthood," *American Journal of Public Health* 103 (2013): S318–23.

4. During everyday conversation, people in the trailer park and the inner city claimed to have no friends or an abundance of them, to be surrounded by supportive kin or estranged from them. Oftentimes, depending on their mood, their accounts of social ties and support varied widely from one day to the next. I came to view these accounts skeptically, interpreting them as a kind of data in their own right but not as accurate evaluations of people's social relationships. Problems arose not only when determining *who* was in someone's network but also when asking what those people *did.* Because giving increases your sense of self-worth and receiving diminishes it—ladling soup at the Salvation Army evokes a very different feeling from having it ladled into your bowl—there is good reason to expect people will overestimate the amount of support they give and underestimate the amount they receive. Ethnography allowed me to distinguish accounts of action from the action itself, and eviction, moreover, provided a unique occasion to compare what people said about the support they received from friends and family with support they actually received during that time of crisis. Eviction had a way of quickening ties, testing relationships, and revealing commitments, thereby drawing to the surface what was often submerged below the level of observation. Matthew Desmond, "Disposable Ties and the Urban Poor," *American Journal of Sociology* 117 (2012): 1295–335.

5. Carol Stack, *All Our Kin: Strategies for Survival in a Black Community* (New York: Basic Books, 1974), 93, 33, 43.

6. Public programs like SSI and food stamps continue to incentivize living alone. If you live under another's roof and eat at her or his table, your SSI income is reduced by one-third. Larger households receive more food stamps—but not as much as members of that household would receive if they lived separately. For example, a couple that registered as a household could receive a maximum of $347 a month to spend on food. A couple that registered separately could receive a maximum of $189 a month each, or $378 combined. With some exceptions, everyone living together must apply to the Supplemental Nutrition Assistance Program, rather than separately. See US Department of Agriculture, Food and Nutrition Service, Supplemental Nutrition Assistance Program, *Applicants and Recipients*, December 30, 2013. On SSI living-arrangement requirements, see US Social Security Administration, "Simplifying the Supplemental Security Income Program: Options for Eliminating the Counting of In-Kind Support and Maintenance," *Social Security Bulletin* 68 (November 4, 2008); Brendan O'Flaherty, *Making Room: The Economics of Homelessness* (Cambridge: Harvard University Press, 1996), 222. On kin dependence and AFDC, see M. Lisette Lopez and Carol Stack, "Social Capital and the Culture of Power: Lessons from the Field," in *Social Capital and Poor Communities,* eds. Susan Saegert et al. (New York: Russell Sage Foundation, 2001), 31–59. Milwaukee renters receiving SSI have lower levels of crowding than

their counterparts, even after controlling for income. Milwaukee Area Renters Study, 2009–2011.

7. When it came to meeting basic needs, poor kin had always been greater assets than middle-class relatives. See Desmond, "Disposable Ties and the Urban Poor"; Stack, *All Our Kin*, 77–78.

8. Single mothers like Arleen could not make ends meet on welfare alone: on average, welfare, food stamps, and SSI payments covered only about three-fifths of single mothers' expenses. Even after attempting to make up the difference by working side jobs and seeking help from agencies, many endured severe hardship, going hungry or forgoing winter clothing and medical care. Kathryn Edin and Laura Lein, *Making Ends Meet: How Single Mothers Survive Welfare and Low-Wage Work* (New York: Russell Sage Foundation, 1997).

9. See, for example, Lee Rainwater, *Behind Ghetto Walls: Black Family Life in a Federal Slum* (Chicago: Aldine, 1970), 73; Sandra Susan Smith, *Lone Pursuit: Distrust and Defensive Individualism Among the Black Poor* (New York: Russell Sage Foundation, 2007). For an extended treatment, see Desmond, "Disposable Ties and the Urban Poor." Other ethnographers have documented similar network dynamics in poor neighborhoods: see Elliot Liebow, *Tally's Corner: A Study of Negro Streetcorner Men* (Boston: Little, Brown and Company, 1967), 163–65, 182; Rainwater, *Behind Ghetto Walls*, 73. Of course, these dynamics can be observed at all levels of society. The tendency to rely on perfect strangers for emotional comfort, for example, is fairly common among the middle class, as evidenced by the so-called "stranger on a plane" phenomenon. Although poor people's strategy of relying on disposable ties is not different in kind from the tendency of rich people to rely on strangers, it often is different in degree. It is only the poor who routinely rely on disposable ties to meet basic human needs.

10. People see neighborhoods as much more than school districts and the usual ecological indicators. They see things much too personal to quantify but powerful enough to attract them to or repel them from entire sections of the city.

11. Crystal had allowed her food stamps to lapse after her grandmother died the year before. She remembered her grandmother's death causing her to fall into a dark depression. "I didn't do shit. Sleep all day. Get in the shower. Eat. Go back in the house and go back to sleep. I shut down—on everything and everybody." It was another example of how a trauma exacerbated poverty.

12. That is, Crystal used an insult in place of Jori's name.

13. E-24

1. On the North Side, white landlords often hired black property managers. Said Sherrena, "There's a lot of white boys [who] come down from Brookfield here, and they buy all this inner-city shit. . . . And they will hire a black property manager to handle things for them. . . . The white boy will hire a black guy, maybe that looks a little mean and can keep up stuff, and they'll bawl 'em. It's easy." Sherrena meant the property manager would not hesitate to yell at

tenants ("bawl them out") if they didn't pay up. See Jennifer Lee, "Cultural Brokers: Race-Based Hiring in Inner-City Neighborhoods," *American Behavioral Scientist* 41 (1998): 927–37.

2. Mortgage and release records were retrieved from the Milwaukee County Register of Deeds.

3. Tobin and Lenny's rent records showed that during most months five trailers sat empty and forty tenants were behind, the average amount owed in a month being $340. Five vacancies a month left 126 trailers paying an average of $550 in monthly rent. Subtract from that total missed rent payments in the amount of $163,200 (40 × $340 × 12). This reduction was probably too drastic for two reasons. First, Tobin did not carry out anything close to forty evictions a month; so most people found a way to satisfy their debts. Second, missing payment estimates were based on summer-month totals (the trailer park's rent rolls from April to July 2008) when nonpayments and evictions spiked. Nevertheless, I have kept these likely inflated reductions to generate a conservative estimate. Tobin's overhead consisted of Lenny and Susie, whose combined annual salaries and rent reductions ran just shy of $50,000. Lenny's annual salary and rent waiver totaled $42,600 ($36,000 + $6,600), and Susie's salary and rent reduction totaled $6,400. (Tobin considered Susie a part-time employee, whom he paid $5 an hour for twenty hours a week; or: [$5/hr × 20 hours × 52] + $1,200 in reduced rent.) With respect to maintenance, all but twenty trailers were "owned," which meant tenants footed most repair bills. Estimated regular maintenance costs rarely exceeded $5,000 a month, even after accounting for money paid for grass cutting and litter pickup. But I have kept this likely inflated estimate as well. Tobin's property taxes were $49,457 in 2008, and his water bill was $26,708 that year. (Both figures were pulled from public records.) Tenants paid gas and electricity. Eviction court costs? Tobin averaged three formal evictions a month, and didn't use a lawyer unless cases got tricky, which would mean he paid less than $7,000 a year in eviction court, sheriff, and lawyer fees. (If Tobin evicted an average of three tenants a month, then his annual baseline court costs could come to $3,222 [$89.50 × 3 cases × 12 months]. I doubled that number to account for irregular sheriff, mover, and lawyer fees and rounded up to $7,000.) Trash? Lenny told me that the bill for managing the two Dumpsters ran $800 a month (or $9,600 a year). Lighting? Tobin paid for the outdoor lighting (installed to utility poles) that lit the trailer park at night. Using We Energies standard rates, I budgeted $5,000 a year for this expense (plus the office's electricity bill). Incidentals? I budgeted an additional $15,000 for advertisements and Lenny's rent-collection bonuses. That leaves $446,635 a year. I excluded large, onetime maintenance expenses from this calculation—like when Tobin had speed bumps installed within the park—because they were rare and irregular. Lenny thought my estimate was too low. He believed Tobin took home "more like six hundred thousand" a year.

14. HIGH TOLERANCE

1. John Gurda, *The Making of Milwaukee*, 3rd ed. (Milwaukee: Milwaukee County Historical Society, 2008 [1999]), 174.

2. In my experience, disadvantaged neighborhoods were characterized not by the presence of an "oppositional culture" as much as by a palpable lack of one.

3. Robert Fogelson, *The Great Rent Wars: New York, 1917–1929* (New Haven: Yale University Press, 2014), 85, 86.

4. Frances Fox Piven and Richard Cloward, *Poor People's Movements: Why They Succeed, How They Fail* (New York: Vintage, 1979), 12, 4.

5. Fogelson, *Great Rent Wars*, 88.

6. This finding is based on a negative binomial regression model applied to the full Milwaukee Area Renters Study (2009–2011) sample. To measure "community support," respondents were asked if they ever had helped someone in their current neighborhood (a) pay bills or buy groceries, (b) get a job, (c) fix their housing or car, (d) by supporting them emotionally, or (e) by watching their children. Neighborhood disadvantage was measured by a factor-loaded scale composed of median household income, violent crime rate, and the percentages of families below the poverty line, of the population under eighteen, of residents with less than a high school education, of residents receiving public assistance, and of vacant housing units. In a paper with Weihua An, I found neighborhood disadvantage to be positively associated with community support, net of income, education, residential mobility, race, age, gender, employment status, and network composition. Residents in disadvantaged neighborhoods with strong ties to homeowners and the college educated were just as likely to offer support to their neighbors as those who lacked such ties. This suggests the strong presence of local gift exchange in distressed neighborhoods, one relatively unaffected by the composition of people's extended networks. See Matthew Desmond and Weihua An, "Neighborhood and Network Disadvantage Among Urban Renters," *Sociological Science* 2 (2015): 329–50.

7. Support systems that arise organically in poor neighborhoods help people eat and cope, but they also expose them to heavy doses of trauma and sometimes violence. Bruce Western, "Lifetimes of Violence in a Sample of Released Prisoners," *Russell Sage Journal of the Social Sciences*, forthcoming.

8. Harvey Zorbaugh, *The Gold Coast and the Slum: A Sociological Study of Chicago's Near North Side* (Chicago: University of Chicago Press, 1929), 70.

9. This finding is based on an ordered logistic regression model applied to the Milwaukee Area Renters Study, 2009–2011. The outcome variable is political capacity. Respondents were asked: "How likely is it that people in this neighborhood would ever organize and work together to improve their community and their lives: not at all, a little bit, somewhat, quite a bit, or a great deal?" The primarily explanatory variable is a measure of perceived neighborhood trauma. Respondents were asked: "While you have been living in this neighborhood,

have any of your neighbors ever: (a) been evicted; (b) been in prison; (c) been in an abusive relationship; (d) been addicted to drugs; (e) had their children taken away by social services; (f) had a close family member or friend murdered?" Answers were summed. The full model documents a significant negative relationship between political capacity and perceived neighborhood trauma, controlling for prior political involvement, tenure in neighborhood, neighborhood poverty and crime rates, and a run of demographic factors. See Matthew Desmond and Adam Travis, "Perceived Neighborhood Trauma and Political Capacity," unpublished manuscript, Harvard University, 2015. On the perception of social disorder mattering more than disorder itself, see Lincoln Quillian and Devah Pager, "Black Neighbors, Higher Crime? The Role of Racial Stereotypes in Evaluations of Neighborhood Crime," *American Journal of Sociology* 107 (2001): 717–67; Robert Sampson, *Great American City: Chicago and the Enduring Neighborhood Effect* (Chicago: University of Chicago Press, 2012).

10. During the Milwaukee Area Renters Study, respondents were asked: "What two words would best describe your landlord?" Two independent coders assigned a value to each word, with 1 being the lowest and 10 being the highest. Words like "slumlord" and "asshole" were assigned 1's and words like "excellent" and "loving" were assigned 10's. More muted critiques or compliments were assigned a midrange value. The coders' scores were then averaged to produce an overall rating. The average renter in Milwaukee, according to this ranking, sees her or his landlord as a 6. Renters with extreme housing burden did not rate their landlord better or worse than other renters did. But those who experienced housing problems saw their landlord in a significantly more negative light.

11. Tenants did bind together upon learning that the trailer park might be shut down; this was their "extraordinary moment." But after that moment passed, things went back to normal. They did not question the rent, fight for better housing conditions, or assign a political narrative to evictions. Their quibble had been with their alderman, not their landlord. Once, tenants did circulate a petition. It asked for the removal of a woman seen as a snitch and general troublemaker. "We are asking that Grace in trailer S12 be evicted from the trailer park before matters get worse . . ." the petition read. "We feel the only way to resolve this problem is to remove her before someone resolves it, and we don't need for it to come to that." Forty people signed what came to be known as the Petition Against Grace.

15. A NUISANCE

1. Psychologists have shown that when self-preservation is pitted against empathy, empathy usually loses. See Keith Campbell et al., "Responding to Major Threats to Self-Esteem: A Preliminary, Narrative Study of Ego-Shock," *Journal of Social and Clinical Psychology* 22 (2003): 79–96.

2. "Dot your eyes" means blacken them. "Scary," when used in this way, means cowardly.

3. Throughout the twentieth century, as America modernized and its police force

grew, citizens were instructed to clear the scene, to line up behind the yellow tape. The right to pursue and punish wrongdoers would come to rest with the state alone. But in the 1960s antiwar protesters began bleeding from standard-issue batons, citizens were speaking out against police brutality in minority communities, stories of entrenched corruption were being broadcast, Watts was burning, and violent crime was increasing. Facing this gust of changes, Americans began growing disenchanted with the criminal justice system. The coup de grâce was delivered in 1974 when Robert Martinson reviewed 231 relevant studies and concluded in the pages of *The Public Interest* that "with few and isolated exceptions, the rehabilitative efforts that have been reported so far have had no appreciable effect on recidivism." "Nothing works," politicians and criminologists sighed. Its authority compromised, the justice system responded schizophrenically, at once giving the police more power and resources while also bringing non-police actors into the business of crime control. On the rise and character of third-party policing, see Matthew Desmond and Nicol Valdez, "Unpolicing the Urban Poor: Consequences of Third Party Policing on Inner-City Women," *American Sociological Review* 78 (2013): 117–41; David Garland, *The Culture of Control: Crime and Social Order in Contemporary Society* (Chicago: University of Chicago Press, 2001); Lorraine Mazerolle and Janet Ransley, *Third Party Policing* (Cambridge: Cambridge University Press, 2005).

4. Reinier Kraakman, "Gatekeepers: The Anatomy of a Third-Party Enforcement Strategy," *Journal of Law, Economics, and Organization* 2 (1986): 53–104.

5. Desmond and Valdez, "Unpolicing the Urban Poor," Table S1. Mazerolle and Ransley, *Third Party Policing.*

6. The nuisance ordinance has also been championed as an effective weapon in the drug war. But of the 1,666 nuisance activities listed in all citations distributed in Milwaukee between 2008 and 2009, only 4 percent involved drug-related crimes. For the methodology that resulted in this estimate, see Desmond and Valdez, "Unpolicing the Urban Poor," 122–25.

7. Here, "black/white neighborhoods" refer to census block groups in which at least two-thirds of residents are black/white. And "properties that could have received a nuisance citation" refer to those from which three or more 911 calls were placed within a thirty-day period. If most nuisance citations were addressed to properties in predominantly black neighborhoods, this was not so much because those neighborhoods were more crime-ridden as much as it was because they were blacker. The discrepancy remained even after controlling for crime rate, 911-call volume, neighborhood poverty, and other relevant factors. Imagine that two women called the police at the same time, both reporting domestic abuse. One woman lived in an 80 percent black neighborhood and one lived in a 20 percent black neighborhood. The landlord of the first woman was over 3.5 times more likely to receive a nuisance citation, even after controlling for the prevalence of domestic-violence calls made from properties and a neighborhood's domestic violence rate. Desmond and Valdez, "Unpolicing the Urban Poor."

8. This might lead one to wonder if recent declines in domestic violence should be credited to the increasing criminalization of family abuse or to the proliferation of nuisance property ordinances that discourage reporting. See Cari Fais, "Denying Access to Justice: The Cost of Applying Chronic Nuisance Laws to Domestic Violence," *Columbia Law Review* 108 (2008): 1181–225.

9. Other landlords responded to nuisance property citations by discouraging tenants from calling 911. Some instructed tenants to call them instead of the police. A landlord running a living facility housing "persons with disabilities" posted the following sign around the building: STOP BEFORE CALLING 911 / YOU CAN BE FINED BY THE / POLICE FOR / NON-EMERGENCY CALLS / CALL [414-###-####] / ASK FOR DAWN. Other landlords threatened tenants with eviction or fines if they called 911 again. After receiving a citation, one landlord circulated the following letter to his tenants: "Tenants who place nuisance calls to the Milwaukee Police Department, or abuse the 911 system, will be fined . . . $50.00 PER OCCURRENCE."

10. Wisconsin Coalition Against Domestic Violence, *Wisconsin Domestic Violence Homicide Report: 2009* (Milwaukee: Wisconsin Coalition Against Domestic Violence, September 2010).

11. Milwaukee amended its ordinance in 2011, shortly after I shared my findings with the Police Department, city attorneys, and housing lawyers. Now, citations explicitly state that "nuisance activity" does not include domestic abuse, sexual assault, or stalking. With this step, Milwaukee has joined a handful of other municipalities—Chicago; Madison, Wisconsin; Phillipsburg, New Jersey; and the Village of East Rochester, New York, among them—whose nuisance property ordinance forbids administering citations for repeated calls due to domestic violence. They are the exception to the rule. Will dropping domestic violence from the list of nuisance activities be enough to protect battered women from the ordinance? It will most likely not, for two reasons.

The first is that domestic-violence incidents often hide behind other police designations, antiseptic and context-barren, such as Property Damage (as when an ex-boyfriend kicks down the door) or Subject with Weapon (as when a husband uses a pair of box cutters on his wife). Domestic violence, sexual assault, and stalking were not struck from Milwaukee's original list of nuisance activities; they were never included in the list to begin with. Because the ordinance still lists things like battery, harassment, and misuse of emergency telephone numbers among its thirty-two permissible nuisances, these designations can still be applied to crimes of the home.

A second problem with the city's quick fix is that it relies on landlords, who have been threatened with hefty fines, to reveal if nuisance activities are domestic violence–related. Some will raise this issue with the police, and others will simply evict the tenant, implementing their own quick fix. Roughly 8 in 10 property owners abated nuisance activity, regardless of what it involved, by evicting tenants or by threatening them with eviction if the police were contacted again. One could propose a list of other improvements—more police training could help; cities could aim their ordinances only at drug activity or noise—but maybe this is a case where the hatchet is preferred to the scalpel. Not only can nuisance property ordinances do considerable harm, but they also reveal the extent to which local governments are willing to relax civil rights and circumvent the judiciary process when confronted with a scarcity of resources. "Nuisance tenants" are not prima facie guilty. They are not prima facie anything because questions of guilt and innocence are inconsequential to policies designed to operate beyond the purview of the court. Unless the tenant puts up a serious fuss, the evidence never even sees the inside of a court. Besides these concerns about due process rights, legal scholars have argued that nuisance property ordinances violate constitutional (think Fourth Amendment) and statutory (think Fair Housing Act) protections. Perhaps what Caleb Foote said of US vagrancy laws almost sixty years ago can be said of nuisance property ordinances today: the only reason they are tolerated is because families struggling to make ends meet in the low-income housing market are simply too poor or too vulnerable to assert their obvious rights. See John Blue, "*High Noon* Revisited: Commands of Assistance by Peace Officers in the Age of the Fourth Amendment," *Yale Law Journal* 101 (1992): 1475–90; John Diedrich, "Domestic Violence Victims in Milwaukee Faced Eviction for Calling Police, Study Finds," *Milwaukee Journal Sentinel*, August 18, 2013; Caleb Foote, "Vagrancy-Type Law and Its Administration," *University of Pennsylvania Law Review* 104 (1954): 603–50; Karen Phillips, *Preliminary Statement, Grape v. Town/Village of East Rochester*, No. 07 CV 6075 CJS (F) (W.D.N.Y. March 16, 2007).

16. ASHES ON SNOW

1. I began this evening with Sherrena and Quentin at the casino. The scene of Lamar playing cards with Kamala was reconstructed through interviews with Lamar, Luke, Eddy, and some of the neighborhood boys. I also reviewed court records and reports by medical examiners and fire/safety scientists. The rest of the evening's events were witnessed firsthand.

2. Mothers' cries were heard over a century ago, when flames ravaged tenements, the fireproofing of which was deemed too costly; and they went up throughout the twentieth century, when ghetto housing in city after city ignited in flame or collapsed in decay. In Chicago alone, between 1947 and 1953 fires claimed the lives of over 180 slum dwellers, 63 of whom were under the age of ten. Conditions that invited fires—overcrowding, slipshod construction—also could prevent families from escaping. Throughout the 1960s and early '70s, some landlords torched their own buildings to collect insurance money. Sometimes these buildings were vacant; sometimes they were not. Today, children living in substandard housing are more than ten times more likely to die in a fire than those living in decent and safe homes. Said Jacob Riis, a fire at night is "a horror that has few parallels in human experience." The quote comes from Riis, *How the Other Half Lives: Studies Among the Tenements of New York*

(New York: Penguin Books, 1997 [1890]), 88, but see also 35–36. On fires in the slum, see Jacob Riis, *Battle with the Slum* (Mineola: Dover Publications, 1998 [1902]), 89; Marcus Anthony Hunter, *Black Citymakers: How the Philadelphia Negro Changed Urban America* (New York: Oxford University Press, 2013), chapter 3; Arnold Hirsch, *Making the Second Ghetto: Race and Housing in Chicago, 1940–1960* (New York: Cambridge University Press, 1983), 25–26; Thomas Sugrue, *The Origins of the Urban Crisis: Race and Inequality in Postwar Detroit* (Princeton: Princeton University Press, 2005), 37; Beryl Satter, *Family Properties: How the Struggle over Race and Real Estate Transformed Chicago and Urban America* (New York: Metropolitan Books, 2009), 335; Douglas Parker et al., "Fire Fatalities Among New Mexico Children," *Annals of Emergency Medicine* 22 (1993): 517–22.

17. THIS IS AMERICA

1. On "going homeless" to receive benefits, see Adrian Nicole LeBlanc, *Random Family: Love, Drugs, Trouble, and Coming of Age in the South Bronx* (New York: Scribner, 2004).

2. Humans act brutally under brutal conditions. "People who have never experienced chronic hunger are apt to underestimate its effects," the psychologist A. H. Maslow once wrote. "If they"—the well-fed, the housed—"are dominated by a higher need, this higher need will seem to be the most important of all." So it is with so many thinkers and pundits who try to explain violence in poor communities without considering the limitations of human capacity in the teeth of scarcity and suffering. Look how neighbors, perfectly peaceful when the crop yield is plenty, will claw and trample and bite one another when bread is tossed from a food truck during a famine. Or as Maslow would put it: "It is quite true that man lives by bread alone—when there is no bread." Ideas about aggression in low-income communities that do not account for the hard squeeze of poverty, the sheer emotional and cognitive burden that accompanies severe deprivation, do not come close to capturing the lived experience of people like Arleen and Crystal. A. H. Maslow, "A Theory of Human Motivation," *Psychological Review* 50 (1943): 370–96, 387, 375. For accounts of human behavior under extreme conditions, see, e.g., Elie Wiesel, *Night* (New York: Bantam Books, 1982 [1960]), 95; Tim O'Brien, *The Things They Carried* (New York: First Mariner Books, 2009 [1990]), 64–81.

People respond to structural conditions, like food scarcity or concentrated disadvantage, in cogent ways. The anthropologist Oscar Lewis, who popularized the notion of a "culture of poverty," thought those patterned actions and beliefs themselves become sentient and help to reinforce the conditions that originally produced them. It is in this moment of sentience that those actions and beliefs are thought to constitute something like a "culture"—enduring and shared views and practices—instead of something more fleeting and circumstantially necessary. Omitted from this model are institutions that occupy a space between people and structural conditions and that encode disadvantage in people's language, habits, belief systems, and practices. Resource-poor schools in low-income neighborhoods often leave children with subpar language and critical-thinking skills. Those deficits will remain even if those children relocate to safe and prosperous neighborhoods later in life. To think of those school-conditioned speech patterns and belief systems as evidence of a "culture of poverty," the invention of poor families themselves, is to overlook the influence of broken cultural institutions through which low-income families pass. We do not think that the rich are rich because they invented a "culture of affluence" but because they pass through elite institutions that modify their behavior, habits, and worldviews, and this constellation of skills and ways of being, in turn, eases their entrance into other elite institutions. What might be viewed as a "culture of affluence" is, simply, affluence; and "many of the features alleged to characterize the culture of poverty . . . are simply definitions of poverty itself," as Carol Stack pointedly observed in *All Our Kin: Strategies for Survival in a Black Community* (New York: Basic Books, 1974), 23. On the culture of poverty, see Oscar Lewis, *Five Families: Mexican Case Studies in the Culture of Poverty* (New York: Basic Books, 1959); Michèle Lamont and Mario Luis Small, "How Culture Matters: Enriching Our Understanding of Poverty," in *The Colors of Poverty: Why Racial and Ethnic Disparities Persist*, eds. David Harris and Ann Lin (New York: Russell Sage Foundation, 2008), 76–102; Mustafa Emirbayer and Matthew Desmond, *The Racial Order* (Chicago: University of Chicago Press, 2015), chapter 6; Matthew Desmond, "Relational Ethnography," *Theory and Society* 43 (2014): 547–79.

18. LOBSTER ON FOOD STAMPS

1. Jason DeParle, *American Dream: Three Women, Ten Kids, and the Nation's Drive to End Welfare* (New York: Penguin, 2004); John Gurda, *The Making of Milwaukee*, 3rd ed. (Milwaukee: Milwaukee County Historical Society, 2008 [1999]).

2. On waiting as a lived experience of poverty, see Javier Auyero, *Patients of the State: The Politics of Waiting in Argentina* (Durham: Duke University Press, 2012).

3. Social Security Administration, *Understanding Supplemental Security Income SSI Resources* (Washington, DC: SSA, 2014).

4. "When I write about this, it's going to be a little hard for people to understand," I said.

"You're going to put this in your book?" Larraine asked.

"Yeah, I think so. They'll say, 'What is she doing? She just got evicted. She's practically homeless. She's living with her brother, and who knows how that'll go. She just got out of a meeting to renew her food stamps. What on earth is she doing putting on layaway a fifteen-hundred-dollar sixty-two-inch TV?' They'll say that."

"Well, they don't have to understand it. I don't understand a lot of things other people do, but they do it."

"What would you say to them if they were sitting right here, and they were saying, 'Larraine, why would you do such a thing?'"

"I would say because I wanted to."

5. Some middle-class people can't help feeling incredulous, even furious, upon walking into a low-income household and spotting a big-screen television or fresh Nikes by the door. Conservative think tanks and news outlets publish reports with titles such as "Are You Poor If You Have a Flat-Screen TV?" and *Air Conditioning, Cable TV, and an Xbox: What Is Poverty in America?* Liberals try to change the subject to avoid talking about behavior they wish would go away. That fancy television in the ratty apartment? Those new shoes worn by the kid eating free school lunch? Their owners likely didn't pay full dollar for them. You can take a nice television off a hype for fifty bucks and find marked-down Nikes at the corner store. The price tags in inner-city clothing stores are for white suburban kids who don't know how to haggle. Next to that big-screen television too it is harder to see what is missing. You are almost as likely to find as many televisions in a poor household as in a rich one. But most poor Americans do not own a computer. When Larraine ate her special meal, she didn't even have a phone. See Tami Luhby, "Are You Poor If You Have a Flat-Screen TV?," *CNN Money*, August 13, 2012; Robert Rector and Rachel Sheffield, *Air Conditioning, Cable TV, and an Xbox: What Is Poverty in America?* (Washington, DC: The Heritage Foundation, 2011); US Energy Information Administration, *Residential Energy Consumption Survey*, 2012.

It is an old liberal tradition: ignoring the nastier, more embarrassing aspects of poverty. And because, to paraphrase Carol Stack (*All Our Kin: Strategies for Survival in a Black Community* [New York: Basic Books, 1974], 24), liberal commentators and researchers do not take a hard look at these aspects of poverty, they can only apologize for them. But as William Julius Wilson argued in *The Truly Disadvantaged: The Inner City, the Underclass, and Public Policy*, 2nd ed. (Chicago: University of Chicago Press, 2012 [1987]), 6, 12, "to avoid describing any behavior that might be construed as unflattering or stigmatizing" to poor people is to "render liberal arguments ineffective" because the American public wants answers to questions about that behavior. There are two ways to dehumanize: the first is to strip people of all virtue; the second is to cleanse them of all sin.

6. Would people behave differently if they were provided with a real opportunity to break out of poverty? There is good reason to expect as much. Behavioral economists and psychologists have shown that "poverty *itself* taxes the mind," making people less intelligent and more impulsive. Moreover, when poor families are provided with a meaningful economic uplift, they often respond by building assets and paying off debt. A recent study found that almost 40 percent of parents who received an Earned Income Tax Credit in excess of $1,000 saved a considerable portion of their refund and almost 85 percent used the refund to address debt. The expectation of ongoing refunds gave parents hope, and they responded by saving toward the goal of climbing out of poverty. See

Sendhil Mullainathan and Eldar Shafir, *Scarcity: Why Having So Little Means So Much* (New York: Times Books, 2013), 60, 66; Abhijit Banerjee and Sendhil Mullainathan, "The Shape of Temptation: Implications for the Economic Lives of the Poor," National Bureau of Economic Research Working Paper, No. 15973 (2010); Ruby Mendenhall et al., "The Role of Earned Income Tax Credit in the Budgets of Low-Income Households," *Social Service Review* 86 (2012): 367–400.

7. Eviction is costly, often preventing tenants from saving up first-month's rent and security deposit for a new place.

8. The majority of public housing residents are either disabled or elderly. On the rise of elderly housing, see Lawrence Vale, *From the Puritans to the Projects: Public Housing and Public Neighbors* (Cambridge: Harvard University Press, 2000), 285–90. On the composition of public housing residents, see Alex Schwartz, *Housing Policy in the United States*, 2nd ed. (New York: Routledge, 2010), chapter 6.

9. The practice of denying housing assistance to people based on eviction records and other civil proceedings raises a number of serious concerns. As Larraine learned, court records can be inaccurate; they can display wrongful evictions; and they can reflect landlord discretion, which can have a disparate effect on certain groups like single mothers and victims of domestic abuse. On questionable standards of accuracy in civil court records, see Rudy Kleysteuber, "Tenant Screening Thirty Years Later: A Statutory Proposal to Protect Public Records," *Yale Law Journal* 116 (2006): 1344–88; David Thacher, "The Rise of Criminal Background Screening in Rental Housing," *Law and Social Inquiry* 33 (2008): 5–30.

10. The poverty debate could do more to recognize the powerful effects of rejection on a person's self-confidence and stamina. Applying for an apartment or job and being turned down ten, twenty, forty times—it can wear you out. Theories about neighborhood selection or joblessness often assume low-income people are more or less "rational actors" who recognize trade-offs and make clear choices. The reality is that many are "exhausted settlers" who accept poor housing in a disadvantaged neighborhood or a dead-end or illicit job after becoming depleted and disheartened from trying and trying and failing and failing. The shame of rejection not only can pressure people to accept undesirable circumstances today; it can also discourage them from striving for something better tomorrow. On the experience of rejection when job hunting for entry-level work, see Philippe Bourgois, *In Search of Respect: Selling Crack in El Barrio* (New York: Cambridge University Press, 1995), chapter 4; Katherine Newman, *No Shame in My Game: The Working Poor in the Inner City* (New York: Vintage, 1999), chapter 3.

11. Some months later, Betty received a letter from Tobin threatening eviction for boarding Larraine. Larraine responded by paying Tobin what he said she owed in back rent and court costs. That amount was twice what the court records said Larraine owed. This caused Larraine to fall so far behind with Eagle

Moving that she lost everything she had stored with them. Her furniture, photographs, and layaway jewelry were bought at a public sale for who knows what by some bargain hunter or thrown in the dump.

19. LITTLE

1. Housing insecurity is an important source of employment insecurity among low-income workers. Applying matching techniques as well as discrete hazard models to the Milwaukee Area Renters Study data set with Carl Gershenson, I found low-wage workers who involuntarily lost their homes to be significantly more likely to lose their jobs. When we examined the effects of forced removal for renters with relatively stable work histories and those with fairly unstable employment, we found forced removal to be an actuator of job loss for both groups. Matthew Desmond and Carl Gershenson, "Housing and Employment Insecurity Among the Working Poor," *Social Problems*, forthcoming.

2. Consider Tina's story. A single mother of three, Tina worked part-time for a landscaping company, entering data and making customer-service calls. After serving her an eviction notice, Tobin began calling Tina's work and threatening to carry out the eviction unless she paid him $600. (Tina claimed to owe only $100.) Fighting the eviction, Tina attended several court hearings, sometimes missing work to do so. While her case was still pending, sheriff deputies and an Eagle Moving crew appeared at her trailer. Tina's teenage daughter held them off until she arrived and explained her situation. Tina began looking for another place to live but was turned away by several landlords on account of her open eviction case and poor credit. Soon, Tina's job performance began to falter. Depressed and overwhelmed, she began calling in sick. At work, she began making mistakes, like forgetting to enter service calls into the system, which she attributed to the stress of her eviction case. One day at the office, Tina broke down sobbing at her desk as coworkers and supervisors looked on. A judge would agree that Tina was being overcharged, but she still was evicted. Afterward, she began relying on friends and casual acquaintances for shelter, eventually moving with her daughters into a house owned by a man who showed a romantic interest in her. His house was considerably farther away from Tina's workplace, and her car was unreliable. This situation played a role in increasing her lateness and absenteeism. In late fall, Tina was laid off. Tina's case reveals multiple mechanisms linking eviction to job loss. The consuming and disruptive nature of the eviction caused her to miss work and negatively affected her job performance. Moving under duress and with little control over her circumstances, Tina relocated farther away from her employer, which increased her risk of tardiness and no-showing. And her dependency on a casual acquaintance for shelter introduced a new set of interpersonal complications and demands.

3. Thomas Sugrue, *The Origins of the Urban Crisis: Race and Inequality in Postwar Detroit* (Princeton: Princeton University Press, 2005), 53.

4. These mothers were writing to apply for public housing in Detroit between 1946 and 1948. Detroit Housing Commission, *"Children Not Wanted": The*

Story of Detroit's Housing Shortage Victims Told in Their Own Words (Detroit: Detroit Housing Commission, 1948).

5. Jim Buchanan, *Fair Housing and Families: Discrimination Against Children*, Public Administration Series, Bibliography, P1732 (Monticello: Vance Bibliographies, 1985).

6. Mary Ellen Colten and Robert Marans, "Restrictive Rental Practices and Their Impact on Families," *Population Research and Policy Review* 1 (1982): 43–58, 49.

7. Edward Allen, "Six Years After Passage of the Fair Housing Amendments Act: Discrimination Against Families with Children," *Administrative Law Journal of American University* 9 (1995): 297–359.

8. Unlike with discrimination based on race or gender, most Americans do not even realize that discrimination against children is illegal. Rigel Oliveri, "Is Acquisition Everything? Protecting the Rights of Occupants Under the Fair Housing Act," *Harvard Civil Rights–Liberties Law Review* 43 (2008): 1–64, 5. A report based on a nationwide sample of Americans found that the majority of respondents recognized discrimination based on race, religion, and ability to be illegal, but only 38 percent were "aware that it is illegal to treat households with children differently from households without children." See Martin Abravanel and Mary Cunningham, *How Much Do We Know? Public Awareness of the Nation's Fair Housing Laws* (Washington, DC: US Department of Housing and Urban Development, 2002), 10. See also US Department of Housing and Urban Development, *Live Free: Annual Report on Fair Housing* (Washington, DC: US Department of Housing and Urban Development, 2010). Fair Housing of Marin, *Discrimination Against Families with Children in Rental Housing* (San Rafael: Fair Housing of Marin, 2002); Gulf Coast Fair Housing Center, *An Audit Report on Race and Family Status Discrimination in the Mississippi Gulf Coast Rental Housing Market* (Gulfport: Gulf Coast Fair Housing Center, 2004).

9. Milwaukee Area Renters Study, 2009–2011.

10. Ned might have been homeless and on the run, but he was still compensated, as W. E. B. DuBois would have it, by a "psychological wage" that involved disparaging black people. See *Black Reconstruction in America* (Cleveland: Meridian Books, 1969 [1935]), 700.

11. The weight of the shame, sociologists have long thought, explained why many relationships fell apart in poor black neighborhoods. Especially for jobless men, the indignity of facing your family empty-handed built up to the point where abandonment became the lesser disgrace. To stay in a committed relationship was "to live with your failure, to be confronted by it day in and day out. . . . In self-defense, the husband retreated to the streetcorner." Most single mothers had no street-corner reprieve. Elliot Liebow, *Tally's Corner: A Study of Negro Streetcorner Men* (Boston: Little, Brown and Company, 1967), 135–36. See also Kathryn Edin and Timothy Nelson, *Doing the Best I Can: Fatherhood in the Inner City* (Berkeley: University of California Press, 2013).

12. Orlando Patterson, *Rituals of Blood: Consequences of Slavery in Two American Centuries* (New York: Basic Civitas Books, 1998), 134; Nancy Scheper-Hughes, *Death Without Weeping: The Violence of Everyday Life in Brazil* (Berkeley: University of California Press, 1992), 276.

13. Carl Nightingale, *On the Edge: A History of Poor Black Children and Their American Dreams* (New York: Basic Books, 1993), 76–77; Patterson, *Rituals of Blood*, 133–34.

In the days of slavery and sharecropping, black mothers and fathers often disciplined their children harshly "to prepare them for life in a white-dominated world where all blacks had to act cautiously." Jacqueline Jones, *Labor of Love, Labor of Sorrows: Black Women, Work, and the Family from Slavery to the Present*, rev. ed. (New York: Basic Books, 2010), 96. Later, during Jim Crow, black parents sometimes trained their children to be subservient and docile. "In low-class [black] families," wrote one observer, "a child is taught that he is a 'nigger' and that he must be subservient to white people, since he must work for them." A saying emerged among black families at the time: "It's a white man's world and you just happen to be here, nigger." See Jennifer Ritterhouse, *Growing Up Jim Crow: How Black and White Southern Children Learned Race* (Chapel Hill: University of North Carolina Press, 2006), 98.

Today, poor mothers are less supportive, less emotionally invested, and less solicitous of their children's needs, desires, and dreams. They give fewer hugs and tender fewer compliments. Mothers experiencing severe levels of economic deprivation hit and scold their children more frequently. The sociologist Orlando Patterson has gone so far as to say that "the parenting of boys and girls by the Afro-American lower classes has become increasingly abusive." The standard explanation for these troubling patterns goes like this: poverty diminishes a person's capacity for affirming and supportive parenting because it causes mothers to become irritable, depressed, and anxious. If parents are irritable, depressed, and anxious, that increases their tendency to be punitive and less supportive of their children. The cluster of disadvantages and traumas we call "poverty" can siphon a mother's joy. But poor mothers are not the only ones who are irritable, depressed, or anxious. These conditions are not unique to poverty. What is unique to poverty is poverty. It is the experience of parenting in scarcity itself that impels mothers like Arleen to become harsh caregivers some of the time. Their barbed coolness is a necessary protection, a defense mechanism in the teeth of deprivation. Patterson, *Rituals of Blood*, 133. A vast literature connects nonsupportive and punitive parenting styles to lower self-esteem, aggression, and antisocial behavior in children. See Robert Bradley and Robert Corwyn, "Socioeconomic Status and Child Development," *Annual Review of Psychology* 53 (2002): 371–99; Elizabeth Gershoff, Rashmita Mistry, and Danielle Crosby, eds., *Societal Contexts of Child Development: Pathways of Influence and Implications for Practice and Policy* (New York: Oxford University Press, 2013); Vonnie McLoyd, "How Money Matters for Children's Socioemotional Adjustment: Family Processes and Parental Investment," *Health Disparities in Youth and Families* 57 (2011): 33–72.

In the developing world, it is scarcity that pressures mothers of sickly infants to say that their babies were born "already wanting to die" and to soothe their indifference with the reassurance that "little critters have no feelings." "Here," the anthropologist Nancy Scheper-Hughes has written about a shantytown in Brazil, "good enough mothering can require almost superhuman effort." Scheper-Hughes, *Death Without Weeping*, 342, 128, 361.

20. NOBODY WANTS THE NORTH SIDE

1. I never personally witnessed maintenance men propositioning shelter residents, but Crystal, Vanetta, and other women I met at the Lodge said this happened. In subsequent interviews, Salvation Army staff reported having no knowledge of such interactions between their guests and workers.

2. Institutions charged with managing the poor, those that brought together people with similarly pressing needs, were especially fertile ground for disposable ties. Welfare offices, food pantries, job centers, Alcoholics Anonymous clubs, methadone clinics, homeless shelters, even the waiting areas of eviction court—disposable ties regularly were initiated in such venues. On the role of organizations in network formation, see Mario Small, *Unanticipated Gains: Origins of Network Inequality in Everyday Life* (New York: Oxford University Press, 2009).

3. According to Vanetta, the seizures began after a day-care worker dropped Bo-Bo on his head.

4. Elliot Liebow, *Tally's Corner: A Study of Negro Streetcorner Men* (Boston: Little, Brown and Company, 1967); Matthew Desmond, "Disposable Ties and the Urban Poor," *American Journal of Sociology* 117 (2012): 1295–335.

5. From Vanetta's court records and her own accounting.

6. In its *Admissions and Continued Occupancy Policy* (2011), the Housing Authority of the City of Milwaukee states that it "is not required or obligated to assist applicants who . . . have a history of criminal activity by any household member involving crimes of physical violence against persons or property and any other criminal activity" (page 16).

7. Most of what we know about people's acceptance or rejection of racial integration comes from vignette studies that take place in a lab. These studies consistently find blacks to be strong proponents of integration and whites to be advocates of segregation. One paper found that most black participants reported their ideal neighborhood to be half black and half white, while most white participants said they would move from such a neighborhood. If you step out of the lab and watch families search for housing in real time, you see something different and more unsettling. White movers have strong aversions to living in black neighborhoods—but so do black movers. I never once heard a black renter voice a desire to move into an "integrated neighborhood," although they would be contributing to racial integration simply by moving from a majority-black neighborhood. Instead, I heard them speak of a desire to "get away from these black motherfuckers," as Crystal did. When Arleen

was house hunting outside the inner city, she once said, "The only people I have a problem with is people my own color." Natasha once said, "Black people don't know how to act. . . . If I had a choice, I would move out there [to the suburbs] too! Ain't nobody want to stay out here, and you hear gunshots all the time." In these sentiments you don't find a (positive) desire for integration but a (negative) repulsion directed at majority-black communities. For vignette studies about racial preferences, see Reynolds Farley et al., "Stereotypes and Segregation: Neighborhoods in the Detroit Area," *American Journal of Sociology* 100 (1994): 750–80; Reynolds Farley et al., "Chocolate City, Vanilla Suburbs: Will the Trend Toward Racially Separate Communities Continue?," *Social Science Research* 7 (1978): 319–44.

8. Between 2009 and 2011, half of all Milwaukee renters found their housing through social networks, and 45 percent conducted the search themselves. Only about 5 percent of renters found housing through the Housing Authority or another social-service agency. With respect to renters who found housing on their own, roughly half of white renters relied on the Internet; an additional third found housing after spotting a rent sign. A third of black renters who looked for housing on their own found it through rent signs, and an additional third did so through the newspaper or other print media, like the *RedBook*. Fifteen percent looked online. For most black renters, looking for apartments was an un-digital affair. Fifty-eight percent of black renters found housing through social networks. The same was true for only 41 percent of white renters. The vast majority of tenants who located housing through network ties relied on kin and friends, with white renters almost twice as likely to rely on friends as family members. In sharp contrast to research on finding employment that suggests that black job seekers receive less help from social ties than other groups, evidence from the Milwaukee Area Renters Study finds black house seekers received more. Cf. Sandra Susan Smith, *Lone Pursuit: Distrust and Defensive Individualism Among the Black Poor* (New York: Russell Sage Foundation, 2007).

9. According to the owner, Tim Ballering, Affordable Rentals owned 322 units and managed an additional 484 as of July 2014.

10. "Our government doesn't need to exist to take care of the poor and hungry. That's the Church's job," said Pastor Daryl, adored by Larraine. Conservative politicians often express similar beliefs. In 2013, Republican congressman Doug LaMalfa voiced a sentiment shared by many in his party when he argued that low-income Americans should be helped "through the church . . . because it comes from the heart, not from a badge or a mandate." But after watching people like Larraine and Crystal seek help from their churches, you can't help but wonder if our hearts are really big enough for people with such heavy and persistent needs, people who need a lot more than some groceries now and again, a few hundred dollars here and there. ("My knowledge of social work is next to zero," Pastor Daryl said.) In the biblical telling, the early Church was able to uplift the poor only after believers "sold property and possessions

to give to anyone who had need" (Acts 2:44). Modern-day churchgoers have been less inclined to make such sacrifices. Pastor Daryl was frustrated by what he called Larraine's "poverty mentality," her inability to "buckle down" and "manage her finances." Minister Barber often called Crystal and snapped at her for doing things eighteen-year-olds are prone to do, like staying out late. Both people of the cloth had extended help in the past, and both had reasons why they felt they should not extend help in the future. Government mandates and entitlements are far from perfect, but they are less dependent on the limits of human compassion. LaMalfa was quoted in Michael Hiltzik, "Families on Food Stamps Would Suffer While Farms Get Fat," *Los Angeles Times*, June 14, 2013. On the role today's black church plays in the inner city, see Omar McRoberts, *Streets of Glory: Church and Community in a Black Urban Neighborhood* (Chicago: University of Chicago Press, 2003). On religious experience, see Timothy Nelson, *Every Time I Feel the Spirit: Religious Experience and Ritual in an African American Church* (New York: NYU Press, 2004).

11. Douglas Massey and Nancy Denton, *American Apartheid: Segregation and the Making of the Underclass* (Cambridge: Harvard University Press, 1993); Camille Zubrinsky Charles, "The Dynamics of Racial Residential Segregation," *Annual Review of Sociology* 29 (2003): 167–207.

12. Lewis Mumford, *The City in History: Its Origins, Its Transformations, and Its Prospects* (New York: MJF Books, 1961), 417. See also Lewis Mumford, *The Culture of Cities* (New York: Harcourt, Brace, and Company, 1938).

13. Elizabeth Blackmar, *Manhattan for Rent, 1785–1850* (Ithaca: Cornell University Press, 1989), 199.

14. Mumford, *City in History*, 462–63; Blackmar, *Manhattan for Rent*; Jacob Riis, *How the Other Half Lives: Studies Among the Tenements of New York* (New York: Penguin Books, 1997 [1890]).

15. Landlords exercised this privilege to such an effective degree that judges were pressured to exempt some items from seizure, especially tools used to earn a living. Frank Enever, *History of the Law of Distress for Rent and Damage Feasant* (London: Routledge and Sons, 1931); David Caplovitz, *The Poor Pay More* (New York: The Free Press, 1967), 162–63.

16. Jacqueline Jones, *The Dispossessed: America's Underclasses from the Civil War to the Present* (New York: Basic Books, 2001), chapter 1.

17. In 1928, 99 percent of Milwaukee's blacks rented. Joe William Trotter Jr., *Black Milwaukee: The Making of an Industrial Proletariat, 1915–45*, 2nd ed. (Urbana: University of Illinois Press, 2007), 70.

18. Arnold Hirsch, *Making the Second Ghetto: Race and Housing in Chicago, 1940–1960* (New York: Cambridge University Press, 1983), chapter 1; Marcus Anthony Hunter, *Black Citymakers: How the Philadelphia Negro Changed Urban America* (New York: Oxford University Press, 2013), chapter 3; Allan Spear, *Black Chicago: The Making of a Negro Ghetto, 1890–1920* (Chicago: University of Chicago Press, 1967), chapter 8; Thomas Sugrue, *The Origins of the Urban Crisis: Race and Inequality in Postwar Detroit* (Princeton: Princeton University

Press, 2005), 51–55; Alex Schwartz, *Housing Policy in the United States*, 2nd ed. (New York: Routledge, 2010), 21.

19. Beryl Satter, *Family Properties: How the Struggle over Race and Real Estate Transformed Chicago and Urban America* (New York: Metropolitan Books, 2009), 6; see also Spear, *Black Chicago*, 148; Trotter, *Black Milwaukee*, 180.

20. Michael Bennett, *When Dreams Come True: The GI Bill and the Making of Modern America* (McLean: Brassey's Publishing, 1966); Ira Katznelson, *When Affirmative Action Was White: An Untold History of Racial Inequality in Twentieth-Century America* (New York: Norton, 2005).

21. At 43 percent, blacks have the lowest homeownership rates in the country today. At 73 percent, whites have the highest. Robert Callis and Melissa Kresin, *Residential Vacancies and Homeownership in the Third Quarter 2014* (Washington, DC: US Census Bureau, October 2014), Table 7; Ta-Nehisi Coates, "The Case for Reparations," *The Atlantic*, June 2014.

22. Satter, *Family Properties*, 430n7.

23. Drawing on the Milwaukee Area Renters Study, 2009–2011, Tracey Shollenberger and I designed a lagged OLS model estimating renters' current neighborhood poverty and crime rates, conditioning on their previous neighborhood poverty and crime rates. Examining the most recent move of all renters who moved sometime in the previous two years, we accounted for several important demographic factors—race, education, family structure, housing assistance—and several key life shocks potentially related to neighborhood selection: job loss, the birth of a child. Even after conditioning on a run of important factors and on previous neighborhood characteristics, experiencing a forced move is associated with more than one-third of a standard deviation increase in both neighborhood poverty and crime rate, relative to voluntary moves.

21. BIGHEADED BOY

1. Sherrena had charged Patrice "double damages." Milwaukee landlords could bill tenants twice the rent for each day they remained on the property past the eviction notice expiration (704.27, Wis. Stats.). This was designed to help landlords recoup lost rental income when evicted tenants held up the property and prevented landlords from re-renting it. Sherrena usually didn't do this, but she made an exception for Patrice. "Because she pissed us way off! Her mouth is too slick," Sherrena said.

2. Cf. Elliot Liebow, *Tally's Corner: A Study of Negro Streetcorner Men* (Boston: Little, Brown and Company, 1967), 63.

   Poor housing conditions have been linked to asthma, lead poisoning, respiratory complications, developmental delays, heart disease, and neurological disorders, leading a prominent medical journal to call inadequate housing "a public health crisis." Even limited exposure to substandard conditions could have lasting health effects, especially on children. On the link between housing and health, see Samiya Bashir, "Home Is Where the Harm Is: Inadequate Housing as a Public Health Crisis," *American Journal of Public Health* 92 (2002):

733–38; Gary Evans, Nancy Wells, and Annie Moch, "Housing and Mental Health: A Review of the Evidence and a Methodological and Conceptual Critique," *Journal of Social Issues* 59 (2003): 475–500; James Krieger and Donna Higgins, "Housing and Health: Time Again for Public Health Action," *American Journal of Public Health* 92 (2002): 758–68; Wayne Morgan et al., "Results of a Home-Based Environmental Intervention Among Urban Children with Asthma," *New England Journal of Medicine* 351 (2004): 1068–80; Joshua Sharfstein et al., "Is Child Health at Risk While Families Wait for Housing Vouchers?," *American Journal of Public Health* 91 (2001): 1191–92.

3. Lee Rainwater, *Behind Ghetto Walls: Black Family Life in a Federal Slum* (Chicago: Aldine, 1970), 476.

4. Robert Sampson, *Great American City: Chicago and the Enduring Neighborhood Effect* (Chicago: University of Chicago Press, 2012); Patrick Sharkey, *Stuck in Place: Urban Neighborhoods and the End of Progress toward Racial Equality* (Chicago: University of Chicago Press, 2013).

5. Julie Clark and Ade Kearns, "Housing Improvements, Perceived Housing Quality and Psychosocial Benefits from the Home," *Housing Studies* 27 (2012): 915–39; James Dunn and Michael Hayes, "Social Inequality, Population Health, and Housing: A Study of Two Vancouver Neighborhoods," *Social Science and Medicine* 51 (2000): 563–87. On "territorial stigmatization," see Loïc Wacquant, *Urban Outcasts: A Comparative Sociology of Advanced Marginality* (Malden, MA: Polity Press, 2008), chapter 6.

22. IF THEY GIVE MOMMA THE PUNISHMENT

1. While living with Patricia, Crystal would tell anyone who asked that she was staying with "her mom." Presumably, she would give survey researchers the same answer. Our current analytical toolkit, even with all the white-coated words of network analysis, is ill equipped to capture the complexity of relationships in which people like Crystal are enveloped. See Nan Lin, *Social Capital: A Theory of Social Structure and Action* (New York: Cambridge University Press, 2002); Mario Small, *Unanticipated Gains: Origins of Network Inequality in Everyday Life* (New York: Oxford University Press, 2009); Matthew Desmond, "Disposable Ties and the Urban Poor," *American Journal of Sociology* 117 (2012): 1295–335.

2. I did not personally witness this incident. I reconstructed the scene after multiple interviews with Crystal.

When tenuous but intense relationships between virtual strangers end badly—or violently, as they sometimes do—they foster deep misgivings between peers and neighbors, eroding community and network stability. The memory of having been used or mistreated by a disposable tie encourages people to be suspicious of others. Relying on disposable ties, then, is both a response to and a source of social instability.

Crystal's cousins and foster sisters were around her age. They could not offer her shelter or much money, but they could fly to her side during a fight.

3. On the presence of Child Protective Services in the lives of poor black families, see Christopher Wildeman and Natalia Emanuel, "Cumulative Risks of Foster Care Placement by Age 18 for U.S. Children, 2000–2011," *PLOS ONE* 9 (2014): 1–7; Dorothy Roberts, *Shattered Bonds: The Color of Child Welfare* (New York: Basic Books, 2002).

4. In 2010, the *New York Times* reported that one in every fifty Americans lives in a household with an income consisting only of food stamps. Jason DeParle, "Living on Nothing but Food Stamps," *New York Times*, January 2, 2010.

23. THE SERENITY CLUB

1. From Scott's disciplinary proceedings in front of the Wisconsin Board of Nursing.

2. Consequential and costly policy decisions have been made based on the collective assumption that poor people lack connections to kin and friends who are gainfully employed, college educated, and homeowners. Mixed-income housing is intended to "provide low-income residents with exposure to employment opportunities and social role models." Neighborhood relocation programs, such as Moving to Opportunity, are designed to connect low-income families to more "prosocial and affluent social networks." But many poor people have plenty of ties to the upwardly mobile. Roughly 1 in 6 Milwaukee renters lives in a neighborhood with above average disadvantage but is embedded in networks with below average disadvantage. But simply having ties to the middle class is insufficient. Likely because of the popularity of the term "social capital," researchers tend to think of prosocial connections to important or resource-rich people as something you "have" and that, like money, can be used whenever you'd like. In reality, as Scott's experience shows, those connections matter only insofar as you are able to activate them. On social programs designed to combat "social isolation," see US Department of Housing and Urban Development, *Moving to Opportunity for Fair Housing Demonstration Program: Final Impacts Evaluation* (Washington, DC: Office of Policy Development and Research, 2011); US Department of Housing and Urban Development, *Mixed-Income Housing and the HOME Program* (Washington, DC: Office of Policy Development and Research, 2003). For canonical theories about poverty and community life holding that spatial isolation (residential ghettoization) brings about social isolation (network ghettoization), see William Julius Wilson, *The Truly Disadvantaged: The Inner City, the Underclass, and Public Policy*, 2nd ed. (Chicago: University of Chicago Press, 2012 [1987]); Douglas Massey and Nancy Denton, *American Apartheid: Segregation and the Making of the Underclass* (Cambridge: Harvard University Press, 1993). For a detailed analysis of neighborhood and network disadvantage, see Matthew Desmond and Weihua An, "Neighborhood and Network Disadvantage Among Urban Renters," *Sociological Science* 2 (2015): 329–50.

3. When he was using, Scott would sometimes call it "self-medicating." It wasn't just nurse talk. So many words and phrases exist to help cover over the rotten

thing festering at the base of the root. How often, I wonder, is coping mistaken for culture?

4. The psychiatrist asked Scott, "Do you want to go straight to two hundred in Zoloft, or do you want to work up to it?"

"Straight to two hundred," Scott answered. He didn't think it made sense to drop his dosage, high as it was, since he had been on 200 mgs before.

5. When methadone made the news, it usually wasn't pretty. The year Scott began his treatment program, methadone accounted for less than 2 percent of opioid pain-reliever prescriptions but almost one-third of the overdose deaths caused by opioid pain relievers. The medical community attributed the troubling rise of methadone-related deaths to the increasing use of the drug to treat pain, not addiction. When it comes to treating heroin addiction and its broader social ramifications, methadone has been highly effective since being introduced in 1964. Known as a full opioid agonist, it feeds an addict's cravings and allows him to function without impairment, if the dose is right. The evidence is consistent. Methadone reduces or eliminates heroin use, lowers overdoses as well as criminality associated with drug use, boosts patients' health, and helps many live full, productive lives. When it comes to heroin addiction, the drug simply outperforms abstinence-only programs like AA. "You hear all these harsh stories about methadone," one expert said, "but you never hear about the tens or hundreds of thousands of people who are taking methadone every day, who work, who have largely conquered their habits and lead normal lives." Scott was becoming one of those people. Peter Friedmann, quoted in Harold Pollack, "This Drug Could Make a Huge Dent in Heroin Addiction. So Why Isn't It Used More?," *Washington Post*, November 23, 2013. See also Herman Joseph, Sharon Stancliff, and John Langrod, "Methadone Maintenance Treatment (MMT): A Review of Historical and Clinical Issues," *Mount Sinai Journal of Medicine* 67 (1999): 347–64; Centers for Disease Control, "Vital Signs: Risk for Overdose from Methadone Used for Pain Relief—United States, 1999–2010," *Morbidity and Mortality Weekly Report* 61 (2012): 493–97.

6. Sally Satel, "Happy Birthday, Methadone!," *Washington Monthly*, November/December 2014.

24. CAN'T WIN FOR LOSING

1. This means that to divide the urban poor into two groups, the unstable and the stable, the undeserving and deserving, the decent and street, is often to misrecognize as immutable that which is regularly transitory and tenuous. Stability and instability: these are not fixed states as much as temporary conditions poor families experience for varying periods of time. Problems bleed into each other. The murder of a loved one can lead to depression, which can lead to job loss, which can lead to eviction, which can lead to homelessness, which can intensify one's depression, and so on. Policymakers and their researchers can be prone to aiming a silver bullet at one of these problems. But a shotgun's wide blast might be preferred. On cascades of adversity among low-income families,

see Timothy Black, *When a Heart Turns Rock Solid: The Lives of Three Puerto Rican Brothers On and Off the Streets* (New York: Vintage, 2009); Matthew Desmond, "Severe Deprivation in America," *Russell Sage Journal of the Social Sciences,* forthcoming; Kristin Perkins and Robert Sampson, "Compounded Deprivation in the Transition to Adulthood: The Intersection of Racial and Economic Inequality Among Chicagoans, 1995–2013," *Russell Sage Journal of the Social Sciences,* forthcoming; Bruce Western, "Lifetimes of Violence in a Sample of Released Prisoners," *Russell Sage Journal of the Social Sciences,* forthcoming.

2. Milwaukee neighborhoods with more children had more evictions, even after accounting for their poverty rate, racial composition, and a number of other things. In neighborhoods where children made up less than 10 percent of the population in 2010, 1 renting household in 123 was evicted. In those where children made up at least 40 percent of the population, 1 household in every 12 was. All else equal, a 1 percent increase in the percentage of children in a neighborhood is predicted to increase a neighborhood's evictions by almost 7 percent. These estimates are based on court-ordered eviction records that took place in Milwaukee County between January 1, 2010, and December 31, 2010. The statistical model evaluating the association between a neighborhood's percentage of children and its number of evictions is a zero-inflated Poisson regression, which is described in detail in Matthew Desmond et al., "Evicting Children," *Social Forces* 92 (2013): 303–27.

3. That misery could stick around. At least two years after their eviction, mothers like Arleen still experienced significantly higher rates of depression than their peers. See Matthew Desmond and Rachel Tolbert Kimbro, "Eviction's Fallout: Housing, Hardship, and Health," *Social Forces* (2015), in press. See also Marc Fried, "Grieving for a Lost Home," in *The Urban Condition: People and Policy in the Metropolis,* ed. Leonard Duhl (New York: Basic Books, 1963), 151–71; Theresa Osypuk et al., "The Consequences of Foreclosure for Depressive Symptomatology," *Annals of Epidemiology* 22 (2012): 379–87.

4. Another approach involves surveying a person's resources before trying to access them. Because in poor neighborhoods the most accepted way to say no is to say, "I can't," people sometimes try to take that option off the table. So, for example, instead of asking, "Can I get a ride?" you ask, "You got gas in your car?" Instead of asking, "Could you make me a plate?" you ask, "You eat?" When someone knows you have gas in your tank or food in your refrigerator, it's harder to give a good reason for turning him or her away. Through everyday interaction, the poor have picked up what political fund-raisers and development officers have spent millions of dollars to discover: that there is a delicate art to "the ask." Knowing how to ask for help—and, in turn, when to extend or withhold aid—is an essential skill for managing poverty.

Asking social workers for help comes with its own set of rules. You don't want to ask for nothing, because you'll receive nothing in return. But you also don't want to come off as too needy, too hungry, too on the edge—because

Child Protective Services might soon pay you a visit. I once met a woman, a thirty-three-year-old mother of two teenage girls, who drank a lot. She attributed her drinking to traumatic events that happened to her as a child. "I remember. Down to the smell."

"Have you ever seen a counselor?" I asked.

"No. I thought about it. But they get too deep into your business. I had somebody make a false allegation against me with child services in California. They didn't find nothing, but it was traumatizing just the same, having somebody come through my door . . . and talk to my kids by theyself."

If she told someone how damaged she was, and how she coped, would she be allowed to keep her children? This mother didn't know and wasn't going to find out.

5. I did not personally witness this interaction. Arleen told me about it.

EPILOGUE: HOME AND HOPE

1. Lewis Mumford, *The City in History: Its Origins, Its Transformations, and Its Prospects* (New York: MJF Books, 1961), 13; with special thanks to Rowan Flad and Shamus Khan for etymology insights.

2. Alexis de Tocqueville, *Democracy in America* (New York: Perennial Classics, 2000), 511.

3. Gunnar Myrdal, *An American Dilemma*, vol. 2, *The Negro Social Structure* (New York: McGraw-Hill Publishers, 1964 [1944]), 810.

4. Plato, *The Republic* (New York: Penguin Classics, 1987), 312. I have changed "men" to "people."

5. Mary Schwartz and Ellen Wilson, *Who Can Afford to Live in a Home? A Look at Data from the 2006 American Community Survey* (Washington, DC: US Census Bureau, 2007).

6. Chester Hartman and David Robinson, "Evictions: The Hidden Housing Problem," *Housing Policy Debate* 14 (2003): 461–501.

7. Gary Evans, "The Environment of Childhood Poverty," *American Psychologist* 59 (2004): 77–92; Shigehiro Oishi, "The Psychology of Residential Mobility: Implications for the Self, Social Relationships, and Well-Being," *Perspectives on Psychological Science* 5 (2010): 5–21; Robert Sampson, *Great American City: Chicago and the Enduring Neighborhood Effect* (Chicago: University of Chicago Press, 2012).

8. In fact, one can detect a thick middle-class bias among researchers who assume that moves are deliberate and planned. For a further explanation of the intentionality bias in residential mobility research, see Matthew Desmond and Tracey Shollenberger, "Forced Displacement from Rental Housing: Prevalence and Neighborhood Consequences," *Demography*, forthcoming. On high rates of residential mobility among poor families, see David Ihrke and Carol Faber, *Geographical Mobility: 2005 to 2010* (Washington, DC: United States Census Bureau, 2012); Robin Phinney, "Exploring Residential Mobility Among Low-Income Families," *Social Service Review* 87 (2013): 780–815.

9. This finding comes from a negative binomial model that estimated the number of moves renters undertook in the previous two years, conditioning on household income, race, education, gender, family status, age, criminal record, and three recent life shocks: job loss, relationship dissolution, and eviction. The analysis found that low incomes predicted higher rates of mobility only before controlling for involuntary displacement and that, all else equal, renters who experienced a forced move were expected to have a moving rate 1.3 times greater than those who avoided involuntary displacement. See Matthew Desmond, Carl Gershenson, and Barbara Kiviat, "Forced Relocation and Residential Instability Among Urban Renters," *Social Service Review* 89 (2015): 227–62. By "Milwaukee's poorest renters," I mean renting households in the lowest income quartile (with incomes below $12,204). Milwaukee Area Renters Study, 2009–2011.

10. On Jackson County, Missouri, see Tara Raghuveer, "'We Be Trying': A Multistate Analysis of Eviction and the Affordable Housing Crisis," B.A. thesis (Cambridge, MA: Harvard University, Committee on the Degrees in Social Studies, 2014). In 2012, New York City's Housing Courts processed 28,743 eviction judgments and 217,914 eviction filings for nonpayment. See New York City Rent Guidelines Board, *2013 Income and Affordability Study*, April 4, 2013. Cleveland, a city of approximately 95,702 occupied renter households, saw 11,072 eviction filings in 2012 and 11,031 in 2013—meaning that almost 12 percent of renter households were summoned to eviction court each year. See Northeast Ohio Apartment Association, *Suites* magazine, "Eviction Index," 2012–2013; American Community Survey, 2013. In 2012, an estimated 32,231 evictions were filed in Chicago, which represents 7 percent of the city's rental inventory; see Kay Cleaves, "Cook Eviction Stats Part 5: Are Eviction Filings Increasing?," StrawStickStone.com, February 8, 2013.

11. Matthew Desmond and Carl Gershenson, "Housing and Employment Insecurity Among the Working Poor," *Social Problems*, forthcoming.

12. Evictions also help to exacerbate the problem most responsible for their rise by driving up rents. This is plain in cases where landlords evict tenants from rent-regulated units so that they may offer apartments at market rates. But it is also true of normal evictions of families from unregulated units because it is easier to raise the rent on new tenants than old ones. In Milwaukee, a tenant annually pays almost $58 less in rent for every year she has lived in an apartment, all else equal. Turnover facilitates rent hikes, and evictions create turnover. Matthew Desmond and Kristin Perkins, "Are Landlords Overcharging Voucher Holders?," working paper, Harvard University, June 2015. In San Francisco, Ellis Act evictions—often used to convert rent-regulated apartments into condos or market-rate units—increased by 170 percent between March 2010 and February 2013. Marisa Lagos, "San Francisco Evictions Surge, Report Finds," *San Francisco Gate*, November 5, 2013.

13. Matthew Desmond and Rachel Tolbert Kimbro, "Eviction's Fallout: Housing, Hardship, and Health," *Social Forces* (2015), in press.

14. Desmond et al., "Forced Relocation and Residential Instability Among Urban Renters."

15. Technically, the results of lagged dependent variable regression models showed that experiencing a forced move is associated with a standard deviation increase of more than one-third in both neighborhood poverty and crime rates, relative to voluntary moves. Across all models, the most robust and consistent predictors of neighborhood downgrades between moves are race (whether a renter is African American) and move type (whether the move was forced). Desmond and Shollenberger, "Forced Displacement from Rental Housing."

16. Sampson, *Great American City*; Patrick Sharkey, *Stuck in Place: Urban Neighborhoods and the End of Progress toward Racial Equality* (Chicago: University of Chicago Press, 2013).

17. This finding is documented in a study called "Eviction's Fallout," coauthored with Rachel Kimbro. In that study, we rely on a dichotomous indicator to measure *depressive symptoms* in mothers. Mothers were asked a series of questions, focused on experiences in the previous twelve months, based on the Composite International Diagnostic Interview Short Form (CIDI-SF). Respondents were asked whether they had feelings of dysphoria (depression) or anhedonia (inability to enjoy what is usually pleasurable) in the past year that lasted for two weeks or more, and if so, whether the symptoms lasted most of the day and occurred every day of the two-week period. If so, they were asked more specific questions about: (a) losing interest, (b) feeling tired, (c) change in weight, (d) trouble sleeping, (e) trouble concentrating, (f) feeling worthless, and (g) thinking about death. Mothers were classified as probable cases of depression if they endorsed either dysphoria or anhedonia plus two of the other symptoms in the follow-up questions (leading to a CIDI-SF MD score of 3 or higher). Results are robust to varying the cut-point for the depression scale as well as to negative binomial models estimating the number of depressive symptoms respondents reported. See Ronald Kessler et al., "Methodological Studies of the Composite International Diagnostic Interview (CIDI) in the US National Comorbidity Survey (NCS)," *International Journal of Methods in Psychiatric Research* 7 (1998): 33–55.

18. Michael Serby et al., "Eviction as a Risk Factor for Suicide," *Psychiatric Services* 57 (2006): 273–74. Katherine Fowler et al., "Increase in Suicides Associated with Home Eviction and Foreclosure During the US Housing Crisis: Findings from 16 National Violent Death Reporting System States, 2005–2010," *American Journal of Public Health* 105 (2015): 311–16.

19. Sampson, *Great American City*.

20. This result draws on neighborhood-level data for Milwaukee, 2005–2007. Using a lagged-response model, I predicted a neighborhood's violent-crime rate for one year, controlling for violent crime and eviction rates the *previous year* as well as for the percentage of families in poverty, of African Americans in the neighborhood, of the population under eighteen years of age, of residents with less than a high school education, and of households receiving housing

assistance. The final model documented a significant association between a neighborhood's violent crime rate and its eviction rate the previous year (B = .155; p < .05). See Matthew Desmond, "Do More Evictions Lead to Higher Crime? Neighborhood Consequences of Forced Displacement," working paper, Harvard University, August 2015.

21. Milwaukee Area Renters Study, 2009–2011.

22. United States Conference of Mayors, *Hunger and Homelessness Survey* (Washington, DC: United States Conference of Mayors, 2013); Martha Burt, "Homeless Families, Singles, and Others: Findings from the 1996 National Survey of Homeless Assistance Providers and Clients," *Housing Policy Debate* 12 (2001): 737–80; Maureen Crane and Anthony Warnes, "Evictions and Prolonged Homelessness," *Housing Studies* 15 (2000): 757–73.

On the effects of substandard housing and unsafe neighborhoods on children's health, see Julie Clark and Ade Kearns, "Housing Improvements, Perceived Housing Quality and Psychosocial Benefits from the Home," *Housing Studies* 27 (2012): 915–39; Tama Leventhal and Jeanne Brooks-Gunn, "The Neighborhoods They Live In: The Effects of Neighborhood Residence on Child and Adolescent Outcomes," *Psychological Bulletin* 126 (2000): 309–37.

23. Joseph Harkness and Sandra Newman, "Housing Affordability and Children's Well-Being: Evidence from the National Survey of America's Families," *Housing Policy Debate* 16 (2005): 223–55; Sandra Newman and Scott Holupka, "Housing Affordability and Investments in Children," *Journal of Housing Economics* 24 (2014): 89–100.

24. In other markets, when a commodity gets too expensive, people can buy less of it. When the price of oil shoots up, people can drive less. When a sad corn crop scales up the price of beef, people can eat fewer burgers. But when the price of rent and utilities rises, most poor Americans do not have the option of consuming cheaper or smaller housing, because it doesn't exist in their city. According to the 2013 American Housing Survey (Table C-02-RO), roughly 98 percent of renting households below the poverty line live in apartments with at least one bedroom, and 68 percent live in units with two or more bedrooms. In Milwaukee, fully 97 percent of renters live in a one-, two-, or three-bedroom unit. Milwaukee Area Renters Study, 2009–2011. Smaller housing units have vanished from the American city. In the 1970s and 1980s more than a million single-room occupancy (SRO) hotel units were regulated out by new building standards or upwardly converted to cater to better-off renters. See Whet Moser, "The Long, Slow Decline of Chicago's SROs," *Chicago* magazine, June 14, 2013; Brendan O'Flaherty, *Making Room: The Economics of Homelessness* (Cambridge: Harvard University Press, 1996), 142–47; James Wright and Beth Rubin, "Is Homelessness a Housing Problem?," *Housing Policy Debate* 2 (1991): 937–56; Christopher Jencks, *The Homeless* (Cambridge: Harvard University Press, 1994), chapter 6.

Besides moving away from their job, friends, family, and community, the only way low-income tenants can shrink their housing is by taking in boarders. But many landlords simply do not allow this. Even if they were to overlook maximum-occupancy regulations, more people in an apartment means more maintenance costs and a higher water bill. The majority of Milwaukee renter households (75 percent) are not responsible for the water bill. For insight into how landlords and property managers think about occupancy and cost in relation to that bill, consider what Joe Parazinski, a white building manager who lived and worked in the inner city, had to say: "If I move in [more] people, all of a sudden now there's ten living there. Well, now that's ten showers a day. . . . Now the toilet, instead of being flushed twenty times a day, it's now being flushed two hundred times. Now, how many more loads are going to be run through the washer machine? . . . When you start adding that shit up, it's not petty."

Housing advocates tend to think "doubling up" is a problem, but poor renters tend to think doubling up is a solution—because although overcrowding is not innocent of consequences, the much bigger problem they face is undercrowding, the coerced overconsumption of housing they cannot afford. The majority of poor renting households nationwide are not overcrowded: 24 percent of those households have more than 1.5 persons per bedroom. Only 8 percent of all renter households in Milwaukee have more than two people per bedroom. By this definition of overcrowding—more than two people per bedroom—4 percent of white renters, 8 percent of black renters, and 16 percent of Hispanic renters in Milwaukee live in overcrowded apartments. Almost half of all adult renters in Milwaukee do not live with another adult. African American renters in Milwaukee are particularly isolated when it comes to their living arrangements: only 35 percent live with another adult, compared to 58 percent of white renters and 69 percent of Hispanic renters. Among all Milwaukee renters, 32 percent live alone, 16 percent live only with children, and 53 percent live with another adult. Thirty-nine percent of black renters live alone, compared to 33 percent of white renters and 14 percent of Hispanic renters. Twenty-six percent of black renters live only with children, compared to 9 percent of white renters and 17 percent of Hispanic renters. Some surveyed renters likely failed to disclose other adults living with them, especially if the landlord was unaware of them. In the Milwaukee Eviction Court Study (2011), interviewers asked tenants to list all adults who lived or stayed with them. After explaining how their information would be kept confidential, interviewers told participants: "I'm interested in *all* adults that live or stay with you—even if they are not on the lease and even if your landlord doesn't know about them." Tenants in eviction court listed 375 co-resident adults, including 70 who were not leaseholders. Black men made up the largest group of adults not listed on the Summons and Complaint (N=32), followed by black women (N=24). My estimate of the percentage of black renters who live alone (or without another adult) is probably somewhat inflated, then; but the point about the prevalence of overcrowding among renters not matching the concern about overcrowding among policymakers and analysts remains. American Housing Survey (2013), Table C-02-RO; Milwaukee Area Renters Study, 2009–2011.

Studies have documented an association between crowding and adverse outcomes, but there is not much robust causal evidence of the effect of crowding. See Gary Evans, Susan Saegert, and Rebecca Harris, "Residential Density and Psychological Health Among Children in Low-Income Families," *Environment and Behavior* 33 (2001): 165–80; Dominique Goux and Eric Maurin, "The Effect of Overcrowded Housing on Children's Performance at School," *Journal of Public Economics* 89 (2005): 797–819; Claudia Solari and Robert Mare, "Housing Crowding Effects on Children's Well-Being," *Social Science Research* 41 (2012): 464–76.

25. Alex Schwartz, *Housing Policy in the United States*, 2nd ed. (New York: Routledge, 2010), 23.

26. Louis Winnick, "The Triumph of Housing Allowance Programs: How a Fundamental Policy Conflict Was Resolved," *Cityscape* 1 (1995): 95–118, 97. The quotation comes from the documentary *The Pruitt-Igoe Myth* (2011), directed by Chad Freidrichs.

27. Alex Kotlowitz, *There Are No Children Here: The Story of Two Boys Growing Up in the Other America* (New York: Random House, 1991); Arnold Hirsch, *Making the Second Ghetto: Race and Housing in Chicago, 1940–1960* (New York: Cambridge University Press, 1983).

28. Public housing inventory has fallen by roughly 20 percent since 1991. Peter Marcuse and W. Dennis Keating, "The Permanent Housing Crisis: The Failures of Conservatism and the Limitations of Liberalism," in *A Right to Housing: Foundation for a New Social Agenda*, eds. Rachel Bratt, Michael Stone, and Chester Hartman (Philadelphia: Temple University Press, 2006), 139–62; Rachel Bratt, Michael Stone, and Chester Hartman, "Why a Right to Housing Is Needed and Makes Sense: Editor's Introduction," ibid., 1–19; Schwartz, *Housing Policy in the United States.*

29. More technically, the voucher covers the remaining costs up to the "payment standard," a limit set by the local Housing Authority administering the benefit. The program reserves 3 in 4 available vouchers for households with incomes below 30 percent of the area median income or the poverty line (whichever is higher); the remaining quarter may be distributed to households with incomes up to 80 percent of the area median.

30. Joint Center for Housing Studies of Harvard University, *America's Rental Housing: Evolving Markets and Needs* (Cambridge: Harvard University, 2013); Abt Associates Inc. et al., *Effects of Housing Vouchers on Welfare Families* (Washington, DC: US Department of Housing and Urban Development, 2006); Michelle Wood, Jennifer Turnham, and Gregory Mills, "Housing Affordability and Family Well-Being: Results from the Housing Voucher Evaluation," *Housing Policy Debate* 19 (2008): 367–412.

31. Abt Associates Inc. et al., *Effects of Housing Vouchers*; Alan Meyers et al., "Public Housing Subsidies May Improve Poor Children's Nutrition," *American Journal of Public Health* 83 (1993): 115. See also Sandra Newman and Scott Holupka, "Housing Affordability and Investments in Children," *Journal of Housing Economics* 24 (2014): 89–100.

32. American Housing Survey, 2013, Table C-17-RO. These estimates excluded households classified as "other income verification" (3 percent of renter households below the poverty level) and "subsidy not reported" (1 percent of renter households below the poverty level) because it was unclear whether these households received assistance. Matthew Desmond, "Unaffordable America: Poverty, Housing, and Eviction," *Fast Focus: Institute for Research on Poverty* 22 (2015): 1–6.

33. On public housing capital needs, see Meryl Finkel et al., *Capital Needs in the Public Housing Program, Contract # C-DEN-O2277-TO001, Revised Financial Report*, prepared for the US Department of Housing and Urban Development (Cambridge: Abt Associates Inc., 2010).

34. This estimate is consistent across multiple national data sets, including the American Housing Survey, the American Community Survey, the Survey of Income and Program Participation, and the Consumer Expenditure Survey. Frederick Eggers and Fouad Moumen, *Investigating Very High Rent Burdens Among Renters in the American Housing Survey* (Washington, DC: US Department of Housing and Urban Development, 2010).

The problem of unaffordable housing is not America's alone. Over the last several decades, millions of people around the world have migrated from rural villages and towns. In 1960, roughly one-third of the planet lived in urban areas; today, more than half does. Cities have experienced real income gains that have brought about global poverty reductions. But therein lies the rub, for the growth of cities also has been accompanied by an astonishing surge in land values and housing costs. Urban housing costs have risen around the globe, especially in "superstar cities" whose real-estate markets have experienced an influx of global capital, driving housing prices upward and crowding out low-income residents. In Lagos, Africa's largest city, an estimated 60 percent of all residents dedicate the majority of their monthly income to rent, even as the majority of the city's residents live in one-room dwellings. Rents in Delhi's business district now rival those in midtown Manhattan. A recent report estimated that the global housing affordability gap amounts to $650 billion or 1 percent of the global GDP. Roughly 330 million urban households worldwide live in substandard or unaffordable housing demanding more than 30 percent of their income. By 2025, based on migration trends and global income projections, that number is expected to climb to 440 million households, representing 1.6 billion people. The world is becoming urbanized, and the city is becoming unaffordable to millions everywhere. See Joseph Gyourko, Christopher Mayer, and Todd Sinai, "Superstar Cities," *American Economic Journal: Economic Policy* 5 (2013): 167–99; McKinsey Global Institute, *A Blueprint for Addressing the Global Affordable Housing Challenge* (New York: McKinsey, 2014); Pedro Olinto and Hiroki Uematsu, *The State of the Poor: Where Are the Poor and Where Are They Poorest?* (Washington, DC: World Bank, Poverty Reduction and Equity, 2013).

35. Russell Engler, "Pursuing Access to Justice and Civil Right to Counsel in a Time of Economic Crisis," *Roger Williams University Law Review* 15 (2010):

472–98; Russell Engler, "Connecting Self-Representation to Civil Gideon," *Fordham Urban Law Review* 37 (2010): 36–92.

36. D. James Greiner, Cassandra Wolos Pattanayak, and Jonathan Hennessy, "The Limits of Unbundled Legal Assistance: A Randomized Study in a Massachusetts District Court and Prospects for the Future," *Harvard Law Review* 126 (2013): 901–89; Carroll Seron et al., "The Impact of Legal Counsel on Outcomes for Poor Tenants in New York City's Housing Court: Results of a Randomized Experiment," *Law and Society Review* 35 (2001): 419–34.

37. Seedco, *Housing Help Program, South Bronx, NYC* (New York: Seedco Policy Center, 2009).

38. Nearly half of all forced moves that take place among Milwaukee renters are informal evictions: off-the-books displacements not processed through the court. Since informal eviction is already landlords' favored means to displace tenants, they might be more likely to resort to this strategy if poor families had access to counsel. Tenants could insist on a court hearing, but many prefer informal evictions because an official record does not accompany them. This is why any legal-aid initiative needs to consider current court recordkeeping practices.

The legal system has been drastically changed by the recording and publication of its business: so much so that the threat of an eviction record is daily leveraged, both inside and outside the courtroom, by landlords and judges alike, to incentivize tenants to forfeit their right to be heard. Something has gone very wrong with our justice system when it makes more sense for tenants to skip court and quietly move out when their landlord says go than it does for them to plead their case themselves, which often leads to an order to move and an eviction on their record.

Consider the case of Myesha and Chester, a poor black couple whose landlord had moved to evict them from a house riddled with dangerous and degrading problems. According to the tenants, the landlord had agreed to let them live in the house for free until she was able to fix it up. According to the landlord, no such bargain had been struck. What was not in dispute was the terrible condition of the house—there were exposed wires; in some rooms the floor was caving in; water flowed into the house when it rained—photographs of which had led a commissioner to kick the case up to a judge. When the court date in front of the judge came, the landlord and her lawyer offered the tenants a stipulation agreement, which required that they move. But Myesha and Chester had two teenage girls in school and wanted to stay put and see the house repaired; so they were considering arguing their case in front of a jury. The judge explained their options like this: If they signed a stipulation and agreed to leave, "the eviction part [of the case the landlord] would dismiss. So on your record, which anyone can see, it wouldn't say you were evicted. . . . If you think you really have paid the rent or have some other reason that is a legal defense here, then you can tell me all about that. That's your one choice. Your other choice would be to go ahead with some agreement that you'll leave and save [the landlord] and ultimately yourself some headache. Because . . . if you fail to vacate after the lease no longer exists and if [the landlord] has to pay for the sheriff to come and actually move your things out to the street, then that'll cost her money and she'll just add that on to the balance that you owe. So, it's a really tough, unfriendly, sorry, uncomfortable, terribly disruptive situation, when you're put out like that."

"Just a question," Chester said. "What if we had an agreement that we weren't suppose to pay rent until she fixed stuff up?"

"Then, well, have a trial and we'll find out the truth and make that determination," the judge responded.

Myesha and Chester asked for a few minutes to talk things through. "We still gonna lose," Myesha whispered. "It's just how much we gonna lose."

They took the deal.

Some people who have never been evicted or arrested like to say that accessible court records are necessary to promote "a free and open society." Limiting access to court records, they argue, would pave the way for undemocratic state practices: secret police, undocumented arrests, hidden prisons, and God knows what else. Next to the concrete realities of how records are actually used to make families' lives much harder, these abstract worries seem grossly out of touch. For millions of poor Americans, including those who have never committed a crime, court records severely constrict their opportunities. Let's deal with the real problems we have, not the imaginary problems we don't.

39. Martha Davis, "Participation, Equality, and the Civil Right to Counsel: Lessons from Domestic and International Law," *Yale Law Journal* 122 (2013): 2260–81; Raven Lidman, "Civil Gideon as a Human Right: Is the U.S. Going to Join Step with the Rest of the Developed World?," *Temple Political and Civil Rights Law Review* 15 (2006): 769–800.

40. Quoted in Cass Sunstein, *The Second Bill of Rights: FDR's Unfinished Revolution and Why We Need It More Than Ever* (New York: Basic Books, 2004), 3.

41. Quoted in Beryl Satter, *Family Properties: How the Struggle over Race and Real Estate Transformed Chicago and Urban America* (New York: Metropolitan Books, 2009), 215.

42. "Exploitation" appears but twice in William Julius Wilson's *The Truly Disadvantaged: The Inner City, the Underclass, and Public Policy*, 2nd ed. (Chicago: University of Chicago Press, 2012 [1987]), when Wilson summarizes orthodox Marxist accounts, and again twice in Wilson's *When Work Disappears: The World of the New Urban Poor* (New York: Knopf, 1996), when he describes blacks' aversion to it. In Loïc Wacquant's *Urban Outcasts: A Comparative Sociology of Advanced Marginality* (Malden, MA: Polity Press, 2008), you can find four instances of "exploitation," only one of which refers to the exploitation of the poor by the rich (page 123n7). The word makes a single appearance in Douglas Massey and Nancy Denton's *American Apartheid: Segregation and the Making of the Underclass* (Cambridge: Harvard University Press, 1993), on page 176, in reference to sexual liaisons between inner-city residents; a single

appearance in Sudhir Venkatesh's *American Project: The Rise and Fall of a Modern Ghetto* (Cambridge: Harvard University Press, 2000), on page 150, in reference to housing project tenants being exploited by gangs; and a single appearance in Harrington's *The Other America* (page 32). "Exploitation" does not appear at all in the pages of many other modern classics that take up the plight of the poor, from Kathryn Edin and Laura Lein's *Making Ends Meet: How Single Mothers Survive Welfare and Low-Wage Work* (New York: Russell Sage Foundation, 1997) to Charles Murray's *Coming Apart: The State of White America, 1960–2010* (New York: Random House, 2012).

43. On food prices in poor neighborhoods, see Chanjin Chung and Samuel Myers, "Do the Poor Pay More for Food? An Analysis of Grocery Store Availability and Food Price Disparities," *Journal of Consumer Affairs* 33 (1999): 276–96; Marianne Bitler and Steven Haider, "An Economic View of Food Deserts in the United States," *Journal of Policy Analysis and Management* 30 (2011): 153–76.

44. Lizabeth Cohen, *A Consumers' Republic: The Politics of Mass Consumption in Postwar America* (New York: Knopf, 2008), 40; Elizabeth Blackmar, *Manhattan for Rent, 1785–1850* (Ithaca: Cornell University Press, 1989), 237–38; Jacob Riis, *How the Other Half Lives: Studies Among the Tenements of New York* (New York: Penguin Books, 1997 [1890]), 30; Allan Spear, *Black Chicago: The Making of a Negro Ghetto, 1890–1920* (Chicago: University of Chicago Press, 1967); Matthew Desmond, "Eviction and the Reproduction of Urban Poverty," *American Journal of Sociology* 118 (2012): 88–133. Of all people, Daniel Patrick Moynihan recognized the central importance of exploitation to understanding racialized urban poverty. In his report to the US Department of Labor that would later become infamous, Moynihan wrote: "The Negro situation is commonly perceived by whites in terms of the visible manifestation of discrimination and poverty. . . . It is more difficult, however, for whites to perceive the effect that three centuries of exploitation have had on the fabric of Negro society itself. . . . Here is where the true injury has occurred: unless this damage is repaired, all the effort to end discrimination and poverty and injustice will come to little." Daniel Patrick Moynihan, *The Negro Family: The Case for National Action* (Washington, DC: US Department of Labor, 1965).

45. This point is indebted to Satter's *Family Properties*.

46. On rip-off schemes, see Alan Andreasen, *The Disadvantaged Consumer* (New York: The Free Press, 1975); Michael Lewis, *The Big Short: Inside the Doomsday Machine* (New York: Norton, 2010), 20; David Caplovitz, *The Poor Pay More* (New York: The Free Press, 1967). On payday loans, see Pew Charitable Trust, *Payday Lending in America: Who Borrows, Where They Borrow, and Why* (Washington, DC: Pew, July 19, 2012); Gary Rivlin, *Broke, USA: From Pawnshops to Poverty, Inc.* (New York: Harper, 2010).

47. On markets being embedded in state and social relations, see Mark Granovetter, "Economic Action and Social Structure: The Problem of Embeddedness," *American Journal of Sociology* 91 (1985): 481–510; Karl Polanyi, *The Great Transformation: The Political and Economic Origins of Our Time* (Boston:

Beacon Press, 2001 [1944]). On the relationship between poverty and policing, see Megan Comfort, "When Prison Is a Refuge: America's Messed Up," *Chronicle of Higher Education*, December 2, 2013; David Garland, *The Culture of Control: Crime and Social Order in Contemporary Society* (Chicago: University of Chicago Press, 2001); Loïc Wacquant, *Punishing the Poor: The Neoliberal Government of Social Insecurity* (Durham: Duke University Press, 2009); Bruce Western, *Punishment and Inequality in America* (New York: Russell Sage Foundation, 2006); Alice Goffman, *On the Run: Fugitive Life in an American City* (Chicago: University of Chicago Press, 2014).

48. Oliver Cromwell Cox, *Caste, Class, and Race: A Study in Social Dynamics* (New York: Doubleday and Company, 1948), 238.

49. Katie Dodd, *Quarterly Benefits Summary* (Newcastle-upon-Tyne: Department for Work and Pensions, 2015); Hugo Priemus, Peter Kemp, and David Varady, "Housing Vouchers in the United States, Great Britain, and the Netherlands: Current Issues and Future Perspectives," *Housing Policy Debate* 16 (2005): 575–609; "Housing Benefit: How Does It Work?," BBC News, November 9, 2011.

50. No study has shown that, compared to housing vouchers, project-based assistance can deliver housing at equal quality for less cost. On the cost of public housing compared to vouchers, see Janet Currie, *The Invisible Safety Net: Protecting the Nation's Poor Children and Families* (Princeton: Princeton University Press, 2006), chapter 4; Amy Cutts and Edgar Olsen, "Are Section 8 Housing Subsidies Too High?," *Journal of Housing Economics* 11 (2002): 214–43.

On neighborhood quality of voucher holders compared to public housing residents, see Sandra Newman and Ann Schnare, "'. . . And a Suitable Living Environment': The Failure of Housing Programs to Deliver on Neighborhood Quality," *Housing Policy Debate* 8 (1997): 703–41; Edgar Olsen, "Housing Programs for Low-Income Households," in *Means-Tested Transfer Programs in the United States*, ed. Robert Moffitt (Chicago: University of Chicago Press, 2003), 365–442.

51. Brian Jacob and Jens Ludwig, "The Effects of Housing Assistance on Labor Supply: Evidence from a Voucher Lottery," *American Economic Review* 102 (2012): 272–304; Mark Shroder, "Does Housing Assistance Perversely Affect Self-Sufficiency? A Review Essay," *Journal of Housing Economics* 11 (2002): 381–417; Sandra Newman, Scott Holupka, and Joseph Harkness, "The Long-Term Effects of Housing Assistance on Work and Welfare," *Journal of Policy Analysis and Management* 28 (2009): 81–101.

52. Tellingly, countries with universal housing programs do not have minimum housing standards like America's limited voucher program does. When everyone in the country can afford decent housing, you don't need minimum standards because empowered renters can take their voucher elsewhere. Priemus et al., "Housing Vouchers in the United States, Great Britain, and the Netherlands," 582.

53. Riis, *How the Other Half Lives*, 201.

54. A universal voucher program would not solve all our problems. Especially in tight markets, vouchers cannot fully shield tenants from rent inflation. Only significant government regulation (like rent control) or market alterations (like expanding housing supply) can do that.

In fact, there is some evidence—it is thin—that our current voucher program might be driving up everybody's rent: not only voucher holders' but unassisted renters' too. The main reason is simple. If millions of poor people opt out of the private market for public housing, that will lower demand and, thus, rent at the bottom of the market. If those people are reintroduced to the private market, voucher in hand, that will increase demand and, with it, rent. One study found that cities with more housing vouchers experienced steeper rent hikes and that, on the whole, vouchers have cost unassisted families more than they have saved assisted ones. (See Scott Susin, "Rent Vouchers and the Price of Low-Income Housing," *Journal of Public Economics* 83 [2002]: 109–52.) And landlord how-to guides offer the following advice: "I also like to check the going rate for public housing, i.e., government funded rental subsidies, as a benchmark of what you can command in rent." (Bryan M. Chavis, *Buy It, Rent It, Profit! Make Money as a Landlord in Any Real Estate Market* [New York: Touchstone, 2009], 70.) Studies also have found no relationship between the concentration of voucher holders and the overall price of rental housing. For example, the Experimental Housing Allowance Program (EHAP) found that housing vouchers had a negligible effect on marketwide rents. William Apgar has attributed this result to the fact that markets were insufficiently saturated with vouchers and that rents were artificially depressed during the study's time period. Drawing on the EHAP's findings, simulation studies conducted by the National Bureau of Economic Research and the Urban Institute "suggested that a housing allowance could indeed trigger significant price increases for both recipients and nonrecipients, as well as encourage disinvestment and abandonment of units that do not meet program standards." See William Apgar Jr., "Which Housing Policy Is Best?," *Housing Policy Debate* 1 (1990): 1–32, 9. See also Michael Eriksen and Amanda Ross, "Housing Vouchers and the Price of Rental Housing," working paper, University of Georgia, 2015.

55. Matthew Desmond and Kristin Perkins, "Are Landlords Overcharging Voucher Holders?," working paper, Harvard University, June 2015; Cutts and Olsen, "Are Section 8 Housing Subsidies Too High?"; Olsen, "Housing Programs for Low-Income Households." On housing cost regulation, see Tommy Andersson and Lars-Gunnar Svensson, "Non-Manipulable House Allocation with Rent Control," *Econometrica* 82 (2014): 507–39; Richard Arnott, "Time for Revisionism on Rent Control?," *Journal of Economic Perspectives* 9 (1995): 99–120.

The US Department of Housing and Urban Development recently released a plan to provide voucher holders "with subsidies that better reflect the localized rental market" by proposing "Small Area Fair Market Rents" that "vary by ZIP code and support a greater range of payment standards than can be achieved under existing regulations." See US Department of Housing and Urban Development, "Establishing a More Effective Fair Market Rent (FMR) System; Using Small Area Fair Market Rents (SAFMRs) in Housing Choice Voucher Program Instead of the Current 50th Percentile FMRs; Advanced Notice of Proposed Rulemaking," *Federal Register* 80 (June 2, 2015): 31332–36.

56. Bipartisan Policy Center, *Housing America's Future: New Directions for National Policy* (Washington, DC: Bipartisan Policy Center, 2013), chapter 4. For technical documentation of projected cost estimates, see Larry Buron, Bulbul Kaul, and Jill Khadduri, *Estimates of Voucher-Type and Emergency Rental Assistance for Unassisted Households* (Cambridge, MA: Abt Associates, 2012). In 2012, federal expenditures to homeowners amounted to roughly $200 billion. See Will Fischer and Barbara Sard, *Chart Book: Federal Housing Spending Is Poorly Matched to Need* (Washington, DC: Center for Budget and Policy Priorities, 2013). For another cost estimate of an open-enrollment housing voucher program, see William Grigsby and Steven Bourassa, "Section 8: The Time for Fundamental Program Change?," *Housing Policy Debate* 15 (2004): 805–34. This study estimated that expanding housing vouchers to renting families below the 50th percentile in median income for their area would require an additional $43 billion, which at the time amounted to 2.5 percent of federal outlays.

57. Schwartz, *Housing Policy in the United States*, 45–47.

58. Ibid. Executive Office of the President, *Budget of the United States Government: Fiscal Year 2008* (Washington, DC: Office of the President, 2008).

59. Harrington, *The Other America*, 157–58. A. Scott Henderson, *Housing and the Democratic Ideal: The Life and Thought of Charles Abrams* (New York: Columbia University Press, 2000); Peter Dreier, "Federal Housing Subsidies: Who Benefits and Why?," in *A Right to Housing: Foundation for a New Social Agenda*, eds. Rachel Bratt, Michael Stone, and Chester Hartman (Philadelphia: Temple University Press, 2006), 105–38.

ABOUT THIS PROJECT

1. For a fuller explanation, see Matthew Desmond, "Relational Ethnography," *Theory and Society* 43 (2014): 547–79. See also Mustafa Emirbayer, "Manifesto for Relational Sociology," *American Journal of Sociology* 103 (1997): 281–317; Eric Wolf, *Europe and the People Without a History* (Berkeley and Los Angeles: University of California Press, 1982); Stanley Lieberson, *Making It Count: The Improvement of Social Research and Theory* (Berkeley and Los Angeles: University of California Press, 1985).

2. Mitchell Duneier, *Sidewalk* (New York: Farrar, Straus and Giroux, 1999), 337–39.

3. There's this idea that ethnography is a "method." When we see it this way, we tend to ask methodological questions about it. *How do I get my project approved by the IRB? When should I write field notes?* I tend to think of ethnography as a *sensibility*, a "way of seeing" as the anthropologist Harry Wolcott once put it.

This means that ethnography isn't something we go and do. It's a fundamental way of being in the world. If we think of ethnography this way, then we begin to ask different questions. *How can I get strangers to talk with me? How can I become more observant?* If we approach ethnography as a sensibility, then we can begin cultivating a set of skills or disciplines long before we actually enter the field. It is possible to transform yourself into an ethnographer—day in, day out—so that when the time comes for you to set foot in the field, you already are one. (It also helps to get rid of your smartphone.) Harry Wolcott, *Ethnography: A Way of Seeing* (Lanham: Rowman Altamira, 1999). On the violence of interpretation, see Susan Sontag, "Against Interpretation," in *A Susan Sontag Reader* (New York: Farrar, Straus and Giroux, 1982), 99.

4. When I lived in the trailer park, I didn't know that Scott was so depressed that he was planning on killing himself via overdose. Once, he asked me for a large sum of money. I said no and shudder when I recall that I contemplated saying yes.

5. See Mustafa Emirbayer and Matthew Desmond, "Race and Reflexivity," *Ethnic and Racial Studies* 35 (2012): 574–99.

6. I did not rely on any qualitative data software.

7. The fact-checker was Gillian Brassil. I provided Gillian with all of my field notes after she signed a nondisclosure agreement. Gillian corroborated accounts by conducting background research (e.g., police data, legal statutes), almost thirty independent interviews, and reviewing public records as well as my field notes, photographs, and transcripts of my digital recordings. Besides asking for documentation for several details recorded in this book, Gillian also randomly selected 10 percent of the book manuscript's pages and asked me to show her where she could find corresponding scenes or observations in the field notes. Often, she requested photographs or official documents to support claims.

8. I provided a copy of the manuscript (either the entire work or relevant chapters) to everyone featured prominently in its pages. In some cases, I read relevant portions to people to check factual details.

9. Policy wonks and poverty researchers never tire of debating the details of this or that housing policy. Of policies that serve a sliver of the urban poor, they ask a hundred questions. According to Google Scholar, there are more than 4,800 scholarly articles and books in which the phrase "Moving to Opportunity" appears in the text. This neighborhood relocation initiative designed to move families out of disadvantaged neighborhoods was a bold and important program—which served roughly 4,600 households. In other words, by now every family who benefited from Moving to Opportunity could have their own study in which their program was mentioned. We know much more about public housing, which serves less than 2 percent of the population, than about inner-city landlords and their properties, which constitute the bulk of housing for the ghetto poor. We know much more about housing vouchers, enjoyed by the lucky minority of low-income families, than about how the majority of low-income families make ends meet unassisted in the private rental market.

In 1995, Richard Arnott observed that economists' "focus on rent control has diverted attention from more important housing policy issues. . . . Not a single paper has been published in a leading journal during the last decade dealing with low-income housing problems." Richard Arnott, "Time for Revisionism on Rent Control?," *Journal of Economic Perspectives* 9 (1995): 99–120, 117.

10. Matthew Desmond and Tracey Shollenberger, "Forced Displacement from Rental Housing: Prevalence and Neighborhood Consequences," *Demography*, forthcoming.

11. Matthew Desmond, "Eviction and the Reproduction of Urban Poverty," *American Journal of Sociology* 118 (2012): 88–133.

12. Doubly robust logistic regression models, as well as several matching analyses, were used to estimate the odds of receiving an eviction judgment. Milwaukee Eviction Court Study, 2011. For models, see Matthew Desmond et al., "Evicting Children," *Social Forces* (2013) 92: 303–27.

13. Go to https://thedata.harvard.edu.

14. Just over half of Milwaukee's housing units are occupied by renters, a proportion similar to those in other cities (e.g., Chicago, Houston, Baltimore). In terms of median rent, Milwaukee County ranks 1,420th out of 4,763 counties in the United States and Puerto Rico. Cities with similar rent distributions include Portland, OR; Charlotte, NC; Gary, IN; and Baton Rouge, LA. Cities with a stalwart tradition of tenant unionizing and an economically diverse rental population—e.g., Boston, Los Angeles—tend to boast of toothier tenant protections than those, like Milwaukee, in which most middle- and upper-class households own their home. But most cities' renter protections more closely resemble Milwaukee's than Boston's or Los Angeles's. See National Multifamily Housing Council, *Quick Facts: Resident Demographics* (Washington, DC: National Multifamily Housing Council, 2009); US Department of Housing and Urban Development, *50th Percentile Rent Estimates for 2010* (Washington, DC: US Department of Housing and Urban Development, 2010).

15. To paraphrase Elliot Liebow, *Tally's Corner: A Study of Negro Streetcorner Men* (Boston: Little, Brown and Company, 1967), 15.

16. Clifford Geertz, *Works and Lives: The Anthropologist as Author* (Stanford: Stanford University Press, 1988), 5.

17. The rise of first-person ethnographic narration is the product of the postmodern turn in anthropology, which focused attention on the politics and biases of the author. Before that, much of ethnography was written in the third person. The authors of *The Taxi-Dance Hall* (1932) or *Street Corner Society* (1943) or even *Tally's Corner* (1967) are hardly on the page.

INDEX

Affordable Rentals, 245–46, 252, 384n
African Americans, 76, 125, 251, 257, 395n
Agriculture Department, U.S., 312
AIDS, 83, 86
Aid to Families with Dependent Children, 25, 161
albuterol, 56
Alcoholics Anonymous (AA), 270, 271, 272, 273–74, 276, 319, 321, 383n, 389n
Aldea, Anna, 270, 271, 272, 273, 275–76, 319
Aldea, David, 271–72, 273, 275–76
Aldea, Oscar, 275, 276
Aldea, Pito, 91, 177–78, 270–71
Ali (building manager), 232–33, 234, 239
All Bible Baptist Church, 264
Allis-Chalmers plant, 24
All Our Kin: Strategies for Survival in a Black Community (Stack), 161, 351n, 378n
American Civil Liberties Union, 101
American Legion, 178
American Motors, 24–25
amitriptyline, 275
Amtrak station, 260, 268
Antoine (Terri's boyfriend), 153
Arabs, 53

Arby's, 121–24, 291
Arizona State University, 315–16
"Art of the Double Closure, The" (Sherrena's presentation), 198
asbestos, 29
Atalya, Sister, 248
Athea Laboratories, 24, 27
Atlanta, Ga., 312
McDaniel-Glenn Homes in, 301
Auer Steel and Heating, 284
Azerbaijan, 305

Baltimore, Md., 333
banks, 150
Barber, Minister, 247, 248, 253, 385n
Basilica of St. Josaphat, 1, 179
Bay View, Milwaukee, Wis., 83, 178
Beaker (Robert; Larraine's brother), 111, 121, 132, 133, 167–68, 169, 217, 218, 220–21, 222, 224, 322
Belle, Arleen, 1–3, 9, 19, 53–61, 62–63, 152, 159–60, 161, 162–66, 186–87, 192–96, 208–13, 231–35, 239–41, 242, 243, 282–92, 295, 296, 297, 299, 300, 304, 310, 312, 320–21, 322, 327, 335, 336, 349n, 361n, 362n, 369n, 376n, 382n, 383n–84n, 390n
in eviction court, 100–107
eviction record of, 101

Belle, Arleen, (*cont'd.*)
  Nineteenth and Hampton house of, 235
  Sherrena's eviction of, 94–96, 158–59, 187
  Thirteenth Street apartment of, 53–54, 58, 60–61, 76, 107, 140, 187–90, 207–8, 209, 212–14, 240, 241
Ben (Vanetta's boyfriend), 325
Best Western Hotel, 28
Betty, Ms. (trailer park tenant), 224–26, 379*n*
Bible, 2, 123, 126, 139, 159, 248
Bieck Management, 130, 172–73, 182, 221, 222
Big C (T's brother), 286
Big Kendal (Kendal Jr.'s father), 243
Billy (Heroin Susie's boyfriend), 85–87, 276
Bipartisan Policy Center, 311
black-tar heroin, 86
Bliss (Pam's daughter), 48, 50, 237, 239
Blockbuster, 244
Blue, The (Milwaukee tower), 223
Bo-Bo (Vanetta's son), 243, 259, 260, 264, 266, 267, 383*n*
Branson, Mo., 183
Brittain, Dave, 113, 114, 115, 116, 117, 119–20, 124, 132, 364*n*
Brittain, Jim, 113, 132, 364*n*
Brittain, Tom, 113, 132, 364*n*
Brontee (mover), 116
Bronx, N.Y., 4, 148, 304–5
Brookfield, Wis., 142, 151, 152, 369*n*
Brooklyn, N.Y., 334
Brown Deer, Wis., 156, 319
Brownsville, Tenn., 78, 294, 327
Buck "Big Bro" (Lamar's neighbor), 20–23, 27, 136–37, 139, 140, 198, 201
building codes, 310
building inspectors, 16, 75–76
building managers, 128–29
Bunker, Scott W., 51–52, 80, 81–87,

91–93, 169, 177, 178–79, 180, 182–85, 270–81, 294, 295, 296, 318, 319, 321, 335, 336, 355*n*, 388*n*, 389*n*, 404*n*
  in Alcoholics Anonymous, 270–74, 276
  drug use of, 83–84, 86, 179
Burger King, 161
By Grace Alone (workbook), 139

Caleb Jr. "C.J." (Doreen's son), 64–65, 67, 70–71, 77, 78, 138, 155, 257
California, 215, 391*n*
Cam (Joan's husband), 82
Cambridge, Mass., 326
Caribbean, 144
Clara (Crystal and Vanetta's friend), 262
Carol (landlord), 208–10, 212
C.C. (rooming house neighbor), 323
Celebrex, 42
Charleston, S.C., 334
Charney, Tobin, 36–37, 38–40, 41–43, 44–47, 50, 51, 52, 80, 81, 85, 87, 88, 111, 128, 129–30, 131, 169–70, 171, 172, 173, 174–76, 177, 182, 218, 221, 228, 317, 318, 319, 320, 321, 335, 348*n*, 364*n*, 370*n*, 379*n*, 380*n*
Chelsea (Sherrena's tenant), 156, 157
Chicago, Ill., 5, 87, 141, 148, 251, 252, 296, 374*n*, 375*n*, 392*n*
  Gold Coast in, 148
  Robert Taylor Homes in, 243, 301, 302
  South Side of, 148
child care, 25
Child Protective Services (CPS), 68, 181, 230, 234, 244, 262, 263, 289, 291, 320, 322, 335, 391*n*
children, 227–31, 299, 332
Children's Hospital, 232
Chris (Trisha's boyfriend), 140, 141, 186, 187–88, 190, 193, 290
Christianity, 126–27
Chuck E. Cheese's, 35
Church of the Gesu, 107

Cincinnati, Ohio, 333
civic life, 294
Civil Rights Act (1964), 34
Civil Rights Act (Fair Housing Act;
    1968), 34, 230, 252, 375*n*
Civil War, U.S., 250
Clarissa (Scott's sister), 82
Clement, Sissell, 99
Cleveland, Ohio, 5, 296, 392*n*
Clinton, Bill, 25
Cloward, Richard, 180
Cobras (gang), 177
Coco (Hinkston family dog), 64, 78,
    79
Colin (preacher), 139–40
"collective efficacy," 70
College Mobile Home Park, 32–33,
    34–43, 44–47, 48, 50, 51–52, 80,
    81–82, 85–86, 87–88, 92–93,
    111–12, 121, 124, 126, 127–31,
    132–33, 168–76, 179, 180–81,
    182–83, 220, 221–22, 224–25,
    228, 237, 281, 317–18, 319, 321,
    322, 330, 348*n*, 349*n*, 363*n*, 364*n*,
    368*n*, 370*n*, 372*n*
    E-24 trailer in, 173–74
    profit from, 175–76
    reputation of, 85
Columbia St. Mary's Hospital, 57
Columbus, Ga., 315
Common Council (Milwaukee city
    council), 36, 38, 44–45
community, eviction's effect on, 252,
    298
Community Advocates, 112, 346*n*,
    353*n*, 358*n*–59*n*, 362*n*
"Community Key" (installation),
    215–16
Confederacy, 250
Confederate flag, 48
Congress, U.S., 34, 230, 231, 349*n*,
    363*n*, 366*n*, 384*n*
Consolidated Court Automation
    Programs (CCAP), 87, 88, 145,
    208

Cousins Subs, 73, 77, 99, 256
crack cocaine, 27, 49, 53, 60, 161, 179
crime, 70, 89
Cudahy, Wis., 121, 218, 236, 238
Culligan, 82

Dabbs, Mr., 126
Daryl, Pastor, 126–27, 218–19, 384*n*–
    85*n*
data-mining companies, 4
Dawn (trailer park tenant), 82, 85, 172,
    181
Dayton, Tenn., 85
*Death and Life of Great American Cities,
    The* (Jacobs), 70
deindustrialization, 25
DeMarcus (Luke's friend), 20, 21–22,
    27
depression, 298
Depression, Great, 3–4, 24
Detroit, Mich., 333
Devon (Kamala's boyfriend), 198, 201,
    202
Digger (Beaker's dog), 111
Dirky (mechanic), 228, 239
Dixon, Bishop, 248
docketed judgments, 103
doctrine of absolute liability for rent, 250
domestic violence, 191–92
Donny (trailer park tenant), 169, 170
Don't Be Afraid to Discipline (Peters), 2
D.P. (Scott's roomate), 177–79, 271
D'Sean (Bo-Bo's father), 260
Dubuque, Iowa, 334
Dunn, Susie "Office Susie," 34–35, 36,
    37, 38, 41–43, 46, 52, 85, 88, 124,
    129, 168–69, 172, 173, 174, 175,
    317, 370*n*
Duragesic patches, 83

E-24 (trailer), 173–74
Eagle Moving and Storage, 113–17,
    119–20, 124–26, 131–32, 168, 218,
    221, 222, 321, 330, 379*n*–80*n*
Earl (Vanetta's boyfriend), 324–25

Earned Income Tax Credit, 306, 350*n*, 378*n*

Ebony (Vanetta's sister), 248, 260, 262, 264, 325

Edinburgh, 250

education, 296, 310

Education Department, U.S., 312

Emergency Assistance, 51, 112

ethnography, 334–35

Ethnography: A Way of Seeing (Wolcott), 404*n*

Evans, Shortcake, 243, 262, 264, 265, 266, 267

Evans, Vanetta, 243–47, 248–49, 252, 253–54, 259–63, 268, 295, 299, 310, 320, 322, 324–25, 335, 383*n*
  sentencing hearing of, 263–67

Everbrite, 117

eviction court, 94–107, 155–56, 331–32

eviction moves, 113–17, 119–20

eviction records, 101, 103

eviction riots, 3–4

evictions, 3–4, 40, 45–46, 89, 90, 158–59, 179–80, 304, 306, 308, 334
  aftermath of, 69–70
  Christmas breaks from, 101
  community effect of, 252, 298
  community resistance to, 4
  as contagious, 51–52
  cost of, 114
  effects of, 5, 296–99, 331
  "informal," 4, 330
  initiated by renters, 74
  and job loss, 227, 296–97
  landlord discretion in, 128–29
  men's tactics for avoiding, 129
  nonpayment of rent and, 128
  nuisance property ordinance and, 190–92
  as precursor to suicide, 298
  rates of, 4, 5, 295–96, 330–31
  summer spike in, 15–16
  tenant denial of, 115
  truck or curb option in, 2
  twenty-eight-day "no cause," 45–46

two parts of, 102
underestimating the prevalence of, 330–31
women and, 97–98, 299
exploitation, 249–52, 305–7

Fair Housing Act (Civil Rights Act; 1968), 34, 230, 252, 375*n*

Fair Housing Council, 322

Fair Market Rent (FMR), 148, 349*n*, 365*n*

Fanny (Doreen's best friend), 67–68

Federal Housing Administration, 156

fentanyl, 83–84

Florida, 72, 312

food stamps (Supplemental Nutrition Assistance Program; SNAP), 25, 216–17, 268, 285, 303, 308

food vouchers, 215

Forbes, 13

Ford Hotel (San Francisco), 315

foreclosures, 4, 11, 91–92, 116, 124–25, 151, 157, 252, 298, 331
  renter-occupied, 150

Fragile Families and Child Wellbeing Study, 331

France, 305

Free Foreclosure List, 151

GAMP (General Assistance Medical Program), 274

Gary, Ind., 333, 405*n*

Geertz, Clifford, 334

General Mills, 257

Geneva, 250

gentrification, 329

George Webb restaurant, 175, 246, 325

Gerald "Ger-Ger" (Arleen's son) 57, 59, 163, 234, 322

Geraldine (Bieck's office manager), 221–22

Gideon v. Wainwright, 303–4

GI mortgages, 251

Gladstone, Phyllis (trailer park tenant), 40, 348*n*

Glen (Larraine's boyfriend), 118–19, 131, 218
Glendale, Wis., 319
Goodwill, 132
Gramling Perez, Laura, 101–3, 104–6
Grand Avenue mall, 279–80, 281
Great Britain, 309
Great Depression, 3–4, 24
Great Migration, 251
Great Recession, 303
Green Bay, Wis., 46, 48, 49
Guest House (shelter), 279, 280, 294

Habitat for Humanity, 316
Hall, Belinda (representative payee), 61–62, 74, 143, 290, 350n, 365n
Harbor Room (gay bar), 85
"hard money," 151
Harvard Dataverse Network, 333
health-care subsidies, 25
heroin, 48, 51, 86–87, 183, 274, 276, 277
Heroin Susie (trailer park tenant), 35, 51, 85–87, 178, 179, 183, 276, 277
Hinkston, Doreen, 14, 26, 64–65, 66–70, 71, 72, 74, 75–79, 99, 107, 154, 197, 199, 200, 203, 255, 256, 294, 304, 320, 327, 367n
  eviction of, 145, 155–56, 157
  monthly income of, 67
Hinkston, Natasha, 64–67, 68, 71, 76–79, 143, 145, 154, 155–56, 198, 200, 255–56, 257, 258, 327, 355n, 384n
Hinkston, Patrice, 14, 26, 30, 64–66, 67, 68, 69, 71–74, 75–76, 77, 78, 98, 99, 134, 135, 142, 143, 154, 155, 200, 201, 256, 257–58, 294–95, 304, 320, 355n, 386n
Hinkston, Ruby, 64–65, 67, 70–71, 72, 77, 78, 79, 154, 155, 200, 257, 302, 367n
Hinkston family, 64–67, 68–69, 71, 77, 143, 144, 145, 157, 200–201, 255,

256–58, 294, 300, 320, 335–36, 367n
Thirty-Second Street apartment of, 66, 67, 68, 69, 70, 74, 79
Hisense air conditioner, 90
Hispanic Mission, 260
Hispanic neighborhoods, 114, 125, 236, 237, 359n–60n
Hispanics, 34, 346n, 395n
home, 293–94, 300
Home Depot, 142
Homeland Security Department, U.S., 312
homelessness, 268, 299, 302, 308
  programs for people facing, 112
Homelessness Prevention Program, 112, 362n
homeownership, 251–52
housing, 5, 301, 329
  costs of, 4, 58
  discrimination in, 34
  high demand for cheapest, 47
  as right, 300–301, 312–13
Housing Act of 1949, 366n
Housing Allowance (Netherlands), 309
Housing and Urban Development, U.S. Department of (HUD), 223, 231, 349n, 362n, 402n–3n
  FMR set by, 148, 349n, 365n
Housing Authority of the City of Milwaukee, 59–60, 148, 267, 297, 350n, 383n, 384n, 396n
  "the List" of, 59
Housing Benefit (Great Britain), 309
housing boom, 151
Housing Choice Voucher Program, 302, 311, 366n
housing courts, 4, 303–4
housing vouchers, 147–49, 302
  expansion of, 308–12
Houston, Tex., 312
How the Other Half Lives: Studies Among the Tenements of New York (Riis), 115, 375n

hypes (crack cocaine addicts), 136–37, 141

Illinois, 29, 67, 243
incomes, stagnation of, 4
India, 305
Indianapolis, Ind., 333
Individualized Education Program (IEP), 55
Internet, 245, 257–58, 384*n*
Iowa, 82, 183, 184, 279, 321

Jackson County, Mo., 296
Jacobs, Jane, 70
Jada (Patrice's daughter), 64, 154
Jafaris (Arleen's son), 1, 2–3, 53, 54, 55–57, 60, 62, 160, 162, 164, 165, 190, 193, 194–95, 209, 212, 213, 231–32, 234–35, 239–41, 283–84, 285, 288, 290, 291
Jamaica, 28, 144, 149, 153, 154
Jayme (Larraine's daughter), 117, 118, 121–23, 217, 220–21
Jenkins, Larraine, 40–43, 92, 111–13, 117–19, 120–24, 126–33, 167–69, 181, 216–26, 296, 300, 318, 319, 322, 328, 335, 363*n*, 364*n*, 377*n*–78*n*, 379*n*–80*n*, 384*n*, 385*n*
Jerry Lee (Larraine's ex-husband), 117–18
Jesus Christ, 126–27, 225–26, 248
Jim Crow, 251, 382*n*
Joan (Scott's mother), 82, 277, 279
Job Corps, 66
job programs, 310
John (Sheriff's deputy), 114, 115, 116, 117, 119–20
Johnson, Elder, 248
Johnson, Lyndon, 34
Jori (Arleen's son), 1, 2–3, 54–55, 57, 58, 60, 62, 160, 162–63, 164, 165, 166, 190, 194–95, 209, 211, 212, 213, 214, 232, 233, 234, 235, 239–41, 282, 283, 284, 285, 286, 287, 288, 289, 291–92, 300, 302, 335

J.P. (Arleen's cousin), 234, 235, 290
Justice Department, U.S., 88, 312

Kamala (Sherrena's tenant), 137–38, 198, 199, 200, 201–3, 255, 375*n*
Kansas City, Mo., 5, 296
Kayla Mae (Patrice's daughter), 64, 154, 200
"Keep Ya Head Up" (song), 54
Keisha (Woo's niece), 323, 324
Kendal Jr. (Vanetta's son) 243, 259, 263–64, 267, 302
Kimball, Officer "Woo," 319–20, 321, 322, 323
King, Martin Luther, Jr., 34, 305
Kings (gang), 177
kin networks, 161–62
Klausner "Lazarus" reclining sofa, 90
Kroll, Kristin, 49, 228, 231, 238
Kroll, Laura, 49–50
Kroll, Ned, 46–48, 49–52, 80, 82, 178, 179, 227–30, 231, 235, 236–39, 319, 324, 325, 381*n*

labor movement, 306
Ladona (prospective tenant), 147–49, 152
Lafayette, La., 68
"La Grange" (song), 47–48
landlords, 4, 9, 10, 12, 13, 28, 89, 102, 128–29, 180, 250, 303, 306, 307–8
  discretion of, 128–29
  discrimination by, 229–31, 249, 252, 310–11
  FMR and, 148–49
  ghetto, 251
  losses of, 11
  maintenance avoided by, 75–76
  nuisance property ordinance and, 190–92
  profits of, 252
  renters' opinions of, 182
  screening practices of, 88–91, 246
  voucher holders overcharged by, 148–49, 311

Landlord Training Program, 88–89,
90–91, 361*n*–62*n*
Landmark Credit Union, 156
Lane (Larraine's brother-in-law), 92,
121, 126, 127, 218, 222
Larry (Arleen's ex-boyfriend), 57–58,
234, 240, 284, 287, 291
Larry Jr. "Boosie" (Arleen's son), 57,
234–35, 291
Lassiter, Abby Gail, 304
late fees, 100
Lawson, Lenny, 32–33, 34, 35–36,
38–39, 42, 45–46, 47, 48, 87–88,
111, 127–29, 130, 168–73, 175,
181, 221, 317, 320, 348*n*, 349*n*,
362*n*, 363*n*, 364*n*, 370*n*
layaway, 217–18, 377*n*
Lead and Asbestos Information Center,
Inc., 29
lead poisoning, 230
legal aid, 303–5
Lena's Food Market, 99
Letter of Authority, 113
Library of Congress, 28, 348*n*
Licenses Committee, Milwaukee, 36,
40
Link, Uncle, 286
Little (Arleen's cat), 55, 195, 209, 212,
240, 241, 288
Local 113 union, 169
Lodge, the (homeless shelter), 2, 51, 84,
212, 242–44, 245, 246, 248, 259,
260, 262, 324, 383*n*
Long, Karen, 88–89, 90–91, 361*n*–62*n*
Lora (Sherrena's friend), 28, 30–31
Los Angeles, Calif., 312, 405*n*
"lot rent," 46
Lowe's, 142
Luminess Air makeup, 121
Lyrica, 42, 133

MacArthur Foundation, 329
McDaniel-Glenn Homes (Atlanta),
301
Madison, Wis., 249, 374*n*

Mainstay Suites, 58
Majestic Loft Apartments, 279–81
Malik (Natasha's boyfriend), 76, 77, 78,
156, 255, 257, 258
Malik Jr. (Natasha's son), 258, 294
Marcia P. Coggs Human Services
Center, 113, 215–16
Marquette University, 319
Martin (Arleen's brother), 163
Mary (trailer park tenant), 37
mass incarceration, 98
material hardship, 297, 331
Mayberry, Crystal, 159–61, 162, 163,
164–66, 186–89, 190, 192–96,
207–14, 241–49, 252–54, 259–60,
261–62, 267–69, 320, 322, 328,
335, 369*n*, 376*n*, 383*n*, 384*n*,
385*n*, 387*n*
Mayfair Mall, 56
Meals on Wheels, 168
Medicaid, 225
Megan (Larraine's daughter), 117, 118,
123, 217
Memphis, Tenn., 34, 334
Menominee River Valley, 25, 33, 114
Merva (Arleen's aunt), 158, 291
methadone, 277–79
Michael "Mikey" (Patrice's son) 64, 65,
66, 70–71, 135–36, 154–55, 257,
355*n*
Miller Brewery, 152
Millsberry (online game), 257
Milwaukee Area Renters Study
(MARS), 329–31, 344*n*, 345*n*,
346*n*, 348*n*, 351*n*–52*n*, 353*n*,
354*n*, 360*n*, 363*n*, 365*n*–66*n*,
371*n*–72*n*, 380*n*, 384*n*, 386*n*,
394*n*, 395*n*
Milwaukee Area Technical College, 82
Milwaukee Code of Ordinances
(MCO), 188
Milwaukee County, Wis., 103, 148,
215, 274, 357*n*, 364*n*, 390*n*, 405*n*
Sheriff's Office of, 41, 42, 113–14,
115, 119, 124, 131, 362*n*

Milwaukee County Behavioral Services Division Access Clinic, 274–75
Milwaukee County Courthouse, 95, 99
Milwaukee County Small Claims Court, 95–100, 101–3, 104–6
Milwaukee Eviction Court Study, 331–32, 358*n*, 359*n*, 360*n*, 395*n*
Milwaukee Police Department, 21, 188, 191–92, 207–8, 353*n*, 374*n*
nuisance property citations of, 332
Milwaukee Public Schools, 211, 327
Milwaukee Real Estate Investors Networking Group (RING), 27–30
Milwaukee Safety Academy, 88
Milwaukee, Wis., 1–3, 4–5, 15, 16–17, 26, 27, 46, 47, 58, 69, 76, 78, 82, 112, 113, 144, 181–82, 189, 207, 223, 245, 277, 278, 295, 296, 297, 298, 299, 316, 319, 324, 327, 328, 329–33, 334, 335, 336, 344*n*, 345*n*, 346*n*, 347*n*, 348*n*, 349*n*, 350*n*, 352*n*, 353*n*, 354*n*, 355*n*, 358*n*, 359*n*–60*n*, 361*n*, 362*n*, 363*n*, 364*n*, 366*n*, 368*n*–69*n*, 372*n*, 373*n*, 374*n*–75*n*, 384*n*, 386*n*, 388*n*, 390*n*, 392*n*, 393*n*–95*n*, 398*n*, 405*n*
African-American 1930 death rate in, 251
Atkinson Ave. in, 208, 235
Common Council of, 36, 38, 44–45
East Side of, 34, 83
employment in, 24–25
eviction court in, 94–107
Fond Du Lac Avenue in, 11, 99, 285
Grand Avenue mall in, 279–80, 281
Hispanic neighborhoods in, 114, 125, 236, 237, 359*n*–60*n*
housing stock of, 17
housing vouchers in, 149
Landlord Training Program in, 88–89, 90–91, 361*n*–62*n*
Licenses Committee of, 36, 40
Majestic Loft Apartments in, 279–81

North Side of, 2, 9–10, 25, 29–30, 33, 34, 37, 95, 99, 114, 119, 137, 150, 152, 163, 208, 223, 232, 235, 238, 245, 260, 284, 286, 319, 322, 326, 369*n*
nuisance property ordinance in, 190–92
population decline in, 10
poverty in, 24–25
rents in, 74–75, 151–52
segregation in, 33–34, 249–50
Sixteenth Street Viaduct in, 33, 80–81
South Side of, 28, 33, 34, 35, 37, 114, 117, 124, 177, 218, 223, 228, 236, 245, 261, 279, 346*n*
Teutonia Avenue in, 88, 163, 284
West Side of, 152
Minneapolis, Minn., 333
Mira (Scott's crew chief), 91, 92, 178, 179, 182–83
money judgments, 103, 105
morphine, 83
Mt. Calvary Pentecostal Church, 246–48, 253, 267
Mud Lake, 222
Multifamily Housing Inventory Report, 223
Myesha and Chester (Milwaukee tenants), 398*n*–99*n*
Myrdal, Gunnar, 294
Mytes, Meredith (Mrs. Mytes's daughter), 173
Mytes, Mrs. (trailer park tenant), 35, 36, 37, 173–74, 179

Narcan, 278
Narcotics Anonymous (NA), 84, 91, 177, 182, 320
Nathaniel (Ladona's son), 147
National Association of Real Estate Boards, 149, 366*n*
National Association of Realtors, 149
Nazis, 48
Neighborhood Services, Department of (DNS), 15, 16, 18, 36, 68, 76, 170

neighborhood trauma, 181–82
Neighborhood Watch, 294
Netherlands, 309
Newark, N.J., 333, 347*n*–48*n*
New Deal, 251
New Orleans, La., 67
New Pitts Mortuary, 62, 285, 286
New York, N.Y., 75, 148, 296, 304–5, 312, 333, 397*n*
    rent wars in, 180
New York Times, 4, 34, 388*n*
$99 meat deal, 163–64
North Carolina, 304
nuisance activity, 188–89
nuisance property citations, 332
nuisance property ordinance, 190–92
nursing license, 272–73, 276

Oak Creek, Wis., 121
Oakland, Calif., 302
Oakland Raiders, 286
Obama, Barack, 46, 155
Odessa (Larraine's sister), 120–21
Old Country Buffet, 244, 266
Onion, The, 277–78
open housing law, 34
"OPM" ("other people's money"), 151
Oregon, 345*n*
Osbourne, Ozzy, 229
Outlaws (biker gang), 39

P.A. (T's cousin), 284, 285, 287
Pabst brewery, 25
Pana (landlord's son), 282–83, 285, 287–88
PARI Proneb Ultra nebulizer, 56
Paris, 250
Patricia (Crystal's roommate), 260, 261, 262, 387*n*
payday lenders, 90
payday loans, 306
Percocet, 83, 179
"perpetual slums," 70
Philadelphia, Pa., 75, 251, 302
Pick 'n Save, 183

Pittsburgh, Pa., 334
Piven, Frances Fox, 180
police, 68, 70, 190, 191
Ponderosa Steakhouse, 284
Potawatomi Casino, 125, 197–98, 199, 246
poverty, 5, 24–25, 89, 285–86, 299, 316, 317
    concentrated, 309
    exploitation and, 305–6
    hopelessness of, 219, 256–57
    persistence and brutality of, 295
PPG Industries, 130
prednisone, 56
prison boom, 161
Prisoner Connections LLC, 13
private housing market, 329–30
"privilege of distress," 250
property damages, 102
property flipping, 151
property management, 28, 129, 252
Pruitt-Igoe Towers (St. Louis), 301, 302
Psychiatric Services, 298
public housing, 13, 59–60, 61, 149, 223–24, 225, 230, 244, 297, 301–2, 309, 329
    wait for, 59
Public Library, Milwaukee, Wis., 107
Public Storage, 211–12, 224, 321

Quad Graphics, 51, 66, 161

racism, 48, 174, 228, 237, 238, 239, 249, 250–52, 382*n*
Raleigh, N.C., 333
Randy Shit-Pants (trailer park tenant), 82
"rapid rescore," 156
Reagan, Ronald, 303
Reconstruction, 250–51
RedBook, 69, 154, 162, 384*n*
Red Cross, 203, 210, 212
Reinke, Pam, 40, 46–47, 48–52, 80, 82, 169, 178, 179, 227–30, 231, 235–39, 318, 319, 324, 335, 349*n*

Rent-A-Center, 90
rental assistance programs, 302
rent assistance, 147–49
rent certificate program, 149
"rent collector" (car), 9–10
rent controls, 180
renters, 180
RentGrow, 88, 356*n*
Rent Recovery Service, 104, 362*n*
rents, 4, 148, 151, 306
  withholding of, 75
rent strikes, 180
rent-to-own ventures, 156
Repairers of the Breach, 60
representative payee, 61
Restoration International Ministries,
  267–68, 269
Resumes for Dummies, 125
Rhoda (Crystal's aunt), 160, 162
Richards, Eddy, 20, 23–24, 26, 27, 137,
  139, 198, 201, 375*n*
Richards, Lamar, 10–11, 13–14, 20–23,
  25–27, 30–31, 64, 69, 71, 76,
  134–40, 142, 152, 197, 198–99,
  200, 201, 202, 203, 255, 320, 321,
  322, 346*n*, 347*n*, 375*n*
Richards, Luke, 20, 23–24, 26, 27, 137,
  138, 139, 140, 198, 200, 202, 375*n*
Ricky One Leg (Sherrena's tenant),
  98–99, 140, 146, 365*n*
Rights and Responsibilities guide,
  Wisconsin Department of
  Children and Families, 25–26
Riis, Jacob, 311, 375*n*
Ritalin, 56, 71
Roaring Twenties, 180
Robbie (trailer park tenant), 169, 170
Robert Taylor Homes (Chicago), 243,
  301, 302
Robitussin, 183
Rodriguez, Mr. (appliance store owner),
  262–63
Roger (DNS inspector), 170–72
Rome, 179
Roosevelt, Franklin D., 305

Rose (trailer park tenant), 181, 330
Ruben (Larraine's brother), 121, 130,
  131, 222
Rufus (junk collector), 38, 172, 174
R-W Enterprises, 117

St. Ben's, 291
St. Joseph's Hospital, *see* Wheaton
  Franciscan–St. Joseph Campus
St. Jude, 287
St. Louis, Mo., 301, 333
St. Peter's (Rome), 179
St. Stanislaus Church, 261
Salvation Army, 368*n*
  shelter (the Lodge), 2, 51, 84, 212,
    242–44, 245, 246, 248, 259, 260,
    262, 324, 383*n*
Samantha (Troy's common-law wife),
  175, 176
Sammy (Larraine's niece), 218, 219
San Francisco, Calif., 315, 333, 392*n*
Sandra (Pam's daughter), 48, 237, 239
Schlitz brewery, 25
Schuster's department store, 215
ScreeningWorks, 88
Seattle, Wash., 302, 312
security deposits, 105
  and collecting money judgments,
    103–4
segregation, 33–34, 249–50, 309, 329
self-storage, 29
Self Storage Brokers of America, 28
senior housing, 223
Serenity Club, 270, 272, 273–74, 276,
  279
sharecroppers, 251
Sheila M. ("nuisance" tenant), 192
Sheriff's Office, Milwaukee County,
  41, 42, 113–14, 115, 119, 124, 131,
  362*n*
Shields, Ken, 28–29
Shorewood, Wis., 151
Silver Spring, Wis., 319
Sixteenth Street Viaduct, 33, 80–81
Skokie, Ill., 36

slavery, 250

slums, 250, 301

Social Development Commission, 112

Social Security, 121, 169, 303, 356n, 359n

Society of St. Vincent de Paul, 280

SoHo neighborhood, New York, N.Y., 148

Sontag, Susan, 324

South, 251

South Bronx, N.Y., 148, 304–5

Southside Church of Christ, 126–27

Stack, Carol, 161, 351n, 378n

stipulation agreements, 40, 96, 157

Suboxone, 274, 275

subprime lending industry, 90, 125

suicide, 298

Sunny (Trisha's boyfriend), 289, 290

Supplemental Security Income (SSI), 23, 24, 32, 35, 40, 60, 61, 67, 85, 120, 147, 153, 157, 158, 161, 168, 174, 181, 208, 268, 308, 368n–69n
"resource limit" and, 217

Supreme Court, U.S., 303–4

Susan (Larraine's sister), 121, 126, 127, 218, 222

Sussex, Wis., 51

Sweden, 305

Tabatha (social worker), 144–45, 154, 157

Tabernacle Community Baptist Church, 291

Tam (trailer park tenant), 172, 181

Tarver, Quentin, 10, 11–12, 13, 14, 15, 18–19, 26, 27, 30, 63, 71–72, 73, 95, 102, 138, 140–43, 144, 145–47, 152, 153–54, 162, 186, 197–98, 199–200, 201–2, 213, 319, 320, 346n, 352n, 375n

Tarver, Sherrena, 3, 9–13, 23, 25, 26–28, 29–31, 55, 62–63, 71, 72–74, 75–76, 77, 98–99, 134–35, 136, 137, 138, 140–41, 142, 143, 144–46, 147–50, 160, 192, 193,
194, 196, 197–98, 233, 242, 256, 257, 284, 289, 319, 320, 321, 327, 335, 346n, 352n, 353n–55n, 361n, 365n, 369n–70n, 375n, 386n
credit-to-home-loan services of, 156–57
decision to evict Arleen and, 94–96, 159, 187
Eighteenth and Wright property of, 20, 21, 64–66, 69, 70, 134, 145, 154, 198–203
in eviction court, 100–107
eviction of Lamar by, 10–11, 13–14
financing of, 151
fire at property of, 199–203, 255
home of, 18
houses bought by, 152
Jamaica vacation of, 144, 153
maintenance by, 73
monthly rents collected by, 152–54
shooting at house of, 14–15
Thirteenth St. property of, 16–19, 53, 60–61, 76, 107, 140, 160, 187, 188–89, 190, 207–8, 209, 212–14

Taye (Natasha's ex-boyfriend), 77

Teddy (trailer park tenant), 51–52, 80–82, 84–85, 87, 91, 92

Tembi (Vanetta's daughter) 243, 259, 264, 267

tenants:
avoidance of landlords by, 128–29
in eviction court, 94–107
garnishing wages of, 29
money judgments against, 103
right to counsel for, 303–5
utilities responsibility of, 15–16

tenant screening reports, 4

tenants' union, 112

tenements, 75, 250

Tennessee, 91, 258

Tenth Street Methadone Clinic, 277–79

Terrance "T" (Larry's relative), 284–85, 286, 287

Terri (Sherrena's tenant), 152–54

Texas, 321
Theo (trailer park tenant), 173, 174
Third Street Pier restaurant, 58
Thomas (trailer park tenant), 224
Tim (mover), 113, 114, 115, 116, 119, 120
Tim (trailer park tenant), 330
Tina (trailer park tenant), 37, 380*n*
Tiny (worker on Quentin's crew), 140, 143
Tocqueville, Alexis de, 294
Travis (Ned's friend), 228, 238
Trisha (Sherrena's tenant), 60, 61, 140, 186–87, 188, 189–90, 212, 285, 288–89, 290
"Trouble with Subjects" (nuisance activity), 191
Troy (trailer park tramp), 175, 176
Turner, Jason, 25
2Pac, 54

underground economy, 141
unemployment, 141
unemployment insurance, 303
unions, 24, 112
University of Wisconsin Survey Center, 329
UPS, 146
urbanization, 250
Utica, N.Y., 333
utilities, disconnecting of, 15–16

vacancy rates, 47
vendor payment, 210
Verne (Quentin's uncle), 140, 142
Veterans Affairs Department, U.S., 312
Vice Lords (street gang), 141
Vicodin, 82, 83, 179
Vietnam War, 22
Voting Rights Act (1965), 34
voucher programs, 147–49, 302
  expansion of, 308–12
  landlords overcharging tenants through, 147–49, 311

Walmart, 25, 219
Warren, Jerry (trailer park tenant), 39–40, 129, 348*n*
Washington, DC, 59, 230–31
Washington Park, 152
Wauwatosa, Wis., 151–52, 319
We Energies, 15, 42, 244, 347*n*, 370*n*
welfare, 58
welfare reform, 25
welfare sanctions, 327
West Allis, Wis., 229, 236
Wheaton Franciscan–St. Joseph Campus (St. Joseph's Hospital), 258, 260, 261, 268
Winnick, Louis, 301
Winona, Minn., 82
Winona State University, 82
Winslow, Ariz., 315
Wisconsin, 25, 84, 87, 175, 192, 225, 243, 333, 345*n*, 347*n*, 351*n*, 355*n*, 364*n*
Wisconsin, University of, 173, 316
Wisconsin African American Women's Center, 287
Wisconsin Board of Nursing, 84, 355*n*
Wisconsin Circuit Court Access, 87
Wisconsin Department of Children and Families, 25–26, 327, 349*n*
Wisconsin Works (W-2), 25, 208, 210, 351*n*
  W-2 T placement in, 58, 208
Witkowski, Terry, 36, 40, 45, 88, 130, 174, 175, 176, 182, 319
women, evictions and, 97–98, 299
Woods Apartments, 222
Wraparound, 19, 158
"writ of restitution," 40–41

Xanax, 36, 278

YMCA, 112

Zambia, 305
Zoloft, 275, 389*n*

A Reader's Guide for

Evicted: Poverty and Profit in the American City

by Matthew Desmond

Questions and Topics for Discussion

1. Have you ever been evicted, or do you know anyone who has? If the answer is yes, what was your/their experience like, and how has it affected your/their life?

2. What was your experience reading *Evicted*? Were you surprised by what you learned? Was any particular scene or person's story emotionally painful for you to witness?

3. Many people have very codified perceptions of "people who get evicted" and suspect that those people are largely responsible—through bad decision making—for their circumstances. Did you feel this way before reading *Evicted*? Why or why not? Did your opinions change after reading the book? If so, how?

4. In *Evicted,* author Matthew Desmond takes a narrative approach to an important topic and follows the stories of several real people. Which person's story were you most drawn to and why?

5. Sherrena Tarver claimed to have found her calling as an inner-city entrepreneur, stating, "The 'hood is good. There's a lot of money there" (page 152). How did Sherrena profit from being a landlord in poor communities? Do you think her profits were justified? What responsibilities do landlords have when renting their property? What risks do they take? Do you sympathize with Sherrena?

6. On Larraine and her late boyfriend Glen's anniversary, she spends her monthly allocation of food stamps on "two lobster tails, shrimp, king crab legs, salad, and lemon meringue pie" (page 218). Can you relate to her decision? How might you have judged her differently without knowing the backstory that Desmond provides?

7. Because they have children, Arleen, Vanetta, and Pam and Ned frequently find themselves shut out of available housing and resort to lies in order to secure a place to live. Are these lies justified? If you have children, how far would you go to shelter your family?

8. Although eviction is the central issue in *Evicted,* affordable housing interacts intimately with many other social issues. For example: Do parents who have trouble finding and providing safe housing for their children deserve to have their children taken away and put in foster care? Would affordable housing make it easier for addicts and recovering addicts (such as Scott) to enroll in programs that increase their chances of rehabilitation? What other major issues that eviction affects can you think of, whether in this book or in the world in general?

9. How does race factor into the types of struggles faced by the individuals profiled in *Evicted*? What about being a woman? Or a single parent?

10. Did reading *Evicted* inspire you to want to help others in positions similar to those of the people in the book? If so, how do you think you might get involved? (Hint: Visit justshelter.org to learn more about groups and organizations in your area who are already fighting the good fight!)

11. Why do you think Crystal made the decision to let Arleen and her sons stay until they found another residence? How did tenants such as Crystal and Arleen rely on friends and extended kin networks to get by? Did this do anything to lift them out of poverty or distress? What limitations do these short-term relationships have? Why do you think agencies such as Aid to Families with Dependent Children seek to limit kin dependence?

12. Landlords repeatedly turned down Pam and Ned's rental applications because they have children. Why? Do you think families with children should have any protection when seeking housing? Why do you think families with children were not considered a protected class when Congress passed the Fair Housing Act in 1968? Do you think it is fair for landlords to charge tenants with children monthly surcharges and children-damage deposits? Why or why not?

13. Why did Doreen choose not to call Sherrena when the house was in desperate need of repair? Do you agree that "The house failed the tenants, and the tenants failed the house" (page 256)? What effects does living in a home that is not decent or functional have on a person's psychological and emotional health?

14. Do you think housing should be a right in America?

15. Many Americans still believe that the typical low-income family lives in public housing. Unfortunately, the opposite is true; only one in four families who qualify for any kind of housing assistance receive it. In *Evicted,* Desmond proposes a universal housing voucher program. What do you think of that idea?

16. The government spends much more money on homeowner tax benefits for affluent families than on housing assistance to poor families. Is this situation justified? How would you address this issue?

JUST SHELTER

To learn more about how you can help families avoid eviction or get back on their feet after being displaced, visit www.justshelter.org.

About the Author

MATTHEW DESMOND is a professor of sociology at Princeton University. After receiving his PhD in 2010 from the University of Wisconsin at Madison, he joined the Harvard Society of Fellows as a Junior Fellow. He is the author of four books, including *Evicted: Poverty and Profit in the American City* (2016), which won the Pulitzer Prize, the National Book Critics Circle Award, the Andrew Carnegie Medal, and the PEN/John Kenneth Galbraith Award for Nonfiction. The principal investigator of The Eviction Lab, Desmond researches poverty in America, city life, housing insecurity, public policy, racial inequality, and ethnography. He is the recipient of a MacArthur Fellowship, the American Bar Association's Silver Gavel Award, and the William Julius Wilson Early Career Award. A contributing writer for the *New York Times* magazine, Desmond was listed in 2016 among the Politico 50 as one of "fifty people across the country who are most influencing the national political debate."